CUSCO &
MACHU PICCHU

ROSS WEHNER & RENÉE DEL GAUDIO

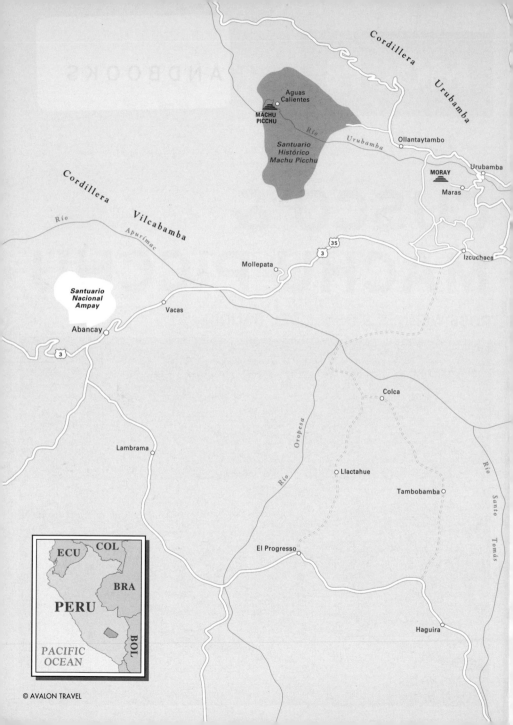

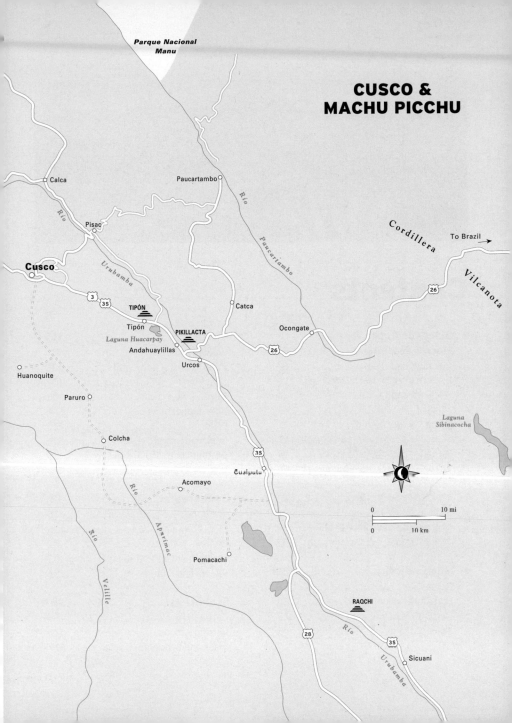

Contents

Discover Cusco & Machu Picchu

The Sacred Valley, Machu Picchu, and Cusco have such an intertwined history and culture that it's impossible to talk about one without referring to the other two. The Sacred Valley's lush hillsides and snowcapped glaciers were regarded by the Inca, who ruled an area of South America larger than the Roman Empire, as paradise on earth. Machu Picchu is the expansive stone city downstream from the Sacred Valley that was carved by the Inca six centuries ago on a remote ridge in Peru's cloud forest. Cusco is the antagonistic blending of the Inca and the Spanish, who demolished the Inca sun temples to make way for Catholic churches.

Together, the Sacred Valley, Machu Picchu, and Cusco tell the stories of the Inca, who evolved from Peru's rich, 7,000-year cultural history; of the Spanish at the height of the European Renaissance; and of the fragmented and difficult union of these old-world and new-world cultures, which developed apart for millennia until they were forced together in the Spanish conquest.

Despite the conquest, Inca culture has proven remarkably resilient over the centuries, which creates the sensation of time standing still. Visitors to the Sacred Valley will still find stone huts, freshly tilled potato and quinoa fields, herds of alpaca, and Quechuan communities. Quechua,

the Inca language that is spoken by six million Andean highlanders, is heard as often as Spanish along the narrow alleyways of Cusco. Inca Trail hikers who arrive at dawn at the Inti Punku, or Sun Gate, will see the fog rise gently from the terraces and perfect stone buildings of Machu Picchu, which was lost for centuries and therefore perfectly preserved.

We suggest that visitors to this region follow a deliberate sequence in order to best enjoy and understand the area. Start by spending a few days in the Sacred Valley to acclimatize to the altitude and experience the incredible natural and cultural world of the Inca. From the Sacred Valley, take an early morning train or hike the Inca Trail to Machu Picchu, the maximum incarnation of the Inca's spiritual beliefs. And, after a full day at the ruins, return in the evening to Cusco and spend the next few days experiencing the complex colonial city, the amalgamation of the Inca and the Golden Age Spanish, which is best understood after spending time in the Sacred Valley and Machu Picchu.

Planning Your Trip

▶ WHERE TO GO

The Sacred Valley

Begin your trip to the Cusco area with the Sacred Valley, which the Inca considered paradise for its fertile earth. Up and down the valley, the Inca built a string of their most sacred sites, including temples and fortresses in Pisac and Ollantaytambo. This charming valley is a destination in its own right, with a great range of lodging and restaurants, day hikes, horseback rides, mountain biking, and more.

Machu Picchu

The Sacred Valley is cut by the Río Urubamba, which rushes toward the Inca's most fabled achievement: Machu Picchu. The fabled lost city is a breath-taking citadel arranged along a jungle-covered ridge. Hiking either the Salcantay route or the Inca Trail, a paved stone highway that culminates in a bird's-eye view of the ruins, is a memorable way to arrive. The train ride in and out also affords incredible views of the area's scenery.

IF YOU HAVE...

- **ONE WEEK:** Visit the Sacred Valley, Cusco, and Machu Picchu.
- **TWO WEEKS:** Visit the Sacred Valley, Cusco, and Machu Picchu, but extend your time in the Sacred Valley to hike, mountain bike, and go horseback riding. Add on an extension to either hike the Inca Trail or make the Salcantay trek to Machu Picchu.

Río Urubamba in the Sacred Valley

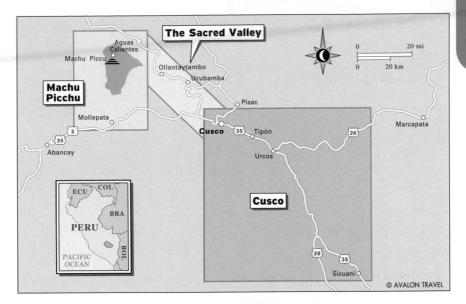

The Sacred Valley

Cusco

After visiting the Sacred Valley and Machu Picchu, travelers are acclimatized to Cusco's high altitude. They are also primed for Cusco's complex culture, which remains today an antagonistic mixture of Inca and Spanish cultures. The Spanish erected more than a dozen baroque churches atop flawless Inca walls. Cusco must-visits are the artisan barrio of San Blas, the fortress of Sacsayhuamán, and the Inca sun temple Coricancha.

Machu Picchu

▶ WHEN TO GO

The traditional time to visit Peru is in the South American winter, June–August, when dry, sunny weather opens up over the Andes. Because Peru's dry months coincide perfectly with summer vacation in North America and Europe, this is also when most travelers visit Peru. Prices for lodging tend to go up during these months, and Machu Picchu can be crowded. Especially crowded times are Inti Raymi, the June 24 sun festival in Cusco, and Fiestas Patrias, the national Peruvian holiday at the end of July.

The bulk of the rainy season is December–April, when trekking and other outdoor activities are hampered by muddy paths and soggy skies. To avoid crowds, we heartily recommend squeezing your trip in between the rainy season and the high tourist months. April, May, September, October, and even November are excellent times to visit Peru. The weather is usually fine and prices for lodging tend to be lower.

Quechua women on the streets of Cusco

weaver in the village of Chinchero

► BEFORE YOU GO

Vaccinations

Most travelers to Peru do get the vaccinations recommended by the Centers for Disease Control (www.cdc.gov), which include hepatitis A and B and typhoid for the Cusco area.

Passports and Visas

Citizens of the United States, Canada, United Kingdom, South Africa, New Zealand, and Australia and residents of any other European or Latin American country do not require visas to enter Peru as tourists at the present time, but they will need to pay departure taxes of US$31 for international flights and US$7 for domestic flights. When visitors enter the country, they can get anything from 30 to 180 days stamped into both a passport and an embarkation card that travelers must keep until they exit the country. If you require more than 30 days, be ready to support your argument by explaining your travel plans and showing your return ticket. Extensions can be arranged at Peru's immigration offices in Lima, Arequipa, Cusco, Iquitos, Puno, and Trujillo for US$21.

Transportation

Most travelers arrive to Peru by plane, and all international flights into Peru arrive in Lima. Travel to Cusco is an additional plane ride. Because of flight patterns, most travelers end up spending a night or a day in Lima either coming from, or going to, Cusco. We recommend travelers spend at least a day in Lima, preferably on the way home, to take in this amazing city.

Explore Cusco & Machu Picchu

▶ THE BEST OF CUSCO AND MACHU PICCHU

This classic loop starts off in the lush surroundings of the Sacred Valley, where you will explore ruins, experience Inca culture, and adjust to the altitude. Then you are off on the train to enjoy the cloud forests and magnificent stonework of Machu Picchu. At the end of the trip, you'll have two days to take in Cusco, the Spanish Renaissance city built atop Inca foundations. There is much to do and see in this colonial town—museums, art galleries, weaving stores, Inca ruins, Spanish architecture, nightclubs, volunteer opportunities, and language schools. Cusco, with its cobblestone streets and unique history, is a place many visitors want to return to again and again. Reserving extra time to explore Cusco's nooks and crannies is a good idea.

Day 1

Begin by flying into Lima, the capital of Peru. Most planes arrive here at night, so you'll have the chance of either overnighting at a Lima hotel or hanging out at the

Cusco's Plaza de Armas

THE SACRED STEPS OF THE INCA

Step designs are found everywhere in important Inca ruins and are versions of the **chacana,** a sacred Andean symbol similar to the Christian crucifix. The *chacana* is the key to understanding the spiritual beliefs of the Inca, which are alive and well today in the syncretic Catholic belief systems of Peru's Andean people. The *chacana* is based on the Southern Cross, a constellation revered by the Inca.

The Andean Cross, or Cruz Andina, is a combination of two figures: an equal-armed cross that indicates the four corners of the Inca world (north, south, east, and west) and a superimposed square indicating the four elements of Inca cosmology (water, air, earth, and fire).

The three steps on each side of the *chacana* correspond to the three levels of the Inca universe. The bottom step is the underworld *(uku pacha),* associated with serpents, death, and the wisdom of ancestors. The middle step is the earth *(kay pacha)* and relates to everyday human life, pumas, and life energy. And the top level is the sky or heavens *(hanan pacha),* linked to condors, stars, virtuous beings, and gods.

You will see the *chacana* symbol displayed in art and jewelry everywhere in Cusco. You can see the *chacana* in different ruins in the Cusco area:

- **Ollantaytambo:** The famous walls of Ollantaytambo's **Temple of the Sun** are decorated with faint step patterns of the *chacana.* At the foot of the temple, the **Princess Baths** are a sequence of fountains decorated with elaborate *chacana* symbols.

- **Pisac:** There is the top half of a *chacana* symbol in front of Pisac's **Intihuatana,** the sacred stone pillar used to measure the sun's movement. Above the *chacana,* sculpted out of rock, is another stone pillar that is easy to miss if you aren't looking for it. During the June 21 winter solstice, the sun casts a shadow from this pillar that hits the *chacana.* The resulting shadow

completes the bottom half of the *chacana* and marks the beginning of the harvest season.

- **Machu Picchu:** *Chacana* step patterns are found throughout the ruins, most notably at the **Funerary Rock, Intihuatana,** and **Royal Tomb.**

- **Q'enqo** and **Sacsayhuamán:** These two ruins, near each other on the outskirts of Cusco, both feature prominent rock outcroppings carved with *chacana* steps. Below Sacsayhuamán is a cave with a *chacana*-shaped entrance.

a sacred *chacana* symbol at the foot of Ollantaytambo's Temple of the Sun

airport for an early morning flight to Cusco. Arrange with your hotel ahead of time for transport from Cusco to either Pisac or Ollantaytambo, two gorgeous villages in the Sacred Valley.

Day 2

On day two settle in and explore your surroundings. If you are in Pisac, see the Inca ruins, which include a sun temple and fortress complex. Then hike down the mountain back into town to check out the market. If you are in Ollantaytambo, head first to the sun temple above town. It's a great place to understand the layout of both Ollantaytambo and the Sacred Valley, and you can see where the Inca and Spanish battled for control over this temple-cum-fortress. In the evening, head out for a meal overlooking the Plaza de Armas.

Day 3

Now that you understand your immediate surroundings, head out and explore farther afield. Both Pisac and Ollantaytambo have excellent day hikes nearby, as well as horseback riding and mountain biking. An excellent option is to explore the weaving village of Chinchero before hiking or mountain biking from the enigmatic circular Inca terraces at Moray to the crystallized salt mines near Maras. From Moray, descend to the Sacred Valley for transport back to Ollantaytambo.

Day 4

Catch an early morning train out of Ollantaytambo to Aguas Calientes, the small town from which to take a bus shuttle to Machu Picchu. Wander around the ruins in the morning before the crowds arrive. Then head off mid-morning to climb the nearby peak of Huayna Picchu and explore the Temple of the Moon. In the afternoon, return to Aguas Calientes for a late lunch and a mug of coca tea. Then board the train to

Huayna Picchu

Ollantaytambo and board a comfortable tourist bus back to Cusco.

Day 5

Now that you're used to Cusco's altitude of 3,400 meters (11,150 feet), you can walk this city's cobblestoned streets all day long. Start with a morning walk through the neighborhood of San Blas and see the Inca sun temple or Coricancha. Save the afternoon for visiting art galleries.

Day 6

Today you choose between shopping and exploring more museums and churches in Cusco (there are plenty) or taking a walk above town from the ruins of Q'enqo and Sacsayhuamán. A late afternoon at Sacsayhuamán, an Inca fortress overlooking Cusco, is a great way to end the trip.

Day 7

Fly from Cusco to Lima as early as you want. Since most planes depart for the United States around midnight, you'll have a day in Lima to explore. Start in central Lima to see the Catedral, Archbishop's Palace, Palacio del Gobierno, and the catacombs at Santo Domingo. If you're hungry and want to shop, skip downtown Lima and head straight to the swanky neighborhood of Miraflores for a *cebiche* lunch overlooking the Pacific Ocean and an interesting variety of museums, shops, and art galleries. In the evening, head back to the airport for the flight home.

► THE 14-DAY ADVENTURE TOUR

The Cusco area has a rich history of conquest and exploration written across a landscape that attracts modern-day adventurers. The altiplano, or high plain, stretches in all directions with endless possibilities for mountain biking, hiking, and horseback riding. The whole area, sandwiched between the snow-covered peaks of the Cordillera Vilcanota and the cloud forests around Machu Picchu, is rich with off-the-beaten-path routes that lead to seldom-visited ruins, Quechua-speaking villages, and soul-stirring vistas.

Day 1

Arrive in Lima and either stay overnight or catch an early morning connecting flight to Cusco. In Cusco, arrange hotel transport to Ollantaytambo, a living Inca village in the Sacred Valley where you can rest and acclimatize.

Hiking through the Cordillera Vilcanota, trekkers approach the massive Nevado Ausangate (20,900 feet).

Day 2

After a leisurely tour of Ollantaytambo's sun temple, hit the trail for an acclimatization hike. Across the Río Urubamba, head up an Inca trail to the quarries from which the rock was hewn to make Ollantaytambo's temples and terraces. If you still have energy, trek another hour uphill to the Inti Punku, or Sun Gate, for spectacular views of the Andes, including the snow-covered Verónica mountain.

Day 3

After a power breakfast of banana pancakes at Ollantaytambo's Pachamama Grill, hop on a mountain bike at the highland village of Maras and cruise across green grasslands to the concentric Inca terraces at Moray. From here, head down a technical single-track past the salt mines of Maras and keep cruising until you get to Ollantaytambo.

stone work at Ollantaytambo's Temple of the Sun

the terraces at Ollantaytambo

TREKKING TO MACHU PICCHU

camping on the Salcantay trek

Most travelers to Peru think there is just one option for trekking to Machu Picchu – the four-day Inca Trail hike. The truth is there are at least four ways to hike to the Inca citadel. If you don't have the time or ability to hike to Machu Picchu you can always opt for train service provided by the Machu Picchu Train (Andean Railways), Inca Rail, and PeruRail, but for the more adventurous travelers, the following treks are really the best ways to enter into this world treasure.

THE FOUR-DAY INCA TRAIL HIKE

This hike, which threads two 4,000-meter passes on the way from the high Andes to the cloud forest, has become a signature experience for arriving at Machu Picchu. Recent regulations and trekker quotas have made the Inca Trail more expensive and at times hard to book.

THE TWO-DAY INCA TRAIL HIKE

If camping is not your thing, or you are short on time, try the new, abbreviated versions of the Inca Trail, which range 2-3 days. With these new variations, trekkers start farther down the trail in order to take in the final set of spectacular ruins and enter Machu Picchu at dawn and through the Inti Punku or Sun Gate. You'll spend your first day hiking the Inca Trail and seeing ruins and your first night sleeping in a hotel in Aguas Calientes, at the base of Machu Picchu. The second day is spent exploring Machu Picchu.

THE SALCANTAY FIVE-DAY TREK

It is true that the trek past sacred Salcantay, a 6,000-meter-plus peak, does not contain the stone paths and Inca ruins of the Inca Trail. But this five-day trek offers a wilderness experience and even better views of the surrounding snow-covered peaks. It's also much less expensive than the Inca Trail, and trekkers are free to trek independently (unlike on the Inca Trail, where all hikers must sign up with a licensed agency). The trek is longer and higher than the Inca Trail, but new sustainable eco-lodges have been built along the Salcantay route to allow trekkers to travel fast and light and stay in relative comfort.

THE INCA JUNGLE TRAIL

This multi-sport option, offered by an increasing number of agencies, is a good choice for backpackers on a budget and with spare adrenaline. This route enters Machu Picchu from the high mountains and cloud forests on its downstream side. Participants are first transported to Abra de Málaga (4,350 meters), a high pass into the jungle, for a stunning mountain bike descent from the alpine zone to lush cloud forest nearly 3,000 meters below. From here, trekkers camp and then head out the second day on a cloud forest trek to Santa Teresa, a riverside village. On the third day, hikers head up the Río Urubamba to Aguas Calientes, the town at the base of Machu Picchu.

the ruins of Runkurakay encountered on the Inca Trail

Day 4

If you've never ridden a *caballo de paso,* get ready for the unbelievably smooth gait of this world-famous horse. Head over to Sol y Luna Hotel to saddle up with a guide and head out on a ride of your choice. That evening, treat yourself to alpaca steaks and a merlot at El Albergue.

Day 5

Head to Piscacucho, a nearby village in the Sacred Valley, and begin the Inca Trail at the ruins of Patallacta. Hike 12 kilome-

ters and set up camp amid the cool winds of Wayllabamba.

Day 6

Start early and climb two high mountain passes amid gorgeous views of snow-covered mountains and two major Inca ruins, Runkurakay and Sayaqmarka. Sleep under the stars at the Pacaymayo campsite.

Day 7

The high mountain passes are behind you now. Drop into the orchids and butterflies

The ruins turn an orange color as the sun rises on Machu Picchu.

of the cloud forest towards the ruins of Phuyupatamarka and Wiñay Wayna. After two frigid nights in the high Andes, you will enjoy camping in the warmer, moist air of the forest.

Day 8

Break camp at dawn and hoof it to Inti Punku (the Sun Gate) to watch the sun rise over Machu Picchu. Explore the ruins and hike up Huayna Picchu before taking the shuttle bus to Aguas Calientes for lunch. Take the train back to Ollantaytambo and board the bus to Cusco.

Day 9

After the Inca Trail, you will need plenty of rest and relaxation, and good food in the magical surroundings of Cusco. Take the time to shop and meander around the Catedral, Iglesia de la Compañía, and Coricancha, Cusco's sun temple.

Days 10-12

For a final dose of adventure, head out on a three-day rafting trip on the upper section of the Río Apurímac. Run Class IV rapids, float past pre-Inca ruins, and camp out on the remote banks of this wild river.

colorful herbal dyes at the Pisac market near Cusco

Day 13

Take a final day to experience Cusco's unique combination of Inca ruins, colonial architecture and museums, markets, and cafés. If the spirit moves you, hike or mountain bike from the ruins of Q'enqo to Sacsayhuamán, or go rock climbing up the 300-meter rock face of the Via Ferrata.

Day 14

Take an early-morning flight to Lima. Hit the sights in central Lima and head to Miraflores for a seaside lunch. True modern-day adventurers can rent a board and wet suit, and hop in the surf there before heading home.

THE SACRED VALLEY

The river that runs past Machu Picchu is the Río Urubamba, which the Inca considered a sacred reflection of the Milky Way. Before reaching Machu Picchu, the Río Urubamba flows through the Sacred Valley, a breathtaking landscape of snowcapped mountains, red granite cliffs, and lush green terraces. The Sacred Valley runs roughly from Pisac to Ollantaytambo and a bit beyond to Piscacucho, a highly fertile region that was the Inca breadbasket and still produces much of the grains and vegetables consumed in Cusco. Compared to the chilly, thin air of Cusco, the Sacred Valley is lush and sunny. For the Inca the Sacred Valley was literally paradise on earth, a vision of Eden made incarnate. Inca palaces, fortresses, and sun temples dot this valley, along with charming Andean villages that produce and sell some of the country's finest handicrafts. Along with Machu Picchu and Cusco, the Sacred Valley is at the top of Peru's must-see list.

Two of the most interesting towns in the Sacred Valley are the Inca villages of Ollantaytambo and Pisac. Ollantaytambo is Peru's best example of a living Inca village, where people still live in the graceful Inca homes and use the same waterways that were used by their ancestors 500 years ago. Ollantaytambo's sun temple towers above town and contains Inca stonework as impressive as that found in Cusco and Machu Picchu. Pisac is best known for its daily handicrafts market, which draws large crowds of travelers each day. But Pisac also has an interesting variety of Inca architecture in town, along with important Inca ruins in the hills above. Pisac's

HIGHLIGHTS

☾ Pisac Market: Peru's most famous crafts market takes place in Pisac daily. This ancient Inca village is nestled in the shadow of an imposing Inca fortress and temple (page 25).

☾ Pisac Ruins: What's unique about Pisac's ruins, apart from their extraordinary beauty, is their range. Here you will find not only religious Inca architecture, but also residential, agricultural, and military (page 26).

☾ Moray and Salineras: This six-hour downhill hike is a gorgeous introduction to the Sacred Valley. Start at Moray, a complex of concentric agricultural terraces, and then head downhill past Salineras, a centuries-old salt mine still in operation today (page 33).

☾ Ollantaytambo Temple: Second in importance only to Machu Picchu, Ollantaytambo includes some of the Inca's best stonework, including a series of ceremonial baths, elegant trapezoidal doorways, and a sun temple that faces the rising sun (page 44).

☾ Inca Granaries (Pinkuylluna): This moderate, 1.5-hour hike will give you a spectacular view of Ollantaytambo, its gleaming sun temple, and interesting grain storehouses, known in Quechua as *colcas* (page 47).

LOOK FOR ☾ TO FIND RECOMMENDED SIGHTS, ACTIVITIES, DINING, AND LODGING.

ruins offer an interesting window into Inca life because they combine religious, civilian, and military architecture in a single location.

A growing body of research proves that much of Inca architecture, especially in the Sacred Valley, was built with the movements of the sun and stars in mind. The temple-fortresses of Pisac and Ollantaytambo both correspond very precisely to lunar and solar events. Moray, an area of terraced natural depressions, was probably designed to use sun and shade to work as an agricultural laboratory. The Inca went to great effort to redirect the Río Urubamba into a stone channel—to maximize farming land, but also probably to reflect the straight shape of the Milky Way. The great care the Inca took in aligning buildings

with the sun, moon, and stars reflects their vision of the Sacred Valley as a sacred, celestial landscape.

Heavy rains in January 2010 caused significant flooding in the Sacred Valley, including the displacement of about 10,000 people in the valley alone. The village of Taray, near Pisac, was nearly completely destroyed.

PLANNING YOUR TIME

The traditional way to visit Cusco, Machu Picchu, and the Sacred Valley is all wrong. Most travelers arrive in Cusco and spend a night or two seeing Cusco. Then they take a whirlwind day tour of the Sacred Valley and then take the train from Cusco to Machu Picchu in one day.

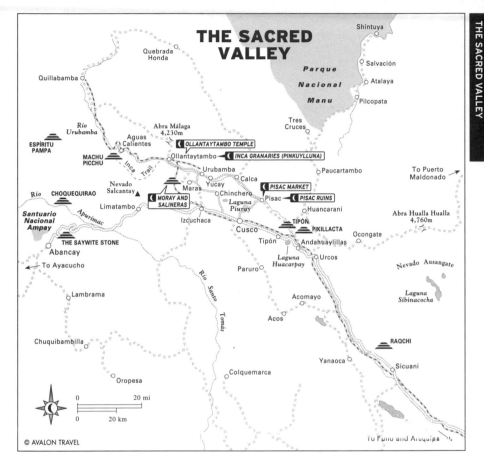

THE SACRED VALLEY

© AVALON TRAVEL

The first thing wrong with this plan is that Cusco is at 3,400 meters (11,150 feet). Most people feel at least some discomfort from altitude sickness, which can feel like the flu and is a heck of a way to start a vacation. A much better plan is to head first for the Sacred Valley, a pastoral paradise with Southern California–like weather that is, most important, 500 meters lower. Few people get altitude sickness here.

Visiting the Sacred Valley first makes sense from a chronological perspective as well. The ruins of Ollantaytambo and Pisac are a good introduction to Machu Picchu. After understanding the Inca side of the equation, travelers

then can return by train to Cusco, which is a Jerusalem-like blend of two opposing cultures—Spanish colonial and Inca imperial.

The standard one-day Sacred Valley tour from Cusco is a mistake. This tour whisks visitors through the Pisac market, lunch in Urubamba, and a visit to the Ollantaytambo ruins. Visitors usually miss the Pisac ruins, some of the finest in Peru, and also get short-changed on Ollantaytambo.

The best plan is to start your Peru trip with 2–3 days in the Sacred Valley and then take a train from the Sacred Valley to Machu Picchu. Return can be from Machu Picchu directly back to Cusco. As of 2010, floods had disrupted normal rail service between Cusco and Machu Picchu. As a result, all trains to Machu Picchu are now starting from Piscacucho, the last village in the Sacred Valley before the Río Urubamba plunges into the narrow gorges leading to Machu Picchu. Normal rail service from Sacred Valley towns such as Urubamba and Ollantaytambo will be restored in the near future.

Pisac and Vicinity

This quaint Andean town, nestled near the top of the Sacred Valley, is best known for a huge crafts market that is probably Peru's number two tourist draw behind Machu Picchu. Every day is market day, with the biggest days being Tuesday, Thursday, and Sunday. Hundreds of travelers descend upon this village as part of a whirlwind day tour from Cusco that begins here in the morning and continues on for lunch at Urubamba and a tour of the ruins at Ollantaytambo.

But there is a lot more to Pisac, and an increasing number of travelers are staying here for a night or two to explore farther afield. There are plans to move the market just out of the plaza, allowing visitors to enjoy the beautiful pisonay trees and colonial church with a backdrop of the ruins. The Inca fortress above town represents the most important Inca ruins in the valley besides Ollantaytambo. The ruins contain a rare combination of residential, military, and religious construction that sheds a deep light onto the daily life of the Inca.

In the high plains beyond the fortress, there are remote villages that can be reached only on foot. Roman and Fielding Vizcarra, owners of Hotel Pisaq, lead recommended trips into the surrounding countryside to visit these Quechuan villages and the remote ruins of Cuyo Chico and Cuyo Grande.

Intihuatana, the main sun temple at Pisac

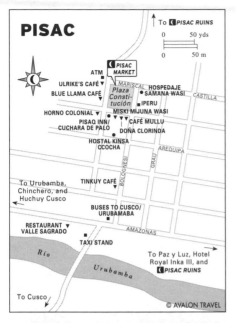

PISAC

To **(PISAC RUINS**

0   50 yds

0   50 m

- **(PISAC MARKET**
- ATM
- ULRIKE'S CAFÉ ▼
- BLUE LLAMA CAFÉ ▼
- MARISCAL HOSPEDAJE
- Plaza
- Consti-
- tución
- SAMANA WASI
- CASTILLA
- IPERU
- HORNO COLONIAL ▼
- MISKI MIJUNA WASI
- PISAQ INN/
- CUCHARA DE PALO
- ▼ ▼ CAFÉ MULLU
- DOÑA CLORINDA
- HOSTAL KINSA
- CCOCHA
- AREQUIPA
- BOLOGNESI
- GRAU
- To Urubamba,
- Chinchero, and
- Huchuy Cusco
- TINKUY CAFÉ ▼
- BUSES TO CUSCO/
- URUBAMABA
- RESTAURANT ▼
- VALLE SAGRADO
- AMAZONAS
- TAXI STAND
- *Río*
- *Urubamba*
- To Paz y Luz, Hotel
- Royal Inka III, and
- **(PISAC RUINS**
- To Cusco
- © AVALON TRAVEL

SIGHTS
(Pisac Market

Pisac has evolved into one of the biggest, certainly the most famous, *artesanía* markets in all of South America. It begins every day at 9 A.M. when the first tour buses arrive from Cusco and winds down around 5 P.M. when the last tourists leave. The town's main square is filled wall-to-wall with stalls selling the full range of Peruvian *artesanía:* carved gourds (*mates burilados*), ceramics, felt hats, alpaca sweaters and mittens, musical instruments, paintings, antiques, a huge variety of trinkets, and, most of all, weavings and jewelry. Even if you are not buying, the café balconies overlooking the market offer superb people-watching: Hundreds of camera-toting tourists, from every conceivable country on earth, haggle with Quechuan-speaking merchants. Quality tends to be in the low to middle range—the good stuff is found in the homes of the *artesanos* themselves or in upscale city galleries—but, after a bit of bargaining, prices can be very reasonable, especially if buying in quantity.

Though touristy beyond belief, the Pisac market has a remarkably deeper side that is rooted in its colonial past and has proven resilient to mass tourism. On Sunday only, campesinos from surrounding villages set up a barter market, or *mercado de treque,* which is an ancient Peruvian custom and an interesting example of the informal economies upon which highlanders depend. Quechuan-speaking Indians sit behind huge piles of potatoes, carrots, herbs, and other vegetables in one corner of the square. They sell these products to buy essentials (salt, sugar, kerosene, matches, medicines) but also trade to acquire other foods, such as oranges from the Quillabamba Valley. It exists side-by-side with the Pisac market but ends by 3 P.M. so that villagers can walk home before dark.

Also on Sunday only, masses in Quechua are held at 6 and 11 A.M. in **San Pedro Apóstol de Pisac,** the colonial church on the main square that was rebuilt after the 1950 earthquake. The early mass is held for townspeople, and the later one is reserved for the *varayocs* and *regidores*

wool on display at Pisac's colorful market

THE SACRED VALLEY

(elected mayors and their appointed deputies) of the 13 villages that are a two- to five-hour walk away through the mountains. After mass, the officials proceed around the square in their Sunday best before baptisms, and sometimes a wedding, are held in the church. Between services, it is possible to enter the church for a glimpse at the Inca foundations and an interesting collection of colonial paintings.

◖ Pisac Ruins

Pisac is one of Cusco's few great Inca ruins that feature all types of architecture—agricultural, hydraulic, military, residential, and religious. It probably began as a military garrison to guard against incursion from the Anti Indians, who occupied the easternmost corner of the empire known as **Antisuyo** (present-day Paucartambo and the Manu jungle). Pachacútec probably built Pisac's imperial architecture, though oddly there is no mention of Pisac in the Spanish chronicles.

There are several ways to see the Pisac ruins (7 a.m.–3 p.m., admission with Cusco ruins

ticket), but the best is to take a US$3–4 taxi up the eight-kilometer highway to the ruins. Instead of going to the main entrance, tell your taxi to go right on the switchback and head farther up to the Pisac ruins of Qanchisracay. From here a trail leads along a ridge, through a tunnel, and down into the **Intihuatana,** or the main sun temple. The walk is steep and exposed to heights, but safe. Or arrive at the Intihuatana via the main path from the main entrance. Allow for one or two hours for Pisac (return to town via taxi) and another two hours for walking downhill all the way to town.

Qanchisracay is one of three residential areas in Pisac. It is composed of rough stone buildings, walls with niches, and small squares. These were probably military garrisons and, in the style of a medieval castle, shelter for villagers in times of war. An easier residential area to visit, below the Intihuatana, is named after the Andean partridge *p'isaqa*—the namesake of Pisac itself.

From Qanchisracay an Inca trail traverses the hillside, arrives at a small pass, then heads

terraces above the Pisac ruins

© BETH FUCHS

up and over a rocky summit to the sun temple, behind and out of sight. At the pass, four purification baths flow with water brought down from a lake at 4,500 meters. Below are five agricultural terraces, once planted with potatoes and *olluco,* the Andean tuber. On the opposing cliff wall, thousands of holes left by grave robbers are all that is left of what was once the Inca's largest cemetery. On the other side of the pass to the left, a 10-minute detour around the corner reveals Inca buttresses, which were once spanned by a hanging bridge made of plant fibers. This is an alternative trail to the Intihuatana and passes a series of fine irrigation canals.

The main path from the pass crosses through a military wall with a perfect trapezoidal door, known as the **Door of the Serpent.** Above is the second residential area, **Hanam P'isaq** (upper Pisac). The path now climbs up steep staircases and niches carved out of the rock itself, alongside a cliff and through the **Q'alla Q'asa** (Split Rock) tunnel. Faced with a vertical rock face, Inca engineers decided to enlarge a rock fissure and bore through the entire cliff—how they did this, with no iron or steel implements, boggles the mind.

The best view of the Intihuatana is from above. Like the sun temple at Machu Picchu, the Intihuatana is an oval building of perfect masonry encasing a votive rock. The pillar atop the rock was used to track the sun's movements. (Most of the finely carved pillar was recently chopped off by thieves—not long before the one in Machu Picchu was chipped during the filming of a beer commercial.) The walls of five other temples surround the temple, including one that was probably devoted to the moon. To the right is a series of restored baths that flow into an underground canal. In front of the Intihuatana is a sacred *chacana* symbol.

Off the easier trail back to the main entrance of the ruins is **P'isaqa,** the third and finest residential area, with its own ritual bath. These were probably homes for the elite, as opposed to the military garrisons closer to the pass. Most people head back at this point to

the main entrance, though there are two trails from here that make for pleasant two-hour walks back to Pisac. One descends directly to the Río Quitamayo, with spectacular views, while the other drops through the lookout towers of Coriwayrachina and an area of steep terracing. Both trails merge on the other side of the river for the final descent into town.

ENTERTAINMENT AND EVENTS

There are no discos in Pisac, but the cafés around the square serve beer and cocktails.

Pisac's big festival is **La Virgen del Carmen,** which begins on July 15 and runs for five days. The first day includes a horse-riding contest followed by a series of religious processions and dances.

SHOPPING

Apart from the Pisac market, there are crafts shops open all week long (10 A.M.–9 P.M. daily) on all the main streets leading from the square, especially **Mariscal Castilla, San Francisco,** and **Bolognesi.** Contemporary art is sold in the first floor of the **Café Art Gallery Mullu** (Plaza Constitución 352) and in a related gallery a block from the square on San Francisco.

ACCOMMODATIONS
Under US$10

The best budget option is **Hostel Kinsa Ccocha** (Arequipa 307, tel. 084/20-3101, US$10 pp), which has several plain, clean rooms a block from the Plaza Constitución. Ask for a newer room, which has higher ceilings. Private baths are an additional US$5.

Hospedaje Samana Wasi (Plaza Constitución 509, tel. 084/20-3018, US$5 s, US$10 d) offers shoebox-size rooms overlooking the plaza, shared bathrooms, and a restaurant (7 A.M.–9 P.M.). Private baths are an extra US$3 per person. **El Artesano** (Calle Vigil s/n, US$8 s, US$11 d) is a family home that has a few rooms for tourists. Luckily, the guest rooms are big and clean, which makes up for having to share the bathroom with the family.

US$25-50

🌑 **Pisac Inn,** formerly Hotel Pisaq (Plaza Constitución, tel. 084/20-3062, www.pisacinn.com, US$45 s, US$55–65 d with breakfast) is a labor of love for Roman Vizcarra and Fielding Wood-Vizcarra, a Peruvian-American couple who founded the hotel in 1993. The adobe building, covered in bright murals, includes the excellent Cuchara de Palo restaurant, with balconies overlooking the market square. Past the building's threshold is a hushed, contemplative atmosphere that recalls Fielding's hometown of Taos, New Mexico. Friezes of turquoise and scarlet fringe the sand-colored walls, and the atmosphere—neither Inca nor Navajo—is billed as a "celebration of indigenous culture all over the Americas." Additional perks include a US$25 Cusco airport pickup, rock-heated sauna, laundry, and a constant supply of water from the hotel's own well—a big advantage, given Pisac's sporadic water supply. Rooms with shared baths are only US$35 for a single to US$55 for a triple. Roman speaks English, Spanish, Quechua, Italian, and German and leads tours throughout the area that combine culture with a bit of spirituality. They have a range of trips described on their related website, www.peruculturaljourneys.com.

New Yorker Diane Dunn's pride and joy 🌑 **Paz y Luz** (off the road to the ruins 2 km outside of town, tel. 084/20-3204, www.pazyluzperu.com, US$35 s, US$55 d with breakfast, cash only) is her collection of earth-colored lodges on the edge of the Río Urubamba above Pisac. The base of her healing center, the inspiration of her book *Cusco: Gateway to Inner Wisdom,* and the starting point of many long walks in the surrounding fields, the lodge truly offers all the peace and light that its name promises. The rooms are comfortable and tastefully decorated, with brand-new bathrooms. A central area has a woodstove, dining table, and polished wood staircase. In the back, in a separate building, is a one-bedroom apartment with its own kitchen. The growing complex includes a restaurant, conference room, meditation room, and rooms for long-term residents.

Prices for long-term guests and descriptions of massage services, spiritual workshops, and other offerings are on the website.

US$50-100

On the outskirts of town, **Hotel Royal Inka III Pisac** (on road to the ruins 1 km outside of town, tel. 084/20-3064, www.royalinkahotel.com, US$53 s, US$80 d) is a charming, converted hacienda with a mid-19th-century chapel. Unfortunately, most of the rooms are in a cold and charmless modern addition. Some rooms have woodstoves, however, and the second and third floors offer views out over the fields. There is a range of services, mostly included in the price, such as an Olympic-size pool (available to nonguests), private whirlpool tub, sauna, tennis court with rented rackets, horses, bikes, game room, restaurant, bar, and videos. There is also a spa, where you can get a massage for US$25 and other treatments. Without a deep discount, this hotel can seem overpriced, especially when compared to other, more charming and considerably cheaper options nearby.

Also outside town is **Melissa Wasi** (on road to the ruins 1 km outside of town, tel. 084/79-7589, www.melissa-wasi.com, US$120 for a bungalow), a charming hotel with separate bungalows built into the hillside. Owners Joyce and Chito have created a beautiful house to accommodate people for a breakfast of homemade bread, eggs, and fresh coffee before sitting in the colorful gardens. Bungalows sleep up to four people, and all have WiFi and a complete kitchen.

FOOD
Cafés, Bakeries, and Ice Cream

🌑 **Ulrike's Café** (Plaza Constitución, tel. 084/20-3195, 7 A.M.–9 P.M. daily, US$4). Ulrike Simic, the classy German owner of this playful establishment, offers a lunch menu (US$7, including vegetarian options) and makes a delectable array of cheesecakes, including chocolate chip, coffee, and lemon. The walls are painted in yellows, greens, and pinks, and a mixture of music drifts through the air, making every sitting nook a perfect respite from the bustling world of commerce outside. **Café Art Gallery Mullu** (Plaza Constitución 352, 9 A.M.–8 P.M. daily, US$4) has an interesting collection of contemporary art on the first floor and a café, with nice market views, on the second.

Blue Llama Café (Plaza Constitución, tel. 084/20-3135, www.bluellamacafe.com, 7 A.M.–9 P.M. daily, US$4) is one of the newest additions to Pisac, offering excellent food and service in its funky restaurant. Great coffee, brownies, and pancakes, along with traditional cuisine, are available all day long. This is a comfy place to hang out with a book or good friends.

Tinkuy Café is another fun place in Pisac, where owners Alfredo and Nancy with their sheep Meli offer a good range of juices, coffee, and vegetarian food. They have a daily menu for US$3. Alfredo speaks excellent English and can help with tours of the area.

If you are in the mood for something quick, tasty, and cheap, try the empanadas made in a few old, wood-fired *hornos coloniales* (colonial ovens) around town. The flaky empanadas—dough filled with cheese, sliced onion, tomato, olives, and oregano—can be had for US$0.50 each on the corner of the main square near the Pisac Inn or on Mariscal Castilla 372, one block away on the other end of the square.

Peruvian

The best place for trout in Pisac, and maybe the whole Cusco area, is **C Restaurant Valle Sagrado** (Amazonas 116, tel. 084/43-6915, 8 A.M.–11 P.M. daily, US$2–5), operated over the last 15 years by the motherly Carmen Luz. During lunch, this place is packed with locals who come not only for the trout but for chicken, soups, sandwiches, and lamb ribs. Restaurant Valle Sagrado is right on the main drag, along with many other lesser restaurants; look for its faux Inca walls.

Despite its humble entrance, **Doña Clorinda** (Plaza Constitución, tel. 084/20-3051, 7 A.M.–7 P.M. daily, US$2–5) serves up safe, flavorful *comida típica*. Highlights are *lomo*

saltado and *rocoto relleno*. There is a basic lunch menu for US$2 or a more luxurious version for US$5.

The gourmet option in town is **C Cuchara de Palo** (Plaza Constitución, tel. 084/20-3062, www.pisacinn.com, 11:30 A.M.–8:30 P.M. daily, US$5–15), inside Pisac Inn. With bright green walls and tree-trunk tables, the atmosphere and the food are all natural. Vegetarians should try the *quinoa chaufa* (fried quinoa), and meat eaters should go for the duck in elderberry sauce or *lomo saltado*.

For dessert, stop by **Miski Mijuna Wasi** (Plaza Constitución 345, tel. 084/20-3266, 7 A.M.–8:30 P.M. daily), where the *crocante de lúcuma* is the house specialty.

Markets

The best supermarkets are **Sofis Market** (Bolognesi s/n, tel. 084/20-3017, 6:30 A.M.–10 P.M. daily) and **La Baratura** (Manuel Prado 105, 6 A.M.–10 P.M. daily).

The fertile Sacred Valley produces much of the grains, vegetables, and fruits consumed in nearby Cusco.

THE SACRED VALLEY

INFORMATION AND SERVICES

The best info about Pisac is available from **Tinkuy Café, Ulrike's Café, Paz y Luz,** or **Pisac Inn,** which also offers laundry, money exchange, and fax services.

There is a clinic and pharmacy above the plaza near the public parking area. Other pharmacies are on Bolognesi and are generally open 8 A.M.–9 P.M. daily, with a midday closure for lunch.

There is a **Global Net ATM** on the corner of the main square, next to Ulrike's Café, and a store that changes foreign currency and travelers checks on the square near the church.

Tourist information is found on the corner of Bolognesi and San Francisco (tel. 084/ 20-3026).

A **mailbox** is on the main square inside the Restaurant Samana Wasi, which also sells stamps. There are **phone booths** at Sofis Market on Bolognesi and near the municipality on the main square. **Internet** is available in several sites around the Plaza de Armas. Hours are usually 9 A.M.–11 P.M. daily.

GETTING THERE AND AROUND

Buses for Pisac leave Cusco from below Tullumayo and Garcilaso every 20 minutes and charge US$1 for the one-hour journey. There are also buses available on Puputi street. For a 45-minute ride, hire a taxi in Cusco's Plaza de Armas for US$10. Buses drop passengers off at the bridge on the main highway, from which it is a three-block walk uphill to the market and main square. Return buses to Cusco leave from the same spot every 15 minutes up until 7 P.M. Buses heading the opposite direction also stop here on the way to Yucay and then Urubamba (US$0.50, 30–40 minutes). Once in Pisac, taxis can be taken eight kilometers to the main Pisac ruins entrance (US$3) or the upper level (US$4).

SIDE TRIPS
Huchuy Cusco

After Ollantaytambo and Pisac, Huchuy Cusco is the next most important Inca ruin in the Sacred Valley. This site features a two-story *kallanka,* or Inca hall, that is nearly

trail at the Pisac ruins

© RENÉE DEL GAUDIO AND ROSS WEHNER

© SCOTT COLLINS, WWW.LIFEUNSCRIPTEDPHOTOGRAPHY.COM

drinking *chicha* at the Sunday market in Chinchero

40 meters long and topped off by a well-preserved third story of adobe—it is easy to imagine this adobe painted, as were the buildings in Cusco, and topped off with a pyramid of thick thatch. There are also terraces, a square, an Inca gate, and many other rougher buildings within a few hundred meters of the hall. The whole site commands a small plateau, 800 meters above the Sacred Valley, with spectacular views.

This was probably the royal estate once known as Caquia Jaquijahuana, where, according to myth, Inca Viracocha hid when the Chancas threatened to invade Cusco in 1438. One of his sons, who later renamed himself Pachacútec, rose up and defeated the Chancas, thus beginning the meteoric rise of the Inca. After the conquest, the Spaniards found a mummy at this site—said to be that of Viracocha.

Reaching Huchuy Cusco is not easy, but it's worth the effort. The shortest way to get there is a three-hour, uphill hike from Lamay, a village between Pisac and Urubamba. The entrance to the footbridge that crosses the Río Urubamba is marked with a large blue sign from the National Institute of Culture.

Another highly recommended option is to approach Huchuy Cusco from the opposite direction in a two-day hike across the high plains from Cusco. The trip starts at Sacsayhuamán in Cusco and follows the original Inca Trail to Calca, heading past finely wrought canals, villages, and several 4,000-meter passes. The total trip is 17 miles, including the final descent to Lamay, where you can catch a bus back to Cusco via Pisac. Both trips are described in detail in Peter Frost's *Exploring Cusco.* For either route, bring plenty of water and food as there is little along the way.

Chinchero

Chinchero is a small Andean village, off the beaten tourist track, that lies along the shortest driving route between Cusco and the Sacred Valley. Chinchero is perched on the high plains at 3,800 meters above sea level and has great views over the snowcapped Urubamba range. It is nearly 400 meters above Cusco, so visitors should be aware of altitude sickness.

Past Chinchero's less-than-appealing street front is the main square, where a handicrafts market is held on Tuesday, Thursday, and Sunday. A number of talented weavers in Chinchero exhibit their wares at this market, which is smaller and less touristy than Pisac. The highlight of the square is an Inca wall with huge niches, which probably formed part of an Inca palace. Above the square is a 17th-century adobe church that was built on Inca foundations, which has deteriorated floral designs painted on its interior. It is open for visitors on market days only.

On market days, you can also catch a weaving demonstration at one of the local workshops. Starting as young as age 5, girls learn to wash wool; a couple of years later they are spinning the wool into thread, and finally by 12 or 15, they are weaving actual pieces. To understand the complexity and incredible skill that goes into creating these pieces, we recommend stopping by **Exposición de Artesanías**

Mink'a Chinchero (Albergue 22, tel. 084/30-6035, minka@hotmail.com, hours vary).

If you're looking for a more active day, and you can leave Chinchero by noon, you'll have time for a nice four-hour hike that drops along an old Inca trail into this valley and ends at Huayllabamba, where *combis* pass in the late afternoon for Urubamba or Pisac. From the church, a wide trail leads up the opposite side of the valley and then gradually descends into the Sacred Valley. Once you arrive at the Río Urubamba, the Sacred Valley's main river, head right (downstream) toward the bridge at Huayllabamba.

There's a hostel or two in Chinchero, but they are very basic and the town's high altitude and bone-chilling nights make the Sacred Valley—almost 1,000 meters lower—a much better option. In Cusco, *colectivos* for Chinchero can be taken from the first block of Grau near the bridge (US$0.75, 45 minutes).

YUCAY

This quiet town, a few kilometers east of Urubamba, consists of a large, grassy plaza where soccer games are played in the shade of two massive pisonay trees reputed to be 450 years old. Various colonial homes, now hotels, front the square along with the restored colonial church of Santiago Apóstol. On the far end of the square, near the highway, lies the adobe palace of Sayri Túpac, who settled here after emerging from Vilcabamba in 1558. Away from the main square lie quiet, dusty streets and extensive Inca terracing on the hillsides near town. There are few services outside the hotels clustered around the square.

Accommodations

The unpretentious **Hostel Y'llary** (Plaza Manco II 107, tel. 084/20-1112, US$27 s, US$33 d with breakfast) has rustic, large rooms with high ceilings and comfortable beds. The views from the flower garden are amazing, and it is also possible to pitch a tent in the yard (US$5 pp).

The luxurious **Sonesta Posadas del Inca** (Plaza Manco II, Yucay 123, tel. 084/20-1107, www.sonesta.com, US$94–170 s, US$99–180 d, prices depend on season and come with breakfast) is like a small village with rooms spread out among plazas and gardens, courtyard fountains, a miniature crafts market, and a chapel. The hotel is built around the charming 16th-century Santa Catalina de Sena monastery, where 21 rooms are located. The modern though colonial-style building next door has another 40 rooms or so with high ceilings, cable TV, lock boxes, and bathrooms with tubs. Amenities include a nice restaurant (US$15 lunch buffet), jewelry shop, ATM, and a full spa. Even if you don't stay here, stop in and see the excellent museum, which has a range of ceramics, *quipus,* and weavings from most of Peru's cultures, from the Chavín to the Inca.

The well-decorated **La Casona de Yucay** (Plaza Manco II 104, tel. 084/20-1116, www.hotelcasonayucay.com, US$85 s, US$105 d with breakfast) is a colonial hacienda that has been converted into a hotel with large rooms and great views. The colonial sitting room is elegant, though the gardens need some work.

Food

The Sacred Valley's best-kept gastronomical secret is 🌓 **Huayoccari Hacienda Restaurant** (Km 64 Pisac–Ollantaytambo highway, call for directions beforehand, tel. 084/22-6241 or cell 084/962-2224, hsilabrador@latinmail.com, US$45 pp). This elegant gourmet retreat, two kilometers up a dirt road near Yucay, is a converted country manor perched high on a ridge overlooking the Sacred Valley. Past a rustic courtyard, the restaurant's walls are lined with colonial paintings, altars, and ceramics collected by José Ignacio Lambarri, whose family has owned the land and nearby hacienda for more than three centuries. The garden terraces offer dazzling views and digestive walks past roses and fuchsias to Inca terraces and some of the most fertile farmland in Peru.

Apart from its privileged location, Huayoccari has the most sophisticated cuisine in all of Cusco. It is completely organic and, best of all, based on the hacienda's original recipes. Lunch begins with *sara lagua,* a cream soup made of local white corn, fresh cheese, and the herb *huacatay.* Main courses include steamed river trout with a sauce of herbs and fresh capers, or chicken rolled with fresh cheese and country bacon and covered with *saucoberry* sauce. The whole meal builds toward the desserts, made of delectable fruits found only in Peru: cheesecake with *aguaymanto* marmalade, chirimoya meringue, or a *sachatomate* compote. Though off the beaten path, Huayoccari is well worth the trek for the food, the country setting, and the private collection of art. There are only a handful of tables, so make reservations well in advance. Huayoccari

is between Pisac and Urubamba and can be reached via taxi from either town.

A more conventional option, but with a diverse menu, is **Allpa Manka** (St. Martin 300, tel. 084/20-1258, www.cuscofood.com, 11 A.M.–3:30 P.M. and 6–9:30 P.M. daily, US$12–15). The US$12 buffet lunch, taken in the sunny patio with live music, can be a restful break from the go-go tourist grind.

Getting There and Around

From Cusco, buses leave for Yucay from the first block of Grau. Frequent buses pass Yucay's main square going one direction to Pisac (30 minutes) or to Urubamba (10 minutes) in the other.

Urubamba and Vicinity

Urubamba lies smack in the center of the Sacred Valley and thus makes a good base for exploring the valley. Ollantaytambo is 20 minutes down the valley one way and Pisac is 40 minutes the other way. From here, another highway climbs onto the high plains toward Chinchero, a weaving center with a Sunday market and Inca ruins, and Cusco.

Despite its location on an atrocious highway strip, Urubamba is a relaxed and friendly town that grows on people who spend time here. The massive flow of tourism through the Sacred Valley—especially strong on the biggest Pisac market days (Sunday, Tuesday, and Thursday)—mostly bypasses Urubamba, which has just one good ruin and little else to attract tourists besides its pleasant square and a colonial cathedral. Other towns, like Ollantaytambo or even Pisac, have more of a Quechua flavor, but none are as mellow as Urubamba. Recently, several hip bars and cafés have sprung up in response to a stream of college students brought here by ProPeru and other student organizations.

The plains above Urubamba are spectacular: The snow-covered Cordillera Urubamba rises over a patchwork of russet and chocolate-brown fields. In the middle is Maras, a dense

cluster of red tile roofs, and two other startling visual anomalies. Moray is a set of huge natural depressions in the earth that were elaborately terraced by the Inca. Salineras is a blinding-white salt mine that sprawls across the mountain slope.

With these sights plus mountain biking, rafting, and horseback riding, it is no surprise that Urubamba is home to the valley's best hotels. Because the day tours through the valley stop here for lunch, Urubamba also has the greatest concentration of good restaurants. A final Urubamba highlight worth mentioning is the Seminario Ceramics studio.

SIGHTS
◖ Moray and Salineras

If you want to soak in the Sacred Valley's spectacular scenery, spend time wandering around the high plains above Urubamba. First stop is **Maras,** a dusty town with a few colonial churches and *chicherías,* fermented corn-beer shops advertised by red plastic bags tied to the end of wooden poles. There is also an ancient hatmaker named Teodosio Argandaño Caviedes—his shop is near the corner of Leguía and Jesús. About five kilometers farther, or a half hour along a good dirt road, lie the four

natural depressions of Moray (7:30 A.M.–
5:15 P.M. daily, US$3). These sinkholes, 150
meters deep, were caused by rain eroding the
calcium-rich soil.

With its perfect terracing, Moray appears
at first glance to be a ceremonial center or a
Greek-style amphitheater. But researchers have
discovered that the pits harbor a cluster of mi-
croclimates. Gradations of sun, shade, and
elevation among the terraces create dramatic
differences in temperature. Irrigation canals
and the discovery of different seeds on the terraces are additional clues that Moray was once
a gigantic crops laboratory. It was here, perhaps, that the Inca learned to grow corn and
potatoes in a variety of elevations, fueling the
expansion of the empire.

On the nearby hills that lead down to the
Urubamba Valley, the Inca once again transformed nature: A spring of warm, salty water
was diverted into thousands of pools, where
sunlight evaporates the water and leaves a thin

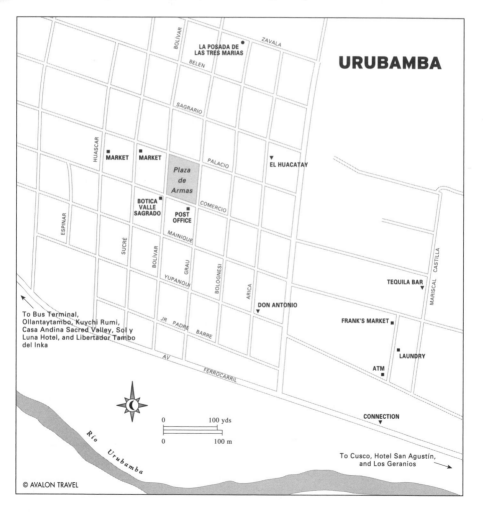

© JORGE RIVEROS CAYO

The concentric circles at Moray are believed to have been an Inca agricultural laboratory.

crust of salt. The salt mines, or *salineras*, continue to be worked by a collective of 260 salt miners from the nearby villages of Maras and Pichinjoto. (You may see this salt marketed overseas as "Peruvian pink salt.") Today there are 5,740 pools, or *pocitos*, each of which yields 150 kilograms of unrefined salt per month. There is a dazzling, and oft-photographed, contrast between the barren hillsides and the snow-white salt pools, which visitors can explore along narrow, crunchy paths.

To reach Moray, take a Cusco–Urubamba bus and get off at the Maras turnoff (say *"ramal a Maras, por favor"*). *Colectivos* wait here and charge US$6–9 for a half-day tour of Maras, Moray, and Salinas. A recommended company is **Empresa Transporte Moray.** To get from Moray to Salinas, car-bound travelers must return to Maras and then proceed another five kilometers downhill to the salt mines. Another option is to get a ride to Maras (four kilometers) and then walk the remaining seven kilometers to Moray (two hours, mostly uphill), through a patchwork of fields. From Moray, it is a two-hour walk—ask for directions along

the way—to the salt mines. A steep but beautiful path continues for another kilometer or two from Salinas to the Urubamba Valley, ending five kilometers down from Urubamba and at the doorstep of the recommended Tunupa Restaurant. This whole circuit makes for an excellent full-day tour on horse, bike, or foot, though many travelers elect to be dropped off at Salineras and take the scenic, one-hour walk to Urubamba.

ENTERTAINMENT AND EVENTS

Urubamba's nightlife has improved with the influx of students. The best way to begin an evening is with an empanada and a beer at **La Esquina** (Comercio 407, tel. 084/20-1554), on the main square. The owner of this pizza-and-empanada bar, a Lima transplant named Lucy, sings whenever the spirit moves her (and her musician friends show up).

Late night, your options are twofold: **Connection** (Mariscal Castilla, 6 P.M.–close) is a laid-back bar with a bit of art on the walls and an owner-DJ who spent the last eight years

WHERE FIESTAS ARE SERIOUS BUSINESS

With a final burst of drinking, dancing, and eating this past weekend we have at last wound up our annual participation in the fiesta of Our Lady of the Nativity, at Huayllabamba, a pueblo just upstream from Urubamba.

It's serious business. We had to scour our section of the Sacred Valley for guinea pigs and barnyard fowl, because the tasteless supermarket chicken is not acceptable to Our Lady. We had been fattening up a flock of ducks and a handful of free-range pigs and earmarked suckling piglets for the fiesta. A steer was dispatched, and many of our guests undertook to bring along sheep, more piglets, maize, and the scores of other items that go into endless days and nights of jolly breakfasts, lunches, suppers, and nonstop Andean music and dancing. Each of the meals is a banquet, some attended by hundreds of guests.

We were *mayordomos*, or sponsors, for one of the dozen groups that, each with its own elaborate costume, its own music, its own ancient tradition, danced for Our Lady. Her dressed-up statue was paraded round town, up the hill to a chapel, all in a tradition-ridden timetable organized by no one. There's no coordinating committee, and if anyone owns an electronic watch, they don't spend much time looking at it.

It would be misleading to say, though, that it's a clockwork operation. When my 12-year-old boy goes along for the rehearsals for the Capac Negro (*Millionaire Slaves of the Virgin*) dance group, in the weeks leading up to the fiesta, he has to wait till everyone else, including the fellow with the taped practice music, arrives. But on the day, you saw a score or so

of lads each in elaborate uniform, dancing with military precision to ancient Quechua tunes and rhythms, with dirges and chants that reach back thousands of years. Our Lady is just the latest in a long line of *apus*, the Andean gods who reside on the snow peaks, some of them visible from Huayllabamba.

A dozen more dance groups come along, with colorful costumes representing jungle Indians fighting the Inca, or the Inca fighting the Spaniards, or even – rather boring this one – barbers in top hats and morning coats, foot-long noses and scissors going snip-snip in time to weird Andean-medieval flute music.

One wonders what the contribution of these fiestas is to the gross domestic product. What do the World Bank people who drift by from time to time in their chauffeur-driven, laptopped Toyota 4x4s think of all this? What say the Inter-American Development Bank, USAID, and the European Union development people with their tax-free incomes and diplomatic passports?

We can be pretty sure that they switch off their satellite-feed cell phones and join in. They may not be having much luck solving our poverty, but that doesn't mean they can't spot the kind of party that, as they would be the first to recognize, none of them could begin to organize for themselves. Huayllabamba's **Virgen de la Natividad** is held September 7-10.

(Contributed by Nicholas Asheshov, M.A., a British journalist who has covered Peru for decades. Asheshov is the Planning Director for Andean Railways Corp. in Urubamba.)

---

in the United States. **Tequila Bar** (third block of Mariscal Castilla, tel. 084/80-1646, tequilaclub@hotmail.com, noon onwards), however, is the wild dance spot. Within the course of a night, this Jekyll and Hyde place can swing from mellow artist pub to Wild West bar, with fists (and beer bottles!) flying.

Urubamba erupts in bullfights, dancing, and partying during the Pentecostal celebration of Señor Torrechayoc in late May or early June and then once again for Urubamba Day on November 9. An even better party, however, is Huayllabamba's Virgen de la Natividad, held September 7–10.

SHOPPING

When in Urubamba, do not miss **Seminario Ceramics** (Barriózabal 111, tel. 084/20-1002, www.ceramicaseminario.com, 8 A.M.–5 P.M. daily). With Pablo Seminario focusing on form and Marilú Behar on color, this husband-and-wife team began to crank out ceramics out of a small home in Urubamba over two decades ago. Thanks to international recognition and lucrative contracts (including a deal with Pier 1 Imports), their original adobe workshop has blossomed into an expansive, garden-filled complex where visitors can pet llamas, watch an educational video, and see the whole ceramics-making process. The couple's workshop produces a range of objects from compotes and coffee cups to sculptures and large painting frames adorned with delicate touches of silver. Everything is handmade, painted with natural mineral oxides, and kiln fired.

For upscale shopping, head to an outlet of **Artenesia Mon Repos** (Cabo Conchatupa s/n, tel. 084/20-1174, www.monrepos-peru.com, 9 A.M.–6 P.M. daily), a Lima-based clothing store with classic designs.

RECREATION
Hiking, Biking, and Horseback Riding
Urubamba is a fast-growing center of adventure sports, including horseback riding, mountain biking, rafting, trekking, and paragliding. There are some highly recommended horseback rides—that can also be done on foot or mountain bike—on both sides of the Urubamba Valley. The sun in the Sacred Valley is intensely bright, so bring a sun hat and sunscreen. It is best to get an early start to avoid the often cloudy (sometimes rainy) afternoons.

To the north (snow-covered mountain side), several mule tracks lead up valleys to high passes on the Cordillera Vilcabamba. On the other side are remote Quechuan villages in the Lares Valley, a journey of several days with an option of returning by car at the end.

One of these valleys, the **Pumahuanca,** is a pleasant half-day trip that combines streams glinting in the morning sun; a series of microclimes, including forests of rhododendrons and native quenua trees; and, at the turnaround point, ruins of several two-story Inca buildings. The other valley above Urubamba

dead-ends at Chicón, the glaciated peak (5,530 meters) that looms above the village. This peak is rarely climbed, even though it is one of the easier summits in the Cusco area.

For those who can take a full day on a horse or on a bike, there is a breathtaking circuit on the south side of the valley that traverses the high plains around Maras and Moray and then descends via the salt mines to Urubamba. The scenery is spectacular.

Wayra (part of the Sol y Luna Hotel outside Urubamba, tel. 084/20-1620, www.wayrasacredvalley.com) rents mountain bikes and has the best selection of *paso* horses in the valley. Another great option for *paso* horses is **Perol Chico** (Carretera Urubamba–Ollantaytambo, tel. 084/974-79-8890, www.perolchico.com). These elegant animals, which kick their feet out to one side for a smooth ride, are best for the Maras–Moray–Salinas loop or a flat loop around the valley (they are not well suited, however, for the steep Pumahuanca ride).

Rafting
All of the Cusco rafting agencies descend the Río Urubamba, which is at its wildest during the high-water months December–May. Day trips run US$40–55. Some trips include one night of camping near Ollantaytambo, mountain biking, and a chance to see ruins the next day.

As the river drops between June and November, the agencies run the steeper, lower section that ends just past Ollantaytambo, though the rapids rarely exceed Class III. The water itself, unfortunately, is somewhat polluted, with plastic festooning the banks.

One of the most professional rafting companies in Peru is **Amazonas Explorer** (Collasuyo 910, Urb. Miravalle, Cusco, tel. 084/25-2846, www.amazonas-explorer.com). **ExplorAndes** (Av. Garcilaso 316-A, Cusco tel. 084/23-8380 or Lima tel. 01/715-2323, www.explorandes.com) also offers high-end rafting trips.

Some less expensive but also experienced agencies are recommended for easier trips. **Apumayo Expediciones** (Jr. Ricardo Palma N-5, Santa Monica, tel. 084/24-6018, www.apumayo.com) is run by Pepe López, a kayaker with a lot of experience on Peru's rivers. He recently built an adventure center on the banks of the Río Urubamba, downstream of Ollantaytambo.

Mayuc (Portal Confituras 211, Plaza de Armas, Cusco, tel. 084/24-2824, www.mayuc.com) is one of the pioneering rafting companies and operates an excellent day trip on Río Urubamba.

Loreto Tours (Calle del Medio 111, Cusco, tel. 084/22-8264, loretotours@planet.com.pe) provides varied rafting itineraries and good-quality equipment.

Terra Explorer Peru (Santa Ursula D-4, Huanchac, tel. 084/23-7352, www.terraexplorerperu.com) is owned by Piero, the youngest of the Vellutino brothers, all dedicated and well known adventure sportsmen and white-water rafters. **Munaycha** (based in the Sacred Valley, tel. 084/984-770-108 or 084/984-770-381, www.munaycha.com) belongs to Duilio, the oldest Vellutino brother, and also offers rafting on Peru's best known rivers.

Climbing

A new adventure in the Sacred Valley is the **Via Ferrata** (tel. 084/98-974-360-260, viaferrata@naturavive.com, www.naturavive.com, US$60 pp), a system of ropes and pulleys that allows you to climb a 300-meter cliff and then rappel, or descend, about 100 meters. The whole experience lasts three–five hours and can even be done by small children. Reservations must be made in advance by emailing or calling Natura Vive.

Paragliding

The best place to get parapenting lessons in the Cusco area is Wayra (part of the Sol y Luna Hotel outside Urubamba, tel. 084/20-1620, www.wayrasacredvalley.com), where owners Marie-Hélène Miribel and Franz Schilter offer paragliding lessons. They are the only internationally certified instructors in Cusco. They charge US$150 for a tandem one-hour flight, taking off from a nearby mountain and landing in the valley itself.

ACCOMMODATIONS
Under US$10

Hotels in Urubamba tend toward upscale, and finding a budget hotel can be tricky. A good option is the shared room at **La Posada de las Tres Marias** (Zavala 307, tel. 084/20-1006, posada3marias@yahoo.com, US$10 pp with breakfast). This converted house has a large dining room, which opens onto a huge garden complete with a patio and tables for an afternoon beer and card playing. The hotel also has private rooms, but they are overpriced for their value.

US$10-25

Los Geranios Hostel (Cabo Conchatupa s/n, tel. 084/20-1093, US$14 s, US$21 d), best known for its lunch buffets, has a few rooms with lots of sunlight, private baths, and hot water. The backyard spills onto the Urubamba riverbanks.

US$25-50

If you've ever wanted to live in a tree house, **Las Chullpas** (Gonzalo Muñoz, tel. 084/20-1568, www.chullpas.uhupi.com, US$45 s/d) is your chance. Chalo, a Chilean, and his German wife, Leonie, have created a lovely set of 10 bungalows, interlaced with gardens, whose tree-trunk floors, tile mosaics, and adobe walls remind you that nature is very playful. One room has a slide in the bathroom, and all beds are covered with homemade alpaca duvets. Sitting in the gardens and watching the hummingbirds is a real treat.

US$100-150

The **Hotel San Agustín Monasterio de la Recoleta** (Recoleta s/n, tel. 084/20-1004, www.hotelessanagustin.com.pe, US$120 s, US$144 d) occupies a stunning, 16th-century Franciscan monastery, though erratic service continues to keep guests away. There is a modern addition with a few spectacular rooms upstairs, outfitted with exposed beams, stone showers, and sun windows. Rooms in the old section are surrounded by a stone courtyard and cannot be renovated because of historical restrictions—they are nicer than the bland modern rooms. All rooms have private baths.

Over US$150

Mexican owner Claudia calls her flower-lined, central walkway the hummingbird corridor. She's right. Walking down it, you're almost guaranteed to see the world's largest hummingbirds. But even better is when the birds flit around your private house, which is what Claudia and her architect husband rent to their lucky guests. ⬛ **Kuychi Rumi Lodging** (Km 74.5 Urubamba-Ollantaytambo Highway, tel. 084/20-1169, www.urubamba.com, US$154 s or d) offers six fully-equipped houses with two bedrooms, a sitting room, and a kitchenette. Tastefully designed and decorated, the houses are meant for a several-day stay, but even if you only have a night, they are worth the privacy and comfort.

Our vote for the most elegant, luxurious hotel in the Sacred Valley goes to the **Sol y Luna Hotel** (tel. 084/20-1620, www.hotelsolyluna.com, US$200 s/d to US$750 for a new deluxe suite, with breakfast), opened in 2000 by Marie-Hélène Miribel and Franz Schilter. This French-Swiss couple have carefully designed every last detail of their 43 bungalows, including terra-cotta tiles, exposed beams, marble bathrooms, and king-size beds. Stay at the newly created luxury bungalows, which include a hot tub on your patio. The US$27 poolside buffet is exquisite, using local produce from the valley. It also has a dessert spread that includes cake made from *lúcuma,* the intoxicatingly tasty fruit. Groups are often treated to *pachamanca* cooking with *marinera* dance demonstrations. Plan on spending time here to stroll through the hotel's gardens, lounge by the pool, work out at the gym, or check into the spa, which includes a whirlpool tub and massage. There are 20 Peruvian horses (*caballos de paso*) lodged in elegant stables in the back and available for half- and full-day rides. If that is not enough, the hotel also rents mountain bikes, coordinates cultural trips to a local school and orphanage, and offers paragliding outings with

the owners, Cusco's only internationally certified instructors. Through an associated non-profit organization, the hotel has also recently created a local school and engaged in other philanthropic efforts.

Another new upscale option is the **Libertador Tambo del Inka** (Av. Ferrocarril, tel. 84/58-1777, www.luxurycollection.com/vallesagrado, US$455 to US$565 s), designed by Bernard Fort on the banks of the Urubamba. The elegant lobby, with 12-meter ceilings, mixed international standards with Peruvian decor. The 128 rooms and suites all have either a balcony or a terrace, and all come with WiFi, cable TV, and iPod docks. This luxury hotel has a 1,800-square-meter spa offering massages, pool and Jacuzzi. At night, hit the Bar Kiri, with its outstanding back-lit onyx wall.

Outside Urubamba

In Yanahuara, just 15 minutes outside of Urubamba on the road to Ollantaytambo, the hotel chain **Casa Andina** has constructed one of its **Private Collection** hotels (5th Paradero, tel. 084/976-5501, www.casa-andina.com, US$200 s d with breakfast). The result is a labyrinth of glassed lobbies, gardens, spa center, and planetarium. You might just have to spend two nights to take advantage of it all. There's so much to do, you'll have to make sure you don't spend all your energy sightseeing. It's also very child friendly with a small playground, llamas, and lots of open space.

In Huayllabamba, the **Aranwa** (tel. 01/434-1452, www.aranwahotels.com, US$160 s/d) chain of hotels has opened a new 100-bedroom, 15-suite complex that includes one of the largest spas in the Sacred Valley. The luxury hotel includes a business center, three restaurants, a sushi bar, and even a cinema. The newer buildings are built around a historic hacienda. There is no formal address for this hotel, but you will find it on the main road between Huayllabamba and Urubamba.

Rio Sagrado (Km 75.8 Cusco–Urubamba Highway, tel. 084/20-1631, www.riosagrado.com, US$205 s) is the latest in the

PERU'S BATTLE WITH THE BOTTLE

Every time travelers buy a plastic water bottle, they are contributing to a solid waste problem that is reaching epic proportions not only in Cusco but all over Peru. The best way to understand the problem is to raft along Cusco's Río Urubamba, where tree roots are blanketed in thick gobs of plastic bags and beaches are completely covered with plastic bottles.

What resources Peru's municipal governments have are used to fight poverty, not improve the environment. There is no plastic recycling in Peru, so everything ends up in open landfills or, as is the case with the Urubamba, floating downstream to the Amazon. Nearly 200 million plastic bottles are produced every month in Peru alone, and a good chunk of these are consumed by tourists – who need a few liters of purified water for each day in Peru.

Recently a boycott campaign has been initiated by longtime Ollantaytambo resident Joaquín Randall, who manages his family's El Albergue Hotel in Ollantaytambo.

Here's how travelers can do their part to resolve Peru's plastic addiction:

· Carry a reusable hard plastic or other water bottle and fill it with treated or boiled water.

· Buy sodas and water in refillable glass bottles.

· Demand that your hotel provide water tanks (*bidones*) or at the very least boiled water for refilling bottles.

· Reuse plastic bags over and over and do not accept new ones.

· Spread the word.

Orient-Express line of hotels, located on the outskirts of Urubamba. It's a newly built hotel with a mixture of high-quality rooms, suites, and two-story bungalows. As seems to be the fashion in the valley, they have also created a spa.

FOOD
Peruvian
The Sacred Valley day tours use Urubamba as a lunch spot, so there are a half dozen restaurants that offer good lunch buffets. The best, and newest, of these is **Alhambra** (Km 74 Urubamba–Ollantaytambo Highway, tel. 084/20-1200, www.alhambrarestaurant.com, noon–3:30 P.M. and 7 P.M.–close daily, US$12–14). The buffet table, full of colors and flavors, is a work of art! Another excellent buffet is available at **Killa Wasi,** the restaurant connected to Sol y Luna Hotel (tel. 084/20-1620, www.hotelsolyluna.com, noon–7 P.M. Tues., Thurs., and Sun., US$27).

If you're looking for a more informal

atmosphere, try **3 Keros** (Sr. de Torrechayoc, tel. 084/20-1701, noon–3:45 P.M. and 6–9:30 P.M. Wed.–Mon., US$12–15). Ricardo, the owner of this laid-back restaurant, dishes up *cuy* specials and Quillabamba mangos while his patrons catch the Michigan game.

Los Geranios (Cabo Conchatupa s/n, tel. 084/20-1093, noon–5 P.M. daily, US$9 buffet) is the least pretentious and most authentic of a group of restaurants on Urubamba's main drag. **Finestra** (Mariscal Castilla 107, tel. 084/20-1005, 8:30 A.M.–4:30 P.M. and 6–10 P.M. Mon.–Sat., US$2–5) is the place to go for a filling midday lunch menu. The service is fast and the decor pleasant.

International
After years of working abroad, first in Spain, then Germany, chef Pio Vasquez has finally returned to his home country, Peru. With the help of his German wife, Iris, they have created an elegant restaurant and garden. Have your passion fruit pisco sour on the patio of

El Huacatay (Arica 620, tel. 084/20-1790, www.elhuacatay.com, 1–10 P.M. Mon.–Sat., US$10–15) before moving into the intimate dining room for a main course based on local produce from arugula to fresh trout. Dessert is Pio's passion, so leave room for the chocolate mousse. Child-friendly.

Another new option is **Don Antonio** (corner of Jr Yupanqui and Arica, tel. 084/20-1501, noon–7 P.M. daily), offering a small menu with pasta, fish, and meat, set in a beautiful garden with fountain.

Markets

For the basics—fruit, cheese, cold cuts, and wine—there's **Frank's Market** (Mariscal Castilla 1032, 7:30 A.M.–2 P.M. and 3–10:30 P.M. daily).

INFORMATION AND SERVICES

There's a **police station** on Palacio (s/n, tel. 084/20-1012). The **town clinic** is on 9 de Noviembre (s/n, tel. 084/20-1032, lab open 8 A.M.–1 P.M.), or visit Dr. Hugo Chavez (Palacios 133, tel. 084/965-5386). There are now a number of tourist clinics in Urubamba, including **SOS Urgent Medical** (Mariscal Castilla, tel. 084/20-5059), which is a modern facility that works with different insurance companies. There are pharmacies all over town, but a good option is **Botica Valle Sagrado** (Bolivar 469, tel. 084/20-1830, 8 A.M.–10 P.M. daily).

On the highway in front of Urubamba, there is a **Banco de Crédito** ATM, and in the Pesca gas station there is a **Global Net** ATM.

The **post office** is on the main square, along with several pay phones under the municipality awning. There are several **Internet** locales, which are generally open 9 A.M.–10 P.M. daily.

Do your laundry at **Clean Wash Laundry** (Mariscal Castilla 100, 8 A.M.–7 P.M. Mon.–Sat.).

Volunteering

ProPeru (Apartado 70, tel. 084/20-1562, www.proworldsc.org) is a highly recommended organization, run by a Peruvian named Richard Webb. The organization arranges homestays for college students (and older folks, too) in Urubamba, Cusco, and other areas in Peru. Students take classes in art, history, anthropology, and Spanish, and work on service projects that range from reforestation to setting up a women's shelter or the town's first Internet café. ProPeru receives rave reviews from its students and is surely one of the better foreign study programs in Peru. Other volunteer organizations in Urubamba include **Casa de los Milagros** (casademilagros@yahoo.com, www.chandlersky.org, U.S. tel. 408/532-0644), which works with children with disabilities.

GETTING THERE AND AROUND

From Cusco, *combis* for Urubamba leave from the first block of Grau near the bridge (US$1.25, 1.5 hours). *Combis* drop passengers at Urubamba's bus station on the main drag, where frequent transport continues for the 20-minute ride to Ollantaytambo and Pisac (10 minutes).

Motocars are ubiquitous in Urubamba and can be contracted cheaply to arrive at the Chicón or Pumahuanca road or for getting to Yucay. **Sol y Luna Hotel** offers a full-day valley tour to Ollantaytambo and Pisac, in a private car with lunch included. Another option is to contract a private driver and car—Ollantaytambo and Pisac together is US$40, while one or the other is US$25. Ask your hotel for recommendations.

Ollantaytambo and Vicinity

Ollantaytambo is the last town in the Sacred Valley before the Río Urubamba plunges through steep gorges toward Machu Picchu. It is the best-preserved Inca village in Peru, with its narrow alleys, street water canals, and trapezoidal doorways. The Inca temple and fortress above town is second in beauty only to Machu Picchu. In the terraced fields above town, men still use foot plows, or *chaquitacllas,* to till fields and plant potatoes. There are endless things to explore in and around Ollantaytambo, which is framed by snowcapped Verónica mountain and surrounded on all sides by Inca ruins, highways, and terraces. Whisking through Ollantaytambo, as most travelers do, is a great shame. Stay and get to know the place.

Ollantaytambo is also in the throes of a tremendous struggle to save its way of life against the mass forces of tourism and development. Trinket sellers have crowded the areas in front of the Inca temple and the train

station. Nondescript pizzerias are creeping onto the main square, which is continually shaken by the passing of massive trucks bound for the Camisea pipeline in the jungle around Quillabamba. One solution to these problems, as resident Wendy Weeks suggests, is to move the train station outside of town and have visitors enter as the Inca did—through the main gate and *on foot.*

The town's saving grace, and what should carry it through its present crisis, is the tremendous sense of community that is palpable to anyone who pauses here. A cadre of researchers, led by English archaeologist Anne Kendall, have spent considerable time researching Inca farming technology and have restored hundreds of farming terraces and aqueducts.

HISTORY

Ollantaytambo was occupied long before the Inca by the Quillques, who built some of the rougher buildings at Pumamarca and on the ridge near the Ollantaytambo temple itself. After Inca emperor Pachacútec conquered this area around 1440, construction began on a ceremonial center and royal estate that housed an estimated 1,000 workers year-round. What Ollantaytambo is most famous for, however, is a 1537 battle in which the Inca defeated a Spanish army—and nearly massacred it altogether.

The battle happened during the 1536–1537 Inca rebellion, when Manco Inca was forced to withdraw his troops to Ollantaytambo after being defeated by the Spanish at Sacsayhuamán. Hernando Pizarro arrived at Ollantaytambo one morning at dawn with 70 cavalry and 30 foot soldiers. But Manco Inca's men were waiting on the terraces of the sun temple, which had been hastily converted into a fort. Pedro Pizarro wrote afterward, "We found it so well fortified that it was a thing of horror." Conquistadors Juan, Francisco, and Hernando Pizarro were brothers and Pedro Pizarro was their cousin.

Río Urubamba outside Ollantaytambo

THE SACRED VALLEY

OLLANTAYTAMBO

From high on the upper terraces, Manco Inca commanded his troops from horseback—co-opting the symbol of Spanish strength—as jungle archers shot volleys of arrows and Inca soldiers fired off slingshots and rolled boulders. Sensing defeat, the Spaniards retreated, but Manco Inca pulled a final surprise. On cue, he diverted the Río Urubamba and flooded the plains below Ollantaytambo, causing the Spaniards' horses to founder in the mud. Manco's forces fought the Spanish all the way to Cusco, where Pizarro waited for

Diego de Almagro to return from his Chile campaign with reinforcements. Manco Inca, meanwhile, recognized the growing strength of the Spaniards and withdrew to Vilcabamba.

After Manco's departure, the whole valley became an *encomienda* for Hernando Pizarro, who pursued Manco deep into Vilcabamba and raided his camp in 1539. Manco narrowly escaped, but his wife and sister, Cura Ocllo, was captured and brought to Ollantaytambo. After Manco refused to surrender, Francisco Pizarro had Cura Ocllo stripped, whipped,

© BETH FUCHS

plowing with oxen in Ollantaytambo

and killed with arrows. To make sure Manco got the message, they floated her body down the Río Urubamba toward Vilcabamba, where Manco's troops found her.

About two-thirds of the inhabitants of the Sacred Valley died of diseases brought by the Spanish. The descendants of the survivors were put to work in the haciendas that sprung up in the valley, often the result of Spaniards marrying Inca elite. One of these, the Hacienda Sillque, is today a ruin of adobe walls and arched doorways, about 20 kilometers west of Ollantaytambo. A road down the Urubamba Valley to Quillabamba was begun in 1895. It was this road that Hiram Bingham took to "discover" Machu Picchu in 1911. In the 1920s, the road was converted into the rail line that now carries travelers to Machu Picchu.

SIGHTS
City Tour
Ask your bus driver to let you off one kilometer before Ollantaytambo at the original Inca Trail, which follows the hillside on the right (north) side of town. To your left is the plain

that Manco Inca flooded in the 1537 battle against the Spanish. The path leads up to the town's restored terraces and through a massive Inca gate, through which a water channel still runs. The path then joins with the road past the Wall of 100 Niches, whose inward slant indicates this was the inside—not the outside—of a roadside building (or maybe the road went through the building).

Once in the main plaza, head a half block north to the original Inca town, named **Qozqo Ayllu,** which is laid out in the form of a trapezoid and bisected by narrow, irrigated alleys. Oversized trapezoidal doorways open in the courtyards of homes, or *kanchas,* occupied continuously ever since Pachacútec's time.

◖ Ollantaytambo Temple
The other half of Ollantaytambo, **Araqama Ayllu,** is across the Río Patacancha. The main square is fronted with a series of monumental buildings, and above is the temple that was being constructed when the Spaniards arrived—and was later converted into a fortress by Manco Inca.

perfect stonework at Ollantaytambo's Temple of the Sun

Two hundred steps lead up terraces to a double-jamb gateway and the **Temple of Ten Niches,** a long wall with odd protuberances. Some say these bumps draw heat away from the slabs, preventing them from expanding. Others say they somehow served in the transport of the blocks. Or perhaps the Inca valued them as we do today, for the graceful shadows they cast across the stone.

Above is the unfinished **Temple of the Sun,** considered one of the masterpieces of Inca stonework. Six giant monoliths of pink rhyolite are perfectly slotted together with thin slices of stone and oriented to glow with the rising sun. Traces of the *chacana* symbols and pumas that once decorated the walls can still be seen. What is unusual about the wall is the long straight lines—and the molten bronze that was poured in the T-joints to hold the wall together. These features indicate the wall was probably the handiwork of Lake Titicaca's Colla Indians, who were brought to work here by Pachacútec as part of the forced labor system known as *mitimayo.* According to J. P. Protzen, the wall was probably intended to be

one side of a great platform, which seems likely with the unfinished blocks, rough walls, and plaza nearby. It is uncertain why the construction stopped—perhaps it was Pachacútec's death, a rebellion of the Colla Indians, the smallpox epidemic of 1527, or the arrival of the Spaniards.

To the left of the plaza, the **Cachicata quarry** appears high on the hillside. The Inca dragged boulders weighing up to 52 tons down the mountain, across the Río Urubamba and the valley floor, and then up a steep ramp—the top of which is at a 25-degree angle, three times that allowed on most U.S. highways! Ollantaytambo expert Vincent Lee used sleds and levers to show how the Inca moved such blocks up the ramp, which still leads up the hillside to the temple. On the ridge above the temple are rougher buildings and the **Incahuatana,** the hitching place of the Inca, where prisoners may have been lashed into human-sized portals.

At the base of the ruins are the **Princess Baths,** a half dozen fountains adorned with *chacana* symbols. Some of the fountains are engineered in such a way as to cause a whirl-pool that allows sediment to drop before the water continues over a delicately shaped spout. On the steep flanks of Pinculluna, the sacred hill that rises above the Inca town, are the ruins of several granaries, which glow in the afternoon sun.

ENTERTAINMENT AND EVENTS

Ollantaytambo has a small but lively night-life scene, due mainly to a community of expats who live in town year-round. Be sure to patronize places that seem respectful of surrounding residents and do not encourage use of drugs, which is an increasing problem in town. **Señor Ganso** (Horno Calle, 1.5 blocks from the square, 9 A.M.–11 P.M. daily) has a great second floor lounge. Bars and clubs change often in Ollantaytambo.

During the **Fiesta de Reyes** (the Celebration of the Kings) on January 6, a revered image of Jesus is brought down to Ollantaytambo from Marcacocha, a town high up in the Patacancha Valley. The event includes a solemn procession around Ollantaytambo's main square, which involves even more images of baby Jesus.

On January 6, over 200 Wallta dancers come down from the hills of Mount Pinkuylluna. These Quechua-speaking communities, dressed in the traditional red outfits, dance and lead processions until the following day.

During the eight-day **Carnaval** season in late January and early February, the upper Patacancha Valley explodes into a series of traditions: cow branding, offerings to mountain *apus* by local priests, *wallata* (the dance of the condor), and ritual battles between towns that are now fought with mature fruit instead of rocks.

The town's most important celebration is the **Señor de Choquequilca,** which happens during the Pentecost at the end of May or early June. The festival dates back to the miraculous appearance of a wooden cross near the town's Inca bridge. A chapel dedicated to El Señor de Choquequilca was completed in the main square in 1995.

SHOPPING

To find authentic, all-natural weavings and hand-icrafts, head to **Awamaki** (Calle Convención s/n, across from the temple, www.awamaki-us.org). All proceeds go to the people of the communities with which Awamaki works.

RECREATION

Several agencies operate trips, including horseback riding, rafting, biking, etc. in this area. One that is highly recommended is **KB Tambo Tours** (Ventiderio s/n, tel. 084/20-4091, www.kbperu.com), run by a long-time resident originally from the United States. **Sota Adventures** (Plaza de Armas s/n, tel. 084/984-080-718), operated by two local brothers; **KB Tours** (Plaza de Armas s/n, tel. 084/20-4133, kbtours_2@hotmail.com); and the NGO **Awamaki** (Calle Convención s/n, across from the temple, www.awamaki-us.org) also organize excursions to the communities outside Ollantaytambo.

Hikes

Ollantaytambo is a great base for a number of excellent hikes, treks, and community visits in

the terraces at the temple in Ollantaytambo

the area. A detailed map of a dozen local hikes is available from the NGO Awamaki (Calle Convención s/n, across from the temple, www. awamaki-us.org) for about US$5. Summaries of these hikes, taken from the Awamaki guide with permission, are listed here. Before setting out on these hikes, check with Awamaki for updated directions.

◖ Inca Granaries (Pinkuylluna)

This moderate, 1.5-hour hike explores the Inca ruins that can be seen from town on the hillside opposite the Ollantaytambo fortress. The larger buildings were used for agricultural storehouses called *colcas*. Along with the multiple Inca sites, this steep hike offers great elevated views of Ollantaytambo and the fortress.

To reach the trailhead from the plaza, take Calle Principal toward Cusco. Take your first left after leaving the plaza completely on Calle Lares. After a few blocks, you will see a stone staircase on your right with a sign for Pinkuylluna. The stone staircase continues up the mountain for 10 to 15 minutes before the trail forks. The trail to the right (with the wooden handrail) will lead you around the corner to the first Inca ruins.

After exploring these, the best option is to descend back down to the fork in the trail and take the trail uphill in the other direction. The trail passes another Inca site and arrives at the large four-tiered storehouse in about 20–30 minutes. From here you can continue up the trail to the four towers that mark the crown of the head of the Tunupa, the god of abundance. If you continue up the mountain from here the views improve but the trail becomes unclear.

Pumamarca

The round-trip hike to the ruins of Pumamarca takes about 4–6 hours from Ollantaytambo on a moderate, steadily climbing trail. The ruins of Pumamarca sit on a hillside overlooking the convergence of the Río Patacancha and the Yuracmayo (White River). The well-preserved site was thought to be a checkpoint to control access to Ollantaytambo.

To reach Pumamarca, follow Patacalle out of town. Shortly after the first bridge, a large path leaves the main road to the right and follows the river. Follow this path for about 15 minutes until it rejoins the main road at the small town of Munaypata. Just up the road you will see an electrical pole on the left labeled 2224 and a path leading behind the adjacent house. Follow this path uphill for 15 more minutes to a blue archaeological marker for the Media Luna terraces in front of you. At this point, follow the switchback up the hill to your right (and not the path in front of you toward the terraces). The trail continues to climb steeply but will soon become more gradual.

After another hour or so of hiking, the trail comes to a clearing with small waterfalls and the beginning of ancient aqueducts. The trail follows an aqueduct and in 20–30 more minutes the ruins of Pumamarca will become apparent on the hillside in front of you. The trail becomes less clear at this point, but you can take multiple routes through the terraced fields up to the ruins (the main entrance is on the right side of the complex). At times there is someone working at the ruins who can provide information, but if not there is currently no entrance fee or hours when the ruins are closed. After exploring the ruins, you can return to Ollantaytambo by the same path or you can descend the hillside to the town of Pallata and take the road down from there.

Inca Quarries (Canteras) and Sun Gate (Inti Punku)

This round-trip walk, which takes 4–6 hours and a few more to reach the Sun Gate, begins at the Inca bridge near Ollantaytambo and along the banks of the Río Urubamba. It follows a fairly well-preserved Inca trail to Cachicata, the stone quarry 700–900 meters above the valley floor that is visible from the Ollantaytambo sun temple. It was here that the great stone blocks were slid down the hillside and hauled across the river to Ollantaytambo. There are three separate stone quarries, within half a kilometer of one another, littered with massive chiseled blocks and small *chullpas,* or burial towers. The western and highest quarry contains mysterious needle-shaped blocks that are up to seven meters long.

From Cachicata, it is possible to see that the terraces below the Ollantaytambo ruins form a pyramid shape, with one 750-meter-long wall aligning with the rays of the winter solstice. New Age theorists Fernando and Edgar Elorieta believe this is the original Pakaritampu, where the four Inca brothers emerged to found Cusco. A few hours' walk above the Cachicata is a perfect Inca gate that frames Salcantay in the background. On the trail approaching the quarries, numerous *piedras cansadas* (tired stones) that never made it to their final destination can be observed. The trail climbs high on the hillside, offering great views of Ollantaytambo and the surrounding peaks. Be prepared; the majority of the hike is fully exposed to the sun, and the only available water is near the beginning of the hike.

Begin by taking a right after the Inca bridge. After about 15–20 minutes take a left at the fork up the hill (a boulder at the fork is labeled "Canteras"). Continue to stay left, following the main path when other trails diverge. In about 20–30 minutes you will reach agricultural terraces and stone building foundations. Follow the trail straight past the foundations, not the smaller trail uphill. You will arrive at the first quarry 1.5–2 hours after starting. Look for small stone buildings built on top of large boulders beneath you. Just after passing through the quarry, look for a smaller path to the left leading uphill from the large trail. If you choose to filter water, a small switchback to the left immediately after this turn will lead to the last water source.

Follow switchbacks up the hillside past the first quarry for one hour. As the grassy trail starts to level out, watch out for a rounded stone resembling a primitive wheel off the trail to your left. As the trail plateaus you will see a much larger quarry to your left and several small fields. These flat fields are a great place to camp if you plan to spend the night. A large boulder in the middle of the quarry has "Instituto National de Cultura" painted in white. Before and to the left of this boulder, a path made of smaller stones leads up though the quarry. Exploring this path, you can find a burial site with skeletons under a large boulder, along with many quarried stones that never made it to Ollantaytambo.

Looking further ahead on the same trail, you can see Inti Punku, or the Sun Gate, on the ridge ahead. To continue to Inti Punku, pass the large boulder with "I.N.C." painted on it and head toward the largest boulder you see. Find the trail on the left side of the boulder and follow it uphill, crossing a scree field. After 30–45 minutes the trail comes to a grass field with Inca ruins (another good campsite). The trail continues just beyond and uphill from these. The trail forks once at a small ravine about 10 minutes from the Sun Gate; take a right through the ravine. About 30–45 minutes from the ruins you will reach Inti Punku. From Inti Punku, return along same path to the last quarry (about 1 hour).

The return route from Las Canteras should take 1.5–2 hours. Follow the trail down switchbacks to the first quarry. Take a left just past the first quarry on a small path and circle back under the quarry. From here you can see two houses with metal roofs on the left hillside. Continue to descend along this ridge toward the houses and the trail improves. From the houses, continue along the trail downhill into the valley. The trail improves and continues downhill through more houses and finally to a bridge. Cross the bridge and follow the railroad tracks on your right. Turn left at a set of stone stairs after 10–15 minutes on tracks and follow the path back to town.

ACCOMMODATIONS
Under US$10

Unlike Urubamba, Ollantaytambo has plenty of good budget options for backpackers taking the morning or afternoon train to Machu Picchu. **Hostel Quilla** (Calle Quiswar s/n, tel. 084/79-5432, US$5 shared bathroom, US$16.50 private bathroom) is the town's best budget option. Rooms are simple and cozy and there is a communal kitchen, equipped with an oven. The shared bathrooms have hot water. Just down the street is another cheap option, **Hostel El Tambo** (Calle Horno, 1.5 blocks from the plaza, tel. 084/77-3262, US$5 pp) The baths are also shared with hot water. According to the owner, Hiram Bingham stayed at this hostel back in 1911.

In the old Inca town, **Hostal Chaska Wasi** (Calle del Medio s/n, tel. 084/20-4045, www. hostalchaskawasi.com, US$5 dorm, US$9 d) has several clean rooms, with wooden floors, arranged around a tiny courtyard. The terrace on the top of the building is a good place to drink tea and look at the Inca granaries. Walking through town, and following the road left (toward the ruins) to the San Isidro neighborhood, you'll find a few families that have turned their homes into hostels under a now-defunct government program. Rooms here cost around US$5 for dorm rooms and shared bathrooms. Private rooms are also available.

US$10-50

An excellent option in this price range is the new **Hostel Iskay** (Patacalle s/n, tel. 084/20-4180, www.hosteliskay.com, US$10–15 s, US$25–30 d with continental breakfast), a small and lovely hostel with a beautiful garden and an astounding view of the ruins. The rooms are clean and simple (the family room on the other end of the garden has a beautiful kapuli tree that grows into the wall of the room). The common living/dining area with sofas, television, books, and board games has real Inca walls and an open kitchen. The friendly Spanish owners are long-time residents of Ollantaytambo. Another comfortable option is **KB Tambo** (Ventiderio s/n, tel. 084/20-4091, www.kbperu.com, US$20 s, US$30 d), which has cozy, unpretentious modern rooms with private bathrooms from singles and doubles to family suites. It has a beautiful small garden and a rooftop with amazing views of the ruins, a Jacuzzi, full bar, and pizza oven. **Hostel Las Orquideas** (Ferrocarril s/n, tel. 084/20-4032, lasorquideas3@hotmail.com, US$20 s, US$30 d with breakfast) has small,

plain rooms with private baths around a courtyard and garden. Spend your afternoon relaxing in the grassy courtyard.

US$50-100

Ollantaytambo's most charming and best-known hotel is **El Albergue** (Ferrocarril s/n, tel. 084/20-4014, www.elalbergue.com, US$58 s, US$74 d with breakfast). The lodge was opened by Wendy Weeks, a painter from Seattle, who arrived here in 1976 after an overland journey with her husband, writer Robert Randall. After her husband's death in 1990, Wendy stayed to raise her two sons here—Joaquín, who now runs the lodge, and Ishmael, who is an internationally recognized sculptor. Wendy Weeks is a beloved member of the community and a passionate spokeswoman for its preservation.

To reach El Albergue, head to the train station, through the gate, and down the tracks in the direction of an arrow and large sign for El Albergue painted on a wall. Or if you are arriving by train, simply disembark, and you'll be there. Compared to the mayhem of the station, El Albergue is a hushed paradise. Blue-and-yellow tanagers flit among datura flowers and a huge Canary Island palm that was planted in the 1920s. The rooms are huge, with white-washed walls, wood tables and beds, and an uncluttered grace. This year, eight new upscale rooms, which cost US$94 per night, have been built in the back. They have floor heating and bathtubs. Decorations include local weavings, Wendy's paintings, a vase of flowers, and a river stone or two. After a breakfast of coffee and French toast, guests browse through the eclectic store, which sells books, weavings, bottles of Matacuy (a homemade *digestif*), and sundry hard-to-find objects—Ekeko dolls, Waq'ullu dance masks, and all the metal fittings for a *sapo* table, the colonial game that is like horseshoes with a twist. Days end with a book on the wood balconies above the garden, followed by an evening steam in the wood-fired sauna. Bottled water, and pisco sours on the house during happy hour, come with the rooms.

Hostel Sauce (Ventiderio s/n, tel. 084/20-4044, www.hostelsauce.com.pe, US$89 s, US$98 d with breakfast) is a serene, upscale establishment with eight sun-filled rooms overlooking the Ollantaytambo ruins. The restaurant, serving salads, meats, and pastas, has a cozy sitting area with a fireplace and couches.

US$100-150

Built in 2000, the luxury **Hotel Pakaritampu** (Ferrocarril s/n, tel. 084/20-4020, www.pakaritampu.com, US$127 s, US$132 d with breakfast) seems a bit out of place in Ollantaytambo. The modern two-story buildings appear overly grand for this humble town and its ruins. But if this doesn't bother you, the hotel does have pleasant gardens and large rooms with wood floors, spring mattresses, goose down duvets, telephones, and small balconies. The nice couches and a fireplace are good for having a drink by, and there is an interesting library. The restaurant is not recommended. Other services include laundry, Internet, and luggage storage.

FOOD
Peruvian and International

For an excellent meal, head down to the train station to the restaurant ((**El Albergue** (Ferrocarril s/n, tel. 084/20-4077, reservations@elalbergue.com, 5 A.M.–9:30 P.M. daily, US$6–10). Using organic vegetables from the Sacred Valley, the menu is inventive and has great vegetarian options. Try the alpaca with *huacatay* mash or the lamb tenderloin with chimichurri and quinoa risotto. Pasta lovers can order a plate of homemade fettuccini with their favorite sauce. Reservations are recommended. The best coffee in Ollantaytambo is also found at the train station, at the El Albergue's **Café Mayu** (Ferrocarril s/n, tel. 084/20-4014, 5 A.M.–9:30 P.M. daily, US$2–15). Order your favorite coffee, be it an espresso, latte, or cappuccino, and drink it to wash down a delicious chocolate chip cookie or brownie. Coffees are also available in the hotel's restaurant.

Kusicoyllor Café-Bar (Calle Convención across from the temple, tel. 084/20-4114,

8 A.M.–10 P.M. daily, US$5–8), located directly in front of the ruins, serves a variety of traditional dishes with a modern flair, as well as croissants, espresso, and homemade ice cream.

((**Pachamama Grill** (Convención s/n, 11:30 A.M.–10 P.M. daily, US$7–10) has amazing trout, pizza, and *lomo saltado*. Local NGO Awamaki can even arrange cooking classes with Zenayda, the charismatic and accomplished chef at Pachamama Grill!

Another good bet is the **Panaka Grill Restaurant** (Plaza de Armas s/n, 7 A.M.–10 P.M. daily, US$7–10), whose second floor tables look down on the plaza, and whose clean kitchen sends out flavorful plates of grilled alpaca, *lomo saltado*, and pizza.

A favorite in town is **Puka Rumi** (Ventiderio s/n, tel. 084/20-4091, 7:30 A.M.–8:30 P.M. daily, US$4–10). The Chilean owner has brought over the traditions from his home country and offers everything from enormous and delicious sandwiches to local dishes including the town's best *lomo saltado*. The menu is extremely varied and has options for all budgets. For dessert, try the brownies.

Vegetarian

Heart's Café (Plaza de Armas s/n, tel. 084/20-4078, www.heartscafe.org, 7 A.M.–9 P.M. daily, US$5–18) was founded by Sonia Newhouse and is about the only place in Ollantaytambo that has a book exchange. This place serves home-cooked meals using mainly organic ingredients and has everything from soups, salads, and sandwiches to main dishes and even afternoon tea with scones. Profits go to Sonia Newhouse's NGO, Living Heart.

Markets

The best minimarket for snacks or a picnic is **Inka Misana** on the Plaza de Armas. But head to the local market for fresh fruit and produce.

INFORMATION AND SERVICES

The best source for information on Ollantaytambo is the information office at **KB Tambo** (tel. 084/20-4091, www.kbperu.com)

or the NGO Awamaki (Calle Convención s/n, across from the temple, www.awamaki-us. org). Awamaki's new U.S. website, www. awamaki-us.org, has tons of great information about Ollantaytambo, as does www.ollantaytambo.org.

The **police** and the **Botica Drugstore** (tel. 084/20-4015, 8 A.M.–9 P.M. daily), which has public phones, are both located on the main square. For medical needs, **Centro de Salud** (Ferrocarril s/n, tel. 084/20-4090) is open 24 hours. Banco de Crédito has an **ATM** in Hotel Sauce, and there is another ATM on the Plaza de Armas.

The **post office** (Principal, 7 A.M.–6 P.M. Mon.–Sat.) is in Tienda Margarita, but there are several places in town to buy stamps and postcards. There are several Internet places on and around the main plaza for about US$2/hour.

Volunteer Opportunities and NGOs

There are several NGOs in Ollantaytambo that you may contact if you're looking for volunteer opportunities and homestay options.

Based in Ollantaytambo, **Awamaki** (Calle Convención s/n, across from the temple, www.awamaki-us.org), founded by American Kennedy Leavens, is a Peruvian NGO partnered with a U.S. NGO of the same name that administers a weaving project with Quechua women and promotes health, education, and sustainable tourism. They have been instrumental in helping weavers in Patacancha and other communities restore their ancient weaving techniques and find sustainable ways to market their products. Awamaki can arrange all kinds of volunteer experiences, Spanish language immersion programs, homestays, excursions to the communities outside of Ollantaytambo, and classes in ceramics, basket weaving, and cooking. A highly recommended experience is Awamaki's weaving class in Patacancha.

Another NGO is **Living Heart** (www.livingheartperu.org), founded by Sonia Newhouse, who also owns **Heart's Cafe** on the Plaza de Armas. Living Heart aims to improve the quality of life for disadvantaged Andean children.

Ollantaytambo's elementary school has a **Tierra de Niños** (Children's Land) organized by **Ania** (www.mundodeania.org), a Lima-based NGO that helps inculcate the love of nature in children. The main force behind Ollantaytambo's Children's Land is Aima Molinari, who can be reached at aimamolinari@gmail.com. More information about the project can be found at www.tiniollantaytambo.blogspot.com

GETTING THERE AND AROUND

To get to Ollantaytambo from Cusco by bus, take the bus from the first block of Grau near the bridge (US$1.50, 90 minutes) to Urubamba and then hop another *combi* for the 20-minute, US$1 ride to Ollantaytambo. However, the most convenient option to get to Ollantaytambo from Cusco is to take a car or *colectivo* from the Paradero Pavitos (US$3.50, 90 minutes) to Ollantaytambo.

The station where you catch the train from Ollantaytambo to Aguas Calientes is a 10- or 15-minute walk from the main square along the Río Patacancha. From Ollantaytambo, various trains leave for Machu Picchu. For up-to-date prices and times, see www.perurail.com. Two new train companies started in 2010 and will be operating from Ollantaytambo—**Inca Rail** (www.inkarail.com) and **Andean Rail** (www.andeanrailways.com). Visit the websites for updated schedules and prices.

Reaching Cusco from Ollantaytambo is easy. *Combis* leave Ollantaytambo's main square for Urubamba, where another *combi* can be taken to Cusco. Direct buses for Cusco (US$1.75, 80 minutes) leave from Ollantaytambo when the evening trains arrive. The most convenient option is taking a car or *colectivo* from the train station or the main plaza (US$3.50).

Buses from Cusco also pass through Ollantaytambo on their way up-and-over the high pass at Abra Málaga and on to the jungle city of Quillabamba, which is the gateway to the biodiverse lower Urubamba basin. Trucks and a few buses headed in this direction stop in Ollantaytambo's main square in the morning and at 8 P.M. Ask local *combi* drivers for more details.

Taxis can be rented for quick trips to Urubamba (US$10) or to the town of Huilloq for a day hike.

PATACANCHA

Patacancha is a traditional Quechua community about an hour's drive above Ollantaytambo on a dirt road. People in Patacancha live much as they have for centuries, weaving, farming, and raising animals.

While in Patacancha please be aware that tourism can be harmful. Be sensitive and discreet in shooting your photos, avoid gaping into people's doorways, and don't go visit the school, as this is very disruptive to classes. Be aware that you will probably be flocked by women trying to sell you things, much of it junk purchased in Cusco. Look for the naturally dyed, hand-woven textiles for which the community is known.

Patacancha is difficult to visit independently, as very little Spanish is spoken and there is no daily public transportation. *Combis* do leave the plaza of Ollantaytambo Wednesday and Friday very early in the morning (6-ish). Or, just head up Patacalle. It's a 4–5 hour walk to the community, and most drivers, if you see any, are willing to pick you up for a few *soles*.

For a deeper understanding of life in Patacancha, the Ollantaytambo-based NGO **Awamaki** (Calle Convención s/n, across from the temple, www.awamaki-us.org) offers alternative community visits. The half-day tour, in English, includes transport, a visit to the Awamaki cooperative's weaving center, a demonstration of the weaving process, and the opportunity to buy top-quality, authentic weavings directly from the women. The tour also includes a visit to a Quechua house with permission, a respectful environment for photo-taking and nutritious snacks and a small tip for the women who participate. All proceeds benefit the project. US$10–30 depending on group size; contact tours@awamaki.org for information. Awamaki can also arrange weaving lessons and home stays in Patacancha.

MACHU PICCHU

Though many photographers have tried, no glossy postcard can capture the sweep and majesty of Machu Picchu. Viewed from above, the city's streets, temples, and stairways sprawl across a jungle ridge that drops more than 300 meters into the Río Urubamba below. Andean peaks, including the horn-shaped Huayna Picchu, rise in the background and frame this mist-drenched island in the sky.

A visit to Machu Picchu is many visitors' main motivation for coming to Peru. The place has a vibrant, spiritual feel and is probably the world's best example of architecture integrating with the landscape. It is in some respects the Inca's lesson to the western world, teaching us how to build our world around nature, not against it.

There is not a stone out of place at Machu Picchu. Terraces, gardens, temples, staircases, and aqueducts all have purpose and grace. Shapes mimic the silhouettes of surrounding mountains. Windows and instruments track the sun during the June and December solstices. At sunrise, rows of ruins are illuminated one by one as the sun creeps over the mountain peaks. The sun, moon, water, and earth were revered by the Inca, and they drive the city's layout.

Adding to Machu Picchu's mystery is the fact that archaeologists still do not know when or why it was built. The ruins of Machu Picchu were known to locals, who led Yale archaeologist Hiram Bingham to the site in 1911. Bingham cleared the site, understood its importance, and announced Machu Picchu to the world.

© GABRIELLA HOLLAND

HIGHLIGHTS

◖ Royal Tomb and Temple of the Sun: This semicircular Temple of the Sun aligns perfectly with the movement of the sun and sits on top of a cave, which the Inca transformed into a sinuous mastery of stone. This cave may have once contained the revered mummy of Inca Pachacútec, the Inca's most powerful and famed ruler (page 60).

◖ Intihuatana: Experts continue to debate over the meaning of this carved stone. There are theories that it's a sun dial, sacrificial altar, or a temple to the surrounding mountain gods. There is no question that it is a profoundly beautiful and spiritual stone sculpture, perhaps the first example of truly abstract sculpture in world history (page 61).

◖ Temple of the Moon and Huayna Picchu: Towering above Machu Picchu is the summit of Huayna Picchu, a sacred summit reached via a two-hour hike up stairs, switchbacks, and, for the final bit, a ladder. Nearby is the enigmatic Temple of the Moon. This nat-

ural cave, sculpted with curving stone walls, is the energetic counterpart to Machu Picchu (page 63).

◖ Inca Trail: For those who hike it, this sacred path is part trek, part religious pilgrimage. It winds down from the windswept mountains to lush cloud forest, passing 30 ruins along the way, then reaching Machu Picchu (page 68).

◖ Two-Day Inca Trail: A great option for those short on time, or not wanting to camp, is the two-day version of the Inca Trail. This hike includes some spectacular ruins and the glorious entry to Machu Picchu via the Inti Punku, or Sun Gate (page 70).

◖ Salcantay Trek to Machu Picchu: This five-day option does not have the stone paths or Inca ruins of the Inca Trail, but does offer stunning views of snow-covered mountains and a true wilderness appeal. This is the way to arrive to Machu Picchu for hard-core trekkers wanting to get a taste of the high Andes (page 71).

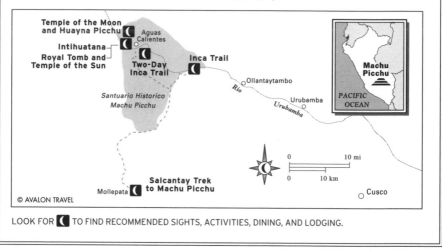

LOOK FOR ◖ TO FIND RECOMMENDED SIGHTS, ACTIVITIES, DINING, AND LODGING.

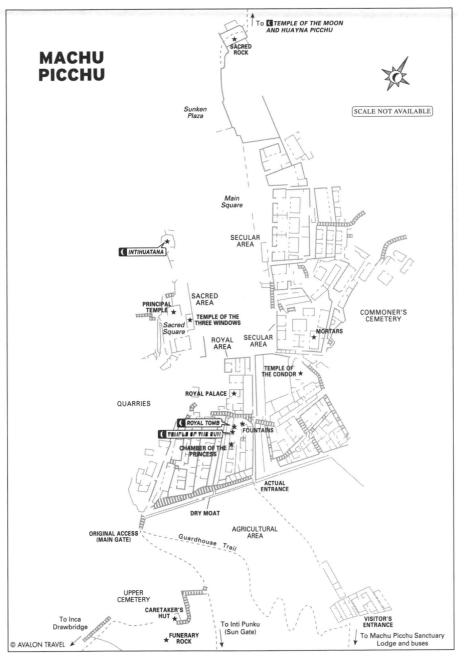

MACHU PICCHU

To **◖** *TEMPLE OF THE MOON AND HUAYNA PICCHU*

★ SACRED ROCK

Sunken Plaza

SCALE NOT AVAILABLE

Main Square

SECULAR AREA

◖ INTIHUATANA ★

PRINCIPAL TEMPLE ★

SACRED AREA

Sacred Square ★ TEMPLE OF THE THREE WINDOWS

SECULAR AREA

COMMONER'S CEMETERY

MORTARS ★

ROYAL AREA

TEMPLE OF THE CONDOR ★

ROYAL PALACE ★

QUARRIES

◖ ROYAL TOMB ★

◖ TEMPLE OF THE SUN ★ FOUNTAINS

CHAMBER OF THE PRINCESS ★

ACTUAL ENTRANCE

DRY MOAT

ORIGINAL ACCESS (MAIN GATE)

AGRICULTURAL AREA

Guardhouse Trail

UPPER CEMETERY

CARETAKER'S HUT ★

To Inca Drawbridge

FUNERARY ROCK ★

To Inti Punku (Sun Gate)

VISITOR'S ENTRANCE

To Machu Picchu Sanctuary Lodge and buses

© AVALON TRAVEL

MACHU PICCHU

Bingham, a 36-year-old adventurer who ended up being both a U.S. Senator and the inspiration for the character Indiana Jones, came to Peru to find Vilcabamba, the legendary lost city of the Inca. This was the jungle enclave, well-described by Spanish soldiers, to which Manco Inca and his followers retreated following their unsuccessful rebellion against the Spanish in 1537. Bingham began his search walking down the newly built road along the Río Urubamba (now the train line) and asking locals if they knew of any ruins along the way.

It was in this way that local resident Melchor Arteaga led Bingham to the vine-covered site, which Bingham would return to in 1912 and 1915 to excavate. He was convinced, to the end of his life, that Machu Picchu was the "lost city of the Inca." But historians are now certain he was incorrect. A wealth of supporting evidence indicates the real Vilcabamba was farther into the jungle at Espíritu Pampa, which Bingham also visited but dismissed at the time as too insignificant.

Bingham discovered more than 100 human skeletons in cemeteries around Machu Picchu, and an inexperienced scientist on his team incorrectly concluded that 80 of them belonged to women. The finding prompted the idea of Machu Picchu as a giant *acllahuasi,* or house for the Inca's chosen "virgins of the sun." Subsequent research on the skeletons proved that there were men, women, and children with women being the majority; however, the sexy idea blazes on (and is still repeated today by Machu Picchu tour guides).

Part of Machu Picchu's power is that it is a riddle, a blank slate upon which generations of historians and explorers have scribbled their theories. Some claimed Machu Picchu was an exclusive religious complex or a giant coca plantation. Others said it was a boarding school for brainwashing the children of leaders conquered by the Inca.

The latest theory, which is gaining widespread acceptance, is that Machu Picchu was a winter retreat built by Inca Pachacútec in the mid-15th century. Scholars had long believed

this, but concrete proof came in the form of a 16th-century suit filed by the descendants of Pachacútec, which University of California, Berkeley, anthropologist Dr. John Rowe found while searching through archives in Cusco. In the suit, the family sought the return of the lands, including a retreat called Picchu.

Many believe that Machu Picchu may have been a sacred site due to the quantities of *huacas* or shrines, and while Machu Picchu certainly had a religious sector, and probably an *acllahuasi* too, its primary purpose is believed to have been pleasure. The Inca could come here to escape the chill rains of Cusco, enjoy the jungle fruits of nearby Quillabamba, and hunt in the surrounding jungle.

PLANNING YOUR TIME

According to an agreement reached by the National Institute of Culture (INC) and UNESCO, only 2,500 people are allowed to visit Machu Picchu a day. That said, large package tours and their megaphone-style guides create a lot of hustle. In order for you to see Machu Picchu by yourself without losing the magic of the ruins, here are a few tips:

- Avoid the busiest months of June–September. The "shoulder" months of April–May and September–October are usually sunny as well.

- Avoid the Peruvian holidays, July 28–August 10. The days around Cusco's Inti Raymi festival, June 24, are also busy.

- Skip solstice days (June 21 and December 21), when the ruins are full by 6 A.M.

- Visit on a Sunday. Although Sundays are discounted for locals, Sundays tend to draw large crowds at the Pisac and Chinchero markets, thereby pulling travelers away from Machu Picchu.

- Stay the night at Aguas Calientes or take the earliest train in the morning in order to beat the train crowds, which arrive at the ruins around 10 A.M. and start departing around 2 P.M. Either arrive early in the morning or linger in the late afternoon. During midday, when Machu Picchu is most crowded, you can hike to Huayna Picchu, the Temple of the Moon, and the Inca bridge.

Machu Picchu admission is expensive by Peruvian standards and only lasts one day, though a second day is half price. Foreigners pay US$46, and nationals and students under 26 with an ISIC card pay US$22. There are no ticket sales on-site. Tickets must be bought in advance in *soles* at the **INC** office in Cusco (Av. el Sol) or in Aguas Calientes at **Centro Cultura Machu Picchu** (Pachacútec s/n, tel. 084/21-1196). A passport is necessary to complete the transaction. The ruins are open 6 A.M.–5:30 P.M. daily.

Shuttle

Buses to Machu Picchu leave every 5–15 minutes from just below Agua Caliente's second bridge. **Consettur Machupicchu** (Hermanos Hayar s/n, tel. 084/21-1134) sells the tickets, US$7 one-way and US$14 round-trip, with the first bus leaving at 5:30 A.M. and the last at 5:30 P.M. If you want to catch the first bus up to Machu Picchu, which is a good idea, arrive at least 45 minutes early as morning lines form. The bus takes about a half hour to wind its way up the switchbacks to the ruins. It is also possible to following the footpath to the ruins, which cuts the switchback. This arduous, all-uphill hike in the moist cloud forest takes about 90 minutes.

Facilities

Outside the gate of the ruins, there are bathrooms and, usually, piles of free walking sticks. **El Mirador Snack Bar** (US$4) sells bottled water, sandwiches, and hamburgers that you can take away or eat at picnic tables overlooking the ruins. The gourmet **Sanctuary Lodge Restaurant** (tel. 084/21-1039, 11:30 A.M.–3 P.M. daily, US$35) serves an extraordinary buffet lunch open to the public that is worth the price if you have a good appetite and want to spoil yourself. There is also a separate dining room with an à la carte menu (US$40–50) serving international and Peruvian food (the ginger-iced

young boy chasing the shuttle bus to Machu Picchu

parfait is especially good). If you plan on eating at Machu Picchu, bring cash with you as you will need it. However, it is advisable to bring snacks and plenty of water with you, as it can be a long day out. There are no ATMs at Machu Picchu so bring cash!

Guides and Tours

During the day there are always guides, of varying quality, waiting at the entrance. A highly recommended guide with 22 years of experience in Machu Picchu is Fernando Luque (hatunchaka@hotmail.com, tel. 084/984-755-200). He can be contacted in advance. Another option is the Machu Picchu Sanctuary Lodge (tel. 084/21-1039, http://machupicchu.orient-express.com), where expensive, top-notch guides can be hired.

Ruins Tour

GUARDS' QUARTERS

From the ticket booth, the path enters the south side of Machu Picchu through the Guards' Quarters, which are two-story storehouses orientated to the June solstice. These buildings now form the modern-day entrance. Instead of going through these buildings, we suggest taking the path, usually marked with white arrows, which you will find on your left just after walking through the ticket area and before arriving at the Guards' Quarters. This 10-minute hike switchbacks up into the forest alongside the terraces and arrives at a lookout offering the oft-photographed view over Machu Picchu. From here, it is easy to understand Machu Picchu's basic layout: A large grassy square divides the city in three areas. To the left are the **Royal and Sacred Areas,** which were probably reserved for the Inca emperor and his court. To the right is the **Secular Area,**

ruins at Machu Picchu

© BETH FUCHS

where the workers lived, and below the lookout itself is the **Agricultural Area.** Running near the lookout area is the main Inca Trail, which comes all the way from Cusco. Looking left, it's possible to see the Inca Trail coming down the terraced hillsides from the **Inti Punku,** or Sun Gate, the ceremonial entrance to Machu Picchu. On the other side of the Inca Trail are smaller paths that lead uphill to the Caretaker's Hut and another that leads across the terraces to the **Inca drawbridge.**

AGRICULTURAL AREA

Beneath the lookout and above the Guards' Quarters are agricultural terraces that face the sun year-round and were used to grow multiple crops. In 2002, Cusqueñan archaeologist Elva Torres took samples from different terraces to determine what crops the Inca cultivated in Machu Picchu. The results showed that they cultivated pumpkins, squash, tomatoes, peppers, and other indigenous tubers, such as *yacon,* which is used to treat diabetes.

CARETAKER'S HUT

This hut is one of the highest points in Machu Picchu, which allowed a caretaker to see a large stretch of the the Río Urubamba in addition to the main entrance from the Inti Punku, or Sun Gate. The Caretaker's House is built in the *wayrana* style, whereby one of the four walls is left completely open to promote ventilation.

FUNERARY ROCK

A carved slab is situated on the left-hand side of the Caretaker's Hut. It is a large, white, granite altar with carvings of three steps and a large flat bed on top. There is also a ring pointing in the direction of the solstice; its significance remains unknown. The Funerary Rock is surrounded by many other foreign rocks such as limestone, which is found in Sacsayhuamán and other quarries far from Machu Picchu. These rocks are believed to have been left over from Inca offerings. Above the rock is a small, four-sided building whose function also remains unknown.

MAIN GATE

Continuing from the Caretaker's Hut, follow the Inca Trail downhill to the Main Gate to Machu Picchu. A gigantic entrance door with locks on the inner part of the door was used to close Machu Picchu. Passing the Main Gate, continue on for about 40 meters, where, to your right, you will find a building with many doors on the first floor. The ground floor of this building was probably used as a meeting area, while the second floor was a storage room where produce was dried by ventilation. Below these storehouses, there are more than 15 constructions on different levels that were used as housing. Going back up to the main trail, continue three minutes until you arrive at an open area with numerous rocks. This area is the quarry of Machu Picchu.

QUARRIES

The main quarry of Machu Picchu lies on the hillside just past the Main Gate. However, there are two more quarries beside the **Sacred Rock** and another below the **Secular Area.**

Some houses are found in the Main Gate quarry, and they probably belonged to the workers. Returning to the main path, walk down the main stairway of the citadel, which has 16 different fountains that are all interconnected. The first fountain is on the right hand side before arriving at the rest hut. From this first fountain, walk downhill following the water into the **Royal Tomb** and **Temple of the Sun,** the most sacred of Machu Picchu's religious areas.

FOUNTAINS

There are two different theories behind the fountains. Some say they were used to supply drinking water to the people of Machu Picchu, and others say that they were ritual baths.

The fountains have two very distinct styles. The first three fountains are constructed in fine stone, and the rest are built in a more rustic style using stone and mortar. Walk down 10 steps, where you will see a small entrance to the right that will take you to the impressive

MACHU PICCHU

natural cave, which the Inca fashioned into the Royal Tomb.

◖ ROYAL TOMB AND TEMPLE OF THE SUN

Here you will find a beautiful chamber where the mummy of Inca Pachacútec may have been stored, although no remains were ever found. The stonework and overall design of the building make it one of the Inca's most famed and elaborate constructions. The rocks are elegantly fitted into the contours of the natural cave, a perfect example of the Inca using carved stone to enhance the beauty of natural stone. The tomb contains three long niches and one smaller one, which has its own altar. At the entrance of the cave, there is bedrock with three long steps believed to have been used to give offerings to the dead. Inside the tomb, you will see a chalk grid, which has been drawn by the INC to determine any seismic movement in Machu Picchu.

Machu Picchu features a series of beautifully sculpted caves, such as the Royal Tomb.

Straight ahead is a wooden stairway next to an Inca stairway; both lead to the Temple of the Sun. Please note: It is forbidden to use the Inca stairway.

The Temple of the Sun, also called El Torreón or The Tower in Spanish, is above the Royal Tomb and is unmistakable thanks to its perfect circular walls, which lean inwards for stability and recall the Coricancha in Cusco. The temple has two windows. One faces the sunrise at Inti Punku, the Sun Gate, on the December solstice and the other is orientated to the June solstice. These windows created rays of light inside the temple during these sacred days.

The temple was recently excavated to strengthen the walls. During this process, three niches were discovered, of which the middle niche has the distinctive double jamb. They have covered this new discovery with glass. On the left side of the temple is a small two-story building that is believed to have been the house of either a princess or a high priest. Near the sun temple is an exquisite fountain that unifies the sacred elements of Inca cosmology (sun, rocks, water, and wind).

ROYAL PALACE

The buildings on the other side of the main staircase are known as the Royal Palace, because it is here that the Inca and his family lived while visiting Machu Picchu. There are a few beautiful trapezoidal doorways and perfect Inca stonework, both tell-tale signs of royal architecture. Follow the doorways and staircases to a large stone patio.

On the right-hand side of the patio there is a large fine door that is presumed to be the entrance to an area where the Inca slept. There are a few other rooms that the Inca and his family used for different purposes.

Climb to the top of the main staircase and turn right before the quarry. Continue about 60 meters to the botanical garden, where you may see various species of native flora. There are orchids, passion fruit trees, and a coca plant.

Beyond the garden to the left is the Sacred Square, containing both the Temple of the Three Windows and the Principal Temple.

SACRED SQUARE AND TEMPLE OF THE THREE WINDOWS

This square has major buildings on three sides, making it one of the more important ceremonial areas of Machu Picchu. As you enter the plaza, the first building on the left is somewhat crude. It probably served a specific utilitarian function and was plastered over to give it a finished look. The temple on the right, which overlooks the main square of Machu Picchu, is known as the Temple of the Three Windows and is built of gigantic stones like the structures in Sacsayhuamán. The three giant trapezoidal windows were perfectly fitted, and there are two additional windows, which were later filled to make niches. Although the exact purpose of this building is unknown, ritual ceramics such as *keros* (drinking cups) were found in the foundations in the 1980s.

The construction here was never completed. We know this because a marker that indicates where a rock should have been chiseled is still visible on the northwestern wall. To the west of this plaza is a circular wall similar to Cusco's Coricancha (sun temple).

PRINCIPAL TEMPLE

This building forms the third corner of the Sacred Square and is composed of enormous horizontal stones hewn from bedrock. The temple faces Cerro Machu Picchu and has an enormous altar on the back wall. Above the altar are very high niches where ceremonial items were placed. The damage sustained to the stonework is due to insufficient foundations (an uncommon problem at Machu Picchu, where an estimate 80 percent of all stonework is underground and used to shore up the buildings on extremely steep and uneven ground).

Directly in front of the temple is a rustic house, believed to have been the house of the priest. Leaving the main square, going west behind the Principal Temple, you will come to a small construction on the right-hand side known as the **Sacristy.**

The Sacristy is the only room within the city

that has the Inca imperial style but that is not a temple or a palace. If you look carefully, you may notice the anti-seismic construction using bedrock, keystones, and the famous 32-sided stone. Also note the unfinished polishing on the rocks.

Leaving the Sacristy, go to your right and climb up the impressive stairway to the top. On your right-hand side, there is a rock that represents the mountains of Putucusi and Yanantin, having the same exact form. Continue upwards to the home of the Intihuatana.

◖ INTIHUATANA

This exquisite four-sided sculpture was likely considered the most sacred place in Machu Picchu because of its unusual form and the three elements of sacred Inca architecture: bedrock to represent mother earth or Pachamama, fine Inca imperial architecture, and three-sided *wayrana* buildings. Without a doubt this was a highly sacred stone, or *huaca,* for

Machu Picchu's Intihuatana is considered by some to be the world's first truly abstract piece of art.

MACHU PICCHU

the Inca. Scholars dispute the function of this stone and have largely dismissed its use as a sun dial. Theories of its use include a solar observatory, sacrificial altar, or a temple aligned with the surrounding mountains and their resident *apus* (gods). What is remarkable about the Intihuatana is that there is no logical explanation for its careful but bizarre shape. We believe the Intihuatana is a deeply sacred work of art, perhaps the world's first abstract sculpture.

In front of the Intihuatana there is a stone on the ground that looks like an arrow and points directly south, similar to a stone found on Huayna Picchu. This observatory is surrounded by two three-walled constructions, one of which is completely intact. Follow the white arrows down the stairs to the bottom. Turn right and cross the plaza. To the north, there are two more *wayrana* buildings that surround the Sacred Rock.

SACRED ROCK

The form of the Sacred Rock, which is flanked by sacred *wayrana* buildings, is identical to the form of the mountain Yanantin located in the foreground. Before this rock was protected a few years ago, hundreds of Machu Picchu visitors would spread their arms across this rock each day to feel its energy. Behind the Sacred Rock to the left is the entrance to Huayna Picchu and the Temple of the Moon, and to the right is a short trail that heads back in the direction of the Guards' Quarters (the entrance to Machu Picchu). This trail leads past a quarry to the Secular Area.

SECULAR AREA

The Secular Area is where the hundreds of workers and servants for Machu Picchu lived and worked. It is divided between *kanchas,* or living compounds, for the *ayllus,* or clans, or Inca elite. The design is broken up and chaotic, and it's difficult to follow a set route through the area. Think of this area as the bustling, populated part of the citadel where most people lived and worked. If you lose track of the directions, head to the general areas indicated by the map.

After the narrow entrance, there is a large open area with two enormous buildings that probably functioned as *kallancas* or great halls. These buildings were used by workers for celebrations, and doubled as large rain shelters.

Returning to the trail and heading in the direction of the Guards' Quarters, continue until you find a series of two-story *colcas* or storehouses. Continue along this trail for about 50 meters until you reach a corner. Head left on the steps and then head right, again in the direction of the Guards' Quarters. Continue ahead for about 60 meters until you reach an area known as the Mortars.

MORTARS

In the open space to the east, there is a large *wayrana*. Mortars that are sculpted in a circular shape with a concave base are found in the ground. While Bingham thought they were grinders, the modern-day hypothesis is that they were filled with water and used as earthquake detectors. Another speculation is that they were mirrors to view constellations.

This area is also the *acllahuasi,* or the "house of the chosen ones." If you explore the area, you will see that it has a large secure doorway. Exiting the principal door, head left to the corner and go down the stairs where you will see a tomb, known as **Intimachay** or Cave of the Sun. This was an important burial site in the citadel, and it contains a window that aligns perfectly with the first sunlight of the December solstice. Next to Intimachay is a large cave that contains a well-carved altar where many remains were found.

Back up the stairs and to your left is a large rock that has a slide on it. On top you will find an altar. From here, go down the stairs to the left, following the arrows to the Temple of the Condor.

TEMPLE OF THE CONDOR

At the entrance, there is an open area with a sculpted rock on the ground known as the head of the condor. Directly behind are the wings of this impressive Andean bird. Below the wings is a cave with stairs and niches on the wall believed to have been a tomb. In 1975, this cave was excavated by Alfredo Valencia, who found the bones of both llamas and guinea pigs. Experts believe the flat rock outside was used as a sacrificial table.

Above the condor, there are three very unusual niches that have two holes on either side. While Hiram Bingham thought this was the prison, it is now believed to have been a place to worship mummies.

To the left of the condor, there is a large two-story building. In order to enter the building, you must climb down the stairs, where you will find another tomb inside the house. Under the stairs, there are small holes in the base of the wall that were used to farm *cuy* or guinea pigs, a method still used in communities throughout the Andes. Returning to the Temple of the Condor and going to the far left, there is another cave. Go inside and you will find yet another tomb. To exit this chamber, duck under the small door, turn left, then go directly to the right, where you will find another secular area that offers a fabulous view of the Agricultural Area and the Temple of the Sun. Climb the stairs in the direction of the Temple of the Sun, but before arriving, turn left and follow the arrows to exit back to the Guards' Quarters, from where you started your walk.

Hikes and Treks

◖ TEMPLE OF THE MOON AND HUAYNA PICCHU

The hike from the Machu Picchu ruins to the summit of Huayna Picchu (elevation 2,740 meters, or 290 meters above Machu Picchu) is a moderate two-hour walk, and approximately 1.9 kilometers round-trip. It starts at the Sacred Rock and passes through a gate that is open 7 A.M.–1 P.M. Only 400 adults a day are allowed to do this climb (children are not allowed). Arrive early if you want to climb Huayna Picchu. It may make sense to climb Huayna Picchu in the morning and then see the ruins afternoon, in order to avoid missing

© BETH FUCHS

peak of Huayna Picchu

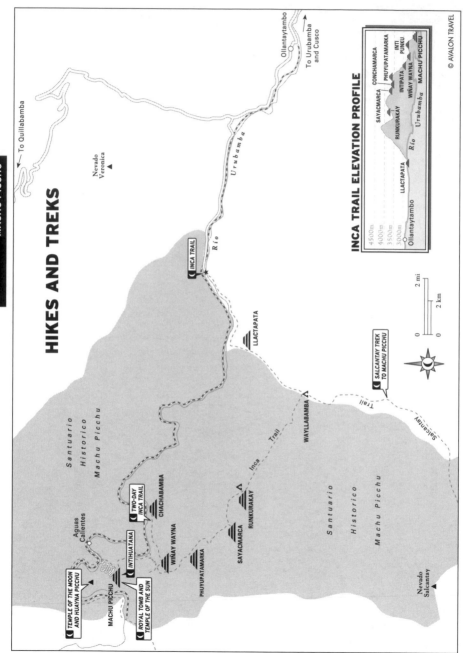

HIKES AND TREKS

To Quillabamba

Nevado Veronica

To Ollantaytambo
To Urubamba and Cusco

Rio Urubamba

INCA TRAIL

LLACTAPATA

Santuario Historico Machu Picchu

Aguas Calientes

TEMPLE OF THE MOON AND HUAYNA PICCHU

MACHU PICCHU

ROYAL TOMB AND TEMPLE OF THE SUN

INTIHUATANA

WIÑAY WAYNA

TWO-DAY INCA TRAIL

CHACHABAMBA

PHUYUPATAMARKA

SAYACMARCA

RUNKURAKAY

Inca Trail

WAYLLABAMBA

SALCANTAY TREK TO MACHU PICCHU

Salcantay Trail

Santuario Historico Machu Picchu

Nevado Salcantay

0   2 mi
0   2 km

INCA TRAIL ELEVATION PROFILE

4500m
4000m
3500m
3000m

Ollantaytambo

LLACTAPATA

SAYACMARCA

RUNKURAKAY

PHUYUPATAMARKA

CONCHAMARCA

INTIPATA

WIÑAY WAYNA

INTI PUNKU

MACHU PICCHU

Rio Urubamba

© AVALON TRAVEL

this hike. While it is steep, the path is in excellent shape, though the last 20 meters include a steep rock slab that must be climbed with a ladder and a rope. The Inca built retaining terraces, buildings, tunnels, staircases, and a shrine on the top of the mountain. Human remains were also found in caves. The splendor of Huayna Picchu is the breathtaking view of the entire complex, which spreads out before the summit like a map.

Farther down on the slopes of Huayna Picchu is the Temple of the Moon, a construction equally as exquisite as the Temple of the Sun but with an entirely different mood. The easiest way to visit the Temple of the Moon is to retrace your steps down from Huayna Picchu and take the marked trail turnoff halfway down, which leads directly to the site. There is also a very steep and technically challenging trail that descends from behind the summit of Huayna Picchu itself. This trail, which can be hard to find, contains a short but near-vertical section climbed with a lashed wooden ladder. Visiting the Temple of the Moon adds about 1–2 hours onto the

Huayna Picchu hike. If you visit both Huayna Picchu and the Temple of the Moon, expect to spend about 3–4 hours, so take plenty of water and food.

The Temple of the Moon is a medium-sized natural cave where rocks have been fitted perfectly in flowing, gentle shapes. Instead of the tower and bright sunlight of the Temple of the Sun, everything here is recessed and dark, with sinuous lines. The Temple of the Moon itself is a wall of doors and windows sculpted perfectly into the space created by a giant overhanging rock. A bit below there is a doorway that leads to other structures, including a lower cave that is near to where the trail from Huayna Picchu descends. The Temple of the Moon is wonderful in part because few people ever visit it. The spiritual energy of the place is palpable.

INTI PUNKU AND INCA DRAWBRIDGE

If you have the time and the energy, head to the Caretaker's Hut and hike up the Inca Trail, which arcs across the mountain slope to a high

MACHU PICCHU

© AMBER DAVIS COLLINS, WWW.LIFEUNSCRIPTEDPHOTOGRAPHY.COM

The Inca drawbridge, about a 20-minute hike from Machu Picchu, spans a gap in an Inca road built on a sheer cliff face.

TREKKING 101

Peru is one of the world's top trekking destinations, and the Inca Trail is Peru's number one trek. Beginning in the high Andes with vistas of sparkling glaciers, the Inca Trail passes a dozen major Inca ruins before plunging into the cloud forest towards Machu Picchu. Apart from the Inca Trail, there are dozens, even hundreds, of incredible treks in Peru's Andes, which are in the same league for trekking as the European Alps, the Alaska Range, or the Himalaya. Apart from the Cusco area, the other main trekking area in Peru is the Cordillera Blanca, the second-highest mountain range in the world, and its lesser-known but equally dramatic sister range, the Cordillera Huayhuash.

PLANNING THE INCA TRAIL

The Inca Trail is the only trek in Peru where all trekkers must hike with a licensed guide and where there is a limit of 500 people per day on the trail, including trekkers. These recent rules are a result of the Inca Trail's popularity and the resulting impact that tens of thousands of trekkers are having on its stone trail and the surrounding ecosystem. For the Inca Trail, your only option is to sign up with a licensed agency – and sign up early, as the Inca Trail fills up six months or more ahead of time.

As a result of these new rules, Inca Trail prices have increased from as low as US$90 in 2000 to a minimum of US$450 today. Walk-in-off-the-street agencies no longer offer last-minute Inca Trail trips. Inca Trail bookings are now done almost exclusively online as the trail's licensed operators have to confirm all reservations several months in advance. To check the official departure availability, visit the website www.nahui.gob.pe. If a date you want is already booked, it's still worth checking with agencies as they often have cancellations on certain days.

PLANNING OTHER TREKS

Any other trek in Peru, including the Salcantay alternative route to Machu Picchu, has a couple of planning options. The easiest, and most expensive, is to sign up with a reputable agency and let it take care of all the details. But you can also custom-design a trip and then hire an agency to take care of logistics such as transport, food, lodging, porters, *arrieros*, cooks, and certified guides. If you can find a reliable trekking or climbing guide, available for US$80–110 per day, he or she can organize all these details for you for an extra fee. Or you can do it all on your own, which is complicated to negotiate properly but possible if you speak Spanish.

WHEN TO GO

The traditional trekking season in Peru is May–August, but the best weather is June and July. Avoid the last week in July when Peru's hotels are often booked solid for the Fiestas Patrias celebration around July 28. If you are gunning for a main trekking route, you will encounter fewer people during the months of April, May, September, and October. These "shoulder months" are the best times to trek in Peru as they are outside of the rainiest months (November–March) and also the busiest tourist months (June–August). April and May, and even March if you don't mind an occasional rain storm, are especially gorgeous as the rainy season has just ended and the highlands are vibrant green.

AGENCIES AND GUIDES

The motto "you get what you pay for" is especially true when it comes to hiring a trekking agency or guide. Go with an established, well-recommended agency. If you skimp on an agency, you can be guaranteed the agency will either skimp on you (poor food, no bathroom tent), the porters (low wages, no health care), or the environment (pit latrines, no regard for Leave No Trace, or LNT, principles).

ACCLIMATIZATION

Plan for at least 3-4 days to acclimatize before heading out on a trek anywhere in Andean Peru. The Cordillera Blanca's most popular trek, the four- or five-day trek through the Santa Cruz Valley, involves at least one high pass, Punta Unión, at 4,760 meters. And the Inca Trail has two passes of approximately 4,000 meters.

Acclimatize by sleeping low and hiking high. A great way to acclimatize in the Cusco area is to spend your first few days in the Sacred Valley and then hike up out of valley floor in places like Pisac, Urubamba, and Ollantaytambo. In Huaraz, good options include day hikes in the Cordillera Negra and Quebrada Quilcayhuanca.

ON YOUR OWN

Because of the altitude, most parties end up hiring an *arriero*, who carries loads on burros, donkeys, or llamas. It's hard to enjoy the scenery while hiking with a full pack at Peru's altitudes, no matter how fit you are. There are other reasons to hire an *arriero* as well: It is a great cultural experience, helps the local economy, and makes your trip safer – *arrieros* often know the routes as well (or better) than a mountain guide, provide evacuation support, and can serve as camp guards.

Arrieros will expect you to pay their wages the day that they return to the main town, usually the day after the end of your trek. This means that for a four-day trek, you will pay the *arriero* five days of wages.

Groups usually hire a cook, too. Peru's cooks pack in fruit, vegetables, sacks of rice, and often a live chicken or two. Pay the people you hire fairly and treat them with respect. You are their employer, so you are ultimately responsible for their health and safety. These are some standard daily wages: US$10 for an *arriero* and US$8 for every mule, US$15 for camp guardian, US$25 for a porter, and US$25-30 for a cook. Also, you are expected to provide shelter and food for your *arriero*, cook, and porters.

If you are on your own, you will have to negotiate the entry and grazing fees that Andean communities increasingly charge trekking groups that pass through their lands. The fees change rapidly and are generally relatively minor. Grazing fees are generally around US$2-5 per horse. Inquire with an agency about fees ahead of time.

MAPS AND GEAR

The best place to get maps is the South American Explorers Club (www.saexplorers.org) in Cusco (Atoqsaykuchi 670, tel. 084/24-5484)

or in the Miraflores neighborhood of Lima (Piura 135, tel. 084/445-3306).

Most people who are trekking or climbing on their own bring all their own gear, but high-quality equipment can be rented for affordable prices in Cusco and Huaraz. Email agencies ahead of time for reservations and prices.

Peru's tropical sun is intense, so bring strong sunscreen, a sun hat, dark glacier glasses, and a long-sleeved shirt. Most trekkers use trekking poles for descending the scree slopes and steep trails. The weather is cold, but extreme storms are rare in the dry months from May to September. On most Peru treks, sleeping bags rated for 0°F and thermal long underwear or fleece pants are fine.

Pretty much all supplies, with the exception of freeze-dried food, are available in markets in Cusco. You'll find pasta, powdered soup, cheese, powdered milk, beef jerky, dried fruit, and more. White gas (*bencina blanca*) is sold at the hardware stores along Calle Plateros in Cusco and at numerous places in Huaraz and Caraz. Get a shop recommendation from an agency or gear store to ensure you find the highest quality gas, and fire up your stove before you go to make sure everything works. Remember that airlines sometimes reject travelers with camp stoves and fuel bottles that have been previously used. It's best to travel with a new stove and bottles, if at all possible.

HAZARDS AND PRECAUTIONS

While the vast majority of trekkers to the Cusco and Huaraz areas never encounter any safety threats, the more popular trekking areas have seen an increase in theft. If you leave your camp for a day hike, make sure to leave a camp guardian, such as an *arriero*, behind. Entire camps of tents have been stolen recently in the Cordillera Blanca while teams were on the mountain.

The main hazards of trekking in Peru, however, are straightforward: sun, altitude, and cold. If you protect yourself from the sun, acclimatize properly, and have the right gear, you will have a great time.

MACHU PICCHU

pass. It is about a one-hour walk to this pass, where there is a stone construction known as the Sun Gate or Inti Punku (2,720 meters).

After visiting Inti Punku, go back down the same trail to the path that branches off for the Caretaker's Hut. Instead of continuing uphill to the Caretaker's Hut continue along via the terraces along an alternative path that heads into the forest before arriving at a path with sheer cliff walls. At one point, it even passes over a man-made ledge, like that found on the upper route at the Pisac ruins. The trail ends near a gap at the stone ledge, where the Inca evidently placed a drawbridge or a series of logs that could be withdrawn if necessary. The path past the drawbridge is overgrown and washed out, but it was an alternative route for reaching the Inca Trail back to Cusco.

CERRO MACHU PICCHU

This moderate three-hour hike is a good alternative to climbing Huayna Picchu if Huayna Picchu has reached its daily quota or if you are afraid of heights (Huayna Picchu has one steep and exposed section). The hike up Cerro Machu Picchu (3,051 meters, or 601 meters above Machu Picchu) offers lots of fresh air, quiet natural surroundings, and a great view at the top. Cerro Machu Picchu is the mountain above Machu Picchu in the direction of the Inti Punku, or Sun Gate. To get there take the Inka Trail out of the Machu Picchu ruins past the Caretaker's Hut and towards Inti Punku. About 150 meters past the Caretaker's Hut, head right up a set of stairs with a sign that says "To Machu Picchu Mountain." Follow the trail for one hour through a habitat of exotic birds, orchids, lichen, moss, and trees, until arriving at the bottom of a set of Inca stairs. From here, it is a steep, 45-minute uphill walk. This is an excellent acclimatization hike for anyone preparing for a post-Machu Picchu trek. Various caves that contained skeletons when found by Hiram Bingham's expedition are located at the base of Cerro Machu Picchu. This area is therefore called **Upper Cemetery.**

◖ INCA TRAIL

Though at times crowded, the hike to Machu Picchu is an unforgettable experience—both a backpacking trip and a religious pilgrimage. There are lots of ways to do it, including walks of 1–4 days, with or without a pack on your back. All trail hikers must go with an agency, to ensure everyone's safety and keep trash off the trail. (The Inca Trail is part of the Machu Picchu Historical Sanctuary, administered by the National Institute of Culture.) There is a wide range in price and quality among Inca Trail agencies, and reservations should be made at least six months in advance.

The two- or even one-day option begins at Km 104 of the railroad line and includes a steep hike to reach the final stretch of the Inca Trail, including the ruins at Wiñay Wayna. Some agencies continue the same day to Machu Picchu and stay overnight in Aguas Calientes, while others camp near Wiñay Wayna to enter Machu Picchu the following morning.

We highly recommend the four-day trip, which passes more than 30 Inca sites along the way and includes the most spectacular scenery.

Trekking Agencies

Peruvian Andean Treks, ExplorAndes, and Tambo Treks are the longest established trekking companies in Cusco; they pioneered the contemporary trekking culture. We recommend them, not only for their unsurpassed experience and professionalism, but also because they consistently recycle their trash, pack out all human waste, treat water carefully, and pay porters fair wages.

Among the more than 150 licensed agencies operating in Cusco, the standard of service and social and environmental responsibilities vary greatly. It is up to the client to be discerning and to research thoroughly before booking. All agencies listed here are recommended.

Peruvian Andean Treks (Pardo 705, tel. 084/22-5701, www.andeantreks.com) is owned by American and long-time Cusco resident Tom Hendrickson. This company was voted Cusco's best tour operator in 2006. **ExplorAndes** (Av. Garcilaso 316-A, tel. 084/23-8380 or Lima tel. 01/715-2323, www. explorandes.com) is Peru's most established adventure sports agency. It offers the traditional Inca Trail hike, as well as variations that combine it with treks above the Sacred Valley or around Nevado Salcantay and Nevado Ausangate. ExplorAndes was voted Peru's best overall tour operator by the Ministry of Tourism in 2005.

Tambo Treks (Casilla 912, tel. 084/23-7718, www.tambotreks.net) is owned by Andreas Holland and has been operating for over 30 years. It offers diverse treks and tours with tailor-made itineraries (six people minimum), which accommodate group specifications and a wide range of special interests. The staff are very knowledgeable, and since its foundation Tambo Treks has had a profound commitment to helping local communities. Most importantly however, the welfare of all their staff has always been a priority as has working in an ecologically sustainable and responsible manner.

Auqui Mountain Spirit (José Gabriel 307, Urb. Magisterial, tel. 084/26-1517, www.auqui.com.pe), run by Roger Valencia, has been operating for over 20 years. This high-end agency has a very experienced team and specializes in customized trips, especially for corporate clients.

Ecoinka (Saphy 456, tel. 084/22-4050, www.ecoinka.com) was founded by Ricky Schiller, who has been involved in the tourism industry for over 30 years. The expert staff provide excellent service.

Perú Sur Nativa (Magisterio 2da Etapa K-7-302, tel. 084/22-4156, www.perusurnativa.com) is owned by long-time Cusco adventurer extraordinaire Raúl Montes.

Enigma (Clorinda Matto de Turner 100, tel. 084/22-2155, www.enigmaperu.com) is one of the newer agencies; it has gourmet cooks. It offers Inca Trail treks combined with Nevado Salcantay, Vilcabamba, and the ruins of Choquequirao.

Inca Explorers (Ruinas 427, tel. 084/24-1070, www.incaexplorers.com) has a range of longer trips to Vilcabamba, Choquequirao, and the Cordillera Vilcanota.

Q'ente (Choquechaca 229, tel. 084/22-2535, www.qente.com) has been running since 1995 and provides a good service and trained staff.

The following Inca Trail operators are at the bottom of the price range but have been reported to be environmentally responsible.

United Mice (Plateros 351, tel. 084/22-1139, www.unitedmice.com) is probably the most recommended backpacker's choice. It also offers a seven-day Salcantay trek.

Peru Treks & Adventure (Garcilaso 265, Of. 11, 2nd Fl., tel. 084/50-5863, www.perutreks.com) is also responsible for the very informative website Andean Travel Web (www. andeantravelweb.com).

Andina Travel (Santa Catalina 219, tel. 084/25-1892, www.andinatravel.com) offers frequent departures for the Inca Trail and interesting sociocultural projects.

Four-Day Inca Trail
DAY ONE
This trip traditionally begins with an early-morning three-hour bus ride to Piscacucho, which is at Km 82 of the train line at 2,700 meters (some agencies use the train instead, which drops backpackers a bit farther down at Km 84). The trail begins in a subtropical ecosystem, with lots of agave plants and Spanish moss hanging from the trees. Many of the cacti along the trail have a parasite that turns crimson when you crush it in your fingers, a trick local woman use for lipstick. The first ruins you pass are **Patallacta,** meaning "city above terraces" in Quechua, a middle-class residential complex used as a staging ground for Machu Picchu. There is 12 kilometers of hiking this first day, with an elevation gain of 500 meters to Wayllabamba, where most groups camp the first night with stunning views of the Huayluro Valley.

DAY TWO

The 12 kilometers covered on this day are much more strenuous because you gain 1,200 meters in elevation and climb two mountain passes back to back. On the backside of the first pass, at 4,200 meters, you will pass by the ruins of **Runkurakay,** a round food storehouse strategically located at a lookout point. This site has an incredible view over a valley and nearby waterfall. The second pass, at 3,950 meters, is named Dead Woman's Pass after a mummy discovered there. In the late afternoon you will see the ruins of **Sayaqmarka** (3,625 meters), with good views of the Vilcabamba range. Sayaqmarka was probably used as a *tambo,* or resting spot, for priests and others journeying to Machu Picchu. The complex is divided into a rough lower section and a more elaborate upper area that was probably used for ceremonial purposes. Most trekkers camp this second night at **Pacaymayo,** with views of snow-covered peaks, including Humantay (5,850 meters) and Salcantay (6,271 meters), the highest peak in the area.

The ruins of Sayaqmarka are encountered on day two of the Inca Trail.

© RENÉE DEL GAUDIO AND ROSS WEHNER

DAY THREE

This is a relatively easy day with plenty of time for meandering and lots of memorable sights. You enter the cloud forest, full of orchids, ferns, and bromeliads, to reach the ruins of **Phuyupatamarka,** a ceremonial site from where you first see the back of Machu Picchu, marked with a flag. Look out for hummingbirds, finches, parrots, and the crimson Andean cock of the rock. Most groups rest at a halfway lookout point that is often shrouded by clouds. From here, it is a two-hour hike straight down, dropping 1,000 meters to the third campsite at 2,650 meters, where there are hot showers, cold beers, and a restaurant. There is usually plenty of time in the afternoon to see the ruins of **Wiñay Wayna,** a spectacular ceremonial and agricultural site that is about a 10-minute walk away. We were lucky enough to see these ruins under the light of a full moon, which was truly mesmerizing. This complex is divided into two sectors, with religious temples at the top and rustic dwellings below. The hillside is carved into spectacular terraces and the Río Urubamba flows far below.

DAY FOUR

Most groups rise very early in the morning in an attempt to reach the sanctuary before sunrise, and it can feel like walking in a herd of cattle. The walk is flat at the start and then inclines steeply up to **Inti Punku** (the Sun Gate), from where you will be rewarded with a 180-degree view of Machu Picchu. Your guide will take you through the ruins, leaving you time to wander on your own and to climb Huayna Picchu if you haven't had enough.

◖ Two-Day Inca Trail

This two-day trip consists of one day of trekking and one day of visiting Machu Picchu. It is a fairly easy hike, and for those who like to avoid camping, there's the advantage of staying in a hotel.

A short train ride from Ollantaytambo brings you to Km 104 (altitude 2,100 meters) of the train tracks. Your trek begins across the river at the ruins of **Chachabamba,** where visits of the complex are usually offered by most trekking agencies. From here, an eight-kilometer ascent through orchids, waterfalls, and hummingbirds in the cloud forest brings you to the impressive site of **Wiñay Wayna.** In Quechua this means "forever young" and it is home to the beautiful, bright purple forever young orchids. Most people stop here for lunch before continuing along the Inca trail to Inti Punku, the Sun Gate, before arriving at Machu Picchu itself. Due to changes in regulations, everyone who does the short Inca Trail now hops on a bus and stays in a hotel in Aguas Calientes. The following day, you return early by bus for a full day to see Machu Picchu and surroundings.

The Inca Trail crosses steep hillsides at times and features dramatic drop offs.

◖ SALCANTAY TREK TO MACHU PICCHU

This five-day trek, which includes one day in Machu Picchu, is one of the latest alternatives in the area. As there are no restrictions, unlike on the Inca Trail, you can do this trek on your own or with a guide or agency. If you don't like camping, there are now high-quality lodges along the route operated by **Mountain Lodges of Peru** (Av. El Sol 948, Centro Commercial Cusco Sol Plaza, tel. 084/24-3636, www.mountainlodgesofperu.com).

Day One

Leaving Cusco, take the road heading towards Lima, to the town of Limatambo and the site of **Tarawasi,** named after the berry *tara,* which grows in the area. Continue on to **Soraypampa** (3,869 meters), which is above the nearby herding village of Mollepata. At Soraypampa there is a campsite and a lodge operated by Mountain Lodges Peru. This company offers luxury high-altitude trekking, with four lodges located along the Salcantay route. Their lodges are all designed with elements of environmental sustainability in

mind. With heating, hot showers, incredibly comfortable beds, and Jacuzzis, this is a great option for trekkers who either do not want to camp or don't want to carry the gear on the way to Machu Picchu.

In Soraypampa, you have wonderful views of both **Salcantay** (6,264 meters) and **Humantay** (5,917 meters) mountains. If you are staying in the lodge, you can hike to the beautiful multi-colored lake at the foot of Humantay glacier as an acclimatization tour. Some trekkers prefer to push on past Soraypampa to a campsite at **Soyroccocha** (4,206 meters). The campsite is at a very high altitude, so come acclimatized and bring plenty of warm clothing.

Day Two

This is the day of the high pass (4,600 meters) and possible sightings of the intriguing Andean chinchilla, a furry rodent that resembles a baby bunny rabbit. Switchbacks take you up to the pass to spectacular snowy

MACHU PICCHU

© FIONA CAMERON

the sacred peak of Salcantay

views of the mountain. From here, it is a steep 3.5-hour downhill walk through both barren high plains and cloud forest to the campsite of **Colpapampa** (2,682 meters).

Day Three

Colpapampa to **La Playa** is a breathtaking trek. You are now well into the cloud forest. This agricultural area is awash with coffee, avocados, citrus fruits, and wild strawberries. This day is the easiest, as it is only a slight descent to La Playa (2,042 meters).

Day Four

Today you get to Aguas Calientes. Follow an old trail for about two hours to the pass (2,743 meters) and down to the Inca town of **Llaqtapata.** Here there is a small archaeological site and a spectacular view of Machu Picchu. After Llaqtapata, the trail is hard, steep, downhill, and super slippery in the rainy season. The elevation decreases 914 meters in three hours to the train station at the hydroelectric plant. From here, to get to Aguas Calientes, most people take the 4:30 P.M. train (US$8); however, some people choose to walk

along the train track to Aguas Calientes, which takes approximately three hours (eight kilometers). Almost all tours offer a night in a hotel in Aguas Calientes before going to Machu Picchu the next day.

INCA JUNGLE TRAIL

The latest route to Machu Picchu is locally known as the Inca Jungle Trail—Peru's version of planes, trains, and automobiles. This is a four-day trip that includes biking, hiking, and trains.

Day One

After 10 years, a decent road to Quillabamba has finally been made. A bus ride of about three hours passes Urubamba and Ollantaytambo to the new road, which leads you to the **Abra de Málaga** (4,350 meters). Most tours bike 80 kilometers down this road to the town of Santa María, which is a vertical drop of 3,000 meters. Be very careful and aware since this road is very busy with speeding minibuses and huge trucks.

Day Two

This day is a six- to seven-hour trek through high

jungle. An old Inca trail has recently been discovered here and is currently being restored. The walk itself takes you through coffee plantations, coca fields, and fruit farms. This walk is a hiker's favorite as it takes you directly to the hot springs in Santa Teresa. Unfortunately, the floods in January 2010 washed the baths out completely, although there is talk of restoring them.

Day Three

This is another day of trekking; the geography is very similar to that of the previous day. After a morning of trekking, you will finally arrive at the hydroelectric plant, where a train will take you to Aguas Calientes. The following day is the normal day tour of Machu Picchu.

Getting There and Around

There are various ways to reach Aguas Calientes, the town at the base of Machu Picchu. You can take the Inca Trail or the Salcantay route, ride the train from Ollantaytambo (90 minutes) or Cusco (2.5 hours), or take the Inca Jungle Trail or bus journey through Santa Teresa. Once in Aguas Calientes, there are frequent bus shuttles to Machu Picchu, though some choose the two-hour forest hike that cuts across the road's switchbacks. There was a government plan

© CYNTHIA BEAMS

Inca Trail porter

some years back to build a Swiss-style tram, but that was, thankfully, rejected after much controversy. Once inside Machu Picchu, the only way to get around is by foot.

During the 1990s, a company named HeliCusco operated huge Russian helicopter trips to Machu Picchu, blowing many of Aguas Calientes's sheet-metal roofs off in the process. Thankfully, helicopters have been banned inside the Machu Picchu Historical Sanctuary, and condors are slowly returning to the area. We saw one cruising in the air underneath the ruins: Watch for fingerlike feathers at the ends of the wings, whitish upper wings, and a white neck.

TRAIN

Two major events have completely recast train service to Machu Picchu. The first was the floods in January 2010, which took out large areas of the train track between Ollantaytambo, in the Sacred Valley, and Aguas Calientes, at the foot of Machu Picchu. Until the tracks are repaired, trains will depart from Piscacucho, about an hour downstream from Ollantaytambo. After the repairs, normal service is expected to be restored to Ollantaytambo, from which all trains to Machu Picchu typically depart.

The second major event is the breakup of the long-time PeruRail monopoly. Only time will tell whether the entry of two new train companies will result in lower prices and better service. Before booking train service to Machu Picchu, or asking your hotel to book trains for

CAMISEA GAS FIELD: THE LAST PLACE ON EARTH

Up until the discovery of the Camisea Gas Field, few outsiders had ever entered the lower Urubamba basin, a vast swath of rainforest downriver from Machu Picchu. A treacherous river gorge deterred boat traffic, and the sheer flanks of the **Cordillera Vilcabamba** hindered would-be colonists.

Thanks to its geographic isolation, the lower Urubamba has evolved over millions of years into one of the world's top 25 megadiversity hot spots, according to Conservation International. Biologists continue to discover an unprecedented variety of endemic plant and animal species in the area.

This swath of mountains and jungles is also the last hiding place for several thousand semi-nomadic Indians who choose to live in complete isolation from the outside world. Some of these indigenous groups fled to these remote headwaters a century ago to escape the disease and slavery of the rubber boom, the last major Amazon bonanza. Their way of life was supposedly protected in the 1970s when the Peruvian government declared the area a cultural reserve for the Yine, Nahua, and Kirineri peoples.

That protection has been crumbling ever since engineers discovered an estimated 11 trillion cubic feet of gas under the jungle floor, now known as the Camisea Gas Field. After more than two decades of negotiations, the Peruvian government signed an agreement to develop Camisea in early 2000. The lower Urubamba has never been the same since.

Dynamite explosions replace the murmur of rivers and shrieking of parrots, as engineers map the contours of the vast gas deposit along a checkerboard of paths spaced a mere 300 yards apart. Chainsaws and bulldozers clear forest to make way for access roads, unloading zones, a processing plant, and drilling platforms, several of which are inside the cultural reserve. Helicopters routinely buzz the canopy. A 25-meter-wide corridor of cleared jungle snakes its way up and over the Cordillera Vilcabamba and down into the jungle below.

The lead Camisea players are Texas-based **Hunt Oil** and the Argentine companies **Plus-Petrol** and **Grupo Techint,** which are leading

---

you, we recommend checking the websites of all three companies.

The first new Machu Picchu train service is the **Machu Picchu Train,** owned by Andean Railways (Av. El Sol 576, Cusco, across from the Coricancha, tel. 084/22-1199, www.machupicchutrain.com). This company is importing a series of fancy coaches and will be price competitive with PeruRail. Once tracks are repaired, the Machu Picchu Train will leave Ollantaytambo at 7:20 A.M. and 12:36 P.M. and arrive in Aguas Calientes 90 minutes later. The train returns from Aguas Calientes to Ollantaytambo at 10:30 A.M. and 4:15 P.M. Prices vary according to time but are approximately US$75 one-way.

The second new service is **Inca Rail** (Av. El Sol 611, Cusco, tel. 084/23-3030, www.incarail.com), which offers three daily departures from Ollantaytambo at 6:40 A.M., 11:35 A.M., and 4:36 P.M. and three daily departures from Aguas Calientes at 8:30 A.M., 2:02 P.M., and 7 P.M. The trains have an executive class (US$50 one-way) and a first class (US$75 one-way).

The traditional option is **PeruRail** (Av. Pachacútec, Cusco, tel. 084/22-8722, www.perurail.com), which offers three train services from Ollantaytambo and Poroy, near Cusco, to Aguas Calientes: the **Backpacker** (US$96 round-trip, US$48 one-way), the **Vistadome** (US$120 round-trip, US$60 one-way), and the luxury **Hiram Bingham service** (US$588 round-trip US$334 one-way). The Backpacker train is nearly as comfortable as the Vistadome, with large, soft seats and plenty of leg room. Food for sale includes sandwiches (US$4) and candy bars (US$2). The perks of the Vistadome include large viewing windows in the ceilings,

the US$1.6 billion effort to drill the gas and then ship it to the coast via two separate pipelines. Hunt is also building a US$2.1 billion liquefied natural gas plant on the coast south of Lima, which will soon be operational. Another Texas company, the KBR division of **Halliburton,** runs a Camisea gas plant next to **Paracas,** Peru's most important marine reserve. Conservationists opposed the project on the grounds that a single tanker spill could wipe out Paracas's already endangered marine life. The project went ahead regardless and began operation in 2004.

During the early stages of the project, U.S. media coverage focused on the behind-the-scenes lobbying, from both the Bush Administration and the Inter-American Development Bank, IDB, which helped make the project happen. The real story, however, is the destruction in the lower Urubamba. The service roads and test paths being built for the project are becoming highways for colonists, illegal loggers, and wildlife poachers – the same pattern of destruction that destroyed most of the Amazon in the 20th century.

Since December 2004, there have been five ruptures of the Camisea pipeline, which sent thousands of barrels of gas into the pristine Urubamba River and polluted local water supplies. Unchecked erosion from the pipeline has also muddied water supplies and decimated fish, the main food source, in some areas. A Peruvian government report estimated that 17 indigenous people had died of diseases brought to the area by oil workers.

The Peruvian government, for its part, says the Camisea project will produce valuable foreign revenue and help Lima make its transition to cleaner-burning fuels. The oil companies, meanwhile, have promised to minimize impact by using lateral drilling technology and oil platforms normally used for deep-sea drilling. And the IDB will also begin to monitor the environmental impacts of Camisea as part of the bank's latest US$800 million loan. "This is a mega project," said Peru president Alan García, of Camisea's liquefied natural gas plant. "In the construction of this plant, it is estimated that Peru's economy will grow nearly one percent per year over the next three years."

MACHU PICCHU

shows put on by train attendants (including fashion walks to promote alpaca clothing), luxurious seats, lights snacks and beverages, and live Andean music.

The Hiram Bingham service is in a whole different league. A full brunch is served on the ride from Poroy (15 minutes outside Cusco) to Machu Picchu, where guests are treated to a deluxe ruins tour and a full tea at the Sanctuary Lodge. On the ride home, pre-dinner pisco sours are served in the elegant dark wood bar, accompanied by a live band and dancing. A gourmet four-course dinner follows at your private table, accompanied by a selection of wines. Afterwards, there is live music and dancing for those with energy. Hands down, this is the most luxurious train service in Latin America. If it feels like the Orient Express, it is—PeruRail has

been operated by Orient-Express Ltd. since the late 1990s.

All trains now depart from Ollantaytambo except the Hiram Bingham service. The Hiram Bingham luxury train avoids the famous (or infamous) switchbacks out of Cusco by leaving from the Poroy station, which is a 15-minute drive from Cusco. It departs at 9 A.M. and arrives in Aguas Calientes at 12:30 P.M. On the return, the train departs Aguas Calientes at 6 P.M. and gets to Poroy at 9:25 P.M.

The Cusco–Machu Picchu train crosses high, desolate plains before descending to meet the Urubamba Valley. Once past Ollantaytambo, the rail enters a gorge that grows narrower and deeper as it continues its descent. Look for occasional glimpses of snow-covered Verónica (5,750 meters) to the right. At Km 88 there is a modern bridge built on

Inca foundations. As the vegetation and the air grow thicker, the train descends into what the Peruvians call the *ceja de selva,* or the eyebrow of the jungle, and the Río Urubamba starts crashing over house-sized boulders. The train continues until reaching the ramshackle town of Aguas Calientes.

BUS JOURNEY FROM SANTA TERESA

The elaborate bus ride to Machu Picchu via Santa Teresa is hardly worth it unless you are really counting your pennies. From the Terminal de Santiago in Cusco, take a bus to Santa María (six hours, US$3). From Santa María, it is a two-hour bus ride to Santa Teresa. From there, shared taxis called *colectivos* will take you across the river to Oroya, where you can take a 5:30 P.M. train to Aguas Calientes (US$8), or where you can walk three hours to the town. No matter what, if you choose this route, you will need to spend the night in Aguas Calientes, which may put another dent in your pocket.

Aguas Calientes

Ever since a landslide destroyed the train line past Machu Picchu to Quillabamba, Aguas Calientes is literally the end of the line for the Cusco–Machu Picchu train. Once a ramshackle town, Aguas Calientes's recent structural improvements have brought paved roads, a colorful crafts market, and a growth in business. New restaurants and hotels are wedging their way into what little available valley space there is. With an economy that lives entirely on tourism, it makes for an interesting stay for a couple of days. Staying overnight in Aguas Calientes will allow you to give Machu Picchu and the surrounding area the time it takes to truly absorb its magnitude. Two nights can be even better, allowing you the opportunity to visit other attractions in the area.

SIGHTS

The town spreads uphill from the tracks, past a square and up the main drag of Pachacútec alongside the Río Aguas Calientes. On the other side of the river, the Orquideas neighborhood is becoming the new hotel zone and is also home to the new stadium.

At the top of Pachacútec are the town's **thermal baths** (US$4, with towels and even bathing suits for rent). The baths are cleanest in the morning and are usually quite grimy by evening. On an uphill dirt trail, past the baths are a few spectacular waterfalls for bathing. This path leads uphill for several hours to a string of remote waterfalls. The baths are actually quite attractive.

Follow the road toward Machu Picchu, and just before the uphill schlep to the ruins, you'll find the new **Museo del Sitio Machu Picchu** (highway to Machu Picchu at Puente Ruinas, 9 A.M.–4:30 P.M. daily, US$7.5). The English-Spanish signs in this small, modern museum lead you geographically, culturally, and historically through Machu Picchu. Dioramas explain a typical Incan day in Machu Picchu, and enlarged photos explain the site's investigation. There is also an attached botanical garden.

ENTERTAINMENT AND EVENTS

Apart from the pizzerias, the best nighttime hangout is **Candela's** (Las Orquideas s/n, tel. 084/976-1173, noon–midnight, US$4), a small art-filled café that's full to the seams with tourists and guides. Happy hour on pisco and coca sours is 8–10 P.M. The disco **Wasicha** (next to the Indio Feliz Restaurant on Lloquey Upanqui, 6–10 P.M.) is the only spot for dancing.

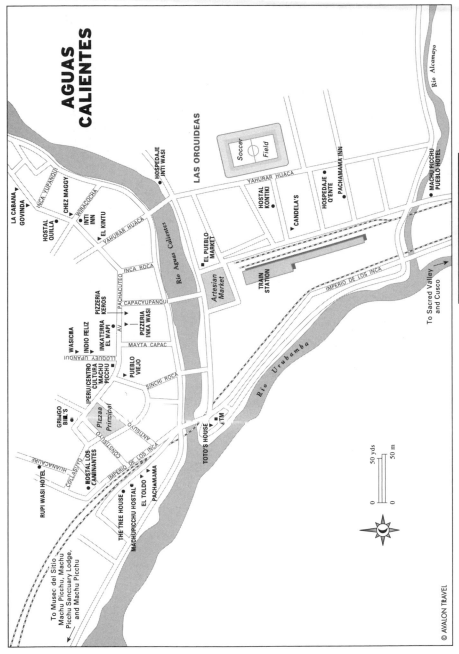

MACHU PICCHU

AGUAS CALIENTES

© AVALON TRAVEL

© SERGIO SCHABELMAN

cleaning the streets of Aguas Calientes, the town at the base of Machu Picchu

SHOPPING

Most Machu Picchu travelers will pass through the Aguas Caliente's market, which lies between the train station and the town itself. The market has a variety of booths covered in plastic awnings with touristy knick-knacks for sale. There is some good jewelry at the market, but better quality jewelry can be found at two jewelry shops in Aguas Calientes. The jewelry shop **Rumi Wasi** (at entrance to thermal baths, hours vary but generally open at night), run by Marcus, who makes silver jewelry on site. The second great option is **Joyeria Maky** (Capac Yupanqui, tel. 084/21-1136, hours vary).

RECREATION
Putukusi

This forested rock dome 400 meters above Aguas Calientes is a superb half-day hike that offers great views of Machu Picchu and a chance to see many different cloud forest birds. The highlight is 200 meters (600 feet) of wooden ladders nailed to the near-vertical

cliff face. The trailhead is signed and is 150 meters past the control point on the railroad tracks. The walk is approximately three hours, allowing you to arrive in leisure and get a very different photo of Machu Picchu.

Mandor Waterfalls

Another option for out-of-town recreation is the Mandor waterfalls. About a one-hour walk (five kilometers) along the railway track in the direction of the hydroelectric plant brings you to a small house where you must pay the entrance fee (US$3.50). From here, it is a 45-minute hike through a banana plantation and jungle that starts from Km 115 off the tracks. Make sure to take the trail on the right-hand side.

Orchid Garden

Operated by four locals, this garden is truly a work in progress, with around 250 different species of orchids. In Las Orquideas, from the left entrance of the stadium, the garden

MACHU PICCHU

© CYNTHIA BEAMS

Those with extra time in Aguas Calientes can try climbing the perilously steep wooden ladders to Putukusi, a peak that offers spectacular views of Machu Picchu.

is at the end of the street at the house of Leonardo Guttierez. He will gladly take you on a one-hour tour for a small donation towards the maintenance of the garden. Those interested in doing research here should email hatunchaca@hotmail.com. Fernando, who speaks English, can assist you in organizing a field study on the endemic orchids for a month or longer.

Alccamayo Waterfall

This hike is perfect for those with little time on their hands. From the top right-hand corner outside the stadium in Las Orquideas, follow a small lane until you reach the chapel. Continue on to the end of the street and take a left behind the last house. The walk takes you through the forest to a 25-meter cascade. If you are looking for a guided tour (in Spanish), ask around for a man named Edwin Escalante, the young owner of the property, who over the past four years has been improving the paths, flora, and fauna.

ACCOMMODATIONS

Compared to the rest of the country, lodging in Aguas Calientes is exorbitantly expensive. The cleanest budget places are in the Orquideas neighborhood, across from the Río Aguas Calientes, which flows from the hot baths and cleaves the town in two. In Aguas Calientes, forking over a bit more dough to be in the US$25–50 range buys a lot of extra comfort, hot water, and river views. The most upscale hotels are slightly outside of town. The Machu Picchu Pueblo Hotel is upstream from town, and the Machu Picchu Sanctuary Lodge is next to the ruins themselves.

Downstream from Machu Picchu, Santa Teresa used to have a few backpacker lodges and a stunning river-side pool that was destroyed in the January 2010 floods. Before heading to Santa Teresa, check on whether these services are once again available.

Under US$10

Hospedaje Inti Wasi (Las Orquideas M-23,

tel. 084/21-1036, jddggk@latinmail.com, US$5 pp) is the nicest budget place in terms of natural surroundings. To get there, walk from the train station all the way up the right side of the Río Aguas Calientes until it dead-ends at a point a few hundred meters below the hot baths. The main sitting area is a plant-filled courtyard, diffused with yellow light from a yellow, semitransparent roof and echo-ing with the sounds of the river nearby. The bunk rooms are small and sparse, with foam beds, and have a tendency to heat up in the sun. Bathrooms are clean, with water heated by electric showerheads.

US$10-25

In the Orquideas neighborhood is **Hospedaje Q'ente** (Las Orquideas near the soccer field, tel. 084/21-1110, US$9 s, US$12 d). Rooms here are basic but clean. Private baths are an additional US$1.50 per person. The main appeal is the neighborhood itself, which has a soccer field and a small-town feel that is a welcome respite from the hustle of Aguas Calientes.

Down by the train tracks, on the other side of town, is the decrepit but classic **Hostal Los Caminantes** (Imperio de los Incas 140, tel. 084/21-2007, US$9 pp). This old wooden building has been receiving backpackers for decades and has friendly management, even if the rooms have foam beds and are in need of renovation. Hot water and rooms with private baths are available (US$12 pp).

Hostal Pirwa (Pachacútec s/n, tel. 084/21-1170, reservaspirwa@gmail.com, US$10 dorm room) is part of the Pirwa chain of hostels found throughout Peru. It is simple, clean, and a good place to meet other backpackers.

Off the road to Machu Picchu, just be-fore Puente Ruinas, there is a **municipal campground** (US$10 pp). If you opt to camp, make sure you have plenty of bug repellent. The campground is right next to the river.

US$25-50

Hostal Quilla (Pachacútec s/n, tel. 084/21-1009, US$25 s, US$35 d) is on Pachacútec be-tween Wiracocha and Túpac Inca Yupanqui. Rooms are plain with tile floors but service is friendly.

Hostal Kontiki (Las Orquideas, MZ A-9, tel. 084/984-296-340, hostalkontiki@hotmail.com, US$20 s, US$30 d) is a clean and friendly hotel. Breakfast is included and English is spoken. For information on a guided tour of the areas and Machu Picchu, ask for Fernando, the hotel owner/manager.

A company named Sierra Andina operates three hotels in Aguas Calientes, all lined up next to one another on both sides of the tracks. We recommend two of them: the **Machupicchu Hostal** (Imperio de los Inca 313, tel. 084/21-1034, sierrandina@gmail.com, US$35 s, US$40 d with break-fast), where rooms are arranged around a plant-filled courtyard overlooking the river. There is a sitting area with a great river view, and the rooms themselves are plain, clean, and comfortable. Next door is the sister **Presidente Hostal** (Imperio de los Inca 135, tel. 084/21-1212, sierrandina@gmail.com, US$60 s, US$65 d), a similar produc-tion with carpeted, bigger rooms. This place has the look and feel of a real hotel; rooms are pleasant, with earth-colored walls—ask for one that overlooks the river.

US$50-100

A great option is the peaceful, clean and modern **Pachamama Inn** (Las Orquideas Chaskatika s/n, tel. 084/21-1141, hostalpachamamainn@hotmail.com, US$60 s, US$80 d, plus US$20 for a Jacuzzi in your room). This hotel comes with all the trimmings: 24-hour hot water, a money exchange, tourist informa-tion, and a restaurant. Strangely enough, all rooms are equipped with mirrors on the bath-room ceiling.

A more mediocre hostel in this price range is **HanaqPacha Orquideas** (Las Orquideas s/n, tel. 084/21-1027, US$70 s US$90 d). It is clean and simple, and breakfast is included. However, the bathrooms tend to be quite small.

US$100-150

The Limeño owner of **Rupa Wasi** (Huanacaure 180, tel. 084/21-1101, www.rupawasi.net, US$70 s, US$100 d) is also a tour guide, so he's quick to give you a tour of the surrounding orchids and point out the view up the gorge. If you strain, you might see Machu Picchu. But perhaps the best place to catch the view is from your room's private balcony. Rooms are rustic but comfortable with down duvet covers, and breakfast is served in the adjoining restaurant complete with yogurt, granola, and even focaccia bread.

The charming **[Gringo Bill's** (signed well off one corner of the main square, tel. 084/21-1046, www.gringobills.com, US$75–130 d with breakfast), one of the oldest hotels in Aguas Calientes, has a treehouse atmosphere and large rooms with balconies and great showers. The downside is that some rooms have overpowering New Age fluorescent paintings, and guests have to make an advance down payment at an office in Cusco. The newer suites on the top floors are the best.

Hostal Restaurant La Cabaña (Pachacútec M-20, tel. 084/21-1048, www.cabanahostal.com, US$110 s/d, with breakfast) is a friendly place at the top of the main street. Rooms have tile floors, textured walls, and wooden ceilings. The owners, Beto and Marta, take an ecosensitive approach. ("We're trying to return to what we've destroyed," Beto told us.) Additional services include guides for walks, security boxes, laundry, and a DVD player with more than 150 movies. They also offer better rates in the restaurant for guests of the hotel.

Over US$150

A formerly state-owned hotel has been taken over by the Inkaterra Group to create **El Mapi** (Pachacútec 109, tel. 084/21-1011, reservas@byinkaterragroup.com, US$200 s or d with breakfast buffet). This hotel is by far the most modern looking of the Inkaterra range, with a beautiful bar, restaurant, and wooden fencing along the windows. To get there from the main square take the main road, Pachacútec, and it is on the right-hand side.

The owners of the Aguas Calientes restaurants Toto's House and Pueblo Viejo have various hotels: **Inti Inn** (Pachacútec s/n, tel. 084/21-1137, www.grupointi.com, US$140 s or d). Although the rooms are impressively small, the furnishings are pleasant, the beds firm and comfortable, and your towels come wrapped up like a Christmas package.

[The Machu Picchu Pueblo Hotel (Railroad Km 110, tel. 084/21-1132, www.inkaterra.com, US$394 s, US$500 d) is one of Peru's most elegant hotels and has been aptly described a "paradise at Machu Picchu's feet." A short walk from the hustle and bustle of Aguas Calientes, this peaceful patch of rainforest echoes the tumbling of the nearby Río Urubamba and the sounds of some 150 different tropical birds. Stone paths wind through the forest past fountains and pools and up to secluded bungalows. Large rooms feature rustic colonial-style furniture, rough tile floors, luxury bathrooms, recessed reading areas, and nice details like fluffy bathrobes, fruit, and the hotel's own line of organic shampoos, soaps, and conditioners. The hotel has grown since 1978 with an earth-friendly philosophy that includes building all of its furniture on-site. It received the Sustainable Travel award from *National Geographic Traveler* in 2002.

Pueblo Hotel is the only Machu Picchu hotel to give visitors a taste of the jungle, and it's the best substitute for those not planning to visit the Amazon. The biologist guides lead early-morning bird-watching walks (we saw a range of tanagers, hummingbirds, motmots, and the Andean cock of the rock in two hours). The hotel's nature walks include the biggest orchid collection in Peru (372 species), a butterfly house, and a miniature tea plantation. The hotel has reintroduced the *Oso anteojos* (Andean spectacled bear) to the area; three bears now live in the grounds of the hotel, and you can also take a tour to visit them. There is an excellent restaurant, a bar, a spa (US$60 for massage and sauna), and a spring-fed swimming pool.

MACHU PICCHU

Guides lead a two-hour walk up into the forest to waterfalls and pre-Inca stone carvings as well as other day hikes in the area.

If you have deep pockets and want to stay within a stone's throw of the lost Inca city, check out the **(Machu Picchu Sanctuary Lodge** (next to the entrance to the ruins, tel. 084/21-1039, res-mapi@peruorienteexpress. com.pe, http://machupicchu.orient-express. com, US$825 s/d with full board). The lodge began as a state-owned hotel in the 1970s, but it was privatized in 1995 and ultimately acquired by Orient-Express Hotels, which also operates Cusco's finest hotel, Hotel Monasterio, and PeruRail. Orient-Express is not allowed to make any additions to the building, so it remains a small, modest hotel on the outside with an elegant interior. The 31 rooms have been outfitted with antiques, king-size beds, and cable TV, and the slightly more expensive rooms have views over the ruins. One advantage of staying here is a night excursion to the ruins, hosted by a local shaman, which is difficult to do from Aguas Calientes. There are two restaurants, one serving gourmet à la carte items (US$40–50) and the other offering an extraordinary buffet (US$29). The hotel also offers trekking, river rafting, and mountain-biking trips; walking paths behind the hotel lead through an orchid garden. In high season, this hotel is booked solid, so make reservations at least three months in advance.

The lastest five-star hotel in Machu Picchu, which took two years to build, is **Sumaq** (Av. Hermanos Ayar s/n, tel. 084/21-1059, reservas@sumaqhotelperu.com, US$480 s, US$600 d). This stunning hotel has been built in an Inca style with large, spacious rooms, each with its own range of amenities, beautiful king-size beds, and bathtubs. The hotel offers cooking classes, bird-watching tours, and access to a spa equipped with a sauna, massage service, and a Jacuzzi. Dinner is also included in the price.

Another option is the upscale **Hatuchay Towers** (Carretera Puente Ruinas MZ 4, tel. 084/21-1201, www.hatuchaytower.com,

US$282 s, US$305 d), which is fully equipped with elevators. Breakfast and dinner are included, and family suites as well as regular rooms are available. While you shouldn't be put off by the garish mural in the lobby, the hotel restaurant, with its delicious buffet, is highly recommended, and fair-trade textiles from a community in Chinchero are for sale at the hotel shop.

FOOD

Along the railroad tracks and up on the main street, Pachacútec, Aguas Calientes is awash with pizzerias and their street salespeople. While quality has definitely risen in the last few years, you must still be cautious and choose carefully—many are not as good a bargain (nor as clean) as advertised.

International

For something different, try **(The Tree House** (Huanacaure 180, in the Rupa Wasi hotel, tel. 084/21-1101, www.rupawasitree-house.com.pe, 5:30 A.M.–3 P.M. and 7–11 P.M. daily). The wooden ecological restaurant brings a fine selection of wines and pisco to accompany its high-quality but affordable food. Try the delicious trout coated in quinoa or the Thai chicken. They can also provide a yummy box lunch for your visit to Machu Picchu.

The strangely named **Paraquachayoc** (Pachacútec s/n, tel. 084/21-1278, 8 A.M.–10 P.M.) has a small trout farm out the back of the restaurant with over 5,000 trout at a time. Owners Victor and Rosemary prepare the fresh trout in an open kitchen overlooking the Río Aguas Calientes. Their specialty is a large, beautifully presented plate of oven-baked trout with bacon and spinach. Since Victor trained at the Hotel Monasterio in Cusco, you can sit back and expect something special.

The French-Peruvian–owned **(Indio Feliz** (Lloque Yupanqui Lote 4 M-12, tel. 084/21-1090, noon–4 P.M. and 6–10 P.M. Mon.–Sat., US$9) serves up some of the best food in town, best described as Peruvian cuisine with French touches, served in American portions. The two-story restaurant has a peaceful, homey feel, with tables in a sunny upstairs dining room. The four-course set menu is huge and, when we were there, included quiche lorraine, *sopa criolla,* lemon or garlic trout, ginger chicken, and apple pie. There is so much food, in fact, that a single meal can be divided for two people, something the kitchen is happy to do. There is real espresso, calla lilies on all the tables, and opera music in the background.

Pueblo Viejo (Pachacútec s/n, tel. 084/21-1193, www.grupointi.com, 10 A.M.–11 P.M., US$3–6) is at the bottom of the restaurant row and has a cozy atmosphere, including live music and a fireplace. There is a huge range of food here, from vegetarian and pizza to grilled meats. There are affordable lunchtime menus here as well. If you like this place, check out **Toto's House** (tel. 084/22-4179, www.grupointi.com, 9 A.M.–11 P.M.), a more upscale restaurant on the tracks nearby with an US$20 lunch buffet and river views.

Farther down the track, **El Toldo** (Av. Imperio de los Incas 147, tel. 084/21-1363, toldosrestaurant@yahoo.com, 10 A.M.–10 P.M., US$8–10) also specializes in pizzas and has a good breakfast for US$7.

Pachamama (Av. Imperio de los Incas 145, tel. 084/21-1141, 9 A.M.–9 P.M., US$8–10) has been part of Aguas Calientes for many years. It offers pizzas, main courses, good desserts, and is a great place for groups. And yet another restaurant on the tracks, **El Kintu** (Av. Pachacútec 150, tel. 084/21-1336, mapijose@gmail.com, 8 A.M.–10 P.M., US$6–10) is an interesting restaurant with an Inca decor, open kitchen, and barbecue. It has a very relaxed atmosphere and is a perfect place to hang out for a drink. There's also a small hostel attached to the restaurant.

Last but not least is the bar at the hot springs, **Paqcha Tarinakuy.** Carlos, the owner, has been here for 13 years and makes one of the best pisco sours in Peru. Hop into the relaxing baths; when you wish for a drink, signal by waving your hands in the air, and the waiters will come and serve you.

Pizza

Restaurant-Pizzeria Inka Wasi (Pachacútec 112, tel. 084/21-1010, www.inkawasirestaurant.com, 9 A.M.–10 P.M. Mon.–Sat., 1–10 P.M. Sun., US$10) offers a US$13 buffet but also serves trout, chicken brochettes, ceviche, pastas, pizzas, and their specialty dish—guinea pig. Along Pachacútec, other recommended places include **Pizzeria Keros** (Pachacútec 116, tel. 084/21-1374, 9 A.M.–11 P.M. daily), which also serves Peruvian dishes like guinea pig and grilled alpaca, and **Chez Maggy** (Pachacútec 156, tel. 084/21-1006, 11 A.M.–4 P.M. and 6–11 P.M. daily, US$7–10). Along with its sister restaurants throughout the country, Chez Maggy has an established reputation for great pastas and wood-fired pizzas. One place to avoid is the pizzeria **Big Brother,** as there have been several reports of food poisoning.

Vegetarian

Excellent vegetarian food is available at **Govinda** (Pachacútec 20, tel. 084/975-3993, 7 A.M.–10 P.M. daily), which has a variety of lunch menus for US$2–8.

Markets and Shops

The biggest minimarket is **El Pueblo,** next to the main market. With juices, yogurts, fresh bread, deli meats, and cheeses, it's a good place to put together a picnic.

Various hotels and restaurants prepare box lunches, including Gringo Bill's, Rupi Wasi, La Cabana, and Machu Picchu Pueblo Hotel.

INFORMATION AND SERVICES

There is a helpful **Iperú** office (Pachacútec s/n, tel. 084/21-1104) just up the main street from the square that hands out free maps. If you haven't bought your Machu Picchu entrance ticket, you can do it at **Centro Cultura Machu Picchu** (Pachacútec s/n, tel. 084/21-1196, US$37). Tickets must be purchased before heading to the ruins. However, at present, there is word from the INC that tickets will

MACHU PICCHU

© SCOTT COLLINS, WWW.LIFEUNSCRIPTEDPHOTOGRAPHY.COM

vista dome train from Ollantaytambo to Aguas Calientes

only be available via Internet; check www.inc-cusco.gob.pe for up-to-date information.

Police are located on the tracks right across from Hostal Presidente.

Where the tracks cross the Río Aguas Calientes is an **EsSalud** clinic (tel. 084/21-1037) with emergency 24-hour service, and on the other side is the **Ministerio de Salud clinic. Señor de Huanca drugstore** (8 A.M.–10 P.M. daily) is on the tracks across from the Hostal Presidente. If they don't have what you need, the **Pharmacy Popular** (Puputi s/n, tel. 084/22-8787, 8 A.M.–10 P.M. daily) is just off the plaza.

Banco de Crédito has an **ATM** on Imperio de los Incas, near Toto's House.

The **post office** is on the Plaza de Armas and open 10 A.M.–2 P.M. and 4–8 P.M. Monday–Saturday.

There are **Internet** places around the main square.

Laundry Angela (Pachacútec 150, tel. 084/21-2205, US$2/kg) will wash clothes the same day.

GETTING THERE AND AROUND

The only way to reach Aguas Calientes is by trekking or taking the **Inca Rail** (www.inkarail.com) or **Andean Rail** (www.andean-railways.com). There are few vehicles and taxis in Aguas Calientes. The place is small enough that most visitors walk everywhere.

CUSCO

Along with the Aztec capital of Tenochtitlán (now swallowed by modern-day Mexico City), Cusco was the other imperial capital of the Americas at the start of the Spanish conquest. Cusco was a dazzling sight, with its temples of elegantly fitted stone, colossal plazas, royal palaces, and the hilltop fortress of Sacsayhuamán, which the Inca somehow built from house-sized stones. This was the capital of the New World's Roman empire and, as in Rome, paved highways fanned out from here through an empire that had stretched in a mere century between southern Chile and Colombia. As Francisco Pizarro marched wide-eyed through this kingdom in 1533, Cusco became the holy grail of his conquest. Two scouts he sent ahead told him the city was as elegant as a European city and

literally covered in gold. Before the scouts left Cusco, they used crowbars to pry 700 plates of gold off the walls of Coricancha, the sun temple.

Despite four centuries of Spanish domination, Cusco still seems to be in a tug-of-war between Spanish and Inca cultures. Though the Spaniards destroyed the Inca buildings in an act of domination, they had enough common sense to leave many of the bulging, seamless stone walls as foundations. These walls line many of Cusco's narrow cobblestone alleys, which thread among the many baroque churches and convents the Spaniards built here. Part of Cusco's power, and the reason visitors linger here, is the uneasy cultural tension evident in places like Coricancha and even hotel lobbies, where seamless Inca walls

HIGHLIGHTS

🌙 **Catedral:** Cusco's baroque cathedral, built atop a former Inca palace, dominates the town's Plaza de Armas and is filled with a huge range of paintings from the Cusco School, elegant carved choir stalls, and a gold-covered Renaissance altar (page 91).

🌙 **San Blas:** This charming neighborhood is our favorite place to stay, eat, and shop in Cusco. Its narrow cobblestone streets, lined with gorgeous colonial architecture, are car-free and blissfully peaceful (page 95).

🌙 **Coricancha and Santo Domingo:** Coricancha, the Inca sun temple, was once covered with thick plates of solid gold. After sacking it, the Spaniards built a Dominican church atop its seamless walls. The bizarre juxtaposition illustrates the religious conflict that agitates Cusco even today (page 96).

🌙 **Sacsayhuamán:** This stone fortress of massive zigzag walls, fashioned from stone blocks weighing hundreds of tons, towers over Cusco and is the ultimate expression of the Inca's military strength (page 98).

🌙 **The Center for Traditional Textiles of Cusco:** This pioneering center not only sells Cusco's finest textiles, but also supports local weavers and helps them recover their ancient weaving techniques in the process (page 103).

LOOK FOR 🌙 TO FIND RECOMMENDED SIGHTS, ACTIVITIES, DINING, AND LODGING.

© AVALON TRAVEL

are nestled incongruously among arcades of Spanish arches.

With its proximity to the standout attractions of Machu Picchu and the Sacred Valley, Cusco is one of the top destinations in Latin America and the mecca of the Gringo Trail, the well-trod backpacker's route through Latin America. The sheer quantity of restaurants, hotels, and cafés indicates the city's dependence on tourism, which somehow has not diminished Cusco's charm. Schoolchildren run through the street yelling in Quechua, and villagers in the surrounding countryside retain their native dress,

festivals, and love of *chicha,* the local brew of fermented corn.

Cusco is at 3,400 meters (11,150 feet), and most people who arrive here feel some form of *soroche,* or altitude sickness, which can range from a headache and the chills to more serious ailments. The best plan is to visit the Sacred Valley and Machu Picchu first and return to Cusco after becoming used to the altitude.

The heart of Cusco is its Plaza de Armas, which stands out for its huge, 16th-century cathedral. Beyond the Plaza de Armas, and opposite the cathedral, are two charming squares, Plaza Regocijo and Plaza San Francisco.

Farther along in this direction lies the market of San Pedro. To the side of the cathedral, a narrow pedestrian street named Procuradores is lined wall-to-wall with restaurants, bars, and cafés. This is Cusco's Gringo Alley, which is crowded with aggressive salespeople. Behind the cathedral, steep alleys lead to San Blas, a bohemian neighborhood that contains most of our favorite hostels and bars.

HISTORY

As with most empires, the foundation of the Inca empire is shrouded in myth. The best-known version is that the empire began around A.D. 1100, when Manco Cápac and Mama Oclla, children of the sun and the moon, arose from the waters of Lake Titicaca and searched the land for a place to found their kingdom. When they reached the fertile valley of Cusco, Manco Cápac was able, for the first time, to plunge his golden staff into the ground. This was the divine sign that showed them where to found the Inca capital city, which was christened Q'osqo, or "navel of the world."

The seeds of truth in this legend are that the **Tiwanaku** (A.D. 200–1000), from the south shores of Lake Titicaca, were the first advanced culture to reach the Cusco area. Around A.D. 700 an even more potent culture, the **Huari** (A.D. 700–1100) from Ayacucho, spread here and built aqueducts, the large city of Pikillacta, and probably, as some archaeologists believe, the first water temple at Pisac. The Inca, sandwiched between these two advanced cultures, rose out of the vacuum created when both collapsed. The Inca combined the Tiwanaku stonework and farming techniques on one hand with the Huari highway system and mummy worship on the other. The result was a potent system of economic and political organization.

Little is known about Inca history, though it is believed Manco Cápac probably existed and was indeed the first Inca. There were 13 Inca emperors, though the empire for all practical purposes began with Inca Yupanqui, the ninth Inca leader and one of the younger sons of **Inca Viracocha.** Around 1440 the Chancas,

the tribe that toppled the Huari, had amassed a large army that was poised to overrun Cusco. Inca Viracocha fled, probably to his estate at Huchuy Cusco in the Sacred Valley, but Inca Yupanqui stayed on to defend Cusco. Of the ensuing battle, mestizo chronicler Inca Garcilaso de la Vega reports that even the stones of Cusco rose up and became soldiers. Against overwhelming odds, Inca Yupanqui and a team of seasoned generals beat back the Chancas.

After the battle, Inca Yupanqui changed his name to **Pachacútec** ("shaker of the earth" in Quechua), took over Cusco from his disgraced father, and launched the Inca's unprecedented period of expansion. Pachacútec created a vision of the Inca people as a people of power, ruled over by a class of elites who were allowed the privilege of chewing coca leaves and wearing large ear plugs. He used a stick-and-carrot strategy, learned from the Huari, of conquering territories peacefully by bearing down on them with overwhelmingly large armies on one hand, and by offering the rich benefits of being integrated into a well-functioning web of commerce on the other.

In the Cusco area, what is most obvious about Pachacútec is that he was a master builder. He fashioned the city of Cusco into the shape of a puma, a sacred animal admired for its grace and strength, with Sacsayhuamán as the head, the city as the body, and the Coricancha sun temple as the tail. He built a huge central plaza, which included both today's Plaza de Armas and the Plaza Regocijo, and also somehow devised a way to move the stones to begin construction of Sacsayhuamán. He is credited for building nearly all of the other major Inca monuments in the area, including Pisac, Ollantaytambo, and probably even Machu Picchu. Pachacútec's armies conquered the entire area between Cusco and Lake Titicaca and also spread north through the central highlands.

His son, **Túpac Yupanqui,** was less of a builder and even more of a warrior. He spent most of his life away from Cusco in long, brutal campaigns in northern Peru against the

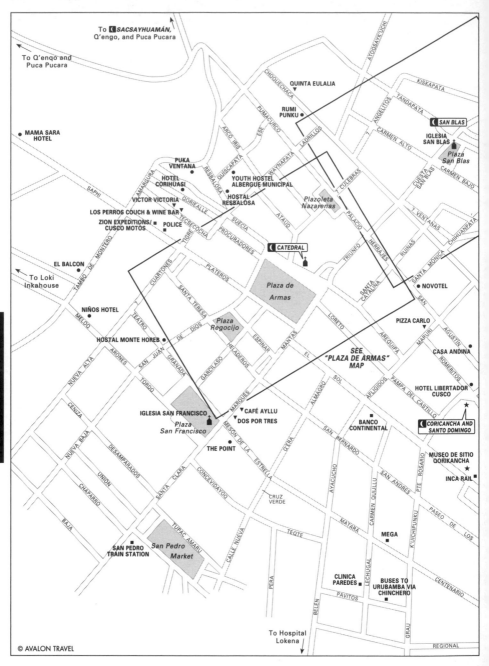

CUSCO

© AVALON TRAVEL

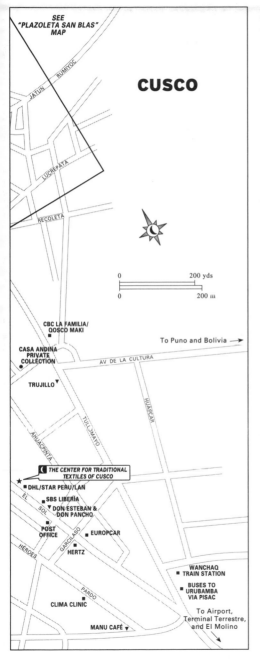

CUSCO

SEE
"PLAZOLETA SAN BLAS"
MAP

RUMIYOC

JATUN

LUCREPATA

RECOLETA

0   200 yds

0   200 m

CBC LA FAMILIA/
QOSCO MAKI

To Puno and Bolivia →

CASA ANDINA
PRIVATE
COLLECTION

AV DE LA CULTURA

TRUJILLO ▾

HUASCAR

TULUMAYO

AHUACPINTA

THE CENTER FOR TRADITIONAL
TEXTILES OF CUSCO

▪ DHL/STAR PERU/LAN

EL ▾ SBS LIBERIA
SOL ▾ DON ESTEBAN &
DON PANCHO

POST
OFFICE   ▪ EUROPCAR

GARCILASO

HEROES   ▪ HERTZ

WANCHAQ
▪ TRAIN STATION

BUSES TO
▪ URUBAMBA
VIA PISAC

PARDO

CLIMA CLINIC ▪

To Airport,
Terminal Terrestre,
and El Molino

MANU CAFÉ ▾

stubborn Chachapoyans. He dominated the entire coastline, including the Chimú empire based at Chan Chan, and pushed all the way to Quito, in present-day Ecuador.

His son, **Huayna Cápac,** the last Inca to rule over a unified empire, seemed to be ruling over a territory that had extended itself almost to the breaking point. Nevertheless he continued the campaign in the north, fathering a son named **Atahualpa** in Quito, and pushed the Inca empire to its last limits, up against what is now the Ecuador-Colombia border. After his death Atahualpa challenged **Huáscar,** the legitimate heir in Cusco, and a disastrous civil war broke out, killing thousands of Inca and badly damaging the empire's infrastructure.

In the end, Atahualpa was victorious. He might have been able to unify the empire again if it were not for the fact that **Francisco Pizarro** and a small Spanish army had begun their march across Peru. Pizarro and his men took Atahualpa hostage in November 1532 and held him until an entire room was filled with gold, much of which was taken from Cusco and carried by llama trains to Cajamarca. Then the Spaniards murdered Atahualpa anyway and continued their march to Cusco.

To maintain stability, Pizarro needed to find a new Inca ruler, and he befriended **Manco Inca,** another son of Huayna Cápac in Cusco, who was grateful to Pizarro for having routed Atahualpa's army of Quito-based Inca. Under the guise of liberators and with Manco Inca's blessing, Pizarro and his men entered Cusco and took full and peaceful possession of the city in November 1533.

It didn't take long, however, for Manco Inca to grow resentful. The Spaniards had sacked Cusco for all of its gold and silver in the first month, picking clean the gold-filled sun temple and even the sacred Inca mummies and melting everything into bars for shipping to Spain. They lived in the palaces of the former Inca emperors and forced Inca nobles to hand over their wives.

Manco Inca escaped from Cusco and by May 1536 had amassed an army estimated at 100,000–200,000 soldiers, who used slingshots

CUSCO

to throw red-hot coals onto Cusco's thatched roofs, burning their beloved city to the ground. Trapped, the Spaniards made a last-ditch effort against the Inca, who had occupied the fortress of Sacsayhuamán. During a battle that raged for more than a week, the Spaniards prevailed against overwhelming odds, causing Manco Inca to retreat to Ollantaytambo and then later to the jungle enclave of Vilcabamba. The Inca resisted for more than three decades until their last leader, Inca **Túpac Amaru,** was captured in the Amazon and executed in Cusco's main square in 1573.

By this time, Cusco had already faded from prominence. After its gold was gone, Francisco Pizarro left for the coast and made Lima the capital of the new viceroyalty. More than two centuries later, an Indian who claimed Inca descent and called himself Túpac Amaru II would rally Inca fervor once again and launch another siege of Cusco. But the Spaniards quickly captured him and hung him in Cusco's main square. His body was quartered and pieces of it were left in the squares of surrounding Inca villages as a warning for the future.

Cusco would have ended up another quiet Andean city like Cajamarca and Ayacucho were it not for Hiram Bingham's discovery of Machu Picchu in 1911. That discovery sparked an international interest in Cusco, which flourished in the 1920s with a glittering café society and a generation of intellectuals that included photographer Martín Chambi. During the 1920s the train line was built past Machu Picchu that still carries travelers today.

A **1950 earthquake,** the most severe in three centuries, destroyed the homes of 35,000 people in Cusco but had the unexpected benefit of clearing away colonial facades that had covered up Inca stonework for centuries. Much of the Inca stonework visible today around Cusco, including the long wall at Coricancha, was discovered thanks to the earthquake. Based on these ruins, and Cusco's colonial architecture, Cusco was declared a **UNESCO World Heritage Site** in 1983.

PLANNING YOUR TIME

Because of its altitude and complex cultural roots, Cusco is best experienced after having visited the Sacred Valley and Machu Picchu. Most of the city can be seen in two days, though we have spent weeks exploring the alleyways of Cusco, and soaking in its incredibly international energy, without getting bored. Cusco's *boleto turístico* gets you into most of the major sites of Cusco and the Sacred Valley for US$45.

As a home base, we prefer staying in the neighborhood of San Blas, which is an uphill hike from the Plaza de Armas but blissfully removed from the noise and traffic of the center. San Blas's narrow streets are difficult for cars to negotiate and therefore very peaceful. The main sights of Cusco are within easy walking distance and concentrated within an area that takes about 10–15 minutes to walk from one side to another. Outlying sights such as Sacsayhuamán and other ruins on the outside of the city require a taxi or bus to arrive, though hiking back downhill into Cusco is an enjoyable way to return.

The traditional time to visit Cusco is during the dry season May–August, but the best weather is in June and July. Avoid the last week in July when Peru's hotels are often booked solid for Peru's Fiestas Patrias celebration around July 28. An increasing number of visitors are enjoying the solitude of Cusco during the rainy season November–March. We definitely recommend the "shoulder months" of April, May, September, and October, which are in between the dry and rainy seasons. You'll find good weather during these months and few crowds.

Taxi hijackings, where taxi drivers kidnap and rob their unsuspecting clients, do happen in Cusco. Examine your taxi carefully before getting inside, especially at night. Have your hotel call a taxi, if at all possible. At night, avoid walking alone in out-of-the-way places or while inebriated, as assaults happen every week.

Sights

PLAZA DE ARMAS

Cusco's Plaza de Armas is surrounded by colonial stone arcades and graced with two extraordinary churches, the Catedral and the Jesuit Iglesia de la Compañía. Though a grove of native trees was unfortunately ripped out in the late 1990s, Cusco's main square is a lively place for locals and tourists alike—full of child shoe shiners, hand-holding schoolgirls, and old men sharing crossword puzzles. Two flags fly over the square, the red-and-white flag of Peru and the rainbow-colored flag of the Inca nation, which is nearly identical to the gay pride flag. It is much older, of course, and its eight colors represent the four corners of Tahuantinsuyo, the Inca empire.

⟨ Catedral

Cusco's baroque Catedral (Plaza de Armas, 10 A.M.–6 P.M. daily, US$8.50 or *boleto religioso*) sits between the more recent church of **Jesús María** (1733) on its right and, on its left, **El Triunfo** (1539), the first Christian church in Cusco, built to celebrate the victory over Manco Inca. The cathedral was built on top of Inca Viracocha's palace using blocks of red granite taken from Sacsayhuamán and took more than a century to construct from 1560 onwards. At least four earthquakes from 1650 to 1986, along with damp and neglect, had taken a serious toll on the building. Fortunately, Cusco's archbishop acquired financial backing from Telefónica for a complete

© AVALON TRAVEL

© RENÉE DEL GAUDIO AND ROSS WEHNER

Plaza de Armas

renovation 1997–2002, which removed much of the grime that had covered chapels and paintings over time. For the first time in a century perhaps, it is possible to make out the unique **Cusco School** paintings, including odd works such as Christ eating a guinea pig at the Last Supper and a (very) pregnant Virgin Mary. There is also an interesting painting, reported to be the oldest in Cusco, showing Cusco during the 1650 earthquake with the townspeople praying in the Plaza de Armas. The church also contains considerable gold- and silverwork, including a silver bier for the **Señor de los Temblores** (Lord of the Earthquakes), patron of Cusco. It also holds a 17th-century carved pulpit and choir stalls and an original gold-covered Renaissance altar. In the bell tower is the huge María Angola bell, one of the largest bells in the world, made with 27 kilograms of gold.

Iglesia de la Compañía

Across the corner from the cathedral is the 17th-century Iglesia de la Compañía (9–11:30 A.M. and 1–5:30 P.M. daily, US$3.50 or

boleto religioso), which was built on top of the palace of Inca Huayna Cápac. This church was built by the Jesuits, who were expelled from Latin America in 1767, but not before they built a series of churches in Peru's principal cities that outshine even the cathedral. This graceful, highly ornate facade is a case in point, behind which is a single nave leading to a spectacular baroque altar. Near the main door is a 17th-century painting depicting the wedding of Inca princess Beatriz Clara Coya to Spanish *captín* Martín García de Loyola, grandnephew of San Ignacio de Loyola.

NORTHEAST OF THE PLAZA DE ARMAS
Museo Inka

Head down the alley to the left of the cathedral to reach this museum (corner of Ataúd and Túcuman, 8 A.M.–7 P.M. Mon.–Fri., 9 A.M.–4 P.M. Sat., US$3.50). This ornate colonial home contains an interesting collection of Inca objects, including jewelry, ceramics, textiles, mummies, and a variety of metal and gold artifacts. It also has the world's largest

Iglesia de la Compañía

CUSCO

CUSCO'S TOURIST TICKET

You will go broke if you pay to get into each museum, church, and archaeological site around Cusco. Even if you are going to visit only a few places, buy a *boleto turístico* for US$45 (US$24 for students under age 26 with ISIC card). The ticket covers 16 sites in and around Cusco, including must-sees like Sacsayhuamán, Pisac, and Ollantaytambo, and you cannot actually get into a lot of the sites if you do not have the ticket. The tickets can be bought at the entrances to most major sites or at **COSITUC** (Av. El Sol 103, #102, www.boletoturisticocusco.com, 9 A.M.–5 P.M. Mon.-Fri.). Unfortunately, the pass only lasts 10 days. There is a process for extending expired passes, but – take it from us – it's not worth wasting a day navigating the halls of the Instituto Nacional de Cultura, which is a harrowing bureaucracy even by Peruvian standards.

The ticket covers these 16 sites: Museo Municipal de Arte Contemporáneo, Museo Histórico Regional, Museo de Arte Popular, Museo de Sitio Coricancha, Centro Qosqo de Arte Nativo, Monumento a Pachacútec, Sacsayhuamán, Q'enqo, Puca Pucara, Tambo Machay, Pisac, Ollantaytambo, Moray, Chinchero, Tipon, Pikillacta.

The Coricancha temple (US$3.50) and the Museo de Arte y Monasterio de Santa Catalina (US$2.50) are not included in the ticket, but if you go to both you only pay US$5. The Catedral (US$8.50), Iglesia de la Compañía (US$3.50), Iglesia San Blas (US$5), and the Museo de Arte Religioso (US$5) are not covered either, but if you plan to go to all four you can buy the *boleto religioso* at the entrance of any of these sites for US$17 (US$8.50 for students under age 26 with ISIC card). Other interesting sites not included are the Iglesia de La Merced (US$2), Museo Inka (US$3.50), and the Museo de Arte Precolombino (US$7).

COLONIAL PAINTING: THE CUSCO SCHOOL

The religious paintings that cover the walls of Peru's colonial churches are more than decoration. For centuries after the conquest, painting was the Catholic church's main tool for converting Peru's native peoples, who for the most part did not read or speak Spanish. The church's religious campaign produced thousands of now-priceless works and renowned schools of painting in Cusco and Quito, in present-day Ecuador.

Shortly after the conquest, the different orders of the Catholic church began importing paintings into Lima from well-known painters of the ongoing European Renaissance. The museum at Iglesia San Francisco in Lima contains works by European painters who influenced the American schools of painting, collectively known as the Spanish American baroque. These 16th-century European masters included the Spanish painters Francisco de Zurbarán and Bartolomé Esteban Murillo and Flemish master Peter Paul Rubens.

By 1580, demand for European paintings had so outstripped supply that European painters began arriving to Lima in search of lucrative commissions. One of these was Italian Jesuit Bernardo Bitti (1548–1610), who was a disciple of Caravaggio and the brightly colored, emotional works of the Italian baroque. He was probably the single most influential European painter to work in Peru, and his paintings can be seen at La Merced in Cusco, La Compañía in Arequipa, and Lima's San Francisco museum. With the guidance of Bitti and other European masters, the church orders set up convent studios around Peru where Indian and mestizo artisans cranked out a staggering quantity of paintings in serial fashion – one painter would specialize in clothing, another in landscape, and still another in face and hands.

Right from the start, the workshops in Cusco began developing a unique style that blended the European baroque with images from Peru, including local trees, plants, animals, and foods. Cusco's cathedral, for instance, contains a painting that shows the Last Supper served with roasted guinea pig and chicha, the local corn beer. In another painting nearby, there is a pregnant Virgin Mary with the lustrous, smooth hair of Andean women. Often the dress of the Virgin Mary has a triangular shape, which art scholars believe is a transformation of the ancient Andean practice of worshipping apus, or sacred mountains.

The painters of the Cusco School also used a lot of gold to highlight their paintings and create a richly decorated surface. Most paintings pictured the Virgin Mary, scenes from the life of a saint, or panoramas of devils and angels. An entirely unique invention of Cusco's painters was the archangels, flying through the air with ornate Spanish clothing and armed with muskets. Far from the tranquil realism of the Flemish baroque, these paintings portrayed a dazzling otherworld, filled with powerful spiritual beings, which were meant to awe, stun, and frighten Indian viewers into accepting Catholicism. The most famous painters of the Cusco School were Diego Quispe Tito, Juan Espinosa de los Monteros, and Antonio Sinchi Roca, though it is difficult to decipher who did what because paintings were rarely signed.

In Quito, new-world painters embarked on a different course. The founder of the Quito School was Father Bedón, who studied with Bitti in Lima but quickly dropped the Italian mannerist style upon returning to Quito. Instead he ushered in a type of religious painting that combined the gold decorations of Cusco School with the colder colors and shadowy depths favored by Peter Paul Rubens and other Flemish painters. The cathedrals in northern Peru, including Cajamarca and Trujillo, often feature paintings from both schools side by side.

collection of *qeros,* wooden cups the Inca used for drinking.

Museo de Arte Precolombino

Farther down the alley to the left of the cathedral, toward the Plaza de las Nazarenas, is the fabulous private Museo de Arte Precolombino (MAP, Plaza de las Nazarenas 231, tel. 084/23-3210, www.map.museolarco.org, 9 A.M.–10 P.M. daily, US$7). MAP opened its doors in June 2003 and contains an exquisite array of ceramics, painting, jewelry, and objects made of silver and gold. Unlike at other archaeological museums, the pieces here are not meant to be viewed as artifacts representative of their cultures. They are ancient works of art, pieces of elaborate craftsmanship and beauty that were handpicked from the Museo Larco in Lima. The museum has an elegant layout designed by Fernando de Szyszlo, one of Peru's most respected contemporary painters, and in the courtyard is an interesting glass box containing the MAP café, one of Cusco's most upscale restaurants. Near the end of the plaza is the 400-year-old **Seminario San Antonio Abad,** which has been converted into the Hotel Monasterio, Cusco's first five-star hotel. Even if you are not a guest, sneak a peak at the courtyard and the 17th-century **Iglesia San Antonio Abad.**

Museo de Arte Religioso

Just one block downhill from Museo de Arte Precolombio along Palacio, this museum (Palacio and Hatun Rumiyoc, 8 A.M.–6 P.M. daily, US$5 or *boleto religioso*) resides in a colonial building that was built by the Marquis of Buenavista and later occupied by Cusco's archbishop. These days its handsome salons showcase religious paintings from the 17th and 18th centuries. Walk up the alleyway Hatun Rumiyoc and you will see that the entire museum is built upon a foundation of Inca stones that fit perfectly into one another. This was the foundation of an early ruler of Cusco, **Inca Roca,** and near the end of the street you will find the famous stone with 12 sides, all of which conform perfectly to their neighbors. Sadly, the stone was badly chipped and scarred by a group of unknown vandals in April 2004.

◖ San Blas

Walk away from the Plaza de Armas along Hatun Rumiyoc and continue walking straight until reaching Cuesta San Blas, which leads to Cusco's San Blas neighborhood. This square, known as **Plazoleta San Blas,** is home to several artisan families who have been operating here for decades. Its steep cobblestone alleys offer excellent views over Cusco.

Iglesia San Blas (Plazoleta San Blas, 8 A.M.–6 P.M. daily, US$5 or *boleto religioso*) is a small, whitewashed adobe church built in 1563. One of the New World's most famous works of art is found here, a carved pulpit made from the trunk of a single tree. There is also a gold-covered baroque altar.

Another interesting place to visit, on top of the fountain in the Plazoleta San Blas, is the family-run **Museo de la Coca** (Suytuk'atu 705, museodelacoca@hotmail.com, 8 A.M.–8 P.M.

San Blas is a great place to stay, stroll, and eat in Cusco.

CUSCO

© RENÉE DEL GAUDIO AND ROSS WEHNER

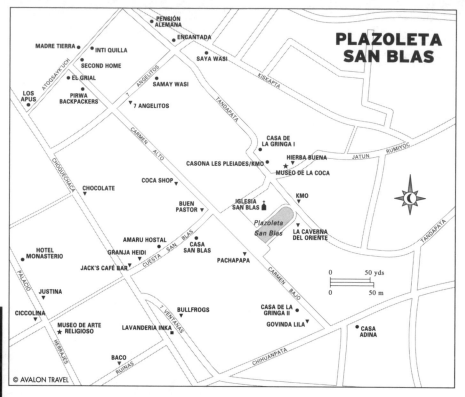

daily, US$3.50). This interesting exhibition demonstrates the history of the coca leaf through to the adulterated production of cocaine. It also has a boutique filled with a large selection of coca products. San Blas is a great neighborhood to find accommodations or just to wander around and have lunch.

EAST OF THE PLAZA DE ARMAS
Museo de Arte y Monasterio de Santa Catalina

From the Plaza de Armas, head down Arequipa to this museum (Arequipa, 8:30 A.M.–5:30 P.M. Mon.–Sat., US$2.50 or US$5 with entry to Coricancha), which was built on top of the enclosure where the chosen virgins of the Inca lived, known as the *acllahuasi*, or "house of the chosen ones." In a strange historical twist, the

Spaniards converted the building into a convent, where 30 nuns remain cloistered to this day. Holy women have thus lived in this building for at least five centuries. The museum has a good collection of Cusco School paintings and an impressive Renaissance altar. A highlight is a trunk containing miniature figurines depicting the life of Christ, which was used by Catholic missionaries for proselytizing in far-flung regions of Peru.

◖ Coricancha and Santo Domingo

The greatest prize in the Spaniards' 1533 sacking of Cusco was Coricancha (Plazoleta Santo Domingo, 8:30 A.M.–5:30 P.M. Mon.–Sat., 2–5 P.M. Sun., US$3.50 or US$5 with entry to Museo de Arte y Monasterio de Santa Catalina), the sun temple. For the Inca, the building had many functions. It was foremost a place where offerings were burnt in thanks to the sun, though there were also rooms devoted to the moon, stars, lightning, thunder, and rainbows. Like so much of Inca ceremonial architecture, the building also served as a solar observatory and mummy storehouse.

The south-facing walls of the temple were covered with gold in order to reflect the light of the sun and illuminate the temple. Inside was the **Punchaco,** a solid-gold disk inlaid with precious stones, which represented the sun and was probably the most sacred object in the Inca empire. Pizarro's scouts had already produced approximately a ton and a half of gold by stripping the inner walls of Coricancha. When the main Spanish force gained Cusco, they gathered hundreds of gold sculptures and objects from the temple, including an altar big enough to hold two men and an extraordinary artificial garden made of gold, including cornstalks with silver stems and ears of gold. Tragically, everything was melted down within a month—except for the Punchaco. It disappeared from the temple and its whereabouts are unknown to this day.

The Dominicans took over the Coricancha and dismantled most of it, using the polished ashlar to build their church and convent of Santa Domingo on top of the sun temple's walls. For centuries, many of the Coricancha's walls were hidden beneath the convent. But in 1950 an earthquake caused large sections of the convent to crumble, exposing Inca walls of the highest quality.

It requires considerable imagination today to picture how the Inca's most important temple must have once looked. The eight-sided sacrificial font, stripped of the 55 kilograms of gold that once covered it, stands in the middle of the Coricancha's main square. The rooms that surround it may once have been covered with silver and dedicated to the moon, stars, and thunder. The wall running along the temple's eastern side is 60 meters long and 5 meters high, and each block is perfectly interlocked with its neighbor. But the highlight is the curved retaining wall beneath the facade of

the church, which has not budged an inch in all of Cusco's earthquakes.

Sharing the same entrance as the Coricancha is Cusco's most serious contemporary art gallery, **Galeria del Convento de Santo Domingo** (Plazoleta Santo Domingo, 8:30 A.M.–5:30 P.M. Mon.–Sat., US$3.50). It is the best place to see young emerging local artists.

Museo de Sitio Coricancha

Reached through an underground entrance across the garden from the Coricancha is this rather unimpressive museum (Av. El Sol, 9 A.M.–6 P.M. Mon.–Sat., 8 A.M.–1 P.M. Sun., entry with *boleto turístico*), which exhibits a few artifacts from the excavation of Coricancha, a model of the sun temple, and blueprints of its floor plans. There are no guides available here, and explanations are in Spanish only.

On your way back to the Plaza de Armas, walk down the narrow alley of Loreto. To your right are the Inca walls of the *acllahuasi,* now the Santa Catalina convent. To the left are the walls of the palace of Huayna Cápac, now the Iglesia de la Compañía.

SOUTHWEST OF THE PLAZA DE ARMAS

From the Plaza de Armas, walk up Mantas one block to the **Iglesia de la Merced** (tel. 084/23-1821, 8 A.M.–12:30 P.M. and 2–5:30 P.M. Mon.–Sat., US$2), which was completely rebuilt following the 1650 earthquake. Inside the church lie two conquistadores, a father and a son who were executed by the Spanish shortly after the conquest. Diego de Almagro the Elder was hung after he rebelled against Francisco Pizarro's authority, and his son, Diego de Almagro the Younger, was executed four years later for murdering Francisco Pizarro in revenge. Hanging on the walls nearby the tombs are paintings by the 16th-century master Bernardo Bitti. The church's elegant cloisters contain a small museum, which showcases a magnificent monstrance made of gold, silver, and precious stones.

From the Iglesia de la Merced, head down Heladeros to the **Plaza Regocijo** and the

Museo Histórico Regional (Heladeros, tel. 084/22-5211, 8 A.M.–5 P.M. Tues.–Sun., entry with *boleto turístico* or US$4.50), which was once the home of one of colonial Peru's most famous and eloquent writers, mestizo Inca Garcilaso de la Vega. The museum provides a fine survey of Peru's pre-Inca cultures, starting with preceramic arrowheads and continuing with artifacts from the Chavín, Moche, Chimú, Chancay, and Inca cultures. The holdings include a Nasca mummy and, on the second floor, colonial furniture and paintings from the Cusco School. Across the Plaza Regocijo in the municipality is the **Museo Municipal de Arte Contemporáneo** (Plaza Regocijo, 9 A.M.–6 P.M. Mon.–Sat., entry with *boleto turístico* or US$4.50), which contains contemporary art of varying quality.

From Plaza Regocijo, walk down Garcilaso to **Iglesia San Francisco** (8 A.M.–noon and 3–5 P.M. daily), a convent and church that stands above the plaza of the same name. This church, with three naves and in the shape of a Latin cross, was built in 1572 and is one of the few churches in Cusco to survive the 1650 earthquake. As a result, its convent is one of the few remaining examples of the highly ornate 16th-century plateresque style, complemented here by *azulejo* tiles imported from Seville. There are two smaller colonial churches down Santa Clara from here toward the market and the train station: The first is **Iglesia Santa Clara** (8 A.M.–noon and 3–5 P.M. daily), which is open only for early-morning mass 6–7 A.M., and the second is **Iglesia San Pedro** (8 A.M.–noon and 3–5 P.M. daily).

OUTSIDE CUSCO

There are four highly recommended Inca ruins outside of Cusco, which many Cusco agencies offer as part of a rushed, half-day tour. The ruins all accept the *boleto turístico* or they charge US$5 per ruin and are open 7 A.M.–6 P.M.; after-hours visits are possible at Sacsayhuamán, the ruins closest to Cusco. Peter Frost's excellent guide to Cusco, *Exploring Cusco,* details some interesting walks around

this spectacular landscape between the four sites, which are littered with aqueducts, Inca roads, caves, shrines, and carvings.

All the ruins lie close to the road that runs between Cusco and Pisac. An enjoyable way to see the ruins is to take a Pisac bus or taxi to the farthest ruins, Tambomachay, and walk the eight kilometers back to Cusco, visiting all the ruins along the way (this walk can be shortened considerably by just walking between Q'enqo and Sacsayhuamán, a distance of one kilometer). Occasional robberies have been reported in this area, so it is better to walk in a group of two or more during the early part of the day.

◖ Sacsayhuamán

Looming over Cusco to the north are the ruins of Sacsayhuamán (7 A.M.–6 P.M. daily), a hilltop fortress with three ramparts of zigzag walls that run for nearly 300 meters on its north side. The largest stones—nearly 8.5 meters high and 361 tons, according to historian John Hemming—were placed at the apex of the walls to strengthen them. Every Inca citizen had to spend a few months of the year working on public works, and the Inca used this tremendous reserve of labor to move the stones, using log sleds and levers. But even engineers have a hard time understanding how the Inca fitted these huge stones so perfectly together.

Only the largest stones of Sacsayhuamán remain. Up until the 1930s, builders arrived at Sacsayhuamán to cart away the precut stone of this apparently limitless quarry, so it is difficult to appreciate how impregnable Sacsayhuamán must have been. Three towers once crowned the top of Sacsayhuamán, and two of their foundations are visible. During Manco Inca's great rebellion, the Spaniards managed to establish a base on the opposing hill and spent two days charging across the plain on horseback and attempting to scale the defensive walls. On the first day, one of the stones fired by the Inca slingshots struck Juan Pizarro, Francisco's younger brother, who died that night. On

The Sacsayhuamán ruins, just above Cusco, are a monument to the Inca's most ferocious battle against the Spaniards.

the evening of the second day, the Spaniards launched a surprise attack with ladders and successfully forced the Inca into the three stone towers. As the Spaniards massacred the estimated 1,500 soldiers trapped inside, many Inca preferred to leap to their deaths from the high tower. The next morning, condors feasted on the dead bodies, and this grisly image is emblazoned on Cusco's coat-of-arms.

These days the flat fields outside of Sacsayhuamán, where the Inti Raymi culminates each June, is a peaceful place to stroll. In the mornings, Cusco residents come here to jog or do yoga on the grassy lawn, which is considerably larger than a soccer field. A huge trapezoidal door leads up a walkway to the top of the ruins, which is a marvelous place to bring wine and watch the sun setting over Cusco. Because many tourists come here in the evening, guards are posted to put visitors at ease as dusk falls. If you have time, visit the top of Rodadero hill,

where the Spaniards based themselves during their assault on Sacsayhuamán. There is a rock outcrop on top, beautifully carved with sacred steps. Sacsayhuamán is a steep, two-kilometer walk from Cusco or a 10-minute taxi ride (US$2). Taxis wait in the parking lot for the return trip to Cusco.

Q'enqo

One kilometer past Sacsayhuamán is the shrine of Q'enqo (7 A.M.–6 P.M. daily), which means "zigzag" in Quechua. It is a large limestone outcrop carved with enigmatic steps leading nowhere, a sacred motif that is found on nearly every *huaca,* the sacred stone revered by the Inca. On the top of the rock are faint carvings of a puma and a condor. Carved into the rock are perfect zigzag channels, which probably flowed with *chicha* or llama blood during ceremonial rituals, much like the Saywite Stone between Cusco and Abancay. Below the rock are caves carved with niches where mummies of lesser nobility may once have been kept. Nearby is an amphitheater with niches centered framing an upright stone, which was probably defaced long ago by Spanish extirpators of idolatry. Between Q'enqo and Sacsayhuamán is a series of soccer fields, where rather pitiful horses can be rented for quick rides in the area (US$5 per half hour, price negotiable).

Puca Pucara

The least significant of the ruins outside Cusco, Puca Pucara (7 A.M.–6 P.M. daily), meaning "red fort" in Quechua, was probably not a fort at all but rather a storage facility or an Inca *tambo,* or lodge. Perhaps when the Inca emperor came to visit the baths of Tambomachay, his court waited here. There are several chambers below and a platform on top with excellent views. The distance between Puca Pucara and Q'enqo is six kilometers along the road.

Tambomachay

Called the Inca's Bath, Tambomachay (7 A.M.–6 P.M. daily) lies about 300 meters off the Pisac road, though it is well marked with a sign. It is a well-preserved example of the sacred water fountains found at nearly every important Inca temple, including Pisac, Ollantaytambo, and Machu Picchu. The Inca took a natural spring and painstakingly channeled the water through three waterfalls, which

continue to work perfectly today. There is a fine Inca wall above with ceremonial niches. The Inca worshiped water as a vital life element, and this site no doubt formed part of a water cult. From here, you can see Puca Pucara, on the other side of the road.

Entertainment and Events

FOLKLORIC MUSIC AND DANCE

The **Centro Qosqo de Arte Nativo** (El Sol 604, tel. 084/22-7901, US$5), founded in 1924, has a highly recommended music and dance show 6:45–7:45 P.M. on most evenings. The Centro was founded in 1924 as the first organized music and dance center in Cusco. Most of the Peruvian restaurants in the Plaza de Armas have live Andean music during dinner.

The once prestigious Garcilaso cinema and theater, has gone through many transformations since its opening in 1963, including

housing a pornographic cinema, evangelical church, and arcade all at the same time. In 2007 it was converted into the **Teatro Kusikay** (Union 117, tel. 084/25-5414, www.kusikay. com, 9 A.M.–9 P.M. Mon.–Sat.), solely dedicated to the show **Paukartanpu,** which is a colorful spectacle based on a religious festival. The show starts at 7:30 P.M. Monday–Saturday and costs US$35. It is a modern and fun insight into Andean culture interpreted through impressive acrobatics, traditional dance, music, and folklore, as well as theater and circus.

CAFÉ BARS

A great place to hang out either at night or during the day is **Los Perros Couch & Wine Bar** (Tecsecocha 436, tel. 084/24-1447, 11 A.M.–midnight daily, US$5). The relaxed atmosphere and comfy couches make an inviting backdrop for a delicious light lunch, an afternoon smoothie over a game of backgammon, a cup of coffee perusing a magazine, or a nice glass of red wine in the evening.

Just up the road is **Indigo** (Tecsecocha 2, 2nd Fl., tel. 084/26-0271, 11 A.M.–2 A.M. daily, US$5), another nice place to slump into a couch in front of an open fire and unwind. Hookahs are available with an impressive selection of exotic tobaccos. The Thai dishes are not bad and reasonably priced.

Known for its raucous private parties, **Fallen Angel Fire & Ice** (Plazoleta Nazarenas 221, tel. 084/25-8184, 11 A.M.–11 P.M. daily, US$5) is the most outrageous place to get a drink. There are glass-covered bathtub fish tanks instead of tables, techno music, and multicolored

indigenous parade in Cusco's Centro

daiquiris. The steaks are the specialty of the creative dinner menu. The owner, Andres Zuniga, has also set up a lavish and flamboyant guesthouse on the same property.

Despite the distracting decor, **The Tea Rooms** (Santa Teresa 364, 2nd Fl., tel.084/23-1317, noon–midnight daily, US$7) is spacious and bright and not a bad place for an evening martini or a classic, though overpriced, afternoon tea for two with sandwiches, scones, and cakes for US$17.

PUBS AND LIVE MUSIC

The English **Cross Keys Pub** (Triunfo 350, 2nd Fl., tel. 084/22-9227, 10 A.M.–2 A.M. daily) recently moved to a new location, but nevertheless continues to be a Cusco classic owned by Barry Walker, British consul and owner of Manu Expeditions. It has dartboards, typical pub fare including chili con carne, and English beer on tap. Happy hours run 6:30–7:30 P.M. and 9:30–10 P.M.

Another good pub in town with nice views over the Plaza de Armas and a great place to play a game of pool or darts is **Nortons** (Santa Catalina Angosta 116, 7 A.M.–2 A.M. daily). There is an impressive selection of imported beers from England, Belgium, and Mexico, including Old Speckled Hen and Abbot Ale on tap. For hangovers a classic English breakfast and a cheap Bloody Mary do the trick.

The atmosphere at **Paddy Flaherty's Irish Pub** (Triunfo 124, tel. 084/24-7719, 11 A.M.–2 A.M.) is a taste of home, at least for those of us who hang out at Irish pubs. It serves Guinness, among other beers, and has a two-for-one happy hour 7–8 P.M. The kitchen offers shepherd's pie, chicken wings, and stuffed potato skins.

For something a little different try **La Chupeteria Shot Bar** (Tecsecocha 400, 8 P.M.–late daily). The imposing picture of Che Guevara and the motto "revolutionary drinking theory" say it all. La Chupeteria adds an exciting twist to a night on the town with its huge array of creative shots. For an impressive spectacle of fire and sparks the Swiss Verbier shot is a must.

Another interesting drinking experience is **El Pisquerito** (San Juan de Dios 250, tel. 084/23-5223, www.elpisquerito.com, 11 A.M.–2 A.M. daily). Owned by one of Peru's most experienced bartenders, Hans Hilburg, this charming little bar specializes exclusively in pisco. There is an extensive menu of delicious designer cocktails and a nice selection of Spanish-style tapas and pizzas.

Hands down the best mojito in Cusco is at **Hierba Buena** (Suytuk'atu 715-B, San Blas, tel. 084/26-0685, 9 A.M.–12:30 A.M. Mon.–Sat.). Make sure to also try the *chicha tu madre,* a drink made with purple maize juice and pisco.

If you are up for some live music there are plenty of places in Cusco. Locals and foreigners head to **Ukukus** (Plateros 316, 8 P.M.–late daily, sometimes a small cover on weekends), a live music venue and bar that has been a classic of Cusco's nightlife scene since it was founded over a decade ago. Shows start at 10:30 P.M. and range from Afro-Peruvian to rock, with affordable drinks.

The hippest place for an evening out is **Bullfrogs** (Warankallki 185, tel. 084/22-1762, 3 P.M.–late daily), a large, two-story, gay-friendly bar with stone walls and colorful beanbags. It has a great atmosphere, the cocktails are good, entertainment options include a pool table, foosball, movies during the day, and live music nightly.

A local expat favorite and a good live music spot that has been around for years is **7 Angelitos** (Siete Angelitos 638, tel. 084/23-6373, 3 P.M.–late daily). Walter, the entertaining owner, prides himself on having some of the best mojitos in town. There are two-for-one happy hours 7:30 P.M.–9:30 P.M. and 11 P.M.–11:30 P.M. just as the bands start playing. If it is late and the door is closed just knock, as it is more than likely the party will still be going on inside.

Above the Plazoleta San Blas, **KMO** (Tandapata 100, tel. 084/23-6009, 3 P.M.–2 A.M. daily), Indigo's sister bar, has been a live music hot spot for years and has happy hour all night.

DISCOTHEQUES

If you still have energy after a pub warmup, there are many places to dance until dawn in Cusco. The Cusco nightclub scene is constantly changing. Clubs open and close monthly and the "in" place has no real criteria. Recently, however, the most frequented dance spot and therefore extremely crowded is **Inkateam** (Portal de Carnes 298, 9 P.M.–6 A.M. daily). Tourists and locals dance to the blasting sounds of techno, reggae, and electro. Happy hour is 9 P.M.–midnight, and there are also free salsa classes every night 9–11 P.M.

Mama África (Portal de Panes 109, 3rd Fl., www.mamaafricaclub.com, 9 P.M.–6 A.M. daily) has been around for a 15 years but is constantly moving and has at various times been the place to go. It still fills up, and every Wednesday at 2 A.M. they have electronic sessions.

Another of Cusco's frequented dance spots is **Roots** (Waynapata 194, 9 P.M.–6 A.M. daily), which also offers salsa classes at 9 P.M. Once you have perfected your salsa moves head to **El Muki** (Santa Catalina 114, 10 P.M.–6 A.M. weekends), the best salsa spot in Cusco, frequented almost exclusively by Cusqueños.

FESTIVALS

Celebrated continuously since the devastating quake of 1650, Cusco's procession of the **Señor de los Temblores** (Lord of the Earthquakes) traditionally begins at Cusco's cathedral on the Monday before Easter.

One of Peru's most enigmatic festivals is **Qoyllur R'itti,** which takes place in May or June before Corpus Christi on the slopes of the Nevado Ausangate at 4,800 meters. During the three-day festival, elaborately costumed men climb in the middle of the night to hew huge blocks of ice, which they carry on their backs down the mountain at dawn. Thousands of campesinos from neighboring communities come to this spot to bring ice down from the mountain or participate in the colorful masked dances. This festival, Christian only on the surface, grew out of the Andean tradition of worshipping mountains, or *apus,* to ensure rains

and good harvests. The pilgrims trek toward the mountain from the town of Tinki, which is several hours away from Cusco on the rough road to Puerto Maldonado. If you are in Cusco during this time, you can find agencies along Plateros in Cusco that sell transport and camping packages.

During Cusco's **Corpus Christi,** which usually happens in early June, elaborate processions fill the streets of Cusco as all the bells in the city ring. Each procession carries a different saint, which is treated as if it were a living person, in the same way the Inca paraded their ancestors' mummies around these same streets five centuries ago.

A country festival that is straightforward for travelers to attend is the June 15–17 festival of the **Virgen del Carmen** in Paucartambo, a pleasant colonial town that is a four-hour bus ride from Cusco on the way to the Manu. The festival includes an extraordinary range of dances and costumes. Many Cusco agencies offer inexpensive lodge-and-transport packages to the festival, which include a dawn trip to Tres Cruces, a fabulous place to watch the sun rise over the Amazon basin.

Cusco's biggest festival is **Inti Raymi,** the Inca celebration of the June 21 winter solstice. The festival, which lasts 10 days on either side of the solstice, was banned by the Spaniards in 1535. But in 1944, a group of Cusco intellectuals re-created the sacred ceremony by studying chronicles and historical documents. Each year, hundreds dress up as Inca priests, nobles, and chosen women, and one man, chosen by audition, gets to be Inca Pachacútec. The main day, June 24, begins at 10 A.M. at the Coricancha (the sun temple) and ends around 2 P.M. at Sacsayhuamán, where thousands of tourists sit on the fort's walls for a good view as Pachacútec speaks with a sun god through a microphone. It is a highly staged, touristy production, completely unlike the more down-to-earth countryside festivals.

Fiestas Patrias, the national Peruvian holiday at the end of July, is one of Peru's most important holidays. The festival honors Peru's independence on July 28 and Peru's armed forces on July 29. A large amount of Peruvians travel in the week that falls around these dates. Hotels, transport, and other services are often booked during this time.

Santuranticuy, on December 24, is one of the largest arts-and-crafts fairs in Peru. Nativity figures, miniature altars, and ceramics are laid out on stalls in the Plaza de Armas by hundreds of artists.

Shopping

Crafts shops are wall-to-wall along Triunfo, which leads from the Plaza de Armas and becomes Rumiyoc and Cuesta San Blas before dead-ending into Plazoleta San Blas, the center of Cusco's bohemian/art district. Several families who have been producing crafts for decades have their workshops here and can often be seen at work.

CERAMICS AND WEAVINGS

The family workshop **Artesania Mendivil** (Plazoleta San Blas 634, 9 A.M.–6 P.M. Mon.–Sat.) is known worldwide for its religious sculptures with long mannerist necks made of plaster cloth, rice paste, and wood. Hilario Mendivil began working as a craftsman at the age of 10 in 1939; though he has passed away, his sons continue the tradition.

World-acclaimed ceramicist Pablo Seminario, whose studio is in Urubamba, has a showroom on the Plaza de Armas. At **Seminario** (Portal de Carnes 244, tel. 084/24-6093, www.ceramicaseminario.com, 9 A.M.–9 P.M. Mon.–Sat., 5–9 P.M. Sun.) there are colonial-style ceramics all designed according to Pablo's unique style.

Another great association run by the altruistic Franco Negri is **Casa Ecológica** (Portal de Carnes 236, interior 2, tel. 084/25-5427, www.casaecologicacusco.com, 9 A.M.–9:30 P.M. daily), which was created to promote sustainable development in rural communities. The shop sells traditional handicrafts produced with natural fibers as well as organic cosmetics and food products.

Another shop whose revenue goes directly to the artists from the communities surrounding Cusco is **Chaska Handicrafts** (Garcilaso 265-1, tel. 084/23-5407, 9 A.M.–1 P.M. and

3–9 P.M. Mon.–Sat.). Just down the road is **Agua y Tierra** (Garcilaso 210, tel. 084/22-6951, 9 A.M.–1 P.M. and 3–9 P.M. Mon.–Sat.), which sells all kinds of jungle handicrafts.

For mainstream touristy products there are crafts markets in Cusco where bargaining is standard procedure. One is right on the Plaza de Armas next to Iglesia de la Compañía (10:30 A.M.–1 P.M. and 3:30–9 P.M. Mon.–Sat., 4–9 P.M. Sun.). A 10-minute walk down Avenida El Sol takes you past many more markets, but the biggest is **Centro Artesanal Cusco** (El Sol and Tullumayo, 8 A.M.–10 P.M. daily).

◖ The Center for Traditional Textiles of Cusco

The highest-quality textiles for sale in all of Cusco are at The Center for Traditional Textiles of Cusco (Av. El Sol 603, tel. 084/22-8117, www.textilescusco.org, cttc@terra.com.pe, 7 A.M.–8 P.M. Mon.–Sat., 9 A.M.–8 P.M. Sun.). Nilda Callañaupa, a weaver and scholar from Chinchero, set up the center with the admirable goal of recovering ancient technologies, showcasing high-quality weaving, and sending revenue straight back to the remote, neglected villages that produce them. Local weavers give daily demonstrations, and there are displays that explain all the plants, minerals, and berries used for natural dyes. The textiles here are far better than those found elsewhere in Cusco and only slightly more expensive.

ALPACA PRODUCTS, CLOTHING, AND JEWELRY

For the finest alpaca clothing, head to **Kuna,** which has shops all over Cusco. The most

CUSCO

central is on the Plaza de Armas (Portal de Panes 127, tel. 084/24-3191, www.kuna.com. pe, 9 A.M.–10 P.M. daily). Another reliable option is **Sol Alpaca** (Plazoleta Nazarenas 167, tel. 084/23-2687, www.solalpaca.com, 9 A.M.–9 P.M. Mon.–Sat.). For up-market, expensive llama products, including leather, **Casa de la Llama** (Palacio 121, tel. 084/24-0813, 9 A.M.–10 P.M.daily) is good.

Werner & Ana (Plaza San Francisco 295-A, tel. 084/23-1076, www.werner-ana.com, 9:30 A.M.–9 P.M. Mon.–Sat.) is a hip clothing boutique with styles in alpaca and other fine materials.

Hilo (Carmen Alto 260, tel. 084/25-4536, 10 A.M.–1 P.M. and 2–6 P.M. Mon.–Sat.) is a funky little shop with original clothes hand-made by self-taught Irish designer Eibhlin Cassidy. Browse through her unique collection of dresses, blouses, and belts while sipping on a cup of tea. For other young new Peruvian designer clothes and jewelry pop into **Pulga** (Carmen Alto 227), **Maracuya** (Tecsecocha 424), or **Claudia Lira** (Choquechaca 162).

There are exclusive jewelry shops all around the Plaza de Armas and up Cuesta San Blas; they mostly sell works of silver. The most well-known and found everywhere is **Ilaria** (Portal Carrizos 258, tel. 084/24-6253, www.ilariainternational.com).

CONTEMPORARY ART AND HANDICRAFTS

Contemporary art can be found in several shops along Triunfo, between the Plaza de Armas and San Blas. **Primitiva** (Hatun Rumiyoc 495, tel. 084/26-0152, www.coscio.com, 10 A.M.–9 P.M. Mon.–Sat.) features the art of Argentine painter Federico Coscio, who captures the landscapes and people around Cusco.

If you are looking for something a little different, **Indigo** (Santa Teresa 317, www.galeriasindigo.com.pe, 9 A.M.–10 P.M. daily) has modern housewares and handicrafts inspired by traditional Andean designs.

There is nothing quite like **Pedazo de Arte**

(Plateros 334-B, tel. 084/24-2967, 9 A.M.–9:30 P.M. daily), a cute shop owned by Japanese artist Miki Suzuki, with unique miniature Peruvian handicrafts.

BOOKSTORES

SBS Bookshop (Av. El Sol 781-A, tel. 084/24-8106, www.sbs.com.pe, 8:30 A.M.–1:30 P.M. and 3:30–7:30 P.M. Mon.–Fri., 8 A.M.–1 P.M. Sat.) is Peru's foremost importer of English books and has a good collection at its small Cusco shop. With choices in English, French, German, Portuguese, Spanish, and Quechua, you'd be hard pressed not to find a book at **CBC La Familia** (Tullumayo 465, tel. 084/23-4073, 10 A.M.–2 P.M. and 4–8 P.M. Mon.–Sat.). Genres include novels, cookbooks, art, and even photography.

The largest book exchange in Cusco can be found at **Libreria Puro Peru** (Heladeros 167, tel. 084/22-1753, librarypuroperu@hotmail. com, 9 A.M.–10 P.M. daily).

If you are nostalgic for a magazine from home you may find it at **Febav Bookstore** (El Sol 106, Galeria La Merced, Stand 109, tel. 084/23-6967).

MUSIC STORES

Director Kike Pinto has collected more than 400 instruments for the **Taki Andean Music Museum** (Hatunrumiyoq 487-5, interior, tel. 084/22-6897, www.takimuseum.org, pinto. kike@gmail.com, 10 A.M.–8 P.M. Mon.–Sat.), some of which are for sale, along with CDs, books, and music lessons.

OUTDOOR AND TRAVEL GEAR

The best shops for getting high-end outdoor apparel and equipment, although expensive, are **Tatoo** (Triunfo 346, tel. 084/22-4797, 10 A.M.–9 P.M. Mon.–Sat., 2–9 P.M. Sun.), **Cordillera** (Garcilaso 210 shop 102, tel. 084/24-4133, 9 A.M.–9:30 P.M. daily), and **The North Face** (Plazoleta Espinar 188, tel. 084/23-2130, 9 A.M.–9 P.M. daily).

Recreation

Along with Huaraz in the Cordillera Blanca, Cusco is Peru's main adventure travel center. The variety of intriguing options and high-quality agencies spur adventurers into Herculean feats of back-to-back sports. One 21-year-old Israeli we met had trekked to Choquequirao, Salcantay, and the Inca Trail, rafted four days down the Class IV **Río Apurímac,** and mountain biked around Maras and Moray above the Sacred Valley. He had just returned from a guided trip down the Río Chilive, just outside the Manu park, where his group floated for 10 days on a homemade balsa raft. He wanted to ride in a hot-air balloon, paraglide over the Sacred Valley, and ride a Peruvian *paso* horse in Urubamba, but by that point he was broke.

For your safety, and for the environment, choose your agency carefully. If you choose to raft a serious river, like the Class IV Apurímac, go with accredited agencies and before departure check the equipment. An average of two tourists a year die on the Apurímac alone, and though not even the best agency can take away all the risk, a new raft, full safety equipment, and most importantly an experienced guide make a big difference.

Fly-by-night agencies, with which Cusco is crawling, offer incredibly cheap prices but usually at the expense of your comfort and safety—and, worst of all, at the expense of the environment. This is especially true on the Inca Trail, where trash and human waste is becoming a serious problem. These low-budget agencies do not tend to follow the principles of sustainable adventure travel, nor do they treat their staff fairly. The porters and cooks are not paid enough, they are not provided with acceptable standards of food and camp accommodation, and they do not receive proper training. Most agencies' websites claim to practice responsible tourism, but these claims are probably unfounded if their prices are low cost.

Dozens of these agencies are closed down each year once the rangers in the Machu Picchu sanctuary catch on. However, the same agency can open again under a new name, which often mimics the high-quality leaders in the field. The excellent Trek Peru, for instance, is often confused with Peru Trek, Peruvian Trek, Trekking Peru, etc. The courts are so backlogged with copyright cases that rarely do agencies defend their name. So the confusion lingers. Travelers who spend a bit more money to go with reputable agencies are helping to push up the bar of quality for all of Cusco's agencies.

Most of the agencies offer a variety of activities, ranging from mountain biking to rafting, but we have organized them according to their main focus. Amazonas Explorer, for instance, is most famous for its rafting trips but does a good range of trekking, mountain bike trips, and cultural tours as well.

TREKKING

The Inca Trail is by far the most popular trekking route in the Cusco area because of its spectacular route of ruins and varied ecosystems. But there are other excellent treks in the Cusco area worth considering. Though they do not have the Inca Trail's variety of ruins or the cachet of leading to Machu Picchu, they are less crowded and plunge into remote areas of Andean villages, tumbling jungle, and out-of-the-way archaeological sites. While all hikers on the Inca Trail must go with a licensed agency, the other routes described here can be done independently by those with enough Spanish to ask directions. The best time to trek in the Cusco area is during the dry winter months April–November; the most crowded months on the Inca Trail are June–August.

Make sure your agency is one of those licensed by INRENA, the government conservation agency. A list of approved agencies can be obtained through Iperú. Before scheduling your trip, ask your chosen agency pertinent questions: What is included in the price (e.g.,

CUSCO

train fares and entry fees), what type of tents and general equipment do they provide, what is the maximum number of trekkers in a group? Also very important is to confirm that your operator is bringing a bathroom tent. The most reputable and responsible agencies do not use the public bathrooms but instead carry PETT toilets, which use organic compounds to break human waste so that it can be packed out of the trail and disposed of properly. Groups are accompanied by porters and there is a legal limit of 20 kilograms (44 pounds) for group gear and 5 kilograms (11 pounds) for personal gear, per porter, which is checked at the beginning of the trail.

Nevado Salcantay, at 6,271 meters, is the sacred mountain that towers above the Inca Trail and eventually drops to Machu Picchu itself. Many agencies offer a four- to five-day trek starting from Mollepata, a town 3.5 hours from Cusco in the Limatambo Valley. If you are trekking on your own it can be reached by any bus heading from Cusco to Abancay. In Mollepata, you can hire mules and local guides. The route traverses part of the Cordillera Vilcabamba, including spectacular views of several snow-covered peaks. It crests the 4,700-meter Salcantayccasa Pass before descending between the stunning glaciers of Humantay and Salcantay. The trek then goes through the lovely Huyracmachaypampa and down through forested slopes to the hot springs at Colpapampa. From here the trail follows the Santa Teresa River to the humid lowlands with the option to trek a little farther to the Inca ruins of Patallacta. From here you descend to the hydroelectric station at Intihuatana, where you can board a train for the short journey to Machu Picchu. The alternative is to walk 2–3 hours along the train track to Aguas Calientes.

Choquequirao is a huge Inca complex perched on a ridge top in the Vilcabamba area that includes many fine Inca walls and double recessed doorways. It was probably built as a winter palace by Inca Túpac Yupanqui, in the same way that his father, Pachacútec,

It's a grueling climb to reach Choquequirao, but it is worth the effort.

probably built Machu Picchu. It was discovered by Hiram Bingham in 1911, though it was lost again until the 1980s when a series of explorers trudged through this rugged territory to find this and other ruins in the area. The Peruvian government (INC), backed by UNESCO, launched a campaign to restore the ruins, and much of the work has been completed to a very high standard. It is worth spending a full day exploring this site as it has some unique features, such as the wonderful stylized white stone llamas.

The most common approach is from Cachora, where guides and mules can be rented, reached by taking a bus to Abancay and getting off at a road past the Sayhuite Stone. The first day is spent hiking down to the Río Apurímac, and the second continues straight up the other side, a long six-hour slog uphill onto the cloud forest ridge. Some agencies offer a combined 10-day trek that leads from Choquequirao all the way to Machu Picchu. Another option is to reach Choquequirao from Huancacalle, near the Inca ruins of Vitcos, a spectacular eight-day traverse of the Cordillera Vilcabamba.

There are various trekking routes through the **Cordillera Vilcanota,** the range to the east of Cusco that is dominated by the sacred **Nevado Ausangate** (6,384 meters). Trekking guides say that this is one of the more untouched and spectacular areas of Peru.

The classic route is a seven-day loop around the peak of Ausangate, which begins at the town of Tinqui in the high puna grasslands and crosses four passes between 4,300 and 5,500 meters. The views include the fluted faces and rolling glaciers of all the mountains of the range, including Colquecruz and Jampa, and the route passes through remote hamlets of llama herders and weavers. This area is famous for its **Qoyllur R'itti** moveable festival in May or June, when thousands of campesinos converge on the slopes of Ausangate.

The truly adventurous and fit may want to try reaching **Espíritu Pampa,** the true "Lost City of the Inca" that served as the base for the Inca's 35-year rebellion against the Spanish. Gene Savoy's discovery of the ruins in 1964 made world news, and several subsequent expeditions have tried, in vain, to keep the jungle from growing over the immense site.

The trip starts from the village of Huancacalle, which can be reached by taking a truck or bus from Cusco over the Abra Málaga to Quillabamba and hopping off at the Huancacalle turnoff. The Cobos family, which has guided all the Vilcabamba explorers since Gene Savoy, operates a small hostel in Huancacalle and rents mules for US$7 a day. From Huancacalle, a path leads to the Inca ruler's original exile at Vitcos, where Manco Inca was murdered by the Spanish, and the exquisite sacred rock of Chuquipalta (the subject, among others, of Hugh Thomson's book *White Rock*). The path heads to **New Vilcabamba,** a colonial-era mining town, and then ascends a 3,800-meter pass before plunging into the jungle below. The path includes sections of fine Inca staircases along a steep and tortuous

© JEFF TREBAC

an Andean homestead on the trekking circuit around Nevado Ausangate, in Cusco's Cordillera Vilcanota

CUSCO

valley to the ruins, which are in mosquito-ridden rainforest at 1,000 meters. Instead of walking back all the way to Huancacalle, it is possible to walk for a day or two alongside the river on good paths until you reach the town of Kiteni on the Río Urubamba. From here, a bus goes back to Quillabamba. This trip takes 7–10 days.

Trekking Agencies

Peruvian Andean Treks, ExplorAndes, and Tambo Treks are the longest established trekking companies in Cusco; they pioneered the contemporary trekking culture. We recommend them, not only for their unsurpassed experience and professionalism, but also because they consistently recycle their trash, pack out all human waste, treat water carefully, and pay porters fair wages. Over the last three decades, these operators have developed ties with a number of Quechua communities in the Cusco area, where they are embarking on a new brand of participatory cultural activities such as harvesting potatoes, building adobe homes, and even herding llamas.

Trekking prices vary greatly based on the season, the number of people in the group, the length of the trek, the trek itself, and other factors. Because of licensing requirements the four-night Machu Picchu trek now costs US$1,500, though most agencies charge US$500–600 for group bookings. The shorter two-day Inca Trail is around $200–250 for group bookings. The alternative five-day Salcantay Trek to Machu Picchu is in the US$300–850 range, though most operators offer group Salcantay treks for around US$500. Other treks in the Cusco area, such as in the Lares Valley, generally run about US$100 per day. Be careful to ask your agency whether the price includes all entry fees (an important consideration for Salcantay in particular).

Peruvian Andean Treks (Pardo 705, tel. 084/22-5701, www.andeantreks.com) is owned by American and long-time Cusco resident Tom Hendrickson. It operates on the Inca Trail and runs treks through jungle areas and the Lares Valley in the Cordillera. It is also the best option for climbing expeditions in the snow-covered peaks around Cusco. This company was voted Cusco's best tour operator in 2006.

ExplorAndes (Av. Garcilaso 316-A, tel. 084/23-8380 or Lima tel. 01/715-2323, www.explorandes.com) is Peru's most established adventure sports agency. It offers the traditional Inca Trail hike, as well as variations that combine it with treks above the Sacred Valley or around Nevado Salcantay and Nevado Ausangate. Kayaking on Lake Titicaca, rafting down the Tambopata or Apurímac, and llama-supported treks around the Cordillera Blanca and Huayhuash near Huaraz are also offered. Recently it has operated a variety of special-interest tours around Peru, focusing on orchids, potatoes and maize, camelids, ceramics, cacti, textiles, coca, and other medicinal plants. ExplorAndes was voted Peru's best overall tour operator by the Ministry of Tourism in 2005.

Tambo Treks (Casilla 912, tel. 084/23-7718, www.tambotreks.net) is owned by Andreas Holland and has been operating for over 30 years. It offers diverse treks and tours with tailor-made itineraries (six people minimum), which accommodate group specifications and a wide range of special interests. The staff are very knowledgeable, and since its foundation Tambo Treks has had a profound commitment to helping local communities. Most importantly, however, the welfare of all their staff has always been a priority, as has working in an ecologically sustainable and responsible manner. Tambo Treks' sister company, Tambo Film (www.tambofilm.com), specializes in outfitting film and television productions throughout Peru.

Two long-standing, reputable and very professional trekking agencies are Auqui Mountain Spirit and Ecoinka.

Auqui Mountain Spirit (José Gabriel 307, Urb. Magisterial, tel. 084/26-1517, www.auqui.com.pe), run by Roger Valencia, has been operating for over 20 years. This high-end agency has a very experienced team and specializes in customized trips, especially for corporate clients.

© GABRIELLA HOLLAND

trekking camp high in the Andes

Ecoinka (Saphy 456, tel. 084/22 4050, www.ecoinka.com) was founded by Ricky Schiller, who has been involved in the tourism industry for over 30 years. The expert staff provide excellent service.

Among the more than 150 licensed agencies operating in Cusco, the standard of service and social and environmental responsibilities vary greatly. It is up to the client to be discerning and to research thoroughly before booking. The agencies listed here are all recommended.

Perú Sur Nativa (Magisterio 2da Etapa K-7-302, tel. 084/22-4156, www.perusurnativa.com) is owned by long-time Cusco adventurer extraordinaire Raúl Montes. Montes has a real eye for adventure and an unflappable sense of humor (we confirmed this after spending two weeks with him on a balsa raft in the Manu jungle eating only green bananas and red-bellied piraña!). Perú Sur Nativa also runs trips in other parts of South America as well as nearby Choquequirao, Carabaya, Vilcabamba, and to the Manu rainforest.

Enigma (Clorinda Matto de Turner 100, tel. 084/22-2155, www.enigmaperu.com) is one of the newer agencies; it has gourmet cooks. It offers Inca Trail treks combined with Nevado Salcantay, Vilcabamba, and the ruins of Choquequirao. Alternative adventures include horseback riding, ayahuasca therapy, and bird-watching.

Inca Explorers (Ruinas 427, tel. 084/24-1070, www.incaexplorers.com) has a range of longer trips to Vilcabamba, Choquequirao, and the Cordillera Vilcanota, as well as participative tourism such as weaving, farming, and traditional healing.

Q'ente (Choquechaca 229, tel. 084/22-2535, www.qente.com) has been running since 1995 and provides a good service and trained staff.

The following Inca Trail operators are at the bottom of the price range but have been reported to be environmentally responsible.

United Mice (Plateros 351, tel. 084/22-1139, www.unitedmice.com) is probably the most recommended backpacker's choice. It also offers a seven-day Salcantay trek.

Peru Treks & Adventure (Garcilaso 265, Of. 11, 2nd Fl., tel. 084/50-5863, www.perutreks.com) is also responsible for the very informative website Andean Travel Web (www.andeantravelweb.com).

Andina Travel (Santa Catalina 219, tel. 084/25-1892, www.andinatravel.com) offers frequent departures for the Inca Trail and interesting sociocultural projects.

RAFTING AND KAYAKING

There are many excellent rafting and kayaking options around Cusco. The easiest, and most common, are day trips along the Class III rapids of the Río Urubamba in the Sacred Valley (US$40–55). They often include one night of camping near Ollantaytambo, mountain biking, and a chance to see ruins the next day. December–May, when the river is swollen, agencies tend to raft the upper section above Pisac. When the water drops after June, they run the section of the river lower down between Ollantaytambo and Chilca. Farther downstream, the water rushes onward to Machu Picchu in great cataracts of unnavigable, Class VI water.

CUSCO

© CYNTHIA BEAMS

Rafting on the Río Apurímac or the Río Urubamba is an excellent day trip from Cusco.

Another day option is the easier stretch of the Río Apurímac below the Cusco–Abancay highway, a gentle stretch that passes the foundations of an Inca hanging bridge made famous by Thornton Wilder in his classic *The Bridge of San Luis Rey.* The Apurímac here is generally sunny and subtropical, so bring sunscreen, a hat, mosquito repellent, and swimwear because a quick dip in local hot springs is often included.

A popular three-day rafting trip is on the upper Apurímac (US$400–650), which can only be run between June and October. The Apurímac plunges through a steep and wild gorge and an endless series of Class III–V rapids. Agencies that operate this section of the river usually also offer trips on Cotahuasi (US$1,950 approximately), a similar though more exacting canyon near Arequipa that takes 10 days to navigate in a full-scale, supported expedition.

Our vote for most spectacular rafting expedition, though, goes to the Río Tambopata (US$1,500–2,500), which is a great way to combine a mountain rafting adventure with world-class Amazon biodiversity. This 10- to 12-day trip begins in cloud forest north of Lake Titicaca with a few days of Class III–V rapids and ends floating on torpid jungle waters through the pristine Parque Nacional Bahuajua Sonene. Participants usually stay at the Tambopata Research Center, a rustic lodge operated by Rainforest Expeditions that is minutes from the world's largest macaw clay lick. Floating silently through this untouched rainforest provides a good opportunity to spot a jaguar or tapir and a huge range of birds and more common animals such as capybara, turtles, and giant otters. The trip includes a flight back to Cusco from the jungle city of Puerto Maldonado.

If you want to go kayaking instead of rafting, agencies will often loan you a kayak on the easier rivers such as the Urubamba and lower Apurímac. Some agencies, such as Erik's Adventures, offer kayaking schools.

Rafting and Kayaking Agencies

Like trekking prices, rafting rates vary greatly based on the season, the number of people in the group, the difficulty of the rapids, and the section of the river. Prices for a daylong rafting trip on the Urubamba River are typically US$25–100 per person per day, including lunch. For the four-day Apurimac River trip, which includes Class III–IV rapids, prices are typically US$300–1,100. Most operators, however, charge US$500–600.

One of the most professional rafting companies in Peru is **Amazonas Explorer** (Collasuyo 910, Urb. Miravalle, tel. 084/25-2846, www.amazonas-explorer.com). It runs a variety of innovative trips in Peru, Chile, and Bolivia, including canoeing, mountain biking, trekking, and rafting. One of the best trips is a 16-day expedition that begins with sightseeing in Cusco and Lake Titicaca and ends in rafting down the Río Tambopata and two nights at the Tambopata Research Center.

ExplorAndes (Av. Garcilaso 316-A, tel. 084/23-8380 or Lima tel. 01/715-2323, www.explorandes.com) also offers high-end rafting trips.

The following are less expensive but also experienced agencies. They are recommended for easier trips. **Apumayo Expediciones** (Jr. Ricardo Palma N-5, Santa Monica, tel. 084/24-6018, www.apumayo.com) is run by Pepe López, a kayaker with a lot of experience on Peru's rivers. He recently built an adventure center on the banks of the Río Urubamba, downstream of Ollantaytambo. The center, which shares profits with the nearby community of Cachiccata, offers hikes and mountain biking for the rafters who arrive here after descending the Río Urubamba. Apumayo runs trips down the Apurímac, Tambopata, and Cotahuasi and offers reforestation cultural treks and the classic Inca Trail.

Mayuc (Portal Confituras 211, Plaza de Armas, tel. 084/24-2824, www.mayuc.com) is one of the pioneering rafting companies and operates an excellent day trip on Río Urubamba. It also does rafting trips on the Apurímac and in Tambopata.

Loreto Tours (Calle del Medio 111, tel. 084/22-8264, loretotours@planet.com.pe)

provides varied rafting itineraries and good quality equipment.

Terra Explorer Peru (Santa Ursula D-4, Huanchac, tel. 084/23-7352, www.terraexplorerperu.com) is owned by Piero, the youngest of the Vellutino brothers, all dedicated and well known adventure sportsmen and whitewater rafters. Terra Explorer offers all kinds of rafting trips including Cotahuasi and Tambopata, mountain treks, and mountain biking. **Munaycha** (based in the Sacred Valley, tel. 084/984-77-0108 or 084/984770381, www.munaycha.com) belongs to Duilio, the oldest Vellutino brother, and also offers rafting on Peru's best known rivers as well as sea kayaking trips off the coast of Arequipa and on Lake Huyñaymarca, a rarely visited part of the Titicaca.

MOUNTAIN CLIMBING

Cusco is surrounded by majestic snow-covered peaks that offer outstanding mountaineering possibilities, though none should be tried by people without mountaineering experience— even with a good guide. Unlike many of the mountains in the Cordillera Blanca, these Andean routes are steep, icy, and complicated. Avalanches are common, especially on Salcantay. Several international climbing agencies operate in Peru.

Mountain Climbing Agencies

Licensed mountain guides in Peru, working on an independent basis, will charge US$100–150 per day. An agency that arranges a technical climb will generally charge twice or three times that rate on a daily basis. For climbing in Cusco, it's a good idea to inquire with agencies in Huaraz, Peru's climbing headquarters. Huaraz agencies are often able to lead climbing trips all over the country.

The best local mountaineering agency is **Peruvian Andean Treks** (Pardo 705, tel. 084/22-5701, www.andeantreks.com), owned by climber Tom Hendrickson. A highly recommended guide in Cusco is **Américo Serrano** (tel. 084/24-7299). Serrano has all the international climbing certifications and is one of the instructors who trains new Peruvian mountain guides in the Cordillera Blanca. In 2003, he assisted Lonnie Thompson, an internationally known glaciologist from Ohio State University, in an expedition to measure glacial recession in Peru's southern Andes.

There are six other internationally certified guides working in Peru. The best way to reach them is through **Camp Expedition** (Triunfo 392, of. 202, tel. 084/43-9859, www.campexpedition.net), which leads rappelling, climbing, and canyoneering adventures in the Cusco area.

BIKING

Nearly all of the rafting and kayaking agencies do bike tours and rent bikes. A highly recommended company is **Loreto Tours** (Calle del Medio 111, tel. 084/22-8264, loretotours@planet.com.pe, US$100 per day for guided tours). Peru's best-known mountain biker, Omar Zarzar Casis (omarzarzar@aventurarse.com), has written a book describing routes in Cusco and across the country. He is a good English-speaking contact for those planning a major ride in the area. **Gravity Assisted Mountain Biking** (Santa Catalina Ancha 398, tel. 084/22-8032, www.gravityperu.com, US$100 per day for guided tours) has great equipment and experienced guides for adventure mountain-biking tours.

Many of the Manu tour operators give clients the option to bike partway down the magnificent dirt-road descent from Acanaju Pass at 3,800 meters into the jungle. This route, which also passes through Pisac and Paucartambo provides a stunning glimpse of more than a dozen ecosystems.

Many agencies also offer mountain-biking in the Sacred Valley, especially on the Chinchero plateau around Moray and Maras, with a final descent past the salt mines (Salineras) to Urubamba. The Abra Málaga (4,600 meters), which lies along the highway between Ollantaytambo and Quillabamba, is another of Peru's spectacular mountain-to-jungle descents. This trip is now part of a bus/biking/walking alternative to the Inca Trail, which takes you past the pristine Colcamayo hot springs in Santa Teresa, from where you can either walk or catch the train to Machu Picchu.

BIRD-WATCHING

The Cusco area has one of the world's highest areas of bird biodiversity, particularly where the high Andes meet the Amazon rainforest. Particularly rich environments are the Abra Málaga (4,200 meters) area, en route to Quillabamba, and the Acanaju Pass (3,800 meters), en route to Parque Nacional Manu. Barry Walker, owner of Manu Expeditions and author of *A Field Guide to the Birds of Machu Picchu, Peru,* leads excellent birding. Barry can be reached through **Manu Expeditions** (Pardo 895, tel. 084/22-6671, birding@manuexpeditions.com, www.birdinginperu.com, US$250 per day for guided tours with more than six people).

The high-quality **InkaNatura** (Ricardo Palma J1, Urb. Santa Monica, tel. 084/25-5255, www.inkanatura.com, US$275 per day for guided tours with more than six people) and **Gran Peru** (www.granperu.com, US$175 per day for guided tours with more than six people) also run birding trips throughout the country. Leo Oblitas is an excellent birding guide and works for some of the leading bird-watching agencies.

HORSEBACK RIDING

Adventure Specialists (U.S. tel. 719/783-2076, www.adventurespecialists.org, prices vary, call ahead) leads highly recommended, custom horse-packing trips all over Peru and especially in the Cusco area. Founder and co-owner Gary Ziegler is a true adventurer, archaeologist, and noted Inca expert.

Manu Expeditions (Pardo 895, tel. 084/22-6671, www.manu-expeditions.com, prices vary, call ahead) offers a range of horse-riding expeditions that explore areas of the Vilcabamba and Choquequirao (17 days), as well as Machu Picchu and the surrounding cloud forest (15 days). Another of its itineraries is from the Andes to the Amazon (14 days). One- and two-day rides around Cusco are also offered.

The best options for riding Peruvian *paso* horses is **Wayra** (part of the Sol y Luna Hotel outside Urubamba, tel. 084/20-1620, info@wayrasacredvalley.com, www.wayrasacredvalley.com, US$195 per day) and **Perol Chico** (Carretera Urubamba–Ollantaytambo, tel. 084/974-79-8890, www.perolchico.com, prices vary, call ahead).

EXTREME SPORTS

A wacky adventure opportunity is **Action Valley** (Santa Teresa 352, tel. 084/24-0835, www.actionvalley.com, US$64 bungee jump, US$20 paint ball). This park, 11 kilometers from Cusco on the road to Chinchero, has a 107-meter bungee drop, a catapult that throws people 120 meters into the air with 3.2 g's of force, a 36-meter climbing pole, a 124-meter rappel wall, and a 10-meter climbing wall.

There are some beautiful paragliding spots in the Cusco area. **Leo Paragliding School** (Triunfo 392, of. 202, tel. 084/23-9477, www.cusco.net/leo-paragliding, US$75 pp) offers tandem flights as well as paragliding training courses. Another recommendable option for tandem paragliding flights over the Sacred Valley is **Viento Sur,** run by the European owners of Sol y Luna Hotel in Urubamba (tel. 084/20-1620, www.hotelsolyluna.com, US$195 pp).

Via Ferrata (tel. 084/984-11-2731, www.naturavive.com, US$45 pp, family rates available) is a 300-meter rock face located in Pacha between Urubamba and Ollantaytambo. It is equipped with wire cables and footholds to allow people with no previous experience to enjoy the adrenaline rush of rock with all the necessary safety equipment.

ESOTERIC EXPERIENCES

Cusco is a center for a range of spiritual and esoteric activities, though the main operators seem to change constantly. A good touchstone and longtime expert is José (Pepe) Altamirano, the owner of the agency **Gatur** (Puluchapata 140, tel. 084/22-3496 or 084/22-7829, www.gaturcusco.com, prices vary, call ahead). Tourists are shown traditional practices by native healers with **Back2Nature** (www.back2nature.no, prices vary, call ahead), owned by Norwegian Irene Kingswick and Peruvian Dennis Alejo.

Many Cusco agencies, including **Enigma,** offer sessions with the ayahuasca hallucinogen. Leslie Myburgh at **Another Planet** (Triunfo 120, tel. 084/22-9379, www.anotherplanet-peru.net, prices vary, call ahead) and Diane Dunn at **Paz y Luz** (tel. 084/20-3204, www.pazyluzperu.com, prices vary, call ahead) in Pisac are other good contacts for ayahuasca and San Pedro ceremonies.

SIGHTSEEING TOURS

There is fierce competition, along with frequent price wars, between Cusco's agencies for general sightseeing tours. Most of the agencies are clustered around the Plaza de Armas and offer competitive prices. There are also luxury tours.

The most popular tours include a half-day city tour and the full-day tour of the Sacred Valley, which includes Pisac market, lunch in Urubamba, Ollantaytambo, and sometimes Chinchero as well. There is also a half-day tour of the ruins outside of Cusco, which include Sacsayhuamán, Q'enqo, Puca Pucara, and Tambomachay. Another half-day tour explores the ruins heading toward Puno, including the magnificent church in Andahuaylillas, Pikillacta, and Tipón.

Several agencies in Cusco cater to groups and also reserve tickets and provide tours for independent travelers. **Condor Travel** (Saphy 848, tel. 084/24-8181, www.condortravel.com, US$35 daylong group tour) is one of the most established and professional operators of traditional tourism.

Gatur (Puluchapata 140, tel. 084/22-3496 or 084/22-7829, www.gaturcusco.com, US$35 daylong group tour) is operated by José Altamirano, one of the most respected authorities on local history.

Orellana Tours (Garcilaso 206, tel. 084/26-3455, orellanatours@terra.com.pe, US$20 daylong group tour) is an inexpensive agency with a good reputation. **Milla Turismo** (Pardo

689, tel. 084/23-1710, www.millaturismo.com, US$32 daylong group tour) is well established and very professional.

Americana de Turismo (Garcilaso 265, tel. 084/24-0999, www.americanadeturismo.net, US$28 daylong group tour) provides excellent sightseeing itineraries.

Attraction (Av. Baja 145, tel. 084/23-2143, www.attraction-voyages.com, price vary, call ahead) is a French-run agency whose main focus is luxury travel. The high-end company offers alternative options for seeing the traditional sites—for example, chauffeur-driven four-wheel drive trips to Lares and special interest travel (photography tours with internationally acclaimed photographer Carlos Nishyama and culinary tours with renowned chefs).

Franco Negri, owner of **Casa Ecológica** (Portal de Carnes 236, interior 2, tel. 084/25-5427, www.casaecologicacusco.com, US$85 per day, prices may vary depending on trip), also runs interesting and innovative community day trips such as visiting an organic farming association in Lamay and using traditional Andean agricultural tools. The day ends with a meal prepared using local ingredients. There are also weaving trips to the community of Amaru, where you can observe and partake in all processes of ancient weaving. The visits directly benefit the people from the communities and indirectly the conservation of their environment and traditional arts and techniques.

JUNGLE TRIPS

Many people who visit Cusco do not realize how close they are to the Amazon jungle. An half-hour plane ride and a few hours in a boat take you to a comfy lodge in Puerto Maldonado, with outstanding opportunities for seeing birds, mammals, and insects. A longer trip to Parque Nacional Manu offers a chance to see a greater variety of animals, especially predators such as the black caiman and the jaguar. See *Moon Peru* for more information on trips to the Amazon.

Accommodations

Our favorite neighborhood in all of Cusco is San Blas, the bohemian district above the Plaza de Armas that is crisscrossed with narrow alleys and teeming with cozy hostels, artisan galleries, and some of Cusco's best bars. San Blas has a relaxing, artsy vibe, and its narrow streets keep out the traffic and smog of central Cusco.

Traffic has made parts of Cusco unpleasant. These areas include the extension of Plateros and Avenida El Sol, where even the back rooms of hotels hum with the noise of taxis and amplified advertisements. Outside of San Blas, Cusco's nicest lodging is along out-of-the-way streets like Suecia, Choquechaca, or Siete Cuartones/Nueva Alta, where classy bed-and-breakfasts are lined up along charming cobblestone streets. Always make a reservation ahead of time in Cusco, and ask for the kind of room you want (e.g., with a view or double bed). Despite a steady increase in Cusco hotels, the best ones are increasingly booked solid May–November. If you arrive and don't like your room, you can usually wriggle out of your reservation after your first night and head elsewhere—there are lots of good options, especially among the newer, lesser-known hostels. It is best not to judge a hotel, especially the more economic accommodations, by the bedding, bathroom tiles, and decor in general.

UNDER US$10

For budget accommodations backpacker hostels are a good option, and there are now quite a few in Cusco. The most popular are **The Point** (Meson de la Estrella 172, tel. 084/25-2266, www.thepointhostels.com, US$8–11 dorm, US$12–15 d) and **LOKI Inkahouse** (Cuesta Santa Ana 601, tel. 084/24-3705, www.lokihostel.com, US$8–11 dorm, US$27 d private bath). Both have locations in Lima and Máncora, dorm rooms (and a few private rooms) that open onto TV rooms, Internet stations, shared kitchens, and bars. They have a reputation for their parties and you are bound to meet other travelers.

Youth Hostal Albergue Municipal (Quiscapata 240, San Cristóbal, tel. 084/25-2506, albergue@municusco.gob. pe, US$5 dorm, US$7 d), part of Hostelling International, has great views from the balcony, clean bunk rooms, and a shared kitchen. A discount is given to youth hostel members.

Pirwa Backpackers (Portal de Panes 151, tel. 084/24-4315, www.pirwahostelscusco. com, US$7.50–10 dorm, US$12.50 d) has four central locations: the Plaza de Armas, Suecia, San Blas, and San Francisco. They all have a variety of dorms and private rooms, most with shared kitchen, common rooms, and a tour/travel desk. **Samay Wasi** (Atocsaycuhi 416, tel. 084/25-3108, Siete Angelitos 675, tel. 084/23-6649, www.samaywasiperu.com, US$7–9 dorm, US$20 d) has two great locations in San Blas. Both offer shared and double rooms and nice gardens. At Siete Angelitos ask about their star room famous for its views.

Probably the best value for money is **Inti Quilla** (Atocsaycuhi 281, tel. 084/25-2659, www.intiquilla.8m.com, US$7 d shared bath, US$9 d private bath, breakfast not included). Also in San Blas, this very basic but clean hostel has two triple rooms and five double rooms around a nice, sunny courtyard. Some rooms have private bathrooms and there is 24-hour hot water. **El Balcón Colonial** (Choquechaca 350, tel. 084/23-8129, balconcolonial@hotmail.com, US$7 s, US$14 d) is a bed-and-breakfast with five clean rooms with firm beds. One has a private bath, and there's a small shared kitchen with breakfast tables, a computer with Internet, and a very friendly and accommodating owner.

US$10-25

The standout feature at **Hostal Resbalosa** (Resbalosa 494, tel. 084/22-4839, www.hostalresbalosa.com, US$16 d shared bath, US$22 d private bath) is the sweeping view over the city from various sunny terraces and common

rooms. The front rooms are older and noisier than the others, but all have hot water and cable TV. Prices are negotiable.

For a location one block from the Plaza de Armas, try **Hostal Rojas** (Tigre 129, tel. 084/22-8184, US$14 d shared bath, US$24 d with private bath), with clean, carpeted rooms around a sunny courtyard.

The charming **Sihuar** (Tandapata 351, tel. 084/22-7435, casasihuar@hotmail.com, US$25 d) is a two-level building that looks out over a nice patio and garden. The rooms are very pleasant and more tastefully decorated than most, with wood floors and woven rugs and gas-heated hot water. Sihuar is great value.

Also in San Blas but a little higher up is the Belgian/Peruvian-run **Hostal Sweet Daybreak** (Pasñapakana 133, tel. 084/22-5776, www.hostalsweetdaybreak.com, US$12 per person, US$24 d private bath, breakfast not included). This cute, family-owned hotel has a variety of rooms ranging from a six-bed dorm with shared bath to double rooms with private baths. Prices are negotiable, especially for groups. It has amazing panoramic views of the city, a lovely garden with rustic wooden tables, free WiFi, cable TV, and hot water 24 hours.

The newly inaugurated **Puca Ventana Hostel** (San Cristobal 109, tel. 084/24-3673, US$25 d) is a small, eight-room hostel all with private bathrooms, WiFi, cable TV, and breakfast. It has a simple rustic feel, a nice living room with great views of the city, and a very friendly atmosphere.

US$25-50

C Niños Hotel (Meloq 442, tel. 084/23-1424, www.ninoshotel.com, US$40 s or d) is a remarkable place with a cause. Its Dutch owner uses hotel revenue to feed, clothe, and provide medical assistance to needy street boys. And as if that isn't enough reason to stay here, just four blocks from the Plaza de Armas, the restored colonial home of Niños Hotel is absolutely lovely. With large, stylish rooms, hardwood floors, and a pleasant courtyard for taking breakfast, it's easy to make yourself at home. There is a second location at Fierro

476 (tel. 084/23-1424) and a Niños Hotel Hacienda in Huasao.

Just one block from the Plaza de Armas, **Hostal San Isidro Labrador** (Saphy 440, tel. 084/22-6241, labrador@qnet.com.pe, US$35 s, US$45 d) is a simple and elegant place with a handful of rooms, each with its own charm. It is right next to the police station and thus is one of the safer locations in Cusco. This hotel is operated by the Lambarri family, who also run the exclusive Huayoccari Hacienda Restaurant in Yucay.

In the center of San Blas are **Casa de la Gringa** (Tandapata 148) and **Casa de la Gringa II** (Carmen Bajo). The houses (tel. 084/24-1168, www.casadelagringa.com, US$28–31 d), owned by Lesley Myburgh, are recommended for their colorful rooms, friendly staff, and small gardens. There is a New Age, spiritual air about the place, and the dedication to such matters, including the imbibing of San Pedro and ayahuasca, is very sincere.

A lovely place in Tandapata is **(Casona les Pleiades** (Tandapata 116, tel. 084/50-6430, www.casona-pleiades.com, US$50 d). Whether it be Melanie or Philip who opens the door for you, the welcome is bound to be warm and friendly. This young French couple have made their seven-room home into a guesthouse, and their aim is to make you feel right at home. That's why there are down comforters on the beds and eggs made to order for breakfast.

In lower San Blas, one of the nicer hotels in Cusco is **(Amaru Hostal** (Cuesta San Blas 541, tel. 084/22-5933, www.cusco.net/amaru, US$33 s, US$43 d). The 27 rooms, with balconies, are spread around two sun-filled patios overflowing with geraniums and roses. The rooms have comfy beds and wood floors, and are small but nice. Rooms here vary dramatically—ask for the corner rooms with sun porches, wicker furniture, and vistas on both sides. For those on a budget there are cheaper rooms with shared bathrooms. The hostel has two more locations in San Blas at Chihuampata 642 (tel. 084/22-3521) and the private Hosteria Anita at Alavado 525 (tel. 084/22-5499).

The very sweet and good value European/Peruvian hotel **Madre Tierra** (Atocsaycuchi 647-A, tel. 084/25-7358, www.hostalmadretierra.com, US$49 d) has seven comfortable carpeted rooms and cozy and inviting communal areas with white sofas, exposed beams, and open fireplaces.

Just down the street is **El Grial** (Carmen Alto 112, tel. 084/22-3012, www.hotelelgrial.com, US$30 s, US$45 d), a small, friendly hostel with basic but comfortable rooms and a sunny, pleasant dining area for breakfast. The **South American Spanish School** is right next door and run by the same owners.

The best value accommodation in San Blas and a great alternative to hotels is **(Saya Wasi Apart Hotel** (Kiskapta 1000, San Blas, tel. 084/25-4160, www.sayawasi.com, US$25 pp). These three sunny, comfortable, and tastefully decorated self-catering apartments include a lounge area with cable TV, kitchenette, bathroom, and floor-to-ceiling windows with incredible views. There is also a lovely communal terrace with even more spectacular panoramic views of the entire city.

US$50-100

(Hostal El Balcon (Tambo de Montero 222, tel. 084/23-6738, www.balconcusco.com, US$55 s, US$69 d) is a lovely restored colonial house with rustic charm and a pretty, flower-filled garden. This 16-room hostel is quaint and homely, and rooms are decorated simply with weavings on the beds.

Charming, German-owned **(Pensión Alemana Bed and Breakfast** (Tandapata 260, tel. 084/22-6861, www.cuzco-stay.de, US$55 d) is the closest thing to a European pension in Cusco. There are 12 light and airy rooms, many with incredible views over the city, very comfortable beds, and great showers. A pleasant garden looks out over the red-tiled roofs of the city, and a nightly fire crackles in the dining room.

The unpretentious **Hostal Corihuasi** (Suecia 561, tel. 084/23-2233, www.corihuasi.com, US$44 s, US$55 d) is a quick, steep walk up from the Plaza de Armas and has old-world charm that befits Cusco. The rooms of this rambling, eclectic colonial house are connected by verandas and walkways. Some of the rooms are nicer with views over the city; others are dark, with porthole windows.

In Santiago, one of Cusco's oldest neighborhoods, is the charming **⟨ Panza del Artista** (Calle Jorge Ochoa 215 interior, tel. 084/26-2610, www.panzadelartista.com, US$40 s, US$60 d). The seven rooms, some with sweeping views of the center of Cusco from their balconies, are spacious and open with natural light. The terraced gardens are perched above the bustling city and provide respite with all-day sun, lush local plants, and a variety of birds. Owners Adam L. Weintraub (who has a good new photography book on the Cusco region called *Vista Andina*) and Xiomara Romero win over guests with their extended Cusqueñan family. Guests can sit for hours in the family kitchen, a welcome respite from the touristy center. The hotel is about a 10-minute walk from downtown, near the San Pedro market.

MamaSara Hotel (Saphy 875, tel. 084/24-5409, www.mamasarahotel.com, US$70 s, US$85 d) is very pleasant and comfortable. The rooms are heated, spacious, and immaculate and come with flat-screen TVs, good showers, and oxygen on request.

Encantada (Tandapata 354, tel. 084/24-2206, www.encantadaperu.com, US$70 s, US$90 d) is a pleasant new hotel in a modern building with great views. The minimalist decor and white comforters are a breath of fresh air. The hotel also doubles as a massage and spa center, and there are special packages: one night's accommodation with two hours of Jacuzzi and massage costs US$150. The owners also have **A Mi Manera,** a nice restaurant on Triunfo, and a recommendable tour agency— **Culturas Peru** (www.culturasperu.com).

An impressive, original Inca doorway, once the entrance to a sacred place, is now the way into the hotel **Rumi Punku** (Choquechaca 339, tel. 084/22-1102, www.rumipunku.com, US$70 s, US$90 d). Light-filled terraces, a garden with an original Inca wall, and a gym and spa make this a pleasant place to stay. The

rooms have all the necessary amenities and the staff are friendly and helpful.

US$100-150

The national and reliable hotel chain **⟨ Casa Andina** (www.casa-andina.com) has three of its "classic" hotels at ideal locations in the center of Cusco. Two are within one block of the Plaza de Armas (Santa Catalina Angosta 149, tel. 084/23-3661, cac-catedral@casa-andina. com, and Portal Espinar 142, tel. 084/23-1733, cac-cuscoplaza@casa-andina.com, US$125 d), and one is near Coricancha (San Agustín 371, tel. 084/25-2633, cac-koricancha@casa-andina.com, US$125 d). These well-designed, comfortable hotels provide excellent service. The aim of the hotels is to reflect the local character of a place and give a genuine experience using local ideology and using local products where possible without sacrificing comfort and convenience. All rooms have down comforters, heating, and cable TV, and a generous breakfast buffet is included.

Guests are greeted by tuxedo-wearing doormen at the upscale, Swiss-managed **Los Apus** (Atocsaycuchi 515, tel. 084/26-4243, www. losapushotel.com, US$89 s, US$109 d). The rooms have wood floors, heating, comfortable beds, and cable TV. Breakfast is served in a nice glass-roofed courtyard.

The **Hotel Arqueologo** (Pumacurco 408, tel. 084/23-2569, www.hotelarqueologo.com, US$120 d standard, US$140 d superior) occupies an old colonial building. Rooms with high ceilings wrap around a rustic stone courtyard or overlook a grassy garden. The hotel tries to maintain a eco-friendly philosophy by having its own bio-veggie garden, recycling rubbish, providing a fountain with drinking water to refill bottles, and only providing TVs in rooms upon request. The first-floor café **Song Thé** has comfortable sofas, a fireplace, and French pastries.

The attractive boutique hotel **Casa San Blas** (Tocuyeros 566, tel. 084/23-7900, www.casasanblas.com, US$110 d, US$156 suite) prides itself on giving a personalized service. It is ideally located, set back off the Cuesta San Blas, and has great views of the city from its sunny roof terrace. Rooms are comfortable, have all the necessary amenities, and are decorated simply with traditional weavings on the walls. There are also self-catering suite apartments with kitchenettes. Sustainability issues are addressed by giving guests the option to reuse bedding and towels and re-fill water bottles, light bulbs are energy-saving, and there are double curtains to reduce the need for heating.

As the name suggests, **Second Home Cusco** (Atocsaycuchi 616, tel. 084/23-5873, www.secondhomecusco.com, US$110 s, 120 d) in San Blas really is a home away from home. This highly recommended bed-and-breakfast, owned by artist Carlos Delfin, son of the famous sculptor Victor Delfin, has three very simple but nicely decorated, light-filled junior suites: the skylight suite, the patio suite, and the balcony suite. Each has its own special charm. There is another great Second Home located in Lima.

US$150-250

The finest of the Casa Andina Classic collection hotels is the 【 **Casa Andina San Blas** (Chihuampata 278, tel. 084/26-3694, cac-sanblas@casa-andina.com, US$156 d standard, US$192 d superior), built around a colonial stone courtyard with some of the best views of Cusco's rooftops and mountains. The cozy sitting areas with wood-burning fires, the rustic bar, and the lovely terrace make this a great place to escape and relax. It has all attributes expected from Casa Andina and more. If you are after an even more luxurious Casa Andina experience you will find it at the 【 **Casa Andina Private Collection** (Plazoleta Limacpampa Chico 473, tel. 084/23-2610, capc-cusco@casa-andina.com US$241 d standard, US$373 suite). Located in a beautiful 18th-century manor house, the hotel centers around three majestic interior patios. The sitting room with its plush red couches is the ideal place to unwind with a pisco sour. There is a nice gourmet restaurant that spills onto the main

patio, where you can dine to the pleasant gurgling of the pretty fountain. The extensive and delicious breakfast buffet includes local, hearty dishes, as well as the standard breakfast fare, which will keep you going for most of the day.

The sophisticated **Novotel** (San Agustín 239, tel. 084/58-1030, www.novotel.com, US$240 d modern room, US$320 d colonial room) is in a restored colonial manor that has a delightful patio lined with stone arches, lamps, and wicker furniture for evening drinks. Undoubtedly the best rooms are those on the second floor around the stone courtyard, with wood floors, high ceilings, king-size beds, sitting areas, and all creature comforts (security box, minibar, cable TV, heating). The other 82 rooms are comfortable but bland, small, and sterile in an unfortunate five-story modern addition.

Equal in elegance and similar in layout, but cheaper and better value is **Picoaga Hotel** (Santa Teresa 344, tel. 084/22-7691, www.picoagahotel.com, US$160 d modern room, US$180 d colonial, US$200 junior suite), which is ideally located one block from Plaza Regocijo and a two-minute walk from the Plaza de Armas. This 17th-century colonial mansion, once belonging to the Spanish noble Marquis de Picoaga, has been well restored with stone archways and columns wrapping around a classic colonial patio. The colonial rooms are most definitely worth the extra US$20 as they are bigger, lighter, more comfortable, and aesthetically more pleasing than the rooms in the characterless modern part.

OVER US$250

The five-star **Hotel Libertador Palacio del Inka** (Plazoleta Santo Domingo 259, tel. 084/23-1961, www.libertador.com.pe, US$305 d standard, US$325 d junior suite, US$385 suite) has a great location next to Coricancha, the Inca sun temple. It occupies the Casa de los Cuatro Bustos, Francisco Pizarro's last home. It is built on the foundation of the *acllahuasi*, "the house of the chosen ones," where virgins picked by the Inca lived in seclusion from society.

The entrance to the Hotel Libertador is spectacular. A stone portal leads into a glass-roofed lobby, lined on one side by Spanish stone arches and on the other by exposed portions of stone Inca walls. There is an excellent buffet breakfast served alongside another large square, ringed with two stories of stone arcades. Throughout the hotel are examples of original colonial furniture, artifacts, and paintings—the owners are avid collectors. Ask for rooms in the colonial section, with views of the sun temple. The suites are larger with sitting areas and marble bathrooms, and are probably worth paying the extra for.

One of the more memorable places to stay in Cusco is **(Hotel Monasterio** (Palacio 136, Plazoleta Nazarenas, tel. 084/60-4000, www.monasterio.orient-express.com, US$634 basic d or US$806–2,232 suites), a 415-year-old monastery that has been converted into a most elegant five-star hotel. The stone lobby leads to a dramatic stone courtyard, graced with an ancient cedar tree and lined with two stories of stone archways. Colonial paintings line long hallways, which wrap around two other fabulous stone patios. The rooms are decked out in old-world Spanish decor, including carved wooden headboards and colonial paintings, and include all the plush five-star comforts. They can even be pumped with oxygen, simulating an altitude 900 meters lower that allows guests to sleep more soundly.

The hotel occupies the former Seminario San Antonio Abad, which was built in 1595 on top of the Inca Amaru Qhala Palace but was badly damaged in the 1650 earthquake. During the restoration, a colonial baroque chapel was added, which remains open to guests and has one of the most ornate altars in Cusco. After yet another damaging earthquake in 1950, the building was condemned and auctioned by the Peruvian government in 1995. It eventually landed in the hands of Orient-Express Hotels, which carefully restored the stonework, planted fabulous gardens, and converted the former cells into 126 plush rooms. These days, guests take lunch in the main square, which is shaded by a giant cedar, scented by a rose garden, and filled with the gurgling of a 17th-century stone fountain. The hotel hosts one of Cusco's three gourmet restaurants, and also includes a small massage room. It's a few minutes' walk from the Plaza de Armas.

Diagonally opposite the Monasterio on Plaza de las Nazarenas is undoubtedly the best hotel in Cusco, **(Inkaterra La Casona** (Plaza de las Nazarenas 113, tel. 084/23-4010, www.inkaterra.com, US$720 patio suite, US$924 balcony suite, US$1,128 plaza suite), the latest masterpiece of the Inkaterra group. This beautiful colonial mansion was first built in 1585 and following the Spanish conquest was possessed by Francisco Barrientos, lieutenant to Diego de Almagro. It has now been officially named a historical monument by the National Institute of Culture. La Casona has been exquisitely restored into 11 luxurious suites, retaining its original heritage right down to the minutest detail. The doors to La Casona are closed off to the outside world, ensuring the utmost privacy and creating a serene and relaxing oasis for guests. The philosophy of the hotel is to provide a personalized service; therefore there is no reception, just a butler and concierge who prioritize individuals' needs and tend to their every whim. Rooms are impeccably decorated with faded frescoes, colonial tapestries, Persian rugs, and antiques, ensuring the original feel of the home without sacrificing modern comfort and luxury. Every suite has thermostat controlled heated floors, flat-screen TV, DVD player, iPod speakers, WiFi, and mini bar. The bathrooms are superbly designed with the most contemporary amenities, including free-standing bathtubs, marble showers with two types of showerheads, lush towels, and handmade toiletries. Special touches such as bowls of fresh fruit, housekeeping service three times a day, and a private spa and massage room make a stay at La Casona truly exceptional. As if this were not enough La Casona prides itself on being one of Peru's first carbon-neutral hotels.

CUSCO

Food

CAFÉS, BAKERIES, AND ICE CREAM

The most popular café in Cusco is ((**Jack's Café Bar** (Choquechaca/Cuesta San Blas, tel. 084/25-4606, 7:30 A.M.–11 P.M. daily, US$5), and with good reason. It is famous for big breakfasts, such as "El Gordo": a huge pile of eggs, home-made baked beans, fried potatoes, bacon, and sausages. For lunch there are great salads and sandwiches made with home-made bread. There is a fully stocked bar, as well as milk shakes, fruit juices, and coffees. In short—a real taste of home.

Along Cuesta San Blas, you'll eventually walk into the warm baking aromas of **Buen Pastor** (Cuesta San Blas 575, tel. 084/24-0586, 7 A.M.–8 P.M. Mon.–Sat.). This bakery run by nuns has warm empanadas and sweet pastries all at very affordable prices. For an authentic French bakery there is **Qosqo Maki** (Tullumayo 465, tel. 084/23-4035, www. qosqomaki.com, 8 A.M.–8 P.M. Mon.–Sat.), which has very good brown country loaves and tasty croissants. It is part of the long-standing and respected NGO Centro Bartolomé de la Casas, and proceeds go to the foundation.

To satisfy a chocolate craving, stop in the tiny ((**Chocolate** (Choquechaca 162, tel. 084/25-8073, 7 A.M.–11 P.M. daily), a shop serving steaming mugs of hot chocolate and chocolates by the piece. If you fancy sampling some creative coca-flavored chocolate and baked goods head to the **Coca Shop** (Carmen Alto 115, 9 A.M.–8 P.M. Mon.–Fri.).

If you are after a hefty sandwich head to **Juanito's** (Qanchipata 596, tel. 01/994-170-852, 12–3 P.M. and 6–11 P.M. Mon.–Sat., Fri. and Sat. open until 3 A.M., US$4). There is a selection of 30 fillings both meaty and vegetarian, including alpaca and *lechon*.

For a lighter lunch on the lovely Plaza de las Nazarenas there is **Mama Oli** (Plaza

A red plastic flag means *chicha*, a fermented corn drink, is for sale.

© GABRIELLA HOLLAND

a woman selling bread inside a *colectivo* station in Cusco

Nazarenas 199, 8 A.M.–8 P.M. Mon.–Sat. and 9 A.M.–4 P.M. Sun., US$4). This Peruvian-French–owned café has great juices, fresh soups, quiches, and desserts.

On the Plaza de Armas, the laid-back ◖ Trotamundos (Portal Comercio 177, tel. 084/23-9590, 8 A.M.–11 P.M. daily, US$5) has balcony seating over the Plaza de Armas and is a great place to wile the day away. It serves some of the best french fries and *pie de limon* you'll find in Cusco.

The classic Cusqueño **Café Ayllu** (Marqués 263, 6:30 A.M.–10:30 P.M. Mon.–Sat., US$4) opened 35 years ago, and its glass display still cases pastries made from the age-old recipes. Be sure to try the *ponche de leche,* a pisco and milk cocktail, or a sliced roast suckling pig sandwich. **Dos Por Tres** (Marquez 271, tel. 084/23-2661, 9 A.M.–9 P.M. daily, US$2.50) is another Cusco classic and artist hangout. The coffee, almost always made by the owner, is cheap and delicious.

No café is better located for postcard-writing than **Don Esteban & Don Pancho**

(Av. El Sol 765-A, tel. 084/25-2526, 8 A.M.–10 P.M. Mon.–Sat., 8 A.M.–8 P.M. Sun., US$5). Directly across from the post office, this café has a varied menu of sandwiches, empanadas (try the *aji de gallina* one), desserts, and bread made on the premises.

Dolce Vita (Santa Catalina Ancha 366, tel. 084/24-7611, 10 A.M.–9 P.M. daily, US$2) is the best place for homemade ice cream. Your only trouble will be deciding on a flavor: *chicha,* pisco sour, *lúcuma,* and coca are just a few of the exotic creations.

PERUVIAN

The area around the Plaza de Armas is over-flowing with Peruvian restaurants. Here are some of the better quality ones. **La Retama** (Portal de Panes 123, 2nd Fl., tel. 084/22-6372, 11 A.M.–11 P.M. daily, US$10) has a great kitchen and wide-ranging Peruvian menu. A nightly buffet accompanied by a live folkloric music-and-dance show makes dinner into theater. On the ground floor of Portal de Panes is **Inka Grill** (Portal de Panes 115, tel. 084/26-2992, www.inkagrillcusco.com, 11 A.M.–11 P.M. daily, US$13), the first restaurant to bring Novoandino cuisine to Cusco and one of passionate restaurateur Rafael Casabonne's six restaurants (all excellent: www.cuscorestaurants.com). The *ensalada de langostinos* has quinoa-encrusted shrimp that literally melt in your mouth. The valley trout is fresh and tasty, and the pepper steak is also a popular choice.

Pucara (Plateros 309, tel. 084/22-2027) has a worthwhile daily US$3.50 lunch menu. The dishes are clean and simple, and the desserts and chocolate truffles are very good. **Café Restaurant Victor Victoria** (Tecsecocha 474, tel. 084/27-0049, 7:30 A.M.–10 P.M. daily) also has a reasonable lunch menu for US$5. The food is homey and there is an ample salad bar.

Pacha Papa (Plazoleta San Blas 120, tel. 084/24-1318, www.cuscorestaurants.com, 9:30 A.M.–10:30 P.M. daily, US$11) occupies a sunny courtyard across the street from the Iglesia San Blas. Peruvian specialties such as tamales, quinoa soup, and an acclaimed *lomo*

STREET FOOD

For the brave of heart and stomach, there are plenty of great street food options in Cusco.

- Start your street food tour with a mid-morning snack of *salteñas*, which are meat-, veggie-, and egg-filled pastries best eaten with a squeeze of lemon and a touch of *rocoto*. The best place for these is **Salteñas Copacabana** (Qeros 220), a small restaurant just off Avenida El Sol.

© GABRIELLA HOLLAND

Anticuchos, or roasted meat, is a favorite Cusco street food.

- At the Portal de Belen, and just outside the Gatos Market, is a lovely lady who sells the best tamales in town. Choose between the sweet *dulce* or savory *salado* option of these maize treats.

- For an evening degustation head to the intersection of Maruri and Loreto where you will find a stand, usually surrounded by people, that has the most tender and flavorful *anticuchos* (marinated meat skewers) in Cusco. The *anticucho de corazon* (heart meat) will melt in your mouth!

- For one of the best Peruvian desserts head to the Ruinas and Tullumayo intersection where you'll find a tiny little restaurant that is renowned for having the best *picarones* in town. These deep-fried sweet potato doughnuts, served hot and covered with syrup, are irresistible.

- To wash everything down, look out for a cart full of glass bottles with colorful liquids at Choquechac aand Cuesta San Blas. These are different herb concoctions that are mixed into a sweet tea called *emoliente*. The gooey texture comes from *linasa*, a gooey but healthy gelatinous linseed extract.

- If you still have room for a last midnight snack, head to Plazoleta San Blas to find a woman who sells rice pudding and *mazamorra morada*, a jelly-like dessert made from purple maize. She is there every day without fail into the wee hours of the night.

saltado are also served. A local favorite in San Blas is **Quinta Eulalia** (Choquechaca 384, 12:30–5 P.M. daily, US$6), which has been serving traditional Andean food since 1941. Prices are very reasonable and servings are massive. Dishes include *cuy, chicharrón,* and *rocoto relleno* (stuffed pepper). Besides the excellent food, this place has a great atmosphere, with tables in a sunny courtyard and live music.

A highly recommended, unpretentious restaurant that serves fantastic Peruvian food is ☾ **Trujillo** (Tullumayo 542, tel. 084/23-3465, restaurant_trujillo@speedy.com.pe, 9 A.M.–8 P.M. Mon.–Sat. and 9 A.M.–5 P.M. Sun., US$10–15). The menu is vast, servings are generous and everything is bound to be genuine and delicious. It is particularly famous for its *ají de gallina,* and the meat of the *asado a la olla* literally melts in your mouth.

INTERNATIONAL

One of Cusco's better Italian restaurants is **Cosa Nostra** (Plateros 358-A, 2nd Fl., tel. 084/23-2992, www.cosanostraristorante.com, noon–3:30 P.M. and 7–10:30 P.M. Mon.–Sat., US$10–15). The pasta is fresh and prepared in the authentic Italian way. The gnocchi, beef carpaccio, and beef filet in balsamic sauce are also good.

Another excellent Italian restaurant with a new and improved menu is ◖ **Incanto** (Santa Catalina Angosta 135, tel. 084/25-4753, www.cuscorestaurants.com, 11 A.M.–11 P.M. daily, US$10–12). The minimalist decor shows off not only the Inca walls, but also the simple and flavorful food. Service is impeccable. The squid ink risotto is divine and the homemade fettuccini with seafood is light, spicy, and extremely tasty. Above Incanto and belonging to the same owner is **Greens** (Santa Catalina Angosta 135, 2nd Fl., tel. 084/24-3379, www.cuscorestaurants.com, 11 A.M.–11 P.M. daily, US$10), a creative organic restaurant. The concept is that the ingredients are separated into food groups for you to mix and match to your liking. The vegetables are prepared simply but well with nice touches such as mashed potatoes made from potatoes roasted in lamb juice. Every single ingredient used in the restaurant is 100 percent organic right down to the whole-meal flour.

If you are after Indian food, **Korma Sutra** (Tandapata 909, tel. 084/23-3023, 5 P.M.–midnight Tues.–Sun., US$8–12) is a good option. While the decorations are a little somber and plain, the curries, although overpriced, are colorful and tasty, especially the onion *bhaji* and the lamb *rogan josh.*

The German-owned ◖ **Granja Heidi** (Cuesta San Blas 525, tel. 084/23-8383, 8:30 A.M.–9:30 P.M. Mon.–Sat.) has farm-fresh produce, including delicious natural yogurt, homemade granola, and a light and tasty midday lunch menu for US$7.50.

At the top of Cuesta San Blas by the fountain in the Plazoleta San Blas is another light, fresh option for lunch. The cute and charming French-owned **La Caverne del Oriente**

(Plazoleta San Blas 646, tel. 084/984-609-045, 9 A.M.–9 P.M. daily, US$4) serves homemade French specialties such as hot goat's cheese salad, *flamenkuche,* and Mediterranean dishes such as couscous. The lunch menu is limited but great value (US$3.50). The Dutch/Argentinian-run **Encuentros Café** (Suecia 320, tel. 084/22-2703, www.encuentroscafe.com) also serves a worthwhile US$3.50 midday menu.

El Gusto Es Nuestro (Tecsecocha 420, tel. 084/25-5060, www.elgustoesnuestrorestaurant.com, 6–10:30 P.M. Mon.–Sat., US$10) is an unpretentious family run restaurant. The friendly Cordon Bleu–trained chef not only cooks the delicious meals but also waits and interacts with the clients. The food is international and ranges from Cobb salad to French onion soup to local favorites like *lomo saltado.*

Australian Tammy Gordon's ◖ **Baco Wine Bar and Restaurant** (Ruinas 465, tel. 084/24-2808, bacorestaurante@yahoo.com, 6 P.M.–midnight Mon.–Sat., US$10–15) has a lovely, relaxing atmosphere. Thin-crust pizzas topped with such options as duck prosciutto and mushroom or blue cheese, marinated figs, and basil are simply delightful. Their organic salads and grilled meats are also delicious accompanied by a great wine from their extensive list.

FINE DINING

At the ambitious **MAP Café** (Plaza Nazarenas 231, tel. 084/24-2476, www.cuscorestaurants.com, mapcafe@cuscorestaurants.com, 11 A.M.–10 P.M. daily, US$16–24) dinner guests sit in a perfectly proportioned glass box, reminiscent of architect Philip Johnson's glass house, which seemingly floats in the stone courtyard of the Museo de Arte Precolombino. The food is a gourmet and sophisticated interpretation of traditional Andean cuisine. The glazed and deep fried *cuy* legs on a *choclo* foam with *tarwi* salad is a tasty and less confronting way to try guinea pig. A favorite dish on the menu is the *capchi de setas,* a mouthwatering creamy mushroom, potato, and broad bean casserole topped with a buttery pastry. The desserts are some of the most creative and delectable in Cusco. The

CUSCO

© FIONA CAMERON

Many of Cusco's restaurants feature singing and dancing in the evenings.

specialty is hot truffle balls with *aguaymanto* and pisco, served with vanilla ice cream and a surprise shot. If you're up for a full three-course meal then the US$50 menu is worth it.

Cicciolina (Triunfo 393, 2nd Fl., tel. 084/23-9510, cicciolinacuzco@yahoo.com, 8–11:30 A.M., 12:30–4 P.M., and 6–11 P.M. daily, US$12–15) is the most happening restaurant in town, popular with tourists and locals alike. A casual lunch here might be a sandwich, salad, and smoothie or their daily menu, but dinner should be taken in the deep red dining room. There, you can truly enjoy the cracked black pepper tagliatelli or grilled scallops in an oriental sauce over your choice of a glass of Peruvian, Argentine, Chilean, French, or Italian wine. For something sweet try the strawberries and port. If you leave satisfied, come back the following morning for breakfast and delicious croissants at the Cicciolina bakery. They also provide a picnic catering service, anywhere you wish, with tables, tablecloths, waiters, and all the trimmings.

For an evening meal with an entertaining operatic twist, **Divina Comedia** (Pumacurco 406, tel. 084/43-7640, info@restaurantcusco. com, 11:30–3 P.M., 6:30–11 P.M. Wed.–Mon., US$12–15) is a lot of fun. The Divine Comedy theme, medieval-influenced decor, and waiters dressed in period clothing are a fitting backdrop to the talented opera singers who entertain you while you dine. The beautifully presented modern and traditional dishes taste as good as they look.

For an all-around great dining experience, the best fusion restaurant in Cusco is **Limo** (Portal de Carnes 236, 2nd Fl., tel. 084/24-0668, www.cuscorestaurants.com, 11 A.M.–3 P.M. and 6 P.M.–midnight daily, US$12–15). Rafael Casabonne's latest project is a tastefully decorated restaurant with a great view over the Plaza de Armas. The service is excellent but most importantly the food is superb. Start the evening with a plate of experimental Peruvian-influenced sushi rolls; the ceviche roll and the tuna rolls can hold their own anywhere in the world. The *tiraditos* and ceviches, especially the *ceviche oriental,* are delicious. As a main, the crab meat and breaded shrimp bathed in *leche de tigre* is a winner.

PIZZA

Pizza Carloía (Maruri 381, tel. 084/24-7777, midnight–3 P.M. and 5–11 P.M. Mon.–Sat., 5:30–11 P.M. Sun., US$10) has traditional Italian woodfire oven pizzas with thin smoky crusts. Those meat lovers who like a bit of spice should try the Diablo.

Babieca Trattoría (Tecsecocha 418-A, tel. 084/50-6940, 11 A.M.–midnight, US$12) has excellent dough, gourmet toppings such as alpaca and trout, and a seriously gigantic pizza called the Kilometriza for US$20.

A very cute, cozy, and affordable pizzeria is **Justina** (Palacio 100, interior, tel. 084/25-5475, 5–11 P.M. daily, US$10). The specialty of the house is the mushroomy and delicious Pizza Justina.

VEGETARIAN

Although most restaurants in Cusco have vegetarian options, there are a few places dedicated exclusively to vegetarian cuisine. A popular option is **Govinda** (Espaderos 128, 8 A.M.–10 P.M. daily, US$3–5), half a block from the Plaza de Armas. This small Indian-inspired restaurant has flavorsome dishes, but the US$8.50 midday menu is overpriced.

For some inexpensive vegetarian and vegan fare head to **Govinda Lila** (Carmen Bajo 228-A, 9 A.M.–9 P.M. daily, US$2–3.50). This cute little place is great value for money. The US$2 lunch menu includes a great salad buffet, a soup, a main, and a simple dessert. The US$3 breakfast buffet has everything you could possibly want except for eggs. The muesli and yogurt are homemade by the friendly owner,

Lojita. For a sweet finish make sure you try the Govinda pie.

A worthwhile and economic option is **El Encuentro** (Santa Catalina Ancha 384, tel. 084/24-7777, 9 A.M.–3 P.M. and 6–9 P.M. Mon.–Sat., US$3.50–5). It has a clean, simple midday menu for US$2, which also has a salad bar, with interesting options such as a vegetarian *ají de gallina*.

MARKETS

The **Mercado San Pedro** (Túpac Amaru, 6 A.M.–7 P.M.), near the San Pedro train station, has amazing fruit and vegetables. Come here to try the unique and delicious granadilla and chirimoya and cheap juices, but keep your eyes out for pickpockets and those who silently slice backpacks with razors to steal the goodies within.

Several blocks past Mercado San Pedro toward Avenida Ejercito is **El Baratillo**, which on Saturday morning is full of the most fascinating secondhand wares. If you have time to browse properly you can find some real treasures, but be careful with your valuables.

El Molino, just behind the central bus station, is Cusco's largest black market and has everything. It is a little out of the center of town, so it's best to catch a cab. Not many tourists come here, but as long as you hang onto your wallet you will be fine.

The largest supermarket is **Mega** (Plaza Túpac Amaru and Matara). **Gato's Market** (Portal Belen 115) and **Market** (Portal Mantas 120) are both on the Plaza de Armas; they're small and pricey but do stock hard-to-find imported products.

CUSCO

Information and Services

TOURIST INFORMATION

The **South American Explorers Club (SAE)** (Atocsaycuchi 670, tel. 084/24-5484, www. saexplorers.org, 9:30 A.M.–5 P.M. Mon.–Fri., 9:30 A.M.–1 P.M. Sat.) is a gold mine of information. It costs US$60 to join as an individual for a year, US$90 for a couple, though nonmembers are allowed to look around as well. This is definitely worth the cost if you will be in Peru for any length of time, and is a recommended first stop in Cusco. No matter how much research you have done, you will always learn something here and, at the very least, meet some interesting people. Club members can peruse trip reports for all over the Cusco area, use the well-stocked library, make free calls to the United States and Canada, and receive discounts at a wide range of restaurants, language schools, hotels, and agencies. It is also the only place in Cusco that sells topographical maps. The club hosts weekly events, and there is a new volunteer room that helps travelers become involved in children's, women's, and jungle projects.

If all you need is some basic tourist information and a map, services are free at the friendly **Iperú** (Portal Mantas 188, tel. 084/26-3176, www.peru.info, 8:30 A.M.–6:30 P.M. Mon.–Fri., 8 A.M.–2 P.M. Sat.) or in the airport (tel. 084/23-7364, 6 A.M. until the last flight).

POLICE

Travelers can contact the tourist police through the Iperú office, but a larger, **24-hour tourist police office** is on Saphi 510 (tel. 084/24-9654), where officers speak some English.

IMMIGRATION

Tourist visa enquiries can be made at the **Immigration Office** (Av. El Sol 314, tel. 084/22-2741, 8 A.M.–noon Mon.–Fri.).

HEALTH CARE

One of the major hospitals of Cusco is **Hospital Lorena** (Plazoleta Belén 1358, in the Santiago neighborhood, tel. 084/22-1581 or 084/22-6511).

A good reliable clinic that accepts international insurance, has adept doctors, and offers 24-hour service is **Clínica Paredes** (Lechugal 405, tel. 084/22-5265, www.clinicaparedes.com). Another recommendable clinic is **Cima Clinic** (Pardo 978, tel. 084/25-5550 or 084/984-651-085, www.cima-clinic.com), which specializes in altitude problems.

Dr. Américo Ortiz de Zevallos Olivera (Urb. El Hogar B-3, San Sebastian, tel. 084/984-743-054 or 084/27-0085, americo_odzo@hotmail.com) is a first-rate private doctor and surgeon who makes house and hotel calls 24 hours a day. He speaks English, has a great bed manner, and charges according to the patient's financial situation. He also works part-time at **SOS Medical Group** (Suecia 368, tel. 084/25-4492).

The best pharmacies are **InkaFarma** (Av. El Sol 210, tel. 084/24-2631, www.inkafarma.com.pe, 24 hours), **Boticas Arcangel** (Mantas 132, tel. 084/22-1421, 7 A.M.–11 P.M. daily), and **Boticas Fasa** (Av. El Sol 130, tel. 084/24-4528, www.boticasfasa.com.pe, 7 A.M.–11 P.M. Mon.–Sat., 8 A.M.–9 P.M. Sun.).

A recommended dental clinic is **Vivadent Clinica Odontologica** (El Sol 627-B, 2nd Fl., tel. 084/23-1558 or cell tel. 084/984-746-581, www.vivadentcusco.com). Dr. Virginia Valcarcel Velarde is expensive but very professional and experienced.

BANKS AND MONEY EXCHANGE

Getting money out of an ATM usually means a stroll down the first few blocks of Avenida El Sol, where **Banco de Crédito** is on the first block and **Banco Continental** and **Interbank** are on the third. The Banco de Crédito and Interbank are open all day 9 A.M.–6:30 P.M. (the others usually close 1–3 P.M.), with Saturday hours 9 A.M.–1 P.M. All the banks

CITY SAFETY

It is a common misconception that traveling through Peru's remote countryside is risky while spending time in a tourist town like Cusco is safe. In fact, the exact opposite is true. Taxi assaults, where cab drivers rob their passengers, are on the rise in Cusco. Most of these are simple robberies, though some have involved violence. Here are some tips for staying out of trouble:

- Take only authorized taxis; these can be easily recognized by a hexagonal yellow sticker on the windshield. Even better is to go with a radio taxi company – these have advertising and phone numbers on their roofs.

- Look at the taxi driver and decide whether you feel comfortable with him. If you feel nervous, wave the taxi on and choose another.

- Always take a taxi late at night, especially after drinking. Night taxis anywhere in town cost US$1.

- Walk in a group at night, and women should never walk alone.

- Carry your wallet in your front pocket and keep your backpack in front of you in a market or other crowded area. In markets, it is often better to leave most of your money and passport at home.

- Walk with purpose and confidence.

- When riding on a bus, store your luggage below or keep it on your lap. Do not put it on the racks above you where others can reach it as you sleep.

- Be wary of new friends at bars and on the street – many scams involve misplaced trust or the lure of drugs and sex and are hatched over the space of hours. Think twice before you go somewhere out of the way with someone you just met.

are closed on Sunday. For wire transfers, there is a **Western Union** (Av. El Sol 627-A, tel. 084/24-4167, 8:30 A.M.–7:30 P.M. Mon.–Fri., 8:30 A.M.–1:30 P.M. Sat.).

There is an overwhelming number of money exchange places, especially along the Avenida El Sol, and they are all much the same. A reliable option is **Panorama** (Portal de Comercio 149, 9 A.M.–10 P.M. daily). The rate is always fair and the bills brand new as they come directly from the bank.

COMMUNICATIONS

Cusco's main **post office** is the Serpost (Av. El Sol 800, tel. 084/22-4212, www.serpost.com.pe, 8 A.M.–8 P.M. Mon.–Sat. and 9:30 A.M.–1 P.M. Sun).

The city is crawling with different Internet places, all of which have cable connections and are generally good. In San Blas, a good place is **SanBlasNet** (Cuesta San Blas 106, 10 A.M.–10 P.M. daily). The owner, Jaime, is super friendly and will help you with just about everything.

Long-distance and international calls can be made at many Internet places, which are all similar in price.

LANGUAGE SCHOOLS

Cusco has more Spanish schools than any other city in Peru, though it is hard to be truly immersed in Spanish unless you can somehow isolate yourself from English speakers. Considering what they include, the school packages are considerably cheap: pre-arranged hostel or homestay with local family, breakfast, airline reservations, volunteer work options, city tour, dance and cooking classes, lectures, and movies. An intensive group class with all these perks runs around US$200–300 per week with 20 hours of classes, while a private package is around US$300–400. A private teacher, without lodging or food, is US$9–11 per hour. All prices quoted are for a week with 20 hours of classes.

CUSCO

Academia Latinoamericana de Español (Plaza Limacpampa Grande 565, tel. 084/24-3364, www.latinoschools.com, US$190 private classes, US$160 group classes) is a professional, family-run business with schools in Peru, Ecuador, and Bolivia. They have great host families in Cusco and offer volunteer programs and also university credits through New Mexico State University. **Amigos Spanish School** (Zaguan del Cielo B-23, tel. 084/24-2292, www.spanishcusco. com, US$120 group) gives half of its income to children with disabilities and has highly recommended teachers.

Centro Tinku (Nueva Baja 560, tel. 084/24-9737, www.centrotinku.com, US$180 group, US$220 private) is a cultural institution that offers standard and custom-made Spanish and Quechua classes. All the teachers are fully certified. Off the Plazoleta San Blas is the affordable and quaint yet professional **Mundo Antiguo Spanish School** (Tandapata 649, tel. 084/22-5974, www.learnspanishinperu. net, US$55 group, US$190 private), run by a friendly Peruvian-Dutch couple. The main aim of this school is to keep it intimate, personal, and welcoming. **Maximo Nivel** (El Sol 612, tel. 084/25-7200, www.maximonivel. com, US$110 group, US$200 private) has schools all over North and South America.

LAUNDRY

Most Cusco hostels offer laundry service for the going rate of US$1.50/kilogram. Otherwise the best place for washing clothes (although a little more expensive) and especially for dry cleaning is **Lavanderia Inka** (Ruinas 493, tel. 084/22-3421, 8 A.M.–1 P.M. and 3–8 P.M. Mon.–Sat.). For just regular washing **Lavanderia Louis** (Choquechaca 264-A, tel. 084/24-3485, 8 A.M.–8 P.M. Mon.–Sat.) is a reliable and economic option at US$1/kilogram.

PHOTOGRAPHY

Digital photographers can download their full media cards to a CD in 20 minutes at many camera shops in Cusco. The catch is that you usually need the USB cord that works with your camera. An exception is **Foto Panorama** (Portal Comercio 149, in front of the cathedral, tel. 084/23-9800, 8:30 A.M.–10 P.M.), which accepts most different media cards. Another highly recommended place for developing or digital services and products is **Foto Nishiyama** (Triunfo 346, tel. 084/24-2922). It also has other locations around town, including on Avenida El Sol.

MASSAGES AND SPAS

There is no shortage of massage therapists (or people claiming to be) in Cusco desperately trying to get your business. Olga Huaman and her team at **Yin Yang** (El Sol 106, Galerias La Merced, Office 302, 3rd Fl., tel. 084/25-8201, cell 084/984-765-390, yinyang_masajes@hotmail.com, 9 A.M.–10 P.M. daily) give very professional massages as well as reiki and offer room service or sessions at their premises. **Angel Hands** (Heladeros 157, tel. 084/22-5159, 6 A.M.–10 P.M.) offers similar services. The **Siluet Sauna and Spa** (Quera 253, Interior 4, tel. 084/23-1504, 10 A.M.–10 P.M. daily) offers massages along with a whirlpool tub and hot and dry saunas.

If you really want to treat yourself to a day of luxurious pampering try **Samana Spa** (Tecsecocha 536, tel. 084/23-3721, cell 084/984-389-332, www.samana-spa.com), in a nicely renovated colonial house. They offer professional massages, steam and dry saunas, Jacuzzis in the lovely stone patio, and all sorts of beauty treatments including facials and manicures. There are special packages such as the Inka Trail Relief, which includes a deep tissue massage, steam/dry sauna, manicure/pedicure, and a Jacuzzi for US$110.

Getting There and Around

AIR

Cusco's airport (tel. 084/22-2611) is 10 minutes south of town and the taxi ride costs about US$2.50. Taxes for domestic flights are US$5.84 pp.

All Cusco-bound travelers must first arrive in Lima and then board another plane in Cusco, for which there are currently three main operators. To approach Cusco's airport, planes must fly at considerable altitude and down a narrow valley, passing ice-covered Nevado Salcantay en route. Because of the tricky approach and winds, afternoon flights are frequently cancelled. If possible, fly in and out of Cusco in the morning.

LAN (Av. El Sol 627-B, tel. 084/25-5552 or Lima tel. 01/213-8200, www.lan.com) is the most reliable airline and has more than 10 Cusco-bound flights a day. It often has very good offers if you book ahead of time. **Star Perú** (Av. El Sol 627, tel. 084/25-3791 or 084/23-4060, www.starperu.com) and **Taca** (Av. El Sol 602-B, tel. 084/24-9921 or 084/24-9922, Lima tel. 01/213-7000, www.taca.com) are also reliable and sometimes have cheaper flights.

In addition, LAN has daily flights from Lima and Cusco to Puerto Maldonado and Arequipa, as well as various other destinations around Peru. Star Perú also flies from Lima or Cusco to Puerto Maldonado and from Lima to other Peruvian destinations.

BUS

There is a new long-distance bus terminal, the **Terminal Terrestre,** on the way to the airport (Via de Evitamiento 429, tel. 084/22-4471). This huge building is busy, safe, and crammed with all of the long-distance bus companies, bathrooms, and a few stores selling snacks. Companies generally open 6 A.M.–9 P.M. and accept reservations over the phone, with payment on the day of departure (you have to speak Spanish, though).

A recommended way to get to **Puno** is with one of the tourist buses that visit the ruins on the way. These buses include a huge buffet lunch, English-speaking guide, and stops at most of the major ruins on the way. **Inka Express** (Plateros 320, tel. 084/24-7887, www.inkaexpress.com, US$50) makes stops in the exquisite colonial church of Andahuaylillas, the Inca ruins of Raqchi, and a buffet lunch stop in Sicuani. In the afternoon the bus stops at La Raya pass and the ruins of Pukará before arriving in Puno. The buses generally leave Cusco at 8 A.M. and arrive at 5 P.M. in Puno, include hotel pickup and drop-off, and even have oxygen tanks on board for altitude problems. There is a 10 percent discount for groups of more than four people.

For direct service to Puno, **Ormeño** (tel. 084/22-7501, www.grupo-ormeno.com) has a daily bus leaving at 9 A.M., which arrives in Juliaca at 1:30 P.M. and Puno at 2 P.M. (US$14 for Royal Class, which has onboard food service and plusher seats than even the Imperial buses). **Imexso** (tel. 084/22-9126, imexso@terra.com.pe), for the most part, has good service and new buses, with English-language videos. **Copacabana** has a bus service leaving at 8 A.M. for US$5.

Many of the above companies offer transfer buses leaving for **Bolivia,** though some go through Desaguadero and others through Copacabana (launching point for Isla del Sol). Ormeño (tel. 084/22-7501) has a direct business-class bus (no meals) through Desaguadero to La Paz, leaving daily at 9 P.M. To head through Copacabana, try Tour Peru, which leaves 10 P.M. daily (US$28). Another recommended company for getting to Bolivia is Litoral, though there are many more options in Puno's excellent Terminal Terrestre. The border crossing, which is open between 8 A.M. and 3 P.M., is quick and easy: Passengers need only get off the bus for a few minutes on each side of the border to have their passports stamped—remember to ask for the maximum number of days (usually 90).

Buses for the 20-hour haul to **Lima** now head to Abancay before crossing the mountains to the coast at Nazca and then heading north for Lima. Ormeño offers the extra-plush Royal Class service, which leaves at 10 A.M. and arrives in Lima the following day at 6 A.M. for US$50. There are also plain, one-story buses with a stop in Abancay. Another recommended company is **Expreso Wari** (tel. 084/24-7217, www.expresowari.com.pe), which has buses with seats that recline into beds. Trips including meals leave at 12:30 P.M. and 8 P.M. for US$52. They also have a less luxurious service leaving at 2 P.M. and 4 P.M. for US$28. **Cruz del Sur** (tel. 084/24-8255) has a good Imperial service leaving at 3:30 P.M. and 6:30 P.M. **Tepsa** (tel. 084/22-4534, www.tepsa.com.pe) is also a reliable option for Lima. The only company with transfer service through Abancay on to **Ayacucho** is **Expreso Los Chankas** (tel. 084/24-2249).

The journey to **Arequipa** via Juliaca takes 8.5 hours. **Cruz del Sur** (tel. 084/24-8255) has Imperial buses that include dinner and bingo leaving at 2 P.M. for US$34, and Ormeño offers a similar-quality service. **Enlaces** (tel. 084/25-5333) and **Cial** (tel. 804/22-1201) also have Imperial buses leaving daily.

Most people who visit Colca head to Arequipa first and then take the three-hour drive to Chivay, the Colca gateway, from there. There is an alternative, spectacular route on rocky roads that branches off from Sicuani and heads past Laguna Languilayo, the Tintaya copper and gold mine, and Condorama Dam on the Río Colca. This Cusco–Chivay route takes at least 11 hours, though more in rainy season, and it is best to do it on Saturday when buses are frequent. First head to Sicuani and scout for a Chivay direct bus or truck. If none is available, take local buses to El Descanso, Yauri, Chichas, and on to Chivay. (This 250-kilometer route between Sicuani and Chivay would also make an excellent mountain-bike journey.) Another option from Colca is provided by the company **Colca** (tel. 084/26-3254), which has daily buses to Arequipa. This bus takes the traditional route through Juliaca

and then stops at Pampa Cañaguas en route to Arequipa. The only direct option for Tacna, the border town for Chile, is **Cruz del Sur** (tel. 084/24-8255), which leaves at 4:30 P.M. and arrives at 8:30 A.M. the following day.

If you are a glutton for punishment you might want to consider the two-day bumpy but spectacular bus journey through Ocongate to **Puerto Maldonado,** the hardest of Cusco's three jungle destinations. The best way to do this is to head to Urcos and take a bus or truck onward from there. Atalaya, the gateway to the Parque Nacional Manu, is similarly hard to reach, but the journey can generally be made in a long day. Travelers must first head to Paucartambo. For Quillabamba, **Ampay** (tel. 084/24-9977) has buses leaving for the 8.5-hour journey for US$7 from the Terminal Terrestre.

Other options for Quillabamba and all other destinations in the Cusco region are the informal *terminales* where buses, *combis*, and *colectivos* leave when full. These are often located in places that are unsafe at night or early in the morning. They generally operate from 5 A.M. until as late as 7 P.M. Here is a list of *terminales* for destinations around Cusco. Most taxi drivers know where they are.

For **Quillabamba,** there is a roadside pickup spot, called a *terminal de paso,* at the last block of Avenida Antoñia Lorena, the principal exit road for the route that goes through the Sacred Valley before heading over Abra Málaga into the jungle (7 hours, US$6).

For **Urubamba,** there are two options. Buses for the shorter, 1.5-hour route, through Chinchero, leave from the first block of Grau near the bridge (45 minutes, US$0.75 for Chinchero; 1.25 hours, US$1.50 for Urubamba). Collective taxis at Pavitos do the same route but go all the way to Ollantaytambo (1.5 hours, US$3.50 pp).

Collective taxis and buses for **Pisac** and **Calca** via Urubamba leave from Puputi and the last block of Tullumayo (one hour, US$1.5 for Pisac; 1.5 hours, US$1.50 for Urubamba).

For **Andahuaylillas** and **Urcos,** on the way to Puno, buses leave from Avenida de la

Cultura in front of the regional hospital (1.5 hours, US$1).

For **Sicuani,** farther along this same route, buses also leave from Cultura but near Manuel Prado (3 hours, US$3.50).

For **Paucartambo,** buses leave from Cultura and Diagonal Angamos (3 hours, US$3).

Buses for **Paruro** leave from Belen and Grau (3 hours, US$3).

TRAINS

The train service between Cusco and Machu Picchu is being transformed by two events, so Peru visitors should check for the latest train information online. First, severe floods in the Sacred Valley in January 2010 destroyed miles of railroad track to Machu Picchu. While the track was being repaired, trains to Machu Picchu were departing only from Piscacucho, a village downstream from Ollantaytambo and at the end of the Sacred Valley.

The second, and very welcome, event is the breakup of the **PeruRail** monopoly and the emergence of two new train companies: **Inca Rail** and **Machu Picchu Train.** Hopefully, new competition will reduce prices and increase train availability to Machu Picchu.

These trains are the only nonstrenuous way to reach Machu Picchu, and a highly interesting way to reach Lake Titicaca as well. A major problem with trains from Cusco, especially during high season, is availability. The easiest way to get tickets is through a hotel or a travel agent. Otherwise visitors should make reservations online. The third, and least desirable option, is to head down to the Cusco train station, a process that, especially during high season, can take an hour or two.

PeruRail still operates trains from Cusco, but most Machu Picchu travelers now depart farther down the line at Ollantaytambo in the Sacred Valley. From Ollantaytambo the train enters the narrow Urubamba gorge, which offers spectacular views of snowcapped Verónica peak (5,710 meters or 18,865 feet) on the right (eastern) side of the train as the landscape transforms into the lush and humid *ceja de selva,* or "eyebrow of the jungle." By the time the train reaches Aguas Calientes, the ramshackle town closest to Machu Picchu, travelers have descended from the dry high plains to mountainous cloud forest.

PeruRail

ENAFER, the former state-owned railroad company, was privatized in the mid-1990s and has been operated since 1999 by **PeruRail** (www.perurail.com), a division of Orient-Express Hotels.

PeruRail offers many train services to Machu Picchu: the **Backpacker** (US$48 one-way, leaves Poroy 7:42 A.M., leaves Aguas Calientes 4:43 P.M.), the **Vistadome** (US$71 one-way, leaves Poroy 6:53 A.M., leaves Aguas Calientes 3:20 P.M.), and the luxury **Hiram Bingham service** (US$334 one-way to Machu Picchu, US$307 one-way from Machu Picchu, leaves Poroy 9:05 A.M., leaves Aguas Calientes 5:50 P.M.). These trains can also be caught from Ollantaytambo. The other services depart only from Ollantaytambo. These include the **Backpacker Cerrojo** (varies in price US$31–43 one-way depending on the departure time, six departures daily), the **Valle Especial** (US$43 one-way earlier train, leaves Ollantaytambo 5:10 A.M. and leaves Aguas Calientes 8:53 A.M., US$60 later train, leaves Ollantaytambo at 8 A.M. and leaves Aguas Calientes 5:27 P.M.), and the **Vistadome Valley** (varies in price US$43–60 one-way depending on the departure time, five departures daily).

For trains to Puno, the PeruRail deluxe Andean Explorer (US$220 one-way)—departs on Monday, Wednesday, and Friday (and Saturday April–October) from Wanchaq Station (Av. El Sol s/n, tel. 084/23-3592) at 8 A.M. and arrives at 6 P.M. in Puno. This spectacular, nine-hour trip winds through the vast altiplano past snowcapped mountains.

Inca Rail

Inca Rail (Av. El Sol 611, tel. 084/23-3030, www.incarail.com) offers three daily departures from Ollantaytambo (6:40 A.M., 11:35 A.M., and 4:36 P.M.) and three daily departures from Aguas Calientes (8:30 A.M.,

2:02 P.M., and 7 P.M.). The trains have an Executive Class (US$50 one-way) and a First Class (US$75 one-way).

Machu Picchu Train

The Machu Picchu Train, owned by Andean Railways (Av. El Sol 576, across from the Coricancha, tel. 084/22-1199, www.machupic-chutrain.com) is importing a series of fancy coaches in a bid to shake up Machu Picchu train service. We like this outfit for a couple of reasons. First, Andean Railways battled PeruRail for years in a David-vs.-Goliath battle that ended in the collapse of PeruRail's monopoly. Second, one of the owners of Andean Railways is Nicholas Asheshov, a British journalist and entrepreneur who has lived in Peru for four decades. Nick knows Peru better than anyone and has also played an important role, along with adventurers Gary Ziegler, Hugh Thompson, and others, in unearthing recent important archaeological ruins in Peru's high Andes. Nick runs the new train service from his adobe electronic home on the grounds of the Libertador Tambo del Inca Hotel in Urubamba.

For the moment, the Machu Picchu Train leaves Ollantaytambo at 7:20 A.M. and 12:36 P.M. and arrives in Aguas Calientes 90 minutes later. The train returns from Aguas Calientes to Ollantaytambo at 10:30 A.M. and

4:15 P.M. Prices vary according to time but are approximately US$75 one-way.

CAR AND MOTORCYCLE RENTAL

Through its Cusco operator, at **Hertz** (Av. El Sol 808, tel. 084/24-8800, www.gygrentacar. com) you can rent a Toyota, be it a Corolla or a Land Cruiser. Rental rates include insurance, taxes, and 250 free kilometers per day. **Europcar** (Av. El Sol 809, tel. 084/22-1010, www.europcar.co.uk) also operates in Cusco. Motorcycles can be rented at **Cusco Moto** (Saphi 592, tel. 084/22-7025, www.cuscomo-totourperu.com), which has 125cc scooters (US$35 per day) and 250cc (US$60 per day) and 400cc (US$100 per day) Hondas. The price includes helmet, gloves, goggles, jacket, and medical and legal insurance. It also offers tours of the Sacred Valley, Maras and Moray, and even Colca Canyon.

LOCAL TRANSPORTATION

A taxi anywhere in Cusco's center costs US$0.85 or US$1 at night. Always be careful with taxis, especially at night. Because Cusco's center is so compact (and congested), few travelers find the need to take buses or *combis*—though the ones that head down Avenida El Sol toward the Terminal Terrestre and airport are useful.

Vicinity of Cusco

There are very interesting ruins along the road that heads south to Lake Titicaca. These cultural sites, from pre-Inca, Inca, and colonial times, form an interesting day tour from Cusco that an increasing number of agencies are offering. These landmarks can also be visited on the highly recommended special tourist buses between Cusco and Puno, which hit all the sights described, head over La Raya Pass, and then keep going to Puno and Lake Titicaca.

Tipón

One of the most elaborate and well-preserved examples of Inca agricultural terracing is Tipón (7 A.M.–5 P.M., US$1.50), which lies 22 kilometers south of Cusco and then another four kilometers up a valley via a switchbacking gravel road. The terraces, finely fitted and impossibly tall, run in straight lines to the head of a narrow valley. They are irrigated by an elaborate aqueduct that still runs from Pachatusan, the sacred mountain that looms over the site, whose name in Quechua means "cross beam of the universe." There are remains of a two-story house on the site and other ruins, possibly a fort, near the top of the aqueduct.

Rumicolca and Pikillacta

Though the Inca refused to admit it, much of their highway network and organizational know-how was based on the **Huari Empire,** which spread across Peru like a wildfire A.D. 500–1000. An example of Huari engineering is Rumicolca, a huge aqueduct that sits on a valley pass on the side of the highway about 32 kilometers from Cusco. The Inca altered the construction, added a few stones, and converted it into a giant gateway to Cusco, though the remains of the old water channels can still be seen.

Nearby is Pikillacta (6 A.M.–6 P.M., US$2), the largest provincial outpost ever built by the Ayacucho-based Huari. This curious walled compound, with nearly 47 hectares (116 acres) of repetitive two-story square buildings, sprawls across the rolling grasslands with little regard to topography. The floors and walls, which are made of mud and stacked stone, were plastered with white gypsum and must have gleamed in the sun. But the Inca so thoroughly erased evidence of the Huari that little about their empire is known today. For many years Pikillacta was thought to be a huge granary, like the Inca site of Raqchi. But excavations have revealed evidence of a large population that left behind refuse layers as deep as three meters. Part of the city caught fire between A.D. 850 and 900, and the Huari withdrew from the city around the same time, bricking up the doors as they went. Whether they abandoned the city because of the fire, or burnt it as they left, is unclear. Some historical information is available at the new museum at the entrance. In the valley below is Lago Sucre and, even farther on, Lago Huacarpay. On the far shores of this lake are the ruins of **Inca Huáscar's summer palace,** much of which continues to be enjoyed today by locals as the Centro Recreacional Urpicanca, the local country club. From the

© RENÉE DEL GAUDIO AND ROSS WEHNER

The Inca converted the Huari aqueduct of Rumicolca into a gateway to Cusco.

shoulder of the highway, it is possible to see ceremonial staircases the Inca built into the landscape above the lake.

Andahuaylillas

The colonial village of Andahuaylillas, 37 kilometers south of Cusco, has a charming plaza shaded with red-flowered pisonay trees and an adobe church, **San Pedro** (8:30 A.M.–noon and 2–5 P.M. Mon.–Sat., 8–10 A.M. and 3–5 P.M. Sun., free), which is built on the foundations from the early Inca empire. Though it's unremarkable on the outside, the doors open to a dazzling painted ceiling, frescoes, and wall-to-wall colonial paintings. This is the most finely decorated church in all of Cusco, probably in all of Peru, though calling it the "Sistine Chapel of the Americas," as some do, is going a bit far. One highlight is a mural by Luis de Riaño depicting the road to heaven and the road to hell, with a full-blown display of all the respective rewards and punishments.

There is a well-known natural healing

CUSCO

center just off the square, **Centro de Medicina Integral** (Garcilaso 514, tel. 084/25-1999, 9 A.M.–7 P.M. daily, medintegral@hotmail.com), with a charming stone courtyard with gardens and plain rooms for US$8 pp. The center attracts a considerable number of overseas visitors for massage, meditation, harmonizing energy therapy, and other treatments.

Urcos

Driving through the main square of this small village, 47 kilometers south of Cusco, it is hard not to notice Urcos's tidy colonial church with a public balcony on the second floor and stone steps in front. On the outskirts of town, there is the beautifully decorated chapel at Huaro, which is on a hilltop overlooking a small lake. According to legend, Inca Huáscar threw a huge gold necklace into these waters to protect the treasure from the Spaniards. The story seemed probable enough that *National Geographic* recently funded an exploration of the lake's bottom by scuba divers—though thick mud prevented them from finding anything.

Raqchi

Raqchi (119 km south of Cusco, 8 A.M.–6 P.M.,

US$3) is a ceremonial center built by **Inca Pachacútec** that offers a fascinating glimpse into the ambition and organization skills of his budding empire. Rising above the humble village of Raqchi, a wall of adobe nearly 15 meters high and 90 meters long sits on a carved Inca wall. This was once the center of a huge hall, the roof of which was supported by adobe columns—one of which has been restored—on either side. On the side are six identical squares, each with six stone buildings, which probably served as a soldiers' barracks. But the most impressive part of Raqchi is line after line of round stone houses—200 in all—that once were filled with a gargantuan amount of quinoa, freeze-dried potatoes, and corn.

Sicuani

There are several nice lunch spots in Sicuani, 138 kilometers south of Cusco. At the **Casa Hacienda Las Tunas** (J.C. Tello 100, tel. 084/35-2480, US$4), Sofia Vásquez serves up a huge, scrumptious buffet of Peruvian food from 11:30 A.M. onwards, when the Inka Express bus pulls in. Her sister, Edith, has good trout and meat dishes at the **Cebichería Acuarios** (Garcilazo de la Vega 141, 2nd Fl., tel. 084/80-9531, US$3) on the plaza.

BACKGROUND

The Land

Peru's foreboding terrain belies its extraordinary fertility. The country's arid coastal climate is caused by the frigid Humboldt Current, which sucks moisture away from the land. But these Antarctic waters also cause a rich upwelling of plankton, which in turn nourishes one of the world's richest fishing grounds. Peru's earliest cultures took root near the ocean and depended on mollusks and fish for their survival.

The snow-covered mountains and high passes of the **Cordillera de los Andes** would appear to be an impediment to the spread of advanced cultures. But the slow melting of the snowpack provides the desert coast with

a vital source of year-round water. Once ancient Peruvians developed irrigation technologies, Peru's early cultures began converting Peru's desert valleys into rich farming areas. The ingenious aqueducts at Nasca, which carry mountain water for miles underneath the desert floor, are still in use today.

In the more moderate topography of North America and Europe, temperature differences and climate zones are largely a question of latitude. Florida, for example, produces oranges, while Kansas produces wheat. But in Peru, climate zones are caused not by latitude, but by altitude. Peru's coast can rise from sea level to over 4,000 meters in less than 100 kilometers,

© GABRIELLA HOLLAND

creating a variety of climates apt for fruits, vegetables, grains, and potatoes. The same phenomenon occurs to an even greater extent where the Andes plunge into the Amazon, a dizzying range of ecosystems that nourish a huge variety of fruits and medicinal plants such as the coca leaf.

Peru's cultural diversity has always been determined by its geography. Trade routes from the Amazon over the Andes to the desert coast were key to the flourishing of Peru's ancient cultures. The Chavín culture, based in the Andes south of the Cordillera Blanca, deified jaguars, snakes, caimans, and other Amazon animals in their enigmatic carvings. They traded their high-altitude grains and potatoes for fruits from the Amazon, dried fish and vegetables from the coast, and the highly valued spondylus seashells brought from Ecuador.

GEOGRAPHY

Peru's total land area is 1.29 million square kilometers, about three times the size of California. Peru's narrow strip of arid desert coast runs 2,400 kilometers between the borders of Ecuador and Chile. Some 50 rivers cascade from the Andes to the coast, though only about a third of these carry water year-round. In these areas, people are entirely dependent on the seasonal rains in the Andes. In Peru's extreme south, the coast forms part of the **Atacama Desert,** one of the driest places on earth.

The Andes rise so abruptly from the coast that they can be seen from the ocean on a clear day. They represent the highest mountain chain on earth next to the Himalayas. **Huascarán,** Peru's highest peak at 6,768 meters, is the world's highest tropical mountain. The Andes are divided into different ranges (called *cordilleras* in Spanish), which often run parallel to each other. In northern Peru, for instance, the Andes rise four separate times to form different *cordilleras* known as the Negra, Blanca, Central, and Oriental.

Between these mountain ranges lie fertile inter-Andean valleys and grasslands between 2,300 and 4,000 meters—the so-called

© GABRIELLA HOLLAND

Peru's Andes are the second-highest mountain range in the world.

breadbasket of Peru, where the majority of its indigenous highlanders live and produce about half the country's food supply. The Inca and other cultures terraced and irrigated this landscape to grow a range of crops, including maize, hardy grains such as *kiwicha* and quinoa, and indigenous tubers such as potatoes, *olluco,* and oca.

On the journey between Cusco and Lake Titicaca, travelers can appreciate the most extreme of Peru's mountain climates, the **puna** or **altiplano.** These rolling grasslands between 4,000 and 4,800 meters look bleak but form rich pasturelands for Peru's variety of camelids, including the wild guanacos, the domesticated llamas and alpacas and the highly prized vicuñas. These animals continue to provide wool, meat, and transport for Andean highlanders.

On the eastern side of Peru, the Andes mountains peter out into a series of ecosystems that cascade into the Amazon basin. Near the top of the eastern edge of the Andes is the montane cloud forest, a mist-drenched, inhospitable place that is one of Peru's most biodiverse habitats. Here live 90 varieties of hummingbirds and over 2,000 types of orchids and butterflies. Clear mountain streams cascade down these slopes, eventually merging to form the broad, muddy, and winding rivers of the lowland rainforest. This carpet of green is the largest jungle on the planet, making up almost 60 percent of Peru's territory, and stretches thousands of kilometers through present-day Brazil to the Atlantic Ocean.

CLIMATE

Peru's weather is a complex set of patterns caused by the Humboldt Current, the Andes, and the jet stream, which blows northwest (not southwest as in the Northern Hemisphere) and picks up the Amazon's moisture as it travels.

On the coast, the southwesterly trade winds that blow toward Peru are chilled as they pass over the frigid waters of the Humboldt Current. When these cold winds hit Peru's sun-baked coast, they gradually warm and rarely release rain because their ability to hold water increases. Clouds form only when the air begins to rise over the Andes, dropping rain over Peru's mountain valleys and high grasslands.

During much of the year, however, a curious temperature inversion occurs along much of Peru's coast. The rising air from the coast is trapped beneath the warm air over 1,000 meters, which is never cooled by ocean breezes. Fog blankets sections of the coast, and drizzle, known in Lima as *garúa,* falls lightly—mainly, but not only, between April and September.

The jet stream heads west over the Amazon basin toward the Andes, picking up transpiration from the Amazon basin. As this warm, humid air rises over the Andes it also condenses into a fine mist that nourishes the cloud forest. As it rises even higher over the puna, it falls as rain.

The heaviest periods of rain in the Peruvian Amazon and Andes occur between December and April, a time that Peruvians refer to as the *época de lluvia* (the rainy season). The first rains, however, begin in October, which is the beginning of the highland planting season. Soon after, rain from the Andes begins to cascade down on the coast, where desert farmers use it for irrigation, and into the Amazon, where rivers become swollen and muddy. The Amazon River can easily rise a staggering 7–14 meters during the brunt of the rainy season in the Andes, which is why most natives live in stilted homes.

ENVIRONMENTAL ISSUES

Peru suffers from a range of environmental problems that are caused in large part by the abuses of mines, fishmeal factories, oil and natural gas wells and pipelines and processing centers, illegal lumber operations, and other extractive industries. These industries have operated with little oversight in Peru for decades as a result of a weak political system that is cash-starved and corrupt. Legislation governing extractive industries, along with regulatory agencies, is improving in Peru but lags well behind other more developed nations.

Peru's zinc, copper, mercury, silver, and gold mines continue to pollute water supplies

ECOTOURISM: LEAVE NO TRACE

Travelers to Peru can either help or hurt the country's long-term survival depending on how they plan their trip and how they behave. A good ecotourism reference in the United States is **The International Ecotourism Society** or TIES (tel. 202/347-9203, www.ecotourism.org), which defines ecotourism as "responsible travel to natural areas that conserves the environment and improves the well-being of local people." A handful of Peru's jungle operators belong to this association. Find out whether the lodge or agency you have chosen lives up to these basic principles set forth by TIES:

· Minimize impact.

· Build environmental and cultural awareness and respect.

· Provide positive experiences for both visitors and hosts.

· Provide direct financial benefits for conservation.

· Provide financial benefits and empowerment for local people.

· Raise sensitivity to host countries' political, environmental, and social climate.

· Support international human rights and labor agreements.

A huge concern in Peru's main trekking areas, such as the Inca Trail and the Cordillera Blanca, is environmental degradation as a result of sloppy camping. A wonderful resource for traveling lightly through wilderness is **Leave No Trace** (www.lnt.org), which has pioneered a set of principles that are slowly being adopted by protected areas around the world. More information on these principles can be found on the LNT web page:

· Plan ahead and prepare.

· Travel and camp on durable surfaces.

· Dispose of waste properly.

· Leave what you find.

· Minimize campfire impacts.

· Respect wildlife.

· Be considerate of others.

Great pains have been made throughout this book to recommend only agencies and lodges that have a solid ethic of ecotourism. But the only way to truly evaluate a company's environmental and cultural practices is by experiencing them firsthand. Your feedback is tremendously valuable to us as we consider which businesses to recommend in the future.

Please send your experiences – both positive and negative – to us at feedback@moon.com (www.moon.com).

with mine tailings, especially in the areas of La Oroya in central Peru and the Cordillera Huayhuash. The U.S.-owned Yanacocha gold mine near Cajamarca has finally taken environmental measures, after being involved in numerous social conflicts with the nearby communities over the last 10 years.

Over the last three decades, gas and oil exploration in the Amazon has caused water pollution and deforestation and had a huge impact on native cultures. The most controversial recent project is the Camisea Gas Field, which is exporting 13 trillion cubic feet of natural gas from the lower Urubamba basin, one of the most remote and pristine areas of the Peruvian Amazon. The project also includes a pipeline over the biodiverse Cordillera Vilcabamba and a natural-gas processing plant next to Paracas, the country's only marine reserve.

Population growth is also exerting tremendous pressure on Peru's resources, especially in the highlands. Overgrazing and the chopping of trees for firewood have caused the area's thin soils to wash away in many areas. The loss of vegetation combines with heavy rains to cause mudslides, known locally as *huaycos*. A series of floods and mudslides in the Cusco area in January 2010 swept away bridges, roads, and the railway that leads to Machu Picchu. The weeks of continuous rains also flooded large areas of fields of the Sacred Valley. As a result, 3,000 tourists were stranded for almost a week in Aguas Calientes, the town near Machu Picchu, and were finally evacuated with helicopters. Worse, thousands of peasants lost their crops and homes.

Flora and Fauna

If in case of a planet catastrophe we would have the choice to choose from one country to save and rebuild the planet from, undoubtedly I would choose Peru.

– English scientist David Bellamy

Peru is located in the heart of the richest and most diverse region in the world. Eleven ecoregions with a unique combination of climate and geography contain a sixth of all plant life in only 1 percent of the planet's land area. The country has 84 of the 114 Holdridge life zones. Few countries can rival Peru's biodiversity, which holds world records for highest diversity of birds (more than 1,800 species), butterflies (more than 3,500), and orchids (3,500). There are at least 6,300 species of endemic plants and animals, along with an estimated 30 million insects. The Andes have relatively low biodiversity but a high rate of endemic species.

ANDEAN FLORA

The high grasslands region or **puna** is home to a collection of bizarre plants with endless adaptations for coping with the harsh climate. Many of them have thick, waxy leaves for surviving high levels of ultraviolet radiation and

THE SUSTAINABLE BRAZIL NUT

Despite the severe depredation generated by the informal gold mining and the unorganized timber industry, the Amazon still has a hopeful model for rainforest development.

Though useful as lumber, the **Brazil nut tree,** locally known as *castaña*, is often the largest tree left standing in the forest because its nuts are more valuable than its wood. The tree's round seedpods look like the pod inside of a coconut and fall to the ground in December and January. Each pod contains between 12 and 24 Brazil nuts, and a single tree can produce as many as 500 kilograms in a year. The nuts are sold as food or for a burgeoning overseas organic products industry that uses its oil in lip balms and skin lotions.

The tough shells prevent birds from eating the seeds before they ripen and are used by natives as candle holders. Only one species of insect – the bee – is physiologically able to pollinate the Brazil nut tree's flowers. Once pollinated, the tree relies on only one animal for the dispersal of its seeds. The brown agouti, a rabbit-sized jungle rodent who collects the seeds and buries them in the ground for later eating. Luckily for the tree, the agouti either forgets where the hole is or returns after the seeds have already germinated. People have often tried to bury and germinate Brazil nut seeds, without success. Apparently the mild-mannered agouti has a few well-kept gardening secrets.

The base of a Brazil nut tree is also a good place to find the deadly bushmaster snake, which is perfectly camouflaged among the leaves as it waits for the agouti. For this reason, Brazil nut workers use a forked pole to pick up Brazil nut seeds off the ground. Otherwise, just imagine.

fine insulating hairs in order to cope with frequent frosts. They grow close to the ground for protection from wind and temperature variations. In Peru's north, wet grasslands known as **páramo** stretch along the northwestern edge of the Andes into Ecuador. The *páramo* has a soggy, springy feeling underfoot and serves as a sponge to absorb, and slowly release, the tremendous amounts of rain that fall in the area.

Peru's most famous highland plant, the *Puya raimondi*—baptized after Antonio Raimondi, the Italian naturalist who studied it—grows in the puna, from Huaraz all the way south to Bolivia. The rosette of spiky, waxy leaves grows to three meters in diameter and looks like a giant agave, even though the plant is in the bromeliad family along with the pineapple. The *puya* lives for a century and, before it dies, sends a giant spike three stories into the air that eventually erupts into 20,000 blooms. Once pollinated, the plant's towering spike allows it to broadcast its seeds widely in the wind.

The spiky tussocks of grass known as *ichu* are the most ubiquitous feature of Peru's high plains. Highlanders use this hardy grass to thatch their roofs, start their fires, and feed their llamas and alpacas. Cattle, which were imported from Europe in the 16th century by the Spanish, are unable to digest it. Cows can only eat the *ichu* when it sprouts anew as a tender green shoot. Hence, highlanders burn large tracts of hillside every year to make *ichu* palatable for cows.

The high deserts of southern Peru, such as those on the way to the Colca Canyon, are so dry that not even *ichu* can survive. Instead, green blob-like plants called *yareta* spread along the rocky, lunar surface. This plant's waxy surface and tightly bunched leaves allow it to trap condensation and survive freezing temperatures. It is currently considered an endangered species.

A few trees can be found in Peru's montane valleys. Eucalyptus, which was imported to Peru from New Zealand, is used widely by highlanders for firewood and ceiling beams. Eucalyptus is useful but also highly invasive;

THE AMAZING LEAF-CUTTER ANT

They crawl, fly, hop, and sting. There is no way to avoid contact with tens of thousands of insect species in the Amazon, which are, so to speak, the real dominators of the rainforest grounds.

The most visible of these is the leaf-cutter ant, which clears neat paths from its colony to the areas where it collects its leaves. These paths are often littered with discarded leaf fragments and can surprisingly stretch a kilometer or more. There are many species of leaf cutters, but all make underground colonies that can reach the size of a living room. The red-colored colonies are made from earth, while black ones are made from partially chewed twig fragments.

Anywhere from 1 million to 2.5 million workers live inside a leaf-cutter colony, divided into five castes:

1. The queen, or egg-layer

2. Male reproducers, who fertilize the queen

3. Leaf-cutters, who chew and transport the leaves

4. Leaf travelers, who remove the waxy cuticle from the leaf and protect the treasure from parasitic *phoridae* flies

5. Cultivators, who tend and fertilize a fungus that grows on the leaves

Biologists believe these leaf-cutters are responsible for nearly half of all herbivore consumption in the neotropics, but the ants do not actually eat the leaves. Instead they pile them up inside their colony to cultivate a fungus, which occurs only in leaf-cutting colonies and is the ants' only food source. The ant and fungus rely on each other for survival, an example of how specific and complex rainforest symbiosis can be.

its rapid spread has greatly reduced the numbers of Peru's most famous highland tree, the *queñual,* currently also endangered. This scraggly, high-altitude, onion skin–like tree can still be seen in abundance, however, in the Parque Nacional Huascarán, especially on a three-kilometer trail known as María Josefa that starts at the shores of Lake Llanganuco.

ANDEAN FAUNA

The most ubiquitous animals of Peru's Andes are the four species of native **camelids** that eat the high-altitude *íchu* grasses and produce wooly coats as protection from the rain and cold. Two of these, the llama and alpaca, were domesticated thousands of years ago by Peru's highlanders, who tie bright tassels of yarn onto the animals' ears. Herds of the much smaller and finely haired vicuña can be seen in the sparse grasslands above Ayacucho, Arequipa, and Cusco. The fourth camelid, the guanaco, is harder to spot because its main range lies south in Chile and Argentina.

Other animals in the Peruvian Andes include **white-tailed deer, foxes,** and the **puma.** The only animal you are likely to see, however, is the **vizcacha,** which looks like a strange mix between a rabbit and a squirrel.

There is a huge range of **birds** in the Andes, the most famous of which is the Andean condor, the world's largest flying bird. Its range extends from the high jungle, including Machu Picchu, all the way to the coast. It can easily be seen in Colca Canyon, along with a variety of other raptors, including the impressive mountain caracara, which has a black body, red face, and brilliant yellow feet. There are also falcons, which have a russet belly and can often be seen hovering over grasslands in search of mice or birds.

© JORGE RIVEROS CAYO

The endangered spectacled bear is the only bear species in South America and can be found in parts of Peru's cloud forest and the Andes.

A variety of water birds can be seen at Lake Titicaca and in the cold, black lakes of the Andean puna. The Andean grasslands are one of the habitats for the Andean goose, a huge, rotund bird with a white belly and black back, and a variety of shimmering ducks including the puna teal and crested duck. There are even flamingos and a few wading birds, such as the red-billed puna ibis. One of the most interesting birds, which can be seen in the river near Machu Picchu and in Colca Canyon, is the torrent duck. This amazing swimmer floats freely down white water that stymies even experienced rafters.

History

Apart from natural diversity, Peru also is the cradle of human civilization in the ancient Americas. Its cultures were far more diverse, for example, than the Mesoamerican cultures that spread through present-day Central America and Mexico.

The first Peruvian states were worshipping at stepped adobe platforms on the coast 5,000 years ago, before the Egyptians were building their pyramids at Giza. And as the Roman empire spread across modern-day Europe, Peru's first empire states were moving like wildfire across the Andes. The **Chavín** and **Tiahuanaco** cultures established patterns of religion, commerce, and architecture that remain alive today among Peru's Quechuan-speaking highlanders.

Western notions of conquest and military-backed empires do not fit easily over Peruvian history. Peru's three large empires—the Chavín, the Huari, and the Inca—spread across Peru in three stages that historians call "horizons." Like the Aztec empire in Mesoamerica, these cultures spread more through commerce and cultural exchange than through military force. Even the Inca, who were capable of raising vast armies, preferred to subdue neighbors through gifts and offers of public works projects. The Inca used military force only when peaceful solutions had been exhausted.

Following the European arrival in the New World, Peru's history follows the same basic stages as other areas of North and South America. There was first a colonial period, which lasted longer and ended later than that of the United States; a war of independence; and then a period of rapid nation building and industrialization in the 19th and 20th centuries.

ORIGINS OF HUMAN CIVILIZATION

Human life in Peru, indeed all over the Americas, is a relatively recent event made possible when the last ice age allowed human settlers to cross the Bering land bridge that connected present-day Russia to Alaska between 20,000 and 40,000 years ago. Another theory, based on Norwegian explorer Thor Heyerdahl's raft expedition in the mid-20th century, suggests that early migration may also have been possible from the Polynesian Islands in the South Pacific. Either way, the first evidence of human civilization in Peru has been dated to as early as 20,000 B.C. at **Pikimachay Cave** outside of Ayacucho, where arrowheads, animal skeletons, and carbon remains were found.

These first human groups began domesticating Andean camelids and *cuys* (guinea pigs) as early as 7000 B.C., establishing small hunter-gatherer villages a thousand years later. The nomadic tribes followed animal migration patterns, exchanging mountain winter for the warmer coastal summers. Potatoes were first cultivated around 6000 B.C. in the Lake Titicaca region. Around 2900 B.C. humans began to plant crops such as manioc, quinoa, lima beans, and cotton at Caral, north of Lima, establishing Peru's long-standing agricultural tradition.

CHAVÍN, THE UNIFIER

Considered the South American counterpart of China's Shang or Mesopotamia's Sumerian civilizations, Chavín flourished around 900 B.C. during the First or Early Horizon era (1000 B.C.–A.D. 200). Chavín managed to unite coastal, highland, and eastern lowland societies with its powerful religious ideology.

The Chavín built an elaborate stone temple at Chavín de Huántar, southeast of Huaraz, decorating it with finely carved stone sculptures and elaborate iconography. These figures depict their worship of a supreme feline deity—the jaguar—as well as other creatures such as snakes, caimans, and natural spirits.

Chavín de Huántar could have been the site of an Andean oracle controlled by a powerful high-priest elite that relied on San Pedro cactus and other hallucinogens to interact with

Chavín stone carvings reflect the powerful religious ideology that unified Peru's different cultural groups 2,000 years before the Inca.

© JORGE RIVEROS CAYO

supernatural forces. This oracle presumably attracted thousands of travelers and pilgrims all the way from Ecuador in the north to the southern Andean region. The discovery of strombus shell trumpets and the highly valued spondylus, which are only found off the coasts of Ecuador, strengthen this theory.

Despite being known for its brilliant and innovative metallurgists, builders, and strategists, Chavín's influence began to fade around 300 B.C. The influence, however, would resonate through Peru's civilizations for the next thousand years.

THE REGIONAL DEVELOPMENT

A variety of cultures sprang up to take the place of the Chavín. On the north coast, the **Moche** (220 B.C.–A.D. 600) began building the Huaca de la Luna, a stepped adobe pyramid south of present-day Trujillo. Highly militaristic and religious, the Moche spread throughout Peru's northern coast. They are best known for finely crafted metallurgy and ceramics, including

artifacts recovered from the Lord of Sipán's intact tomb and the tomb of a tattooed priestess discovered at Huaca Cao Viejo in El Brujo, north of Trujillo.

On the south coast, the **Nasca** (100 B.C.–A.D. 700) began making elegant weavings from cotton and camelid fiber that are considered today the most advanced textiles produced in pre-Columbian America. Their complex cosmography is evident in the Nasca Lines, giant etchings in the desert floor that were likely once used for rain-inducing ceremonies. The Nasca also built Cahuachi, a large temple complex built around A.D. 100 that was probably a pilgrimage site.

In the southern Andean region, the **Tiahuanaco** (A.D. 200–1000) built an elaborate stone urban and ceremonial center on the southern shores of Lake Titicaca. They also developed a system of raised-bed farming that allowed them to cultivate crops despite the area's freezing temperatures. The perfect monumental architecture, witnessed at the Tiahuanaco archaeological site in present-day Bolivia, laid

PERU TIMELINE

20,000 B.C.: First humans arrive in Peru.

15,000 B.C.: Earliest evidence of human life in Peru: Pikimachay Cave, Ayacucho.

7000 B.C.: Andean camelids are domesticated.

2627 B.C.: Sacred city of Caral is built on the coast north of Lima.

900-200 B.C.: Chavín culture flourishes as the unifier of religious ideology from its ceremonial center in the Marañón basin.

900-200 B.C.: Paracas emerges in the desert, producing vividly colored textiles.

A.D. 200-600: Moche, Nasca, and Tiahuanaco flourish as regional civilizations in northern, central, and southern Peru.

A.D. 300: Moche's Lord of Sipán is buried at Huaca Rajada, northeast of Chiclayo.

A.D. 450: Moche's Lady of Cao dies at 25 and is buried in El Brujo complex, north of Trujillo.

A.D. 650: Huari empire starts expanding across most of Peru.

A.D. 900: Sicán culture builds 20 pyramids at Batan Grande.

A.D. 1200: Mythical foundation of the Inca empire by Manco Cápac and Mama Ocllo.

A.D. 1400: Chimú kingdom reaches its maximum expansion.

A.D. 1400: Inca Pachacútec's 33-year reign begins.

A.D. 1450: Chimú kingdom is conquered by the Inca empire. Chan Chan and Túcume are invaded.

1527-1532: Huayna Cápac dies. His two sons Huáscar and Atahualpa plunge into a civil war.

1532: Francisco Pizarro lands in Tumbes with 168 men, meets Atahualpa in Cajamarca, and takes him prisoner.

1533: Atahualpa is tried and executed. Manco Inca, a puppet leader, is installed. Cusco is invaded and sacked.

1535: Pizarro founds Lima.

1536-1537: Manco Inca rebels and subsequently retreats to Vilcabamba.

1538: Diego de Almagro is executed after rebelling against Pizarro's authority.

1541: Almagro's son murders Pizarro in Lima.

1542: Spain's King Charles I establishes the Viceroyalty of Peru.

1542: Potosí mines reach population peak with 160,000 people.

1572: Túpac Amaru I is captured, tried, and executed.

1742: Juan Santos Atahualpa proclaims himself Inca and rebels in the central jungles near Chanchamayo.

1767: Jesuits are expelled from the Spanish empire.

1780-1782: Túpac Amaru II leads a rebellion against the Spaniards but is captured, tried, and executed.

1814: Revolution breaks out in Cusco.

1821: José de San Martín proclaims Peru's independence.

1824: Battle of Ayacucho. Antonio José de Sucre defeats the Spaniards.

1826-1866: Simón Bolívar leaves Peru. A period of political turbulence starts with 35 presidents in 40 years.

1840: Peru signs lucrative contract for exporting guano, or bird dung.

1849-1874: Cotton and sugar plantations on Peru's north coast import 100,000 Chinese coolies to replace freed slaves.

1879-1883: War of the Pacific. Peru loses the war against Chile.

1911: Hiram Bingham discovers Machu Picchu.

1919-1930: Augusto B. Leguía's 11-year civil dictatorship is marked by strong foreign investment and restriction of civil rights.

1927: Víctor Raúl Haya de la Torre founds the Alianza Popular Revolucionaria Americana (APRA) from political exile in Mexico.

1941: Peru enters a seven-week war over disputed border territories with Ecuador.

1955: Women vote for the first time.

1963-1968: President Fernando Belaúnde Terry begins land reform, heading a very unpopular administration.

1968: Belaúnde is overthrown by socialist-leaning General Juan Velasco Alvarado.

1968-1980: Twelve years of military dictatorship. Velasco nationalizes foreign-owned companies.

1970: A 7.9 earthquake kills 70,000 in Áncash, including 18,000 covered by a landslide in Yungay.

1975: General Francisco Morales Bermúdez, presumably supported by the CIA, overthrows Velasco Alvarado.

1980: Belaúnde is reelected. Sendero Luminoso (Shining Path), a pro-Maoist terrorist organization, launches in Ayacucho a 20-year internal war that plunges Peru into violence and chaos.

1982-1983: El Niño floods devastate northern Peru.

1985: APRA candidate Alan García Pérez is elected president, pushing the country into hyperinflation and a downward economic spiral.

1985-1988: The Accomarca massacre (1985); execution of 200 inmates during prison riots in Lurigancho, El Frontón Island, and Santa Bárbara (1986); and Cayara massacre (1988) mark a period of constant human right violations under García's administration.

1990: World-renown novelist Mario Vargas Llosa leads protests against García's intention of nationalizing the Peruvian bank system.

1990: Outsider Alberto Fujimori defeats Vargas Llosa to become president of Peru. He applies a radical economic program tagged the "Fuji-shock."

1992: Fujimori dissolves congress in his "self-coup." Shining Path bombs a building in middle-class Miraflores district. Abimael Guzmán, Shining Path's leader, is captured.

1993: Peru's economy picks up and becomes the fastest-growing in the world.

1996-1997: MRTA terrorist group assaults the Japanese ambassador's residence, taking 700 hostages, finally keeping 71 for four months. Peruvian military operation rescues all hostages but one, killing all MRTA members.

1998: El Niño storms ravage the north coast.

2000: Fujimori reelected president under allegations of electoral fraud. He leaves the country after scandal implications in extortion, corruption, and arms trafficking. Valentín Paniagua leads transition government.

2001: Alejandro Toledo is elected president.

2003-2004: Calls for Toledo's resignation heighten as Peru's largest union, the General Confederation of Workers, holds nationwide strikes.

2006: Fujimori, en route to Peru to run for president, is detained and jailed in Chile with human rights violation charges. Alan García is reelected president.

2007: An 8.0 earthquake hits the Ica region.

2009: After being successfully extradited and taken to trial, Fujimori is sentenced to 25 years imprisonment.

the base for Inca architecture nearly a thousand years later.

Though influences from the Chavín and Tiahuanaco had spread throughout Peru's highlands, the **Huari** culture (A.D. 600–1100) was the first in South America to establish a true empire. They also built the first well-populated cities, like their capital, Huari, north of Ayacucho. This capital covered nearly 300 hectares with aqueducts, warehouses, temples, and elaborate mausoleums for storing mummies. Archaeologists believe 70,000 people lived here comfortably.

Around A.D. 650 the Huari spread south toward the Tihuanaco culture near Lake Titicaca and Cusco, where they built the huge walled city of **Pikillacta.** The city spreads across 47 hectares of rolling grasslands and contains a maze of walled stone enclosures of the city and elaborate stone aqueducts. In the south, near Arequipa, the Huari built the remarkable stone fortress of **Cerro Baúi** atop a sheer-sided mesa. The Huari spread as far north as the edge of the Moche capital near present-day Trujillo and built a walled city near Huamachuco, in the highlands above Trujillo.

By the time the empire faded around A.D. 900, the Huari had left an indelible pattern of organization over Peru that would be repeated in larger scale by the Inca.

THE KINGDOMS OF THE LATE HORIZON

Once again, as happened after the Chavín culture, Peru splintered into various independent kingdoms after the fall of the Huari. The most important of these were spread along the coast and included the Chimú, Sicán, and Ica-Chincha cultures.

The **Chimú** built their mud city, Chan Chan, north of Trujillo and a short distance from the adobe stepped platforms built earlier by the Moche. Chan Chan is the largest city ever built by Peru's pre-Hispanic cultures, and its walled plazas, passageways, temples, and gardens spread over nearly 20 square kilometers. Over time, the kingdom would spread along the coast of Peru from Chancay, a valley

north of Lima, to the present-day border with Ecuador.

As the Chimú were flourishing, other descendants of the Moche culture known as the **Sicán** were building adobe pyramids at Batán Grande, farther north near Chiclayo. Discoveries of royal Sicán tombs there in 1991 revealed a wealth of gold masks, scepters, and ceremonial knives, along with elegant jewelry made from spondylus shell imported from Ecuador. After a devastating El Niño flood destroyed the center, the Sicán began building even larger pyramids a bit farther north at Túcume, which remains an enigmatic and largely unexcavated site today. By 1350, the Sicán culture was conquered by the Chimú.

Peru's south coast was dominated by the **Ica-Chincha** kingdom, which spread along Peru's southern desert valleys. This culture developed elaborate aqueducts for bringing water from the mountains under the desert floor. The ceremonial center of La Centinela, close to Chincha, was an adobe complex painted with sparkling white gypsum and decorated with ornamental friezes.

During this time, other cultures flourished throughout the highlands. The largest of these was the **Chachapoya,** a mysterious federation of city-states that spread across the cloud forests of northeastern Peru. The Chachapoya's most celebrated city is Kuélap, a stone citadel perched atop a sheer limestone bluff, but there are dozens of other major city sites.

Other cultures included the **Caxamarca** near present-day Cajamarca, the **Huanca** and **Chancas** in the central highlands, and the **Colla** and **Lupaca** near Lake Titicaca. One of these groups, almost too small to mention, was a diminutive tribe of highlanders in the Cusco area known as the **Inca.**

THE INCA EMPIRE

The Inca empire (referred to in Quechua as the Tahuantinsuyo, or "Four Corners") and its origins are obscured by myth. Historians believe that Manco Cápac, the first Inca leader, began his rule around A.D. 1200. For more than two centuries the Inca developed slowly in the

Cusco area, until 1438, when the neighboring Chancas tribe threatened to overrun their city. Though Inca Viracocha fled the city, his son Inca Yupanqui beat back the Chancas, took over from his disgraced father, and changed his name to Pachacútec, the "Shaker of the Earth." He launched the meteoric rise of the Inca empire, which within a century would stretch for more than 4,000 kilometers from southern Chile to northern Ecuador and include huge chunks of Bolivia and Argentina as well. Pachacútec was also responsible for much of the Inca's monumental architecture, including the fortress of Sacsayhuamán and, in the Sacred Valley, Pisac and Ollantaytambo. Historians also believe he built Machu Picchu, which may have been a *llacta* or administrative center.

Though the Inca are known for their fine stonework, their greatest accomplishment was the organization of their empire. Cusco was actually smaller than other capitals of pre-Hispanic Peru, including Tiahuanaco, Huari, and Chan Chan. But the Inca imperial city was at the center of a paved road network that led throughout the empire. Inca runners known as *chasquis* would run along these roads carrying messages recorded in *quipus,* knotted bundles of string that store information. The *chasqui* would run at near-sprint speed until reaching a *tambo* or rest house, at which point a new Inca runner would continue. In this way, *quipus* recording harvests, weather, population data, and numerous other statistics could pass from Quito to Cusco in a few days.

As the Inca expanded they built a network of satellite centers that allowed them to support their far-flung conquests. Like most everything in the Inca world, these miniature cities were divided into *hanan* (upper) and *hurin* (lower) parts. The cookie-cutter pattern, which can be seen all over Peru, included one or two plazas; an *ushnu,* a stone-made platform where ceremonies took place; an *acllahuasi,* a compound for the chosen women of the Inca; a *kallanka,* a large hall; and *colcas,* or grain storehouses.

The Inca offered rich economic and cultural benefits to neighboring cultures that submitted peacefully to their rule. When the Ica and Chincha lordships were integrated into the empire, the Inca helped build a vast aqueduct near present-day Chincha that is still used. Though the Inca changed the names of places they conquered and encouraged the spread of their religion and language, they accepted a wide degree of cultural diversity. Spanish chroniclers such as Pedro Cieza de León were impressed with the tremendous variety of languages and native dress in Cusco at the time of the conquest. The Inca also behaved brutally to those who opposed them. After waging a long war against the Chachapoya, the Inca deported half the population to other parts of the empire as part of the forced-labor scheme known as *mita.*

Pachacútec's son and grandson, Túpac Yupanqui and Huayna Cápac, spent most of their lives abroad, extending the Inca empire to its farthest limits. Huayna Cápac, born in Tumipampa (present-day Cuenca, Ecuador) died in 1527 during a smallpox epidemic that devastated Peru's population and was probably spread by the Spaniards, who had set foot on the northernmost fringe of the Inca empire during a preliminary trip in 1526. His sudden death led to a devastating civil war between his two sons, Huáscar and Atahualpa, which had just ended when the Spaniards began their march from Tumbes.

SPANISH CONQUEST

Francisco Pizarro and his men rode through desert and into the Andes and found Atahualpa and an army of 80,000 Inca soldiers at Cajamarca. Atahualpa had just crushed the forces of his half-brother Huáscar and was returning, jubilant and victorious, to his home city of Quito.

The Spaniards invited Atahualpa to a meeting the next day in Cajamarca's square and planned a bold ambush. Firing their arquebuses and charging with their horses and lances, the Spaniards sparked a massive panic, killed at least 7,000 Inca soldiers, and took Atahualpa hostage. The Inca offered to pay a ransom that, when melted down six months later, amounted to an astounding 6,100 kilograms of 22-karat gold and 11,820 kilograms of good silver. The Spaniards executed Atahualpa anyway.

The Spaniards achieved their successes over far superior Inca forces not only because of their guns, dynamite, steel, and horses but also because Pizarro understood how to play Inca politics. After Atahualpa's death, the Spaniards befriended Manco Inca, another son of Huayna Cápac, and declared him the new leader of the Inca empire. Manco Inca did not remain a docile puppet for long, however, after the Spaniards sacked Cusco for all of its gold and raped the wives of Inca nobles. After the gold was gone, Francisco Pizarro left Cusco and headed for the coast to found Lima, which would soon become the capital of the newly declared Spanish Viceroyalty of Peru.

By 1536 Manco Inca had launched a rebellion and laid siege to Cusco with an estimated army of 100,000 soldiers. Against overwhelming odds, the Spaniards routed the Inca from their fortress of Sacsayhuamán during a week of constant fighting. Manco Inca repelled an army of Spaniards at Ollantaytambo in the Sacred Valley before retreating to the jungle of Vilcabamba. For the next 35 years, the Inca would use this jungle stronghold to continue their resistance against the Spaniards until the last Inca leader, Túpac Amaru, was captured and executed in 1572.

Just after the Inca rebellion, the Spaniards themselves erupted into civil war after differences arose between Francisco Pizarro and his junior partner, Diego de Almagro. After a series of bloody clashes, Pizarro's forces won out over the *almagrista* faction in 1538, and Pizarro shocked the king in Spain by executing Almagro. A few years later, Pizarro himself was murdered by a group of *almagristas* that included Almagro's son.

THREE CENTURIES OF VICEROYALTY

Cusco became a center of religious art during the viceroyalty but otherwise fell out of the spotlight after the conquest as the Spaniards turned their attention to mines. In a cynical use of Inca tradition for Spanish ends, Viceroy Francisco de Toledo in 1574 legalized the Inca's old labor scheme of *mita* in order to force huge numbers of Indians to work at the Potosí silver mine, in present-day Bolivia, and the Santa Bárbara mercury mine near Huancavelica. Far from home, thousands of Indians perished while working in virtual slavery at these mines.

Indians in other parts of Peru were not being treated much better. Some were forced to relocate to *reducciones* or new settlements that allowed the Spaniards to better tax the Indians and convert them to Christianity. Rich farmland was divided into *encomiendas* and all the Indians living on it became slaves to the Spanish owner, known as the *encomendero*. Other times Indians were herded into sweatshops (*obrajes*), where they made textiles and other objects for export under prisonlike conditions.

Given the abuse, it is not surprising that an uprising spread across Peru in the late 18th century. The leader of the 1780–1781 revolt was Túpac Amaru II, who claimed to be a direct descendant of the last Inca, Túpac Amaru. After a year-long rebellion, the Spaniards finished off Túpac Amaru II as they had his ancestor two centuries before: He was garroted in Cusco's main square, and then his body was ripped apart by teams of horses pulling in opposite directions.

INDEPENDENCE

After nearly three centuries of being administered from Spain, the native-born people of the Peruvian viceroyalty began to itch for independence. News of the American revolution in 1776 and French revolution in 1789 filtered to Peru and encouraged a groundswell of reform that was inspired by the European Enlightenment.

The descendants of Europeans born in Peru, known as *criollos*, were increasingly resentful of the privileges according to Spaniards, or *españoles*, who held all the powerful positions in the viceroyalty. Colonial society was rigidly classified into a hierarchy that attempted to make sense of, and control, the uncontrollable mixing between races in colonial Peru. The main categories included *mestizo* (European-Indian), *mulato* (European-African), *negro* (African), *zambo* (Indian-African), and *indio* (Indian). Dozens of labels were applied to all the possible combinations and proportions of different ethnic mixtures, and some categories even included bizarre animal names such as *lobo* (wolf), which was used to describe certain types of *mulatos*. Despite the apparent rigidity, recent scholarly work has revealed that racial lines in the viceroyalty were surprisingly fluid and had more to do with wealth than skin color. Wealthy *mestizos* were usually considered *criollos*, for instance.

When Napoleon forced Spain's King Charles IV to abdicate in 1808, independence movements erupted across South America. By 1820, the last bastion of Spanish control was Peru, which for centuries had served as the main Spanish port and administrative center for South America. After liberating Chile, Argentine general José de San Martín routed the royalist forces from Lima in 1821 and proclaimed the symbolic independence of Peru. But he ceded control over the independence struggle to Venezuelan general Simón Bolívar, whose troops won two separate battles in Peru's central highlands in 1824 against the last strongholds of Spanish forces.

Bolívar envisioned a grand union of South American states known as Gran Colombia, which was modeled on the United States. After serving as Peru's first president for two years, he returned to Bogotá, Colombia, in a last-ditch attempt to hold the federation together. Bolívar's scheme fell apart as the former colonies bickered among themselves, and Peru plunged into a half century of chaos. During the four decades following Bolívar's departure, more than 35 presidents came and went.

Despite the chaos, Peru's rising class of merchants found new opportunities for making money besides mining. The biggest business was guano, the huge piles of bird droppings that covered the islands off Peru's coast. This natural fertilizer fetched exorbitant prices in Europe. The guano boom helped finance the ambitious project, spearheaded by American entrepreneur Henry Meiggs in 1870, to build a railroad line into the steep valleys above Lima to La Oroya mine. Following the abolishment of slavery in the mid-19th century, hacienda owners in the north began importing large numbers of Asian indentured workers, or coolies, to work on cotton and sugar plantations.

Despite all the abundance, Peru was devastated by the War of the Pacific against Chile (1879–1883), during which time Chilean armies sacked most of Peru's major cities. After surrendering, Peru was forced to cede an entire southern province to Chile—Tarapacá—which contained valuable fields of nitrate, used to make fertilizer. After the war, Peru plunged into bankruptcy and had to negotiate with its British creditors, who agreed to forgive the debt in exchange for 200 million tons of guano and a 66-year concession over the country's railroads. The British-owned Peruvian Corporation was set up in Arequipa in 1890 and built the current railroads that lead to Arequipa and Cusco. British families poured into Arequipa at this time to grab a share of the booming alpaca wool business. Following the completion of the Panama Canal in 1904, U.S. investors set up a series of mines and factories in Peru, including the Cerro de Pasco mine in the highlands above Lima.

THE 20TH CENTURY

As foreign investors increased their grip over Peru's main industries, worker dissent began to simmer following the October Revolution in Russia. In 1924, exiled political leader Víctor Raúl Haya de la Torre founded the Alianza Popular Revolucionaria Americana—APRA, a workers' party that continues to exert a tremendous influence over Peruvian politics. When Haya lost the 1931 elections, his supporters accused the government of fraud and attacked a military outpost in Trujillo, killing 10 soldiers. In response the Peruvian military trucked an estimated 1,000 APRA supporters out to the sands of Chan Chan and executed them in mass firing squads.

Peru's economic development in the mid-20th century was hampered by the hacienda system of land ownership inherited from the days of the viceroyalty. The independence movement had passed leadership from the *españoles* to the *criollos*, but otherwise Peru's economic structure remained the same—a minority of Peruvians, of direct European descent, still controlled the bulk of Peru's land and wealth. As Peru moved from an agricultural economy to an industrial one, campesinos flocked to Lima in search of a better life and built sprawling shantytowns, or *pueblos jóvenes,* around the city. Pressure for land reform began to grow.

Fernando Belaúnde, architect and politician, was president of Peru during much of the 1960s and instituted a few moderate reforms, but he was overthrown in 1968 by General Juan Velasco, who despite being a military man launched a series of radical, left-wing reforms that stunned Peru's white elite and transformed the Peruvian economy. He expropriated nearly all of Peru's haciendas and transferred the land to newly formed worker cooperatives. Velasco kicked foreign investors out of the country and nationalized their fish-meal factories, banks, oil companies, and mines. He introduced food subsidies for urban slum dwellers and, in a profound gesture of recognition to Peru's Indians, made Quechua the official second language of Peru.

Velasco's restructuring was so rapid and ill-planned that nearly all of Peru's major industries plunged to new lows and the country entered a severe economic crisis. Velasco was overthrown—some historians assure the CIA was behind the coup—and replaced by another pro-U.S. military leader, Francisco Morales Bermúdez, who attempted to control the economic chaos of the 1970s. Amid widespread strikes in the late 1970s, APRA politician Haya de la Torre headed a constituent assembly that finally secured full suffrage for all Peruvian citizens and the return to democracy.

TWENTY YEARS OF POLITICAL VIOLENCE

Peru's first full democratic election in 12 years, in 1980, coincided with the first actions of

an artistic rendering of a Shining Path terrorist

Sendero Luminoso (Shining Path), a terrorist group based on Maoist ideology that rose out of the country's economic chaos and social inequity. Shining Path rose alongside the smaller **Movimiento Revolucionario Túpac Amaru,** MRTA for short. Both organizations terrorized Peru's countryside over the next two decades and began receiving significant financial support from the cocaine business, which had just begun to grow rapidly in the upper Huallaga Valley.

Between 1980 and 2000, Andean villagers were frequently caught in the crossfire between these terrorist organizations and the Peruvian army. The Shining Path would force the villagers to give them food or supply information, and the army in retaliation would massacre the whole village, or vice versa. People in the city were largely uninterested and protected from the countryside war and were shocked to hear the official results of the Truth and Reconciliation Commission's report in 2003. More than 70,000 people were killed during the terrorism years, and 75 percent of them were Quechua highlanders. Half were killed by Shining Path, a third by government forces (police and armed forces), and the rest are so far unattributed.

The worst massacres of the Shining Path were between 1983 and 1984, the same year that Latin American economies collapsed under a debt crisis and that Peru's north was devastated by El Niño rains. The APRA candidate, Alan García, at age 35, won the 1985 elections because he offered a jubilant, hopeful future for Peruvians. He promptly shocked the international finance community by announcing that Peru would only be making a small portion of its international debt payments. García's announcement sparked a two-year spending spree followed by Peru's worst economic collapse ever, with hyperinflation so extreme that restaurants were forced to increase their menu prices three times each day. Peru's struggling middle class saw their savings disappear overnight.

The García administration unsuccessfully sought a military solution to the growing terrorism, allegedly committing human rights violations that are still under investigation. The most important cases include the Accomarca massacre (1985), where 47 peasants were executed by the Peruvian armed forces; the Cayara massacre (1988) in which some 30 were killed and dozens disappeared; and the summary execution of around 200 inmates during prison riots in Lurigancho, El Frontón Island, and Santa Bárbara in 1986. An estimated 1,600 forced disappearances took place during García's presidency.

Peruvian novelist Mario Vargas Llosa led a series of middle- and upper-class protests against García's plan to nationalize Peru's banking system. Vargas Llosa appeared likely to win the 1990 election but was defeated at the last minute by Alberto Fujimori, a low-profile university rector of Japanese descent who appealed to Peru's mestizo and Indian voters mainly because he was not part of Lima's elitist white society. Former president García, meanwhile, fled Peru in 2002 under a cloud of allegations of extortion and corruption.

THE FUJIMORI REGIME

Soon after winning the elections, Fujimori reversed his campaign promises and implemented an economic austerity program that had been championed by his opponent, Vargas Llosa. His plan aimed to stimulate foreign investment by slashing trade tariffs and simplifying taxes. Fujimori also began the process of privatizing the state-owned companies that President Velasco had nationalized in the late 1960s–early 1970s. This program, which was nicknamed "Fuji-Shock," caused widespread misery among Peru's poor populations as food prices shot through the roof. Fortunately, the program also sparked an economic recovery. Inflation dropped from 7,650 percent in 1990 to 139 percent in 1991.

After struggling to convince Peru's congress to pass legislation in 1992, Fujimori strained international relations with the United States and other countries after he dissolved the congress in his famous *autogolpe* or "self-coup." That same year, Peru's level of terror reached a high point when Shining Path detonated two car bombs in Tarata street, right in the heart of the middle-class Miraflores neighborhood, killing 25 people and injuring more than 250.

That same year, Fujimori's popularity shot through the roof when the Peruvian military captured both Shining Path leader Abimael Guzmán and the main leaders of the MRTA. The economy began to pick up and, by 1995, was one of the fastest-growing in the world. Fujimori launched a new constitution and recovered international credibility by reopening Peru's congress.

Having tackled Peru's twin nightmares of terrorism and inflation, Fujimori was riding a wave of public support and easily beat former U.N. secretary-general Javier Pérez de Cuéllar in the 1995 elections. The following year, 14 MRTA terrorists led by Néstor Cerpa took 800 prominent hostages after storming a cocktail party at Lima's Japanese ambassador's residence. After releasing most of the hostages, the terrorists held 72 prisoners and maintained a tense standoff with the military for four months, until April 1997. As the situation grew desperate, Fujimori authorized Peruvian commandos to tunnel under the embassy and take it by surprise. The operation was an amazing success. One hostage died during the operation—of a heart attack—and one military commando was killed under fire. Except for human rights organizations, most Peruvians raised few objections to the fact that all 14 MRTA members were shot to death—including the ones who had surrendered.

Fujimori ran for a controversial third term in 2000, even though he himself had changed the constitution to allow presidents to run for only one reelection. Once again, Fujimori fell out of favor with the international community when he strong-armed his way into the elections against economist Alejandro Toledo. After alleging vote fraud in the main election, Toledo refused to run in the May 2000 runoff election, and the international community also threatened sanctions. Fujimori went ahead with the election anyway and was, despite the flawed process, elected president.

A huge scandal broke in September, when hundreds of videos were leaked to the media. The videos showed Fujimori's head of intelligence, Vladimiro Montesinos, bribing a huge cross-section of elite Peruvian society, including generals, journalists, politicians, and business executives. The resulting investigation uncovered more than *US$40 million* in bribes paid to subvert the three key institutions of democracy: the judiciary, the legislature, and the media.

Montesinos's grip on the media was so tight that he even held daily "news meetings" with their editors to formulate news headlines and decide which stories should be covered. In the judiciary branch, 21 top justices, including members of the Supreme Court, received bribes. Montesinos also bribed a range of politicians, even those within Fujimori's own party, for as much as US$10,000–20,000 per month. Others received cars or houses. To make matters worse, Peruvian investigators also concluded that both Fujimori and Montesinos amassed huge personal fortunes through extortion, arms trafficking, and the drug trade.

Fujimori conveniently resigned from the presidency, via fax, while on a state visit to Japan. Back in Peru, an international warrant for his arrest was issued because of his involvement in paramilitary massacres of left-wing political activists in the early 1990s. In 2005, when Fujimori left Japan to return to Peru and launch a campaign for the presidency, he was arrested in his stopover city of Santiago, Chile. He was held for six months in jail, on charges of corruption and human rights' violations, and was extradited to Peru. At the end of a 15-month trial, Fujimori was sentenced in April 2009 to 25 years in prison for ordering security forces to kill and kidnap civilians.

Montesinos was also arrested in Venezuela after being on the run for eight months and is in a high-security prison near Lima—one he helped design to house Peru's most feared criminals. About US$250 million in his funds have been recovered from bank accounts in the Cayman Islands, Panama, and Switzerland. Following Fujimori's departure, congressman Valentín Paniagua became interim president before Alejandro Toledo was elected in 2001.

RETURN TO DEMOCRACY

Toledo's political inexperience and lack of strong leadership caused his popularity to plunge among Peruvian voters, many of whom missed the dramatic results and bold programs of Fujimori. Toledo, however, did establish a stable and growing economy, which is precisely what newly elected President Alan García, with more charm and political experience than his predecessor, is out to maintain. García barely won the 2006 election against the populist Ollanta Humala, who was inspired if not financially supported by Venezuelan president Hugo Chávez. García's return to presidency was a result of "voting against" Ollanta, a turn of events not many Peruvians were happy with. Nevertheless, Peru's economic growth has favored him, despite the cases of corruption in his political party that have been exposed by the local media.

Government and Economy

President Alan García, in office for a second time after serving as the nation's leader from 1985 to 1990, has continued to develop the political and economic policies of his predecessor Alejandro Toledo. The result has been a bursting economy and a relatively conservative but democratic and stable political atmosphere. This is quite a contrast to the authoritarian years of the Fujimori regime, 1990–2000.

Fujimori dissolved Peru's bicameral legislative system during his *autogolpe* in April 1992 and launched a new constitution with a single congress with 120 seats. Fujimori's new constitution allowed the president to run for two consecutive terms, a law that was changed after he resigned. In the current system, the president appoints a council of ministers, which is presided over by the prime minister. Apart from the president, Peruvian voters also elect two vice presidents. Voting is compulsory between the ages of 18 and 70, and those who do not vote can be fined. Members of the military were not allowed to vote in the past, but now they can.

The weak point of Peru's democracy is its judicial branch, which is rife with corruption. It is still common to read in the media about scandals involving judges who have been bribed to free prisoners or make a favorable ruling. The country's top courts include a 16-member supreme court and a constitutional tribunal. Each of Peru's regions also has a superior court that serves as a court of appeals for the lower courts. There is a huge backlog of cases in the Peruvian court system, and temporary courts have been set up.

© CAROLINE BOES

A typical elementary school classroom in Peru, such as this one in Ollantaytambo, has around 40 students per class.

SACRED LEAF, WHITE GOLD

Peru continues to be the second-largest producer of cocaine worldwide, second only to neighboring Colombia. Peru's cocaine industry rakes in anywhere between US$300 and US$600 million per year in under-the-table money and employs an estimated 200,000 Peruvians, mainly in remote jungle areas of the country. And despite long-standing efforts of both the Peruvian government and the U.S. Drug Enforcement Agency (DEA), Peru's cocaine industry continues to grow. The 2009 report of the International Narcotics Control Board states that illicit coca bush cultivation increased in Peru for the third year in a row, especially in the Apurímac Valley area in southern Peru. In 2009, Peruvian authorities dismantled over 1,200 coca paste laboratories – the highest number since 2000 – and 19 laboratories manufacturing cocaine hydrochloride.

The truth is, coca – scientifically known as *Erythroxylum coca* – has not always been a curse for Peruvians. Probably best known in the world through cocaine, its most popular derived product, the plant has been used for thousands of years in the Andean world, mainly for its medicinal properties and religious significance. Archaeologists have found supplies of coca leaves in mummies 3,000 years old. The Moche might have been the first to chew the leaves, a custom spread widely afterwards by the Inca, who decided that planting coca should be a state monopoly, limiting the use of it to nobles. During the colonial period, Phillip II of Spain recognized the drug as an essential product for the well-being of the Andean inhabitants but urged missionaries to end its religious use.

Viewed as having a divine origin, coca has been an extremely important part of the religious cosmogony in the Andean world – from southern Colombia all the way down to northern Argentina and Chile – since pre-Hispanic times. Coca leaves play a crucial part in offerings made by shamans to the *apus* (mountain spirits), Inti (the sun god), and the Pachamama (mother earth). Leaves are also often read in a form of divination by *curanderos*, in similar ways to reading tea leaves in other cultures. They are also placed inside coffins at burials.

But coca is also used in various everyday activities. Men chew leaves as they work in the fields, and women use it to ease the pain while giving birth. When a young man is about to ask a woman to marry him, he first must present a bag of leaves to his future father-in-law. Coca leaves have been used for thousands of years as a stimulant to overcome fatigue, hunger, and thirst. Once you arrive at Cusco's airport, you will likely be greeted with a hot cup of *mate de coca,* an infusion made from the leaf, considered particularly effective against altitude sickness, known as *soroche.*

The effects of the coca leaf were discovered in Europe during the 19th century, when Albert Niemann (a promising PhD student of Friedrich Wöhler, one of the most celebrated chemists of the century) was able to isolate the active constituent of coca, which he baptized as "cocaine." But it was Paolo Mantegazza, an Italian doctor, who after experimenting with coca leaves in 1859 wrote, "one starts to become more and more isolated from the exterior world, and one is plunged into a consciousness of blissful pleasure, feeling oneself animated with overabundant life." Angelo Mariani, a Corsican chemist who lived in Paris, saw coca's potential to make serious money, in 1863 making a wine with the coca leaves that he named Vin Mariani, a pleasant-tasting alcoholic brew with a real edge.

The success of the product inspired a number of wine imitations in the United States, including one that was converted into a carbonated soft drink known as Coca-Cola after the temperance movement hit Atlanta, Georgia, in 1885. By 1903 a public outcry over the ill effects of cocaine forced the company to remove cocaine from its beverage. What is not generally known is that Coca-Cola today continues to use flavoring from coca leaves, which have been "decocainized."

Making and taking cocaine today remains a nasty business. Villagers in the impoverished Huallaga Valley and other areas of Peru grow the plant because they can get as much as US$2 per kilo for the leaves, many times more than they would receive for selling wheat, potatoes, or corn. Cultivating coca takes a lot out of the soil, and fields therefore have to be changed constantly. The Huallaga Valley, once covered in cloud forest, is nearly denuded and covered with a patchwork of eroding fields.

The process of making cocaine is even worse. The leaves must first be crushed underfoot and soaked in water to remove their essence. This water is then mixed with kerosene and other toxic chemicals and stirred until a white substance floats to the top. This substance, known as *pasta básica* or *bruta*, is

further refined to make pure cocaine, known officially as cocaine hydrochloride. About 400 kilograms of coca leaves produces one kilo of cocaine. The villagers who help stir the *pasta básica* can readily be identified by their scarred arms, which are burned pink by the toxic chemicals.

The cocaine industry has also wreaked havoc on Peru's cities. Though cocaine is widely available in Peru and used often by young Peruvians, the real problem lies in the dusty shantytowns, or *pueblos jóvenes*, on the outskirts of Lima. Because cocaine is too expensive, teenagers smoke cheap cigarettes made from the unrefined *pasta básica*, which is different from crack cocaine but equally as powerful. People become addicted immediately to the US$0.30 cigarettes, and, like crack smokers in the United States, their lives head downhill fast.

Experts say that the collapse of the Medellin and Calí cartels in the mid-1990s probably boosted Peru's cocaine business by fragmenting the industry and allowing players who were in the shadows to grab new market share. According to recent reports of the Peruvian army, one of the new leaders in the cocaine industry is the FARC, the Revolutionary Armed Forces of Colombia, which began cultivating coca in northern Peru near the Colombian border, and which is also behind a dramatic rise in Peru's cultivation of poppy, used to make opium and heroin. Remnants of the Shining Path, Peru's notorious terrorist group, which was crushed in the mid-1990s, are also reported to be involved in trafficking in the Apurímac Valley.

People and Culture

Even before the Spaniards arrived, Peru was covered by a patchwork of diverse cultures created by Peru's extreme geography. Valleys on the coast are separated by long stretches of barren desert. The canyons and peaks of the high Andes created such a degree of isolation that one anthropologist likened them to an archipelago. But the most culturally diverse area of Peru is the Amazon, where at least 65 different ethnic groups live today.

Peru's population, especially on the coast, is an exotic cocktail of world cultures that have been mixing for nearly five centuries. The mixing of Peruvian culture began with the Inca's forced-labor scheme, *mita,* where rebellious tribes were moved to other parts of the empire where they would cause less trouble. The Spaniards continued *mita* and moved highlanders long distances to work in different mines.

The mixing between the Spanish and Peruvian cultures began the moment the conquistadores landed on the shores of Peru, giving rise to Peru's first mestizo population. The cocktail of racial mixes got richer when African slaves were imported to Peru during the viceroyalty. After slaves were freed in the mid-19th century, large numbers of Chinese and Japanese coolies were brought to work in plantations and on the railroad lines from 1850 to 1920. There were also waves of Italian and Palestinian immigrants, and a pocket of German and Austrian colonists established themselves in the jungle at Oxapampa, in the Chanchamayo area. From the 1960s onward, huge waves of immigrants from the Andes settled in the shantytowns around Lima, especially during the height of Shining Path terrorism during the 1980s.

© MYLENE D'AURIOL, PROMPERU

The Q'eros people, who live in the Cordillera Vilcanota outside of Cusco, are struggling to maintain the ancient ways of the Inca despite contact with tourism.

DEMOGRAPHICS

Peru's population today is around 28 million and growing about 1.6 percent each year. Nearly half the people, or 45 percent, are of indigenous blood and reside in the Peruvian highlands. Of the remaining population, 37 percent are mestizo and 15 percent are of European descent. The remaining 3 percent of the population comprises those of African, Japanese, and Chinese descent and also includes a tiny pocket of 250,000 Amazon natives who are divided into 65 ethnic groups. There remains a cultural and economic divide, passed down from colonial times, between the upper class of European descent and the middle and lower classes of mestizos and Indians. But Peru's racial dividing lines have, even since the colonial times, been based more on economics than skin color. Marriage certificates from the 18th century, for instance, reveal that affluent mestizos were automatically considered *criollos* because of their wealth. In the same way, a full-blooded Indian in today's society goes from being an *indio* to a mestizo the moment he or she abandons native dress and puts on western clothing.

During Peru's economic growth of the mid-1990s the average wages of Peruvians also increased. The Fujimori government built new schools throughout Peru's impoverished regions, and the illiteracy rate has dropped below 10 percent (though it is still about 13 percent for women). Medical care also spread, dropping infant mortality rates from 57 per 1,000 births in 1991 to 31 in 2006. An estimated 98 percent of all infants in Peru now receive immunizations.

Despite these advances, Peru remains a crushingly poor country. More than half of Peru's population, or 51 percent, live beneath the poverty line of US$54 per month, and 24 percent live in extreme poverty, earning under US$32 per month. Nearly 40 percent of the people live in the informal economy—that is, they live in isolated country hamlets or disenfranchised city slums and eke out a living outside of government taxes and services.

a woman in indigenous clothing in Peru's Sacred Valley

© GABRIELLA HOLLAND

LANGUAGE

Peru's official language is Spanish, though about four million people in Peru's highland population speak Quechua, the language of the Inca, also known as *runa simi.* Among Quechua speakers, there is a huge range of variations depending where they are located. These mini dialects have grown as a result of the isolating effects of Peru's extreme geography. In the Lake Titicaca area, there is a smaller group of Peruvians who speak Aymara, the language of an ethnic group that spreads into Bolivia. In the Amazon lives 11 percent of Peru's population, divided into 65 ethnic groups and about 14 linguistic families.

RELIGION

The Spanish conquest dotted Peru with magnificent cathedrals, a plethora of churches, and a long-lasting and also certainly conflictive relationship with **Catholicism.** About 90 percent of the current population consider themselves Catholic. Although that number is far from the actual number of practicing parishioners,

© GABRIELLA HOLLAND

The religious beliefs of Peru's Quechua-speaking people are a complex blend of Catholicism and the millennia-old spiritual beliefs of the Inca, Huari, and other Andean cultures.

it does indicate the connection Peruvians feel toward the religion, more by tradition than by real practice. Festivals like Lima's day of Santa Rosa mean a citywide holiday, and the day of San Blas invites horns and processions in Cusco.

Catholicism, though, is a relatively recent addition to Peru's long list of religions. Peru's first civilization began around 2000 B.C., and it, along with the country's other major civilizations, was based on a set of unifying religious beliefs. These beliefs often incorporated **nature worship.** Deities like the sun, the ocean, the mountains, and mother earth appear in the imagery of several successive cultures. Representations of serpents, felines, and birds also make repeated appearances in pre-Hispanic religious iconography. Serpents symbolize the ground, felines the human life, and birds (often in the form of eagles) the air or gods. The religion of the **Chavín** culture, which existed 4000 years ago, incorporated that series of deities. Northern Peru's **Moche** culture did as well, but, unlike the Chavín, the

Moche were clear to distinguish between the spiritual world and the everyday world. The **Chimu** worshipped the sun, moon, and ocean, and were clear to separate the secular and nonsecular worlds. In its pottery, the southern Nasca culture depicted felines, orcas, anthropomorphized birds, and serpentine creatures. And the **Inca** gave offerings to the surrounding mountains, the bright sun, and fortifying Pachamama, the mother earth.

As cultures rose and fell, and even when the Spanish conquered the Inca empire, Peru's religions tended to adapt, fluctuate, and blend. The Inca were known for allowing their conquered cultures to continue their own religious practices as long as they also followed Inca religion. When the Spanish arrived and imposed Catholicism, the Inca quietly integrated their imagery. A grand Last Supper painting in Cusco's cathedral shows Jesus eating a guinea pig.

Nearly 500 years after the Spanish conquest, this fusion of religious beliefs continues to define Peru's spiritual and religious customs, and the subject is a draw for many tourists. In areas like Cusco and Lake Titicaca, the traditional mountain cultures continue to use **shamans** to bless their homes and purify their spirits. In turn, travelers contract with shamans to perform offering or cleansing ceremonies. The Sacred Valley is known for its **energy centers,** and people come from around the world to meditate there. In the jungle, ayahuasca is an essential part of sacred ceremonies and again, curious travelers can contract with experts to help them experience it.

On the flip side, completely new religions are making headway. **Protestant groups, Jehovah's Witnesses, Mormons,** and **Adventist groups** have started small but vigilant communities throughout the country. If history holds true, these new groups should blend with the old to offer an increasingly diverse religious practice.

FOOD

One thing Peruvians are undeniably proud of is their food. Peru's biodiversity offers the country with a generous and varied amount of fresh ingredients. These include a range of seafood, sweet corn, *ajíes* (peppers) and tubers— of the 3,000 varieties of potatoes documented in Peru, only 40 are eaten—exotic fruits, succulent river fish, palm hearts, and wild game.

The Spanish conquest of Peru brought together two great culinary cultures of the 16th century: the Mediterranean cooking techniques and the Andean ingredients. When Pizarro's men landed in Peru, they had their first taste of corn, tomatoes, avocados, potatoes, peanuts, alpaca meat, and blistering *ají* peppers. The Spaniards brought olive oil, lime, and garlic to the table and shortly thereafter created a local supply of lamb, beef, pork, wheat, rice, and sugar.

Things got even more complex with the arrival of Africans and North African Arabs during the viceroyalty, Chinese coolies in the mid-19th century, and successive waves of Italian and Japanese immigrants. Such a succulent mix in the pot created a bewildering range of dishes and entire subsets of Peruvian cuisine, such as *chifa,* a mixture of Cantonese and local *criollo* cooking.

Peruvian cuisine is still evolving and is difficult to classify into pat categories. Because Peruvian cooks work only with ingredients at hand, there do tend to be styles of Peruvian cooking separated by geography. Here are some highlights you should not miss.

Peru's coast is known for *comida criolla* or creole cuisine, which is based mainly on a huge range of seafood, including *corvina* (sea bass), *lenguado* (sole), *cangrejo* (crab), *camarones* (freshwater shrimp), *calamar* (squid), *choros* (mussels), and *conchas negras* (black scallops).

One of the more famous dishes is *cebiche:* chunks of raw fish marinated in lime juice, spiced with *ají,* and served with sliced red onions, slices of sweet potato, and *choclo* (boiled maize kernels) or *cancha* (roasted maize kernels). A delicious variation of *cebiche* is *tiradito,* which can be easily explained as a fish carpaccio topped with a *ají* and *rocoto* sauce over the cuts. Fish fillets can be served in a variety of ways, including *sudado* (steamed), *a la chorillana* (basted with onion, tomato, and white wine) or *a lo macho* (fried with yellow peppers or *ají amarillo*).

Peru's Andean cuisine stands out for a range of meats, *choclos,* high-altitude grains such as *kiwicha* and quinoa, and a huge variety of more than 200 edible tubers, including potatoes, freeze-dried *chuño* (actually dehydrated potatoes), and tubers like *olluco* and *oca.* The high point of mountain cooking is *pachamanca,* which means "earth oven" in Quechua and consists of a variety of meats, tubers, corn, beans, and native herbs roasted underground with red-hot rocks. Andean restaurants often serve *trucha,* which is fried mountain trout, and *cuy* (guinea pig), either roasted (in Cusco), stewed (in Huaraz), or fried (in Arequipa).

Soups and broths are widely consumed in the highlands at any time of the day but especially during the early morning. Lamb, beef, hen, or certain parts of these animals are all good to make a tasty broth. For vegetarians a good option is *sopa de quinua,* made with potatoes and quinoa grains. Lastly, make sure to sample *choclo con queso,* which is an ear of steamed corn with a strip of Andean cheese. Gulp it all down with *chicha de jora,* corn beer that can be *fresco* (fresh) or fermented.

In the Amazon jungle, you will have a whole new type of cuisine to sample. At the top of the list are the roasted fillets of succulent jungle fish, including *paiche, doncella,* and *dorado. Patarashca* is fish fillets wrapped in banana leaves and seasoned with spices before being baked over coals. There is also *paca* fish steamed inside a bamboo tube. Iquitos is famous for *juanes,* a rice tamale stuffed with spices, chicken, and rice. A common game meat is *majá,* also called *picuro,* which is a medium-sized rodent that can be grilled, stewed, or fried.

MUSIC AND DANCE

Traditional Peruvian music can be easily divided between *música criolla,* music from the coast, and *música folklórica,* known as music from the mountains and the jungle. The best-known example of the latter is Simon & Garfunkel's 1970s hit "El Cóndor Pasa (If I Could)," arranged from an original song composed by Daniel Alomía Robles in 1913.

The *huayno* is the most popular dance form in Andean music. It originated in Peru as a combination of traditional rural folk music and popular urban dance music. High-pitched vocals are usually accompanied by a variety of instruments, including the *quena* (Andean flute), *charango* (a small mandolin), harp, saxophone and percussion. In the last few decades *huayno* has undergone a huge change with the introduction of electronic instruments, including synthesizers and electric guitars. Nevertheless, the dance form utilizes a distinctive rhythm in which the first beat is stressed, followed by two short beats. The *huayno* is pop music for an audience of millions of listeners across the Andes. Despite constant evolution, its themes remain the pain of love lost and being far from home.

Andean music sounds different from Western music in part because it relies mainly on the pentatonic scale instead of the diatonic scale.

The instruments include different types of *quenas, zampoñas* (double-row panpipes including the *sicus,* which can be as tall as the musician playing it), *tarkas* (squared flutes that produce an eerie sound), and *antaras* (single-row panpipe). There is also a huge range of rattles, bells, and drums, such as the *tambor* and *bombo,* which are made from stretched animal skins. Most of these instruments, as excavations prove, have been used at least 5,000 years.

In the last five centuries Peru's highlanders have incorporated a range of wind and brass instruments, including clarinets, saxophones, trumpets, euphoniums, and tubas. But the most important European contributions were stringed instruments like the violin, the guitar, and the harp, which was transformed into the Andean harp. This instrument looks like a western harp with 36 strings but has a half-conical, boatlike base that gives it a rich, deep sound. The 10-stringed *charango* is about the size of a mandolin and is made from wood or the shell of an armadillo.

In these last 40 years, Peruvian music has evolved rapidly. In the late 1960s and 1970s, the traditional *huayno* fused with the tropical *cumbia.* As a result, *chicha* was born, the iconic music of highland immigrants living in Lima, having in Chacalón y la Nueva Crema the maximum exponent of this genre. Around the same period of time, hundreds of rock-based bands in the jungle were turning to *cumbia,* either *tropical* or *psicodélica.* Legendary bands such as Juaneco y su Combo and Los Mirlos have been revived in U.S. and European compilations and through local bands in Lima, such as Bareto.

HANDICRAFTS

A stroll through any of Miraflores's handicrafts markets will show you the depth and variety of handicrafts in Peru. Weavings, knittings, pottery, jewelry, and carved gourds have made the long haul from the provinces into Lima. Each piece is modern but carries with it a tradition that has existed for centuries.

World-renowned for its textiles, Peru's **weaving** tradition is over 4,000 years old.

Using the wool of alpacas, llamas, and the precious vicuñas, the pre-Columbian cultures wove their stories into textiles. Abstract figures, deities, and colors described the lifestyles of these people, who had no written language. In turn, the quality of the textile and the wool reflected one's social status and power. When the Spanish arrived, they introduced sheep's wool and silk into the custom. Now, contemporary weavers have the advantages of machine-spun yarn and even woven fabrics. While those are undeniably used, there are still plenty of traditional weavers who continue to use natural dyes, drop spindles, and handmade looms.

The weaving culture exists primarily in the mountainous regions of Cusco, Huancayo, and around Lake Titicaca. In these areas, you are likely to see women walking through the streets, toting a basket of wool that they are aptly dropping and spinning into yarn. Guided by memory and years of experience, women then dip the wool into dyes and then thread it into a weaving. The start-to-finish process can take anywhere from a month to several months and, consequently, the minimum going price for a cloth is about US$100.

Knitting is another important aspect of Peru's textile tradition. *Chullos* (hats), *mangas* (arm warmers), *polainas* (leggings), *medias* (socks), and *monederos* (change purses), are all typical products of the Quechua and Aymara cultures. As with weaving, the most prominent knitting cultures live in Lake Titicaca's Isla Taquile, Cusco, and Huancavelica. Although customs change between communities, knitting responsibilities are typically divided between men and women. Women spin the yarn and men knit it into clothing, most often hats.

Ceramics have also played an important historical role. Cultures as ancient as the Chavín left behind ceramic remains, and even later cultures like the Moche, Nasca, and Chimú were renowned for their craftsmanship and unique styles. The **Moche** perfected the skill of capturing human features and emotion; the **Chimú** pottery is recognized for its black surface; and **Nasca** ceramics are particularly prized because of their intricate paintings. When the Spanish

arrived, they introduced a European form of pottery, which has been particularly influential in the designs of Urubamba-based ceramicist **Pablo Seminario.** Ceramics are best seen in the areas of Piura, Cusco, and Ayacucho.

Other important handicrafts, like carved gourds, jewelry, and even instrument-making, are best seen in the mountain areas. Again, Cusco, Ayacucho, and Huancayo make excellent bases to begin your exploring.

LITERATURE

Like the Greeks, the ancient Peruvians had a rich tradition of oral **poetry,** as there were no known writing systems at the time. It consisted of two main poetic forms: *harawis,* a form of lyrical poetry, and *hayllis,* a form of epic poetry. Both forms described the daily life and rituals of the time and were recited by a poet known as the *harawec.*

A variety of 16th-century Spanish chroniclers, most notably **Bernabé Cobo** and **Pedro Cieza de León,** attempted to describe the exotic conditions of the New World through the confining looking glass of the Spanish worldview and lexicon. An entirely different perspective was presented by indigenous writer **Felipe Guamán Poma de Ayala,** whose decision to write the king of Spain, Philip III, blossomed into a 1,179-page letter titled *Nueva Crónica y Buen Gobierno.* The letter was written between 1613 and 1615 but only discovered in the Royal Library of Copenhagen in 1908. Apart from a detailed view of Inca customs, what is most fascinating about this work is the blend of Spanish and Quechua juxtaposed with a series of 400 ink drawings that portray the bloodiest moments of the Spanish conquest, as well as Inca festivities and traditions.

Inca Garcilaso de la Vega (1539–1616) was educated in Cusco as the son of a Spanish conquistador and an Inca princess. He emigrated as a young man to Spain, where he spent the rest of his life writing histories and chronicles of his Inca homeland. His major work, *Comentarios Reales,* written in 1609, is a highly anecdotal and personal view of the Inca empire. Throughout the text Garcilaso employs a variety of rhetorical strategies to ennoble the Inca aristocracy—and in the process, himself—in the eyes of the royal Spanish court. It is the first example of a *mestizo* author from the New World grappling with the complexities of a torn identity.

During the viceroyalty, **theaters** in Lima and Cusco were at the center of the social life of the Peruvian aristocracy. Most of the productions were imported and written by Spain's Golden Age authors, who had no problem being approved by Peru's Catholic censors. Local playwrights were occasionally approved and their works, though innocuous on the surface, often contain subtle critiques of the viceroyalty's racial and political power structure. Scathing **poetic satire** was circulated secretly throughout upper-class Peruvian society and reflected the growing tensions as Peru's creole elite strained against the straitjacket of Spanish rule.

Following the 1821 independence, literary Romanticism took root in Peru, evolving in an entirely different direction from its European counterpart. Instead of a preoccupation with personal identity and freedom, Peru's Romantic writers fell into the task of nation-building and describing what it meant to be Peruvian. Some renowned authors of the period were **Carlos Augusto Salaverry** and **José Arnaldo Márquez**. At the same time, *Costumbrismo* developed as a literary or pictorial interpretation of local everyday life, mannerisms, and customs. Peru's best-known writer of this style is **Ricardo Palma** (1833–1919), whose most famous work is a descriptive collection of legends and personality sketches known as *Tradiciones peruanas.* Palma was a man of letters, a former liberal politician, and later the director of the National Library of Peru; he rebuilt the collection after it was sacked by the Chilean army during the War of the Pacific.

Peru's best-known female writer is **Clorinda Matto de Turner** (1852–1909), born in Cusco, who wrote both in Quechua and Spanish. She edited a series of acclaimed literary journals, including *Peru Ilustrado,* and wrote a trilogy of novels, the best known of which is *Aves sin nido* (*Torn from the Nest*), translated into English

in 1904 and republished recently by Oxford Press and the University of Texas Press. Matto de Turner was forced into exile in Argentina after being excommunicated by the Catholic church and having her house burnt down. She died in 1909 and was forgotten for decades, though she is slowly gathering critical acclaim and recognition as one of the pioneers of Latin American feminism.

César Vallejo (1892–1938), poet, writer and journalist, is considered one of the great poetic innovators of the 20th century. His main works include *Los Heraldos Negros* (1918), the revolutionary *Trilce* (1922), and *Poemas Humanos* (published posthumously in 1939). Always a step ahead of the literary currents, each of Vallejo's books was distinct from the others and, in its own sense, revolutionary. Born in Santiago de Chuco in Peru's northern highlands, he moved to Paris in the 1920s, where he spent the rest of his life immersed in the vanguard movement and the rise of international communism. His complete poetry has been published in English by the University of California Press.

The growing industrialization of Peru in the 20th century and the continued oppression of the Indian population gave birth to a new genre of socially conscious literature known as *indigenismo*. **José María Arguedas** (1911–1969) was born to a white family but was raised by a Quechuan-speaking family in Andahuaylas, in Peru's southern Andes. He ended up in Lima, where he was educated at the prestigious University of San Marcos. His works of social realism portray the oppression of Indian communities and helped inspire the liberation theologies that continue to cause conflict in Peru's Catholic church. Two of his most famous novels, *Yawar Fiesta* and *Los Ríos Profundos* (Deep Rivers), are in English and have been published by the University of Texas Press.

Ciro Alegría (1909–1967) was a mestizo born in the Marañón Valley of northern Peru whose lyrical novels, like those of Arguedas, portray the suffering of Peru's Andean peoples. His best-known works are *La Serpiente de Oro* (*The Golden Serpent*) and *El Mundo Es*

Ancho y Ajeno (*Broad and Alien Is the World*), which became widely known outside Peru in the mid-20th century and were translated into several languages.

Mario Vargas Llosa (born 1936) is one of Latin America's most significant novelists and essayists, and one of the leading authors of his generation. Some critics consider him to have had a larger international impact and worldwide audience than any other writer of the "Latin American Boom" of the 1960s. Latin America's boom writers dropped the regionalist, folkloric themes of their predecessors and experimented wildly with form and content. Nearly all of Vargos Llosa's novels, including his world-acclaimed *Conversación en la catedral* (*Conversation in the Cathedral*), *La guerra del fin del mundo* (*The War of the End of the World*), and *La fiesta del chivo* (*The Feast of the Goat*), have been translated into English and make an excellent introduction for those wishing to explore Peruvian literature. Once a supporter of Castro and communism during his youth, Vargas Llosa led a middle and upper-class revolt against President Alan García Pérez in the late 1980s and then ran for president in 1990. After being defeated by Alberto Fujimori, Vargas Llosa went to Spain. Nowadays he lives back in Lima's Barranco neighborhood and is actively involved in Peruvian politics and social issues. A prolific writer and columnist in newspapers around the world, Vargas Llosa is a die-hard defender of neo-liberalism and unquestionably a seeker of freedom through his writing.

Alfredo Bryce Echenique (born 1939) is Peru's other best-known novelist. He has produced a dozen novels and numerous collections of short stories. After spending much of his life in Europe, he now resides in Peru.

Several middle-aged and young Peruvians are making waves on the international literary scene. **Alonso Cueto** and **Santiago Roncagliolo** both won international prizes for their 2006 novels, *The Blue Hour* and *Red April,* respectively. The works deal with Peru's history of terrorism and war. More recently, **Daniel Alarcón** (born 1977), a promising Peruvian-born writer raised in the U.S., has published *War by Candlelight* and *Lost City Radio,* his debut novel.

SPORTS

Peruvians go wild about *fútbol* or soccer, which is the main social activity in small towns across Peru. Matches, such as a *clásico* between Alianza Lima and Universitario de Deportes ("La U"), will fill stadiums throughout the year in major cities across Peru. Cienciano, an underfunded team from Cusco, made world news when it defeated huge, internationally acclaimed teams such as River Plate in Argentina and Santos of Brazil—Pele's old team. In December 2003 Cienciano became the first Peruvian team ever to win the coveted Copa Sudamericana.

ESSENTIALS

Getting There

The most common way to arrive to Peru is by plane, and all international flights arrive in Peru's capital, Lima. Because of flight patterns, most visitors either spend a night in Lima upon arrival or spend a day in Lima upon departure, or both.

AIR

Because Peru lies in the same time zone as the East Coast of the United States and Canada, North American travelers feel no jet lag after arriving in Peru. Depending on where you are flying from in North America, the flight can be anywhere from 6 to 10 hours, and many people fly in the evening in order to catch early-morning flights on to Cusco. The cheapest tickets to Lima in high season start around US$590 from Fort Lauderdale through Spirit, and around US$500 from Miami through American.

Most Europeans find it cheaper to travel to Peru via flights with stopovers in the United States or the Caribbean, though there are direct flights from Madrid and Amsterdam. The cheapest flights from major European cities start around US$1,000. Travelers from Asia, Africa, New Zealand, and Australia will also need to make at least one layover en route to Lima.

The most expensive times to fly to Peru are the Christmas vacations and the high tourist

months from June to August. Prices begin to drop around May and September and are at their lowest during the shoulder seasons from October to December and January to April.

From North America

Direct flights from Miami are available, on a daily basis, through **LAN** (www.lan.com) and **American Airlines** (www.aa.com). Airlines with flights from Miami with one layover to Lima include **Avianca** (www.avianca.com), with a stop in Bogotá, Colombia; **Copa** (www.copaair.com), with a stop in Panama City, Panama; and **Taca** (www.taca.com), with a stop in San José, Costa Rica.

From Fort Lauderdale direct flights are available on **Spirit Airlines** (www.spiritair.com), from Los Angeles and New York on LAN, from Dallas–Fort Worth on American, from Houston and Newark on **Continental** (www.continental.com), and from Atlanta through **Delta** (www.delta.com).

From Toronto **Air Canada** (www.aircanada.com) offers direct flights to Lima.

Recommended U.S. agencies that deal with a number of consolidators include **World Class Travel** (U.S. tel. 800/771-3100, www.peruperu.com), **eXito Latin American Travel Specialists** (U.S. tel. 800/665-4053, www.exitotravel.com), and **Big Sky Travel** (tel. 800/284-9809, info@bigskytvl.com).

From Mexico, Central America, and the Caribbean

Direct flights from Mexico City are available through **Aeromexico** (www.aeromexico.com). Taca, Copa, Avianca, and other airlines operate a range of direct and layover Lima flights from Cancún, Mexico; Santo Domingo, Dominican Republic; La Havana, Cuba; Panama City, Panama; San José, Costa Rica; and San Salvador, El Salvador.

From Europe

The only direct flights to Lima from Europe are from Amsterdam through **KLM** (www.klm.com), and from Madrid though LAN, **Iberia** (www.iberia.com), and **Air Europa**

(www.aireuropa.com). Carriers that make one stopover en route to Lima also include LAN, American, Delta, and Continental.

In the United Kingdom, good consolidators include **North-South Travel** (U.K. tel. 01245/608291, www.northsouthtravel.co.uk), which gives part of its proceeds to an international development trust it has set up. Others include **Travel Bag** (U.K. tel. 0800/804-8911, www.travelbag.co.uk) and **Quest Travel** (U.K. tel. 0871/423-0135, www.questtravel.com). **Flight Centre International** (U.K. tel. 0870/499-0040, www.flightcentre.co.uk) is good for tickets between the United Kingdom and the United States only.

From France, good consolidators include **Last Minute** (France tel. 0899/78-5000, www.fr.lastminute.com), **Nouvelles Frontiéres** (France tel. 0825/00-0747, www.nouvelles-frontieres.fr), and **Voyageurs de Monde** (France tel. 0892/23-5656, www.vdm.com).

From Germany, a good option is **Last Minute** (Germany tel. 01805/77-7257, www.de.lastminute.com) or **Just Travel** (Germany tel. 089/747-3330, www.justtravel.de). In the Netherlands, try **Airfair** (Netherlands tel. 0900/771-7717, www.airfair.nl), and in Spain, there is **Barcelo Viajes** (Spain tel. 902/116-226, www.barceloviajes.com).

From Asia, Africa, and the Pacific

From Asia there are no direct flights at this time to Lima. All flights from Hong Kong, Tokyo, and other Asian cities first stop in the United States. Good Asian consolidators include **Japan's No 1 Travel** (Japan tel. 03/3200-8977, www.no1-travel.com), Hong Kong's **Four Seas Tours** (Hong Kong tel. 2200-7777, www.fourseastravel.com), and India's **STIC Travels** (India tel. 79/2642-3518, www.stictravel.com).

From New Zealand and Australia, flights usually have stopovers in Los Angeles or Miami, or in Santiago or Buenos Aires, before heading to Lima. A good agency for flights to the United States is **Flight Centre International** (tel. 0870/499-0040, www.flightcentre.co.uk).

LIMA ESSENTIALS

Lima is a big and bustling city that starts the moment your taxi drives out of the airport gates. We recommend visiting at the end of a Peru trip once you have learned to navigate a smaller Peruvian city, such as Cusco. Though Lima takes some getting used to, it's one of Latin America's most fascinating cities, offering food, a unique cultural mix, museums, art scene, nightlife – did we mention food? Depending on your interests, Lima can be seen in a day's dash or several days to take in most of the museums, churches, and surrounding sights.

Lima can be thought of as a triangle, with the center at the apex. The base begins with the port of **Callao** and the nearby airport and runs along the coast through the neighborhoods of **Miraflores, Barranco,** and **Chorillos.** Other neighborhoods, such as **Pueblo Libre** and **San Isidro,** are in the middle of the triangle.

Most Lima visitors stay in San Isidro, Miraflores, and Barranco, neighborhoods near the coast with the best selection of hotels, restaurants, and nightlife. There is little to see here, however, except for giant adobe platforms that were built by the Lima culture (A.D. 200-700) and now rise above the upscale neighborhoods. The main events are the restaurants and shops in Miraflores around Parque Kennedy, which any taxi driver can take you to.

SIGHTS

Lima is jam-packed with sights, but most interesting to many people are either the colonial churches, convents, and homes in Lima's center or the restaurants and shops of Miraflores, Lima's upscale coastal neighborhood.

There are so many sights to see in downtown Lima that you would need a few days to see them all. The best idea is to start as early as possible at the **Plaza Mayor** to see the **Catedral** and its interesting museum (9 A.M.-4:30 P.M. Mon.-Fri., 10 A.M.-4:30 P.M. Sat., US$5). Other historic buildings on the square include the **Archbishop's Palace** and

the president's residence, **Palacio del Gobierno.** Around the main square are a handful of colonial churches that are easy to visit and offer a fascinating glimpse into Lima's past.

Our favorite church is **San Francisco** (Ancash and Lampa, 9:15 A.M.-5:45 P.M. daily, US$3.50, US$1.75 students) a 16th-century convent featuring a patio lined with centuries-old *azulejos* (Sevillean tiles) and roofed with *machimbrado,* perfectly fitted puzzle pieces of Nicaraguan mahogany. But the highlight is the catacombs, or public cemetery, where slaves, servants, and others without money were buried until 1821 (rich citizens were usually buried in their home chapels).

The center of Lima is perfectly safe, but it is a good idea not to stray too far outside these main streets – except for a lunchtime foray to **Chinatown** or a taxi ride to **Museo de los Descalzos,** on the other side of the river. Keep your passport and airplane tickets in a money belt under clothing.

Lima's best museums are spread out, set in neighborhoods that are sandwiched between the coast and the center. Excellent collections of pre-Columbian gold, textiles, and ceramics can be found at the **Museo Larco** (Bolívar 1515, tel. 01/461-1312, www.museolarco.org, 9 A.M.-6 P.M. daily, US$11) in Pueblo Libre, **Museo de la Nación** (Javier Prado Este 2465, tel. 01/476-9873, 9 A.M.-6 P.M. Tues.-Sun., US$4, US$3 students) in San Borja, and **Museo de Oro** (Molina 1110, tel. 01/345-1271, 11:30 A.M.-7 P.M. Mon.-Sun., US$11.50) in Monterrico. English-speaking and sometimes French-speaking guides are usually available at these museums. Miraflores has a few interesting private archaeological collections that are worth checking out, such as the **Museo Enrico Poli** (Lord Cochrane 466, tel. 01/422-2437 or 01/440-7100, 4-6 P.M., by appointment only, US$12).

ACCOMMODATIONS

If you want or need to stay the night in Lima, you have two basic options: Either pay for the new four-star hotel inside the airport, or take a 20-40 minute cab ride (depending on the

© PROMPERU

Lima's Catedral, built in the late 16th century, is a must-see.

time of the day) into Miraflores, San Isidro, Barranco, or central Lima. There are a few midrange options near the airport, but the area is unappealing and unsafe and we recommend taking a cab into town instead. The hotels recommended are in different price ranges and provide reliable airport pickups.

Inside the airport is the new **Costa del Sol-Ramada** (Av. Elmer Faucett s/n, Aeropuerto Internacional Jorge Chávez, tel. 01/711-2000, www.costadelsolperu.com, US$250 s, US$265 d with buffet breakfast included), with a good restaurant, sushi bar, pool, spa, gym, and all the normal amenities. The hotel is literally right across the taxi lanes in the airport.

Near downtown Lima is the **Hostal de Las Artes** (Chota 1460, tel. 01/433-0031, www.hostaldelasartes.net, US$5 for dorm bed, US$9 s, US$18 d), a clean, well-managed,

gay-friendly place with Dutch owners. Sevillean-style tiles line the entrance off a quiet street that is a 10-minute walk from Plaza San Martín. Rooms are simple with whitewashed walls, dark wood, comfy beds, and near silence. A book exchange, gardens, and two patios round out the hostel. There are good restaurants down the street.

In Miraflores, the charming **Hostal El Patio** (Diez Canseco 341, tel. 01/444-2107, www.hostalelpatio.net, US$40 s, US$50 d with breakfast) is a memorable colonial home overflowing with plants and flowers and cheerfully painted walls. Large rooms have either tiled floors or carpet, as well as homey furnishings and large windows. Ask for a mini-suite for an additional US$5 – you'll get your money's worth with a kitchenette. Rooms are interspersed with terraces, which are great places for reading or sunbathing.

(continues on next page)

LIMA ESSENTIALS *(continued)*

3B Barranco's Bed & Breakfast (Centenario 130, tel. 01/247-6915, www.3bhostal.com, US$55 s and d) is the newest addition to a group of comfy and well-equipped hostels and bed-and-breakfasts in Barranco. With a neat, minimalistic design and decor, the rooms are clean, bright, and spacious with very comfy beds and impeccable bathrooms. The hostel is on a very busy street but two blocks away from the ocean and a few more from all of Barranco's nightlife.

Our favorite upscale hotel in Lima is the charming **Hotel Antigua Miraflores** (Grau 350, tel. 01/241-6166, www.peru-hotels-inns.com, US$79 s, US$94 d with breakfast). This turn-of-the-20th-century mansion has all the comforts of a fine hotel and the warmth of a bed-and-breakfast. The rooms are large, cozy, and handsomely decorated with hand-carved furniture, local art, and warm colors. Plus, the remodeled bathrooms have big tubs. There are plush couches in the downstairs sitting room, and the six types of breakfast are served in a sunny, black-and-white-tiled café. It is worth paying another US$20 for a room in the old part of the house, and suites are also available with kitchens and whirlpool tubs.

FOOD

If you have a few hours downtime, head into Lima and grab a world-class meal. Here are a few mind-blowing restaurant suggestions in the Miraflores area, which is fun to stroll around, and central Lima. There are dozens of other incredible options, which are too numerous to mention here.

In Miraflores, budget eaters flock to **Rincón Chami** (Esperanza 154, tel. 01/444-4511, 9 A.M.-9 P.M. Mon.-Sat., 9 A.M.-5 P.M. Sun., US$7) for ceviche, tamales, *brochetas*, and *lomo saltados*, dished up in a dinerlike atmosphere. Each day there is a different special of the house (Sunday, for instance, is *chupe de camarones*, a cream-based soup with sea shrimp).

Ceviche is elegantly served in martini glasses at Gaston Acurio's **La Mar Cebichería** (La Mar 770, tel. 01/421-3365, 11 A.M.-5 P.M., US$15-20) in Miraflores. No reservations are accepted and lines can get long, so plan for a leisurely lunch over several types of ceviche, cold beer, grilled fish, and crisp white wine.

Our vote for best restaurant in Peru is **Astrid y Gastón** (Cantuarias 175, tel. 01/444-1496, 1-3 P.M. and 7:30-11:30 P.M. Mon.-Sat., US$35-40). This adventurous gourmet restaurant, set in an elegant republican home, is the labor of love of a Peruvian-German couple who met at the Cordon Bleu in Paris. The evening begins with creative pisco drinks such as the *aguaymanto* sour, made with *pisco puro* and the tangy juice of *aguaymanto* fruit. Then, as diners watch through a glass wall, chefs concoct never-before-sampled entrées such as kid goat basted in *algarroba* honey and marinated in *chicha de jora*, or river prawns served with red curry, coconut milk, and jasmine rice. Save room; the desserts are the best part: *blanco mousse* with a sauce of *sauco* and blackberries.

On the way from the airport to Miraflores is **Pescados Capitales** (La Mar 1337, tel. 01/421-8808, 12:30-5 P.M. Tues.-Sun., US$10), a witty play on words (*pescados* means fish but rhymes with *pecados*, or sins) that makes sense when you see the menu. Each dish is named for a virtue or sin; Diligence will bring you a ceviche of tuna and *conchas negras*, while Patience will bring you a ceviche of shrimp with curry and mango chutney.

In central Lima, there are some great restaurants in the pedestrian walkways right off the Plaza Mayor. One of these is **T'anta** (Pasaje Nicolás de Rivera el Viejo 142-148, tel. 01/428-3115, 9 A.M.-9 P.M. Mon.-Sat., 9 A.M.-6 P.M. Sun., US$7-14), a Gaston Acurio restaurant, which serves up refined plates of the Peruvian favorites *lomo saltado* and *recoto relleno*, as well as creative new inventions like *ají de gallina* ravioli.

GETTING THERE **169**

GETTING THERE AND AROUND
Airport
All overseas flights from Europe and North America arrive in Lima at **Jorge Chávez International Airport** (tel. 01/511-6055 24-hour flight info, www.lap.com.pe). From here flights continue on to Cusco and other cities. Most planes from overseas arrive in the middle of the night, and flights to Cusco begin from about 5 A.M. onwards. Some travelers wait in the airport for connecting flights, while the majority head to Miraflores, San Isidro, Barranco, or even Lima's historic center, where there is a good selection of hotels. On the return, most flights from Cusco arrive here in the midday and leave for the U.S. at night – so many visitors have at least a half day in Lima.

Jorge Chávez has come a long way and is actually a pretty modern airport. It has a range of services, including banks, money exchange booths, ATMs, a post office, stores, café, two food courts, duty-free shops, a rent-a-cell service, and a recommended Quattro D ice cream shop with playground, among other services. There is even the **Sumaq VIP Lounge,** voted as the Lounge of the Year 2009 by Priority Pass. If you want to store your luggage, go to **Left Luggage** (tel. 01/517-3217, at the side of Domestic Arrivals, US$1.25 per piece of luggage per hour, US$7.5 per piece of luggage per 24 hours).

There is a US$6.82 tax on all domestic flights leaving Lima and a US$31 tax on all departing international flights. Both taxes can be paid in either U.S. or Peruvian currency, according to the exchange rate of the day, which is normally posted outside the cashier's window. On your way home, arrive at the airport 2-3 hours in advance for international flights and 1-2 hours for domestic flights.

Velasco Astete International Airport in Cusco has flights arriving from Santa Cruz and La Paz, Bolivia, with **Aerosur** (www.aerosur.com), and Benigno Ballón Farfán International Airport in Arequipa has flights from Arica, Chile, with **Sky Airline** (www.skyairline.cl).

Taxis
Pushy taxi drivers will be waiting for you outside the airport. The best thing to do is contract a taxi through **Taxi Green** (tel. 01/9826-7148), a private company that has stands just outside luggage claim. Have your destination address written down. Taxi prices from the airport to the center should be around US$12, and to Miraflores about US$15. You may be able to get a cheaper taxi if you negotiate with a driver in the airport parking lot, but be sure to know where you are going. Hard-core budget travelers will walk outside the gate of the airport and save a few dollars by taking a taxi, *combi*, or collective taxis on the street. Be very careful with your luggage if you do this!

Day Tours
Our favorite travel agency in Lima is **Fertur Peru** (www.fertur-travel.com), run by the enterprising Siduith Ferrer, with offices in central Lima at the Plaza Mayor (Junin 211, tel. 01/427-2626, 8:30 A.M.-8 P.M. Mon.-Sat.) and Miraflores (Schell 485, tel. 01/242-1900, same hours). This agency can arrange to pick you up at the airport for a day tour of Lima.

Private drivers can also be hired for the hour, day, or for a trip such as to the Nasca Lines. Many travelers who are only in Lima for a single day would greatly benefit from a driver who recommends museums and restaurants and then drops them off at the airport in the evening. A highly recommended driver is **José Salinas Casanova** (tel. 01/9329-2614, casanovacab@hotmail.com, US$7/hr), based out of the Hotel Antigua Miraflores. Also try **Miguel Vásquez Díaz** (Carlos Izaguirre 1353, central Lima, tel. 01/9809-2321, sumisein@latinmail.com) or the English-speaking **Mónica Velasquez** (tel. 01/9943-0796 or 01/224-8608, www.monicatourism.da.ru). **Fidel Loayza Paredes** (tel. 01/533-1609, armandoloayza280671@hotmail.com) does not speak much English but is trustworthy.

From Africa, travelers to Lima head to Europe first, though **South African Airways** (South Africa tel. 0861/359-722, www.flysaa.com) has a flight from Johannesburg to São Paolo, Brazil. A good African agency is **Rennies Travel** (South Africa tel. 0861/100-155, www.renniestravel.com).

Within South America

More than a dozen South American cities have daily flights through **LAN** and **Taca,** to and from Lima, the regional hub for both airlines. Taca flies from/to Quayaquil and Quito in Ecuador; Bogotá, Cali, and Medellín in Colombia; Caracas in Venezuela; La Paz and Santa Cruz in Bolivia; Montevideo in Uruguay; Santiago in Chile; Buenos Aires in Argentina; São Paulo and Rio de Janeiro in Brazil. LAN also flies to/from Lima to all cities mentioned for TACA. **Aerolíneas Argentinas** (www.aerolineas.com) flies from Buenos Aires. **Avianca** (www.avianca.com) flies from Bogotá, and **TAM** (www.tam.com.br) from Rio de Janeiro.

Cheap Fares

The best way to get a cheap fare to Peru is to travel outside the high season months of June through August. Within Peru's three-month high season, it will be difficult to find a discount fare to Peru and onward to Cusco and other main destinations.

The easiest way to start a search for airfare is to use an airfare price comparison website like **Kayak** (www.kayak.com), which compiles the best prices from hundreds of sources, including online travel engines like Travelocity, Expedia, CheapTickets, and Orbitz. Other options include **FareChase** (www.farechase.com), **SideStep** (www.sidestep.com), **Mobissimo** (www.mobissimo.com), and **Bookingbuddy** (www.bookingbuddy.com).

BUS

It is possible to reach Peru by international bus service from the surrounding countries of Paraguay, Uruguay, Ecuador, Bolivia, Chile, Brazil, and Argentina. The major buses that run these routes can be quite comfortable, with reclining seats, movies, and meals. The longest international bus trips leave from Lima. Some major neighboring cities from which buses travel to Lima are: Santa Cruz in Bolivia, Asunción in Paraguay, Córdoba and Buenos Aires in Argentina, Montevideo in Uruguay, São Paulo and Rio de Janeiro in Brazil, and Santiago in Chile. Buses leave frequently from/to La Paz, Bolivia, for the five-hour direct journey to/from Puno and on to Cusco. The main international bus companies are **Cruz del Sur** (Lima tel. 01/311-5050, www.cruzdelsur.com.pe), **Ormeño** (Lima tel. 01/472-1710, www.grupo-ormeno.com), **Caracol** (tel. 01/431-1400, www.perucaracol.com), and **El Rápido** (Lima tel. 01/425-1066, www.elrapidoint.com.ar).

Getting Around

Peru's diverse landscape includes long stretches of desert, high Andean passes, and endless tracts of swampy jungle. Not surprisingly, Peru can be a complicated country to navigate. Nearly all of Peru's major jungle destinations require a flight unless you want to spend a few days on a cargo boat or one day, sometimes three, riding in a bumpy bus. Train service is limited, except in the Cusco area, but new highways have made traveling by bus much faster and more comfortable than it was a decade ago.

AIR

If you are on a tight schedule and want to see a range of places, flying is the best way to go. In Peru, a round-trip fare can be less expensive than one-way, but that depends on the season and the airline. The best way to buy tickets or reconfirm them is through the airline's local office or website, where you can buy tickets online for almost all domestic flights. Finding tickets around Christmas, Easter, and the national holiday of Fiestas Patrias in the last weekend of July is expensive and difficult.

The major Peru airlines are **LAN** (www.lan.com); **Star Perú** (www.starperu.com), **Peruvian Airlines** (www.peruvianairlines.pe), and **LC Busre** (www.lcbusre.com.pe).

BUS

Because most Peruvians travel by bus, the country has an incredible network of frequent, high-quality buses—much better, in fact, than in the U.S. or Europe. You will be safer if you avoid the dirt-cheap bus companies that pick up passengers along the way. Some of these buses have been adapted (stretched) to the point where they are structurally unsound.

Bus companies in Peru have a confusing variety of labels for their deluxe services, which include Imperial, Royal Class, Cruzero, Ejecutivo, Especial, and Dorado. The absolute best services, comparable to traveling business class on an airplane, are Cruz del Sur's Cruzero or Cruzero Suite class and Movil's better service 180° Bus-Cama class, which unfortunately only serves Huaraz. Deluxe bus service means nonstop (only for driver shifts), more legroom, reclining seats, onboard food and beverage service, videos, safe drivers, and clean bathrooms.

Reputable bus companies in Lima are **Cruz del Sur** (Lima tel. 01/311-5050, www.cruzdelsur.com.pe), **Ormeño** (tel. 01/472-1710, www.grupo-ormeno.com), **Movil Tours** (tel. 01/332-9000, www.moviltours.com.pe), and **Oltursa** (tel. 01/225-4499, www.oltursa.com.pe).

Bus travel is easier in cities like Arequipa, Puno, and Cusco, where all the bus companies are consolidated in a main bus station, which is usually known as the *terminal terrestre*. Travelers can arrive there, shop around, and usually be on a bus in an hour or two. In other cities, such as Lima, each bus company has its own bus terminal, some even with VIP lounges, and travelers can save time by buying a ticket through an agency or at a Wong or Metro supermarket through **Teleticket.**

Luggage theft can still be a problem for bus travelers, especially for those who travel on the cheap bus lines. Always keep your hand on your luggage at a bus station. Once on the bus, the luggage that is checked underneath is usually safe because passengers can only retrieve bags with a ticket. The big problem is carry-on luggage. Place it on a rack where you can see it. Some people bring oversized locks to chain their luggage to a rack, but thieves will just razor through your bag and take what they want.

Assaults on night buses are still a problem in Peru, especially on less expensive buses. Highway bandits either hold the bus up by force or sometimes board as normal passengers and hijack it en route. Passengers are not hurt, but are shaken down for their money and passports. Though some companies use a camcorder to film all passengers getting on board, no company can eliminate the risk entirely.

TRAIN

The decade-long monopoly enjoyed by Orient-Express–owned **PeruRail** (www.perurail.com) is finally breaking up. New entrants into the market to provide train service from Cusco to Machu Picchu include **Machu Picchu Train,** owned by Andean Railways (www.machupicchutrain.com) and **Inca Rail** (www.incarail.com). Check the websites for expected competitive fares, fancier coaches, and better service. PeruRail also operates trains from Cusco to Puno.

During high season, it is best to reserve tickets online ahead of time to travel to Machu Picchu. Buying tickets once you arrive in Cusco is a hassle, but many of Cusco's nicer hotels will purchase them for their guests.

COMBIS AND COLECTIVOS

The cheapest way to move around a major city like Lima, Cusco, Iquitos, Trujillo, Arequipa, or Chiclayo is by public transportation. There are buses, *combis* (imported Asian vans that dart along the roads), and *colectivos* (station wagons with room for five passengers). The buses are cheap but slow, *combis* are a bit faster but tend to be very cramped, and *colectivos* are the fastest of all.

Bus fares usually hover around US$0.40–0.60; *colectivos* are about twice that, but fares go up on weekends and evenings. You can tell where buses and *combis* are going by the sticker on the front windshield, *not* by what is painted on the side. Before you take public transportation, ask a local for specific directions to where you are going. It can be a fun, inexpensive way to travel around. To get off a bus or *colectivo* simply say *"baja"* ("getting off") or *"esquina"* ("at the corner"). Fares are collected during the ride or right before you get off, by the *cobrador* or the man (seldom a woman) who also shouts out the route or destination the bus or *combi* is leading to, practically hanging out the bus door.

TAXI

The fastest but still not too expensive way to get around Peru's cities is via taxi or *motocar,* the three-wheeled canopied bikes that buzz around cities in the jungle and the coast (not Lima, though). The typical fare for in-city travel is US$0.40–1 for a *motocar* and US$1.50–5 for a taxi.

Assaults on taxi passengers can be a problem in Cusco, Lima, and Peru's other tourist hot spots. The best way to avoid this is to have your hostel call for a taxi or to flag down only registered taxis on the street. Avoid young, suspicious-looking drivers and beat-up cars with tinted windows and broken door handles. When traveling, sit on the backseat diagonally opposite the driver's.

Bargaining is an essential skill for anyone taking a taxi, because taxis in Peru do not use meters. Know approximately what the fare should be and stand somewhere where your taxi driver can pull over without holding up traffic. Always negotiate the fare before getting in the car. A typical bargaining conversation would start with you asking *"¿Cuánto cuesta a Barranco?"* (or wherever you're going); the taxi driver replies, *"Ocho soles."* You bargain with,

"No, seis pues," and so on. You get the picture. If you can't get the fare you want, wave the driver on and wait for the next taxi. Have in mind that rates can rise during rush hours and the evenings.

Private drivers can also be hired for the hour or day, or for a long-distance trip. The fee can often start at US$7 per hour and go up to US$60–70 for all day. Ask at your hotel for recommended drivers.

RENTING A CAR OR MOTORCYCLE

Renting a car does not usually make sense cost-wise in Peru because taking taxis or hiring a private car can be cheaper. Also, gas is expensive (about US$4–5 per gallon, depending on the grade), and distances between cities are considerable. Your best bet is to get to your destination and then rent a car to get around.

The phone book of any major Peruvian city is filled with rental car options, which are usually around US$70 per day once you factor in extra mileage, insurance, and other hidden costs. Four-wheel-drive cars are usually US$100–120 per day. Major rental companies include **Hertz** (www.inkasrac.com), **Avis** (www.avisperu.com), and **Budget** (www.budgetperu.com). All these companies have offices in Jorge Chávez International Airport, Lima, Arequipa, and Cusco. Smaller companies operate in many other cities. To rent a car, drivers usually need to be at least 18 years of age, have a driver's license from their country, and have a credit card.

BIKE

Biking is a great way to explore Peru's back roads and get to know local people along the way. Many of Peru's adventure agencies, especially those that offer rafting trips, rent **mountain bikes** starting at US$15 per day and up, though quality varies tremendously and the bikes are generally meant for local use only. Adventure agencies in Lima, Arequipa, Huaraz, Cusco, and Puno offer multiday bike expeditions with tents, a support vehicle, and a cook. These trips follow fabulous single-track routes up and over the mountains with mind-boggling descents on the other side.

Dozens of cyclists pass through Peru each year, during their epic Alaska–Patagonia pilgrimage. Those who want to start their tour from Peru will have to box their bike up and fly it with them, as good bicycles are extremely expensive in Peru. Some airlines provide a box in which your bike will fit once you take the handlebars off. If your bike is or looks new, smear mud on it so you can get through customs without having to pay duty taxes. Most people use mountain bikes to travel on dirt roads, often with slicks for road and highway travel.

When planning your route, keep in mind that the Pan-American Highway (Carretera Panamericana) is a dangerous bike route because buses pass at high speeds and the shoulder is cluttered with debris. The same applies for major routes into the mountains, including the Cañon de Pato near Huaraz. The best trips are on remote back roads, which are invariably spectacular and much safer. Keep in mind altitude, weather extremes, drinking water, and the complete lack of repair parts outside of major cities.

Good sources of information include the Adventure Cycling Association in the United States (www.adventurecycling.org) and the loads of trip journals from people who have biked in Peru, which can be found at www.geocities.com/thetropics/island/6810/. One of Peru's best known bikers, **Omar Zarzar Casis** (www.aventurarse.com), has written a book in Spanish, called *Por los camino de Perú en bicicleta,* describing 10 of Peru's most beautiful mountain bike circuits, available in many Peruvian bookstores.

HITCHHIKING

People in Peru are not afraid to flag down whatever transport happens to pass by, and drivers usually charge them a bit of money for gas. Instead of sticking a thumb up, Peruvians in the countryside swish a handkerchief up and down in front of them to attract drivers' attention. We think hitchhiking is fairly safe on country roads where there are no other options. When near cities or large highways, though, always take buses. If you hitchhike, do it with a companion, and make sure your driver is sober before getting in.

TOURS

Organized tour groups are a good idea for travelers leery of traveling on their own or who long for a hassle-free, action-packed tour. A range of excellent, though often expensive agencies operate in Peru and offer anything from general tours with a bit of soft adventure to well-tailored adventures for trekkers, climbers, birdwatchers, spiritual seekers, or just about any other group.

With the right company, tours can be safe and enlightening, and a great way to make new friends. Common complaints include a lack of flexibility on meals and lodging options, a go-go schedule that allows no time for relaxation, and a large up-front payment.

Before booking, read the fine print and ask a lot of questions. Find out what hotels you are staying in and then check them with this book. Look for hidden expenses like airport transfers, meals, and single rooms if you are traveling alone. Find out who your guide will be and what his or her experience and language skills are. Ask about the size of the group, the average age of the other passengers, and the cancellation policy. Get everything in writing and add up what all the costs would be using this book. Peru is a relatively inexpensive place to travel in and you may be able to do it cheaper on your own.

Day-Tour Operators

Because of all the public transport in Peru, independent travelers can usually find their way even to the country's most remote sites, if they don't mind waiting around for an hour or two, walking, and sometimes hitchhiking.

No one likes to be in a group of obvious tourists, but taking a day tour is the fastest, easiest, and sometimes cheapest way to see a given area's sights, like taking a group taxi. In most cities, tour agencies are clustered together on the main square or along a principal street. Before paying, confirm how good your guide's English is and get tour details confirmed in writing, including sites visited, how many people maximum will be in the group, and whether the cost includes lunch and admission fees. If your guide does a good job, make sure to give him or her a reasonable tip (US$10–25 for a day tour).

Package Tours

Package tours typically include airfare, hotels, and some meals—but you choose what to do and where to eat. Many Peru-bound airlines offer package tours, including **American Airlines Vacations** (tel. 800/321-2121, www. aavacations.com), **Delta Vacations** (tel. 800/654-6559, www.deltavacations.com), and Continental **Airlines Vacations** (tel. 800/301-3800, www.covacations.com, operated by Solar Tours). The web page of the **United States Tour Operators Association** (www.ustoa. com) has a search engine to find package tours and specialty tour operators.

Many of the package operators are based in Miami, including **Analie Tours** (tel. 800/811-6027, www.analietours.com), which offers rock-bottom prices. To get these rates, however, you have to travel on a specific date and stay in the hotels they have reserved—otherwise expect add-on costs. Resort hotels including Ica, Tarapoto, Puno, Cusco, Máncora, and Cajamarca often promote specials for Lima weekenders on their web pages. These all-inclusive packages can be an excellent value for foreign travelers.

Overland Journeys

Many companies in the United States and the United Kingdom offer overland backpacking trips for large groups. You and 39 others hop on a retrofitted Mercedes bus for a one- or two-month tour that could begin in Santiago, Chile, or São Paolo and end in Lima, visiting Cusco, Machu Picchu, and all the other sites along the way. These companies strike bargains with hotels ahead of time and take care of all food, lodging, and transport.

These trips move like an army, camp on beaches, advance along the Inca Trail and leave behind a litter of soap opera romances. With a two-month trip costing around US$3,000 these trips are about as good of a value as you are likely to find. A pair of budget-minded travelers could, however, do the same trip for the same cost or less. Last-minute web specials often offer 25 percent discounts on these trips.

The best agencies to look at are **Kumuka** (www.kumuka.co.uk), **Bukima Adventure Travel** (www.bukima.com), **Dragoman Overland** (www.dragoman.com), and **South American Safaris** (www.southamericansafaris.com). A final highly recommended option is Australia-based **Tucan Travel** (www.tucantravel.com), which offers a range of trips including language schools and custom packages for independent travelers.

International Tour Agencies

Peru has a huge range of good tour operators with overseas agents, who can work with you regardless of what country you are calling from. The operators in Peru will be the ones you meet when you arrive there. The local operators are listed throughout this book. Contacting these operators directly can sometimes be cheaper, though they are officially supposed to offer the same price to you as their agent overseas does. Many of the agencies listed will organize a tour for as few as two people, with options for trip extensions. In the Cusco area, for instance, tour operators generally offer trip extensions to Lake Titicaca or the jungle.

Adventure tourism is growing fast in Peru, and new tour operators appear every year. To keep abreast of the latest operators, watch the classified ads sections of adventure magazines such as *Outside* and *National Geographic Adventure* or online resources such as www. andeantravelweb.com.

World Class Travel Services (U.S. tel. 800/771-3100, www.peruperu.com) is a leading seller of consolidated tickets and arranges professional, organized tours. It works with the best operators in Peru, such as **Amazons**

Explorer and **InkaNatura.** World Class offers tours all over Peru, including a US$672 four-day package that includes all but a few meals for visiting Cusco, Sacred Valley, and Machu Picchu. World Class owner Bob Todd personally inspects all the hotels to which he sends clients and is willing to work with groups as small as two people.

CULTURE AND SOFT ADVENTURE

The Seattle-based nonprofit travel organization **Crooked Trails** (U.S. tel. 206/383-9828, www.crookedtrails.com) offers excellent travel programs, culturally sensitive and with exciting off-the-beaten-path destinations around Peru for families, schools, universities, and almost any type of group. There are at least 10 different packages, such as The Andes and the Sacred Valley, a 15-day tour including Cusco and Machu Picchu, along with homestays with villagers and their families in Vicos (Cordillera Blanca) or Chinchero (Cusco). La Gran Ruta Inca is a seven-day trek extension on one of the Inca highway's best preserved segments southeast of the Cordillera Blanca.

Far Horizons Archaeological & Cultural Trips (U.S. tel. 800/552-4575, www.farhorizon.com), a California-based agency, is the right choice for those with a passion for archaeology. Tours hit all of Peru's major ruins and are guided by an American university professor. Along the way, guests attend lectures by Peru's most noted archaeologists, including Walter Alva, who excavated the Lord of Sipán tombs. Their tours often include a complete tour of the north coast, Chavín ruins in the Cordillera Blanca, Cusco, Machu Picchu, and Lima's main museums.

Nature Expeditions International (U.S. tel. 800/869-0639, www.naturexp.com) has been in business for more than three decades and runs a range of upscale trips throughout Peru. Its 12-day Peru Discovery trip passes through Lima, Arequipa, and the whole Cusco area and includes stays in top-notch hotels like the Hotel Libertador in Cusco and the Machu Picchu Pueblo Hotel. It works with groups of just two people and can arrange lectures

on a range of topics, from natural healing to Peruvian cuisine.

For a more luxurious trip, **Abercrombie & Kent** (U.S. tel. 800/554-7016, www.abercrombiekent.com) pampers its travelers with small groups, the top hotels of the country, and luxury train travel. The trips are expensive, but there are occasional discounts available on its website.

Seattle-based **Wildland Adventures** (tel. 800/345-4453, www.wildland.com) is renowned worldwide for its diverse international trips. In Peru alone, it offers 16 distinct trips that cover the three major geographic zones: coast, mountains, and jungle. In addition to the more traditional Inca Trail and Cordillera Blanca treks, the company also offers trips designed especially for families. On a trip like the lodge-based Andes & Amazon Odyssey, kids and their parents visit and interact with local schools and markets.

Guerba Adventure & Discovery Holidays (U.K. tel. 01373/82-6611, www.guerba.co.uk) is a long-established U.K. operator that offers a good range of hotel-based culture tours and gentle treks. Its tours range from one week to four months and have won international awards for environmentally responsible tourism.

ADVENTURE AND NATURE TOUR OPERATORS IN NORTH AMERICA

Our top choice for treks anywhere in Peru is **Andean Treks** (U.S. tel. 800/683-8148, www.andeantreks.com). It is affiliated with the highly recommended Peruvian Andean Treks in Cusco, and its treks range from a six-day/five-night Inca Trail trek (US$695), to a Salcantay trip (US$920), to an 18-day Vilcabamba expedition (prices vary, contact tour operator for price quote). It has been around since the 1970s and has been a leader in taking care of the environment and porters—it's probably the only agency in Peru that pays retirement to its porters!

Adventure Specialists (U.S. tel. 719/783-2076, www.adventurespecialists.org) is based out of a spectacular ranch in Westcliffe, Colorado, and has operated quality educational and creative adventure programs in Peru since 1971. Founder and co-owner Gary Ziegler, a fellow of the Royal Geographical Society and Explorers Club, is a true adventurer, archaeologist and noted Inca expert. His expeditions have rediscovered and surveyed the important Inca sites Corihuayrachina, Cota Coca, and Llaqtapata. The company specializes in archaeology-focused horse trips around Cusco, but Ziegler and his crew can custom-design nearly any adventure you are looking for.

Adventure Life International (406/541-2677, U.S. tel. 800/344-6118, www.adventure-life.com) is a company based in Missoula, Montana, that is a good bet for budget-minded trekkers. Its 10-day Machu Picchu Pilgrimage includes Cusco, Machu Picchu, and a well-run Inca Trail trek for US$1,775. It also offers affordable trips to the fabulous Tambopata Research Center. It uses three-star, family-run hostels and local guides, and gives independent travelers flexibility on where they eat. Maximum group size is 12, though it often sends off groups as small as two people. It has recently set up a fund (www.earthfamilyfund.org) to give back to the countries it visits.

South Winds (U.S. tel. 800/377-9463, www.southwindadventures.com) is based in Littleton, Colorado, and offers a range of eco-adventures from the jungle to the high Andes. It comes highly recommended from people who have done the trips and from *Condé Nast Traveler* magazine.

The Miami-based **Tropical Nature Travel** (U.S. tel. 877/827-8350, www.tropicalnaturetravel.com) works with a variety of conservation organizations across Latin American to plan jungle trips. In Peru it works with InkaNatura, the owner of some of Peru's best jungle lodges. Your choices range from the Manu Wildlife Center and Cock of the Rock Lodge in the Manu area, or the Sandoval Lake and Heath River lodges around Puerto Maldonado.

KE Adventure Travel (U.S. tel. 800/497-9675, www.keadventure.com) is based in Avon, Colorado, and offers a range of high-quality climbs and treks—at considerably lower prices than its competitor, Mountain Travel Sobek. It works with top international trekking guides and is best known for treks around the Cordillera Huayhuash and Nevado Ausangate near Cusco. It also guides peaks in the Cordillera Blanca and leads multi-sport trips that combine rafting, trekking, and mountain biking.

GAP Adventures (U.S./Canada tel. 800/708-7761, www.gapadventures.com) stands for Great Adventure People and is one of Canada's lead tour outfits. It is a good choice for independent-minded travelers who prefer small groups. Groups stay in locally owned hotels, and GAP is known for socially responsible tourism that includes a good deal of interaction with communities.

Our vote for best international climbing agency in Peru goes to Seattle-based **Alpine Ascents** (U.S. tel. 206/378-1927, www.alpineascents.com). The company's Peru guide, José Luis Peralvo, splits his time between Everest, his home in Ecuador, and Peru and has been guiding the world's toughest peaks for about two decades. Alpine Ascents is extremely responsible about acclimatization and small rope teams.

Other Peru adventure options can be found through the **Adventure Center** (U.S. tel. 800/277-8747, www.adventurecenter.com), which sells the packages of various operators from its offices in Emeryville, California.

For esoteric tours and ayahuasca sessions, check out **El Tigre Journeys** (U.S. tel. 303/449-5479, www.biopark.org/peru.html). This for-profit company has been in business since 1997 and is associated with the nonprofit **International Biopark Foundation** in Tucson, Arizona. It leads ayahuasca ceremonies in the Amazon, spirit journeys, and solstice celebrations throughout the year.

ADVENTURE AND NATURE TOUR OPERATORS IN THE UNITED KINGDOM

Amazonas Explorer (U.K. tel. 01437/89-1743, www.amazonas-explorer.com) has tons of local experience in Peru and an unmatched array of adventure trips that integrate kayaking, rafting, mountain biking, and trekking. It is constantly innovating new trips, with a team full-time in Cusco.

Based in Edinburgh, Scotland, **Andean Trails** (U.K. tel. 0131/467-7086, www.andeantrails.co.uk) was cofounded in 1999 by a former South American adventure guide. The company leads interesting, small-group mountain-bike and trekking adventures throughout Peru.

Journey Latin America (U.K. tel. 020/8747-8315, www.journeylatinamerica.co.uk) is the United Kingdom's largest operator of specialty tours and has been in business for more than 25 years. It does rafting, kayaking, trekking, and cultural tours that can either be escorted groups or tailored for two people. It also sets up homestays and language classes.

Exodus (U.K. tel. 0870/950-0039, www.exodus.co.uk) is one of the United Kingdom's larger adventure tour operators, with more than 25 years of experience and trips in countless countries. Its 28 Peru trips often include visits to Bolivia or Ecuador.

World Challenge Expeditions (U.K. tel. 0208/728-7200, www.world-challenge.co.uk)

is a London-based adventure company for student groups in Peru. Its coordinator in Peru, Richard Cunyus, is a full-time resident, takes great care of the students, and tracks down excellent adventures such as trekking in the Cordillera Huayhuash or paddling a dugout in the Reserva Nacional Pacaya Samiria. The company also works with many students from the United States.

ADVENTURE AND NATURE TOUR OPERATORS IN AUSTRALIA

World Expeditions (Australia tel. 1300/720-000, www.worldexpeditions.com.au) is Australia's leader in adventure tours and treks to Peru. It works with Tambo Treks, a small and reputable trekking outfit in Cusco. In Peru, trips include treks through the Lake Titicaca grasslands, forays into Colca Canyon, and longer trips that take in Peru, Bolivia, and the Amazon jungle. It has representatives in the United Kingdom (enquiries@worldexpeditions.co.uk), the United States (contactus@worldexpeditions.com), and Canada (info@worldexpeditions.ca).

Visas and Officialdom

VISAS AND PASSPORTS

Citizens of the United States, Canada, United Kingdom, South Africa, New Zealand, and Australia do not require visas to enter Peru as tourists at the present time, nor do residents of any other European or Latin American country. When visitors enter the country, you can get anything from 30 to 180 days stamped into both a passport and an embarkation card that travelers must keep until they exit the country. If you require more than 30 days, be ready to support your argument by explaining your travel plans and showing your return ticket.

Extensions can be arranged at Peru's immigration offices in Lima, Arequipa, Cusco, Iquitos, Puno, and Trujillo for US$21. There are also immigration offices on the border checkpoints with Chile, Bolivia (Desaguadero

and Yunguyo), and Ecuador, though at this point it is easier just to leave the country, stay the night, and reenter on a fresh visa.

Always make a photocopy of your passport and your return ticket and store it in a separate place. Carry yours in a money belt underneath your clothing, or leave it in a security box at your hotel. If your passport is lost or stolen, your only recourse is to head to your embassy in Lima. If you have lost or had your passport stolen before, it may take up to a week while your embassy runs an international check on your identity.

PERUVIAN EMBASSIES AND CONSULATES ABROAD

If you are applying for a work visa or other type of special visa for Peru in the United States,

the flag of Peru

contact the consular section of the Peruvian embassy (tel. 202/833-9860, www.peruvianembassy.us), located in **Washington D.C.** Additionally, there are consulates in Atlanta, Boston, Chicago, Dallas, Denver, Hartford, Honolulu, Houston, Los Angeles, Miami, New Orleans, New York, Paterson, Phoenix, Sacramento, Salt Lake City, San Francisco, San Juan, Seattle, St. Louis, and Tulsa.

The Peruvian embassy in **Canada** is in Ottawa (tel. 613/238-1777, www.embassyofperu.ca), with consulates in Calgary, Montreal, Toronto, Vancouver, and Winnipeg. In the United Kingdom the embassy and consular section are both in **London** (tel. 020/7235-1917, www.peruembassy-uk.com). In **South Africa,** the Peruvian embassy and consulate are in Pretoria (tel. 27-12/348-8744, embaperu6@telkomsa.net).

In **Australia** the embassy is in Barton, Canberra (tel. 612/6273-7351, www.embaperu.org.au), with consulate offices in Brisbane, Melbourne, Sydney. In **New Zealand** the embassy is in Wellington (tel. 64-4/499-8087, embassy.peru@xtra.co.nz), and there are two honorary consulates in Auckland and Christchurch. There is a complete list of Peruvian embassies and consulates around the world (www.rree.gob.pe/portal/misrree.nsf/webdiremb?OpenForm) on the Foreign Relations Ministry website.

FOREIGN EMBASSIES IN PERU

Many foreign travelers are surprised by how little help their own embassy will provide during an emergency or a tight situation abroad. If you have been robbed and have no money, expect no help from your embassy, apart from replacing your passport. The same applies if you have broken Peruvian law, even by doing something that would be legal in your own country. Go ahead and contact your embassy in an emergency, but don't wait for them to call back.

These embassies are all in Lima: **United States** (Av. La Encalada, Block 17, Surco, tel. 01/434-3000, http://lima.usembassy.gov/, 8 A.M.–5 P.M. Mon.–Fri.), **Canada** (Libertad

130, Miraflores, tel. 01/444-4015, www.cana-dainternational.gc.ca/peru-perou/, 8–11 A.M. and 2–4 P.M. Mon.–Fri.), **United Kingdom** (Av. Larco 1301, 22nd Fl., Miraflores, tel. 01/617-3000, http://ukinperu.fco.gov.uk/, 8 A.M.–1 P.M. Mon.–Fri.), and **South Africa** (tel. 612/4848, www.dfa.gov.za/foreign/sa_abroad/sap.htm). **Australia** does not have an embassy in Lima—the closest is in Santiago, Chile (www.chile.embassy.gov.au), but it does have a consulate (tel. 01/222-8281, www.aus-tralia.org.pe).

If you find yourself in trouble, your best hope for finding a lawyer, good doctor, or a bit of moral support may not be with your embassy, but with the **South American Explorers Club (SAE)** (www.saexplorers.org), which has offices in Cusco (Choquechaca 188, #4, tel. 084/24-5484, cuscoclub@saexplorers.org, 9:30 A.M.–5 P.M. Mon.–Fri., 10 A.M.–1 P.M. Sat.) and Lima (Piura 135, Miraflores, tel. 01/445-3306, limaclub@saexplorers.org, 9:30 A.M.–5 P.M. Mon.–Fri., 9:30 A.M.–1 P.M. Sat.).

TAXES

Foreign travelers are required to pay a US$31 exit tax before boarding an international flight and US$6.82 for all domestic flights.

As of 2001, foreigners no longer have to pay a 19 percent value-added tax, commonly known as **IGV** or *impuesto general a las ventas* on rooms or meals purchased at hotels. When you check into a nice hotel, the receptionist will require to photocopy your passport. Check your bill upon leaving.

Foreigners still have to pay the 19 percent IGV at upscale restaurants that are not affili-ated with hotels. These restaurants often tack on a 10 percent service charge as well.

CUSTOMS

Peru's customs office (*aduana*) is notorious for being strict with travelers coming back from Miami with loads of imported goodies. That is why you will see a line of Limeños nervously waiting to pass through the stoplight at the Peruvian customs checkpoint. If you get the unlucky red light, you should know the rules.

Travelers are allowed to bring three liters of alcohol and 20 packs of cigarettes into Peru duty-free. You can also bring in US$300 worth of gifts, but not to trade or sell.

On your way home, it is illegal to leave Peru with genuine archaeological artifacts, historic art, or animal products from endangered spe-cies. If you're caught you will surely be arrested and prosecuted. Your home country will not let you bring in coca leaves but rarely do they hassle you about coca teabags.

BORDER CROSSINGS

Peru has around 10 official border crossings with Chile, Ecuador, Brazil, and Colombia. They are open year-round and are not usually a hassle as long as one's passport and tourist card are in order.

POLICE

Peruvian police officers are incredibly helpful and, for the most part, honest. Always carry your passport with you or a photocopy of it if you decide to leave your passport where you are staying. Other means of identification are pretty much worthless, unless you're renting a car and need to show your international driv-er's license. If you are stopped on the street, the only thing police are allowed to do is check your Peruvian visa or passport. If police hassle you for a bribe for whatever reason, politely refuse and offer to go to the police station or just act like you don't understand. Police will usually just give up and let you go.

Police corruption is much less common now in Peru than it was a decade ago. If you have an encounter with a crooked cop, get the officer's name and badge number and call Peru's 24-hour, English-speaking tourist police hotline (tel. 01/574-8000).

Peru has set up tourist police offices in Arequipa, Ayacucho, Cajamarca, Chiclayo, Cusco, Huancayo, Huaraz, Ica, Iquitos, Lima, Nasca, Puno, Tacna, and Trujillo. In Lima, the emergency number for the police is **tel. 105,** but English-speaking operators are usu-ally not available. Your best bet is to call the 24-hour hotline.

mounted police on parade in Cusco

© GABRIELLA HOLLAND

Conduct and Customs

ETIQUETTE

Peruvians invariably exchange a *buenos días* or good morning, a *buenas tardes* or good afternoon, or a *buenas noches* or good evening. Women and men greet each other with a single kiss on the right cheek, though highland Indians generally just offer a hand—sometimes just a wrist if they have been working.

The title *señora* is reserved for older or married women with children and can be quite insulting if addressed to a younger girl. *Señorita* is for younger, usually unmarried women. *Señor* is used to address men, and *don* or *doña* is used for elder men or women as a sign of respect.

Machismo in rural areas especially is very much a part of Peruvian culture. Men will often direct dinner conversation only toward other men. Women can handle this situation by directing conversation at both the men and women alike at the table.

Peruvians typically dress nicely and conservatively, especially when dealing with official business or entering a church. Women in these cases should consider wearing pants or a skirt that is longer than knee length, and men should avoid shorts or casual T-shirts. Despite that, fashion in Lima and Amazon towns is more relaxed. You are likely to see men in shorts and women in shorts or short skirts. You should feel comfortable doing the same. Away from Lima or the jungle, shorts can be worn when participating in an athletic activity that requires them: trekking, beach volleyball, or even running. Foreigners will call less attention to themselves if they wear generally inconspicuous clothing.

CULTURE

Family is still the center of Peruvian society. Extended families often live in neighboring houses, and young cousins can be raised together as if they were brothers and sisters, especially in rural areas and small cities and towns. Women travelers over the age of 20 might be asked whether or not they are married or have children.

Many Peruvians seem to not be bothered with high noise levels, a cultural difference that most Western foreigners find grating. Shops will blare merengue, *tecnocumbia,* and other Latin pop music to the point where conversation becomes impossible but commerce goes on as usual. Radios tend to be turned up at the first sign of morning light, and workmen start hammering at dawn, so sleeping in is often out of the question. Ear plugs can be handy under these circumstances.

Most Peruvians are also used to crowded spaces and don't mind sitting close to one another on buses and *colectivos.* While at the bank, they will stand just inches away from one another even though there is plenty of space around. In the highlands, houses tend to be small, often with many family members sleeping in the same room. Women travelers often think that men are pressing in on them, when actually they just have a different sense of space.

Peruvians also have a very different relationship toward time, taking things relaxed and slow without the hectic attitude of Westerners. If you agree to meet somebody at noon, expect to wait at least 15–30 minutes. You will inevitably sit in a restaurant longer than anticipated, waiting for your food, waiting for your bill, and then waiting some more for your change. You are never going to change this, so just sit back, be patient, and smile.

PANHANDLING

Whether or not to give money to those asking for it on the street is a personal decision. The hardest to turn down are the street kids with rosy, dirt-covered cheeks and an outstretched hand. In the countryside, children will frequently ask for money in exchange for having their picture taken. Remember that when you give them money, you are encouraging the practice in the future. Also, know that parents often have their children working as teams to collect money in the street. Instead of money, the best-prepared travelers give pens, notebooks, or other useful items.

© FIONA CAMERON

A Peruvian family prepares to serve *chicha*, a fermented corn beverage.

Tips for Travelers

ACCOMMODATIONS

Choosing the right place to stay is key to having a relaxed, enjoyable trip to Peru. The quality of lodging ranges dramatically in most Peruvian cities and often has no correlation whatsoever with price. If you plan well, you should usually be able to find a safe and quiet room, with a charming environment and a helpful staff.

Because where you stay makes a huge difference in the quality of your experience, we recommend making advance reservations by email—especially in hot spots like Lima, Arequipa, Huaraz, Cusco, and Puno and especially between the busy months May–September. Rates can increase as much as 50 percent during local festivals or national holidays such as the July 28 Fiestas Patrias weekend.

Walk-in travelers often get better rates than those who make reservations over email, but those with a reservation often get the corner room with a view, the quieter space off the street, or the room with a writing desk—especially if you ask for it in advance.

Lodging rates can be negotiated at budget hotels. That said, most hotels except for the top-end ones will probably have a low-season rate posted October–April, considerably lower than the usual rate posted year-round. But this depends on the city and can actually vary month to month.

Before you pay for a room, ask to see one or two rooms to get a sense of the quality standard at the hotel. Look carefully at how safe a hotel is, especially what neighborhood it is in, and avoid lodging around discos, bars, bus stations, or other places nearby that might make your room noisy at night. Inspect the bathrooms carefully and turn on the hot water to make sure it exists. If you are in a cold area, like Puno or Cusco, ask if the hotel provides electric heaters. If you are in a jungle city, ask if there are fans. If you are planning to make calls from your room, ask if there is direct-dial service that allows the use of phone cards—otherwise you will have to wait for the receptionist to make your call at a hefty rate that can be as much as US$0.50 per minute for local calls.

Budget Hotels

The cheaper establishments are called *hospedajes,* and the *hostales* are usually a bit fancier. There are government rules that define

---

WHAT TO TAKE

Travel light and have a carefree vacation – drop-off laundry is common in Peru, so bring five days' **clothing** and put it all in a medium-sized backpack. For the warmer weather of the Sacred Valley and Machu Picchu, we recommend light, fast-drying clothing that protects your arms and legs from sun and insects. Protect yourself from the sun with a wide-brimmed hat, bandanas, sunscreen, and sunglasses. For the colder weather of Cusco, or the Inca Trail, add a lightweight rain jacket, fleece jacket, and silk-weight long underwear.

Miscellaneous items include a Leatherman-style folding knife, small roll of duct tape for repairs, mending kit, hand sanitizer, headlamp with extra batteries, camera, voltage adapter, water bottle, roll of toilet paper (Peru's public bathrooms are always out), binoculars, pocket English-Spanish dictionary, book, journal, and a tiny calculator for confirming money exchanges. Don't forget your **medical kit** with standard medicines, insect repellent, and water purification tablets.

Paperwork should include valid passport, plane ticket, student card if you have one, a yellow vaccinations card, travelers checks, ATM card and credit card, and a copy of your travel insurance details. Email yourself numbers for travelers checks, passport, and credit cards in case these things get stolen. Photocopies of the first few pages of your passport and your plane ticket are also a good idea.

the difference between both and a hotel. Key things to look for with a budget place are the quality of the beds, nifty perks like shared kitchen or free Internet, or even WiFi nowadays, the cleanliness of the bathroom, and how the water is heated. A few hotels use water heaters with a limited supply of hot water. A few others use electric showerheads, which heat water with an electrical current like that of a toaster oven. Often the device needs to be turned on at the showerhead or via a circuit breaker in the bathroom. The whole concept is unnerving, but the devices are surprisingly safe. The problem is they often only make the water lukewarm. Fortunately, the majority have switched to gas water heaters.

Midrange Hotels

This category of lodging tends to encompass modern, charmless buildings with a fancy reception area and average rooms with tacky decorations. But they are usually a sure bet for hot water, safe rooms, phones, WiFi Internet, and refrigerators.

High-End Hotels

Nearly all major Peruvian cities have high-end hotels with the full range of international creature comforts, including swimming pools, WiFi Internet, spring mattresses, alarm clocks, refrigerators, loads of hot water, bathtubs, and direct-dial phones. The fancier establishments often have kitchenettes, slippers, bathrobes, and complimentary toiletries. Often suites are just a bit more expensive but much more luxurious. These hotels invariably charge a 19 percent value-added tax, which by law must be refunded to travelers as long you require so and the hotel has a copy of your passport.

DINING

Nowadays, a traveler's experience of Peruvian food can be a unique experience, considering that Peru has the best, most interesting and varied food offer in Latin America. It can also be a double-edged sword, especially if you have a sensitive stomach. Many travelers return with fond memories of the exquisite and surprising range of flavors, while others return with their stomachs crawling with bacteria or parasites. Choose where you eat carefully and work from the recommendations in this book or from fellow travelers. Peruvians often recommend *huariques,* or hole-in-the-wall restaurants that work well for their hardy stomachs, but not necessarily for yours.

Service at Peruvian restaurants is broken down into various steps, which include receiving the menu, ordering, waiting for food, waiting for the bill, and then waiting for change. If you are eating lunch, you can order from the *menú,* the fixed menu of the day, usually a list of prepared entrées and main courses that can be served quickly. À la carte items are more expensive than the *menú.* Many travelers choose to make their own breakfasts by buying yogurt, cereal, and some fruit if they have the facilities at the hostel. If you get good service it is encouraged to leave around 10 percent of the bill as a gratuity.

EMPLOYMENT

Jobs teaching English in Peru are easy to find and can often be arranged in-country without a work visa (which doesn't mean you will be legal). You should first scan expatriate bulletin boards in Lima, where language schools often advertise jobs for around US$8 per hour. One of Lima's better language schools is **El Sol** (http://elsol.idiomasperu.com).

International organizations that help find teaching positions include **Amerispan** (www.amerispan.com) and **TEFL** (www.tcfl.com). These organizations are also worth contacting: **International Schools Services** (U.S. tel. 609/452-0990, www.iss.edu), **Británico** (Lima tel. 01/447-1192, www.britanico.edu. pe), **American Language Institute** (alisac@terra.com.pe, contact Joseph Phrower in Lima), **Teaching Abroad in the U.K.** (www.teaching-abroad.co.uk), or **EFL** (efl. institute@terra.com.pe) in Lima. Wherever you work, make sure you get a contract in writing.

Other paid employment can be found through the **International Jobs Center** (www.internationaljobs.org). This organization collects information on current international job openings with governments, government contractors, United Nations agencies, private voluntary organizations, and student exchange organizations. Membership, including posting your credentials in its database and access to profiles of major employers, is US$26 for six weeks.

For tips on living in Peru see **Living In Peru** (www.livinginperu.com) or **Expat Peru** (www.expatperu.com); both webpages have resourceful information for expatriates with everything from apartments to tips on how to deal with cultural differences.

VOLUNTEERING

There are hundreds of volunteer opportunities in Peru, involving art and culture, community development, disability and addiction services, ecotourism and the environment, education, health care, and services for children and women. Although these organizations do not pay salaries, they often provide food or accommodation in exchange for your time.

The most common complaint with volunteer work is that the organization is disorganized, there is not enough meaningful work, or that organizations are exploiting eager beavers for their own bottom line. For that reason, do research and try to speak with people who have worked with the organization in the past.

One source for volunteer information in Peru is the Lima office of the **South American Explorers Club** (Piura 135, Miraflores, tel. 01/445-3306, www.saexplorers.com, 9:30 A.M.–5 P.M. Mon.–Fri., 9:30 A.M.–1 P.M. Sat.). If you're a member, you can even access the volunteer database online. If you're not, you can send an email or buy a phone card and talk to someone in person. Another organization in Lima that hooks up volunteers with organizations is **Trabajo Voluntario** (www.trabajovoluntario.org). A

good global resource for finding volunteer organizations is www.idealist.org.

There are many Spanish-language schools that combine teaching with volunteering. If you take morning language lessons, the school will often set you up with volunteer work for a minimal administration fee.

There are also many Peru-based volunteer organizations. Check out **Lucho Hurtado's** programs in Huancayo (www.incasdelperu.org); the organization **Center for Social Well Being** (www.socialwellbeing.org) in Carhuaz in the Cordillera Blanca; and **Awamaki** in Ollantaytambo (www.awamaki.org).

Crooked Trails (U.S. tel. 206/383-9828, www.crookedtrails.com) is a nonprofit, community-based travel organization with excellent 3–4 week volunteer travel programs in communities located in countries such as Peru, Ecuador, Guatemala, India, Nepal, Thailand, Bhutan, and Kenya, creating true cultural exchange bonds that make positive contributions to host countries and achieving lasting effects on their travelers.

Cross-Cultural Solutions Peru (U.S. tel. 800/330-4777, U.K. tel. 01237/66-6392, www.crossculturalsolutions.org) runs highly professional volunteer programs mainly for students from the United Kingdom and the United States in Lima, Trujillo, and Ayacucho. In Lima, the company works in Villa El Salvador, the shantytown that was a Nobel Peace Prize nominee for its community organization. The program is quite expensive but recommended for its professional staff. Costs are US$2,489 for two weeks with every additional week costing US$272.

World Leadership School (U.S. tel. 303/679-3412, www.worldleadershipschool.com) helps middle and high schools in the U.S. create global programs with schools in Peru. During the 3–4 week programs, volunteers focus on a single global issue, such as climate change, education, or public health. Volunteers understand and develop competence with each issue by working on solutions at the community level. The programs include a leadership

© CRAIG GEMMELL

High school and college students are increasingly participating in volunteer experiences in the Sacred Valley and other areas of Peru.

curriculum and mentorship from local leaders, who share their perspective and wisdom.

ProWorld (U.S. tel. 877/429-6753, U.K. tel. 870/750-7202, www.myproworld.org) has locations in Peru, Belize, and Mexico. In Peru, ProWorld is based out of Urubamba, where, since 2000, it has built schools, irrigation systems, and bridges; replanted forests; helped developed sustainable industries like agro-tourism; and sent volunteers to work with countless local nonprofits. They have programs ranging from two weeks to a semester in length and they offer academic credit. Prices begin at US$1,795 for two weeks.

World Youth International (www.worldyouth.com.au) organizes volunteer programs in Cusco such as the Clínica San Juan de Dios, which is a well-organized resident program for children with disabilities.

Kiya Survivors (U.K. tel. 01273/72-1092, www.kiyasurvivors.org) works with special-needs children, abandoned women, and young single mothers. It is run by British citizen Suzy Butler out of Cusco and offers volunteer placements of 2–6 months. A standard six-month placement includes in-country tours, accommodations, and a tax-deductible donation to the organization.

The highly recommended nonprofit **Mundo Azul** (Lima tel. 01/447-5190, www.mundoazul.org/english) is dedicated to conserving natural biodiversity, and its volunteers play a first-hand role in helping that mission happen. The two-week to month-long volunteer programs take participants to the ocean to research dolphin populations or dive into open water to collect marine species. (Only experienced divers can apply for the latter option.) A rainforest trip to Manu involves researching tapirs, macaws, and giant river otters.

Ania (Lima tel. 01/628-7948, www.mundodeania.org) is an innovative nonprofit founded by Peruvian Joaquín Leguía in 1995. The nonprofit has focused mainly on helping children across Peru, and the world, connect with their love for nature through a creative, grass-roots effort that includes Ania, a cartoon character, and a series of Tierra de Niños natural areas. These "Children's Lands" are owned, designed, and maintained by children and range from only a few meters squared to a giant nature reserve near Puerto Maldonado. Leguía, who has been awarded the prestigious Ashoka fellowship, plans to begin working with volunteers, so check for available placements.

OPPORTUNITIES FOR STUDY

Peru has a variety of great Spanish-language programs in Lima, Huaraz, Cusco, Urubamba, Arequipa, Huancayo, and Puerto Maldonado. These programs offer either private instruction for US$7–15 per hour or much cheaper group classes that last between a week and a month. Many of these programs will also set up homestays, hikes, classes, and other activities. The schools vary in quality, so we recommend asking the school for email addresses of former students in order to contact them. Many of the schools also engage in volunteer projects, which is a great way to immerse into Spanish. When choosing a school, think carefully about what situation will provide the most immersion. We recommend a homestay where you will not be able to speak English and a city where there are few foreigners.

Council on International Educational Exchange (www.ciee.org) organizes study-abroad programs and has links to a variety of programs.

BSES Expeditions (U.K. tel. 0207/591-3141, www.bses.org.uk) runs annual science expeditions for British teenagers, though Americans also sign up. The trips usually include science "base camps" in unusual areas of Peru, along with trekking, rafting, and other adventure activities.

WOMEN TRAVELING ALONE

Machismo is alive and well in Peru, so women traveling in Peru should know what to expect. Most Latin men assume that a woman traveling on her own, especially a blonde, must be promiscuous. So you have to set the record straight.

At some level, there is the larger issue that some men feel threatened by women who travel abroad, study, work, and are generally independent because it conflicts with their perceptions of how women should be.

How you interact with men makes a huge difference. Speak with men you do not know in public places only. Treat them neutrally and avoid intimate conversation and behaviors, like friendly touches that might be misinterpreted. Wear modest clothing. Some say a fake wedding ring or a reference to a nonexistent husband or boyfriend helps, but that can also result in the reply *"no soy celoso"* ("I'm not jealous").

Peruvian men, and often teenagers, will ingratiate themselves with a group of female gringas and tag along for hours, even if they are completely ignored. The best way to deal with this is by telling them early on that you want to be alone: *"quiero estar sola, por favor."* The next step would be a loud and clear request to be left alone: *"déjeme, por favor."* The final step would be to ask passersby for help" *"por favor, ayúdeme."* The bad side of machismo is harassment, but the flip side is protection.

Be especially careful at night. Choose a hotel in a safe, well-lit part of town. Take care when flagging down a taxi and do not walk around alone at night, especially in tourist towns like Cusco. Walk with confidence and purpose, even if you do not know where you are going. Women who look lost are inevitably approached by strangers. Peruvian women ignore catcalls, aggressive come-ons, and flirtatious lines called *piropos,* which are almost a form of poetry among men. You should do the same.

Do not walk alone in out-of-the-way places in the countryside. We have heard reports of women who have been assaulted while walking alone on popular travelers' routes. Trek or hike in the daylight and with at least one other person. If you are robbed, surrender your purse rather than risk physical harm. Mace, whistles, alarms, and self-defense skills are effective tools that are likely to catch most assailants off-guard.

GAY AND LESBIAN TRAVELERS

Peru is far from progressive for gay and lesbian travelers, and Lima's gay scene is considerably smaller than that in other major South American capitals. There are a variety of well-hidden and exclusively gay bars, restaurants, and clubs in cities like Lima, and a growing number in Iquitos and Cusco—though none cater exclusively to lesbians. Most gay men in Peru's *machista* society are still in the closet and maintain heterosexual relationships as well as homosexual ones.

The only way to find about gay and lesbian establishments is online. The concept of gay rights is still relatively new in Peru, so gay and lesbian travelers are advised to be discreet and exercise caution. The best resource is the bilingual website **Gay Lima** (http://lima.queercity. info), written by a U.S. citizen living in Lima. It gives a good overview of gay and lesbian life in Peru and is updated constantly with the latest bars, nightclubs, and hotels, and also includes chat rooms and links. Another good online resource is **Gay Peru** (www.gayperu.com), a great site on gay travel, including gay-oriented package tours, although it is in Spanish only.

For those interested in learning about gay rights in Peru, check the website in Spanish of the **Movimiento Homosexual de Lima** (www. mhol.org.pe), one of the oldest gay movements in Peru.

The San Francisco–based **Now Voyager** (www.nowvoyager.com) is a worldwide gay-owned, gay-operated full-service travel agency, as is **Purple Roofs** (www.purpleroofs.com). The **International Gay and Lesbian Travel Association** (www.iglta.org) has an extensive directory of travel agents, tour operators, and accommodations that are gay and lesbian friendly. **Above Beyond Tours** (www. abovebeyondtours.com) is a California-based gay travel specialist offering independent and group travel packages.

ACCESSIBILITY

Facilities for people with disabilities are improving in Peru but are far from adequate. Most bathrooms are impossible to enter in a wheelchair. Hotel stairways are usually narrow and steep, and ramps are few and far between. Peru's sidewalks are hard to navigate with a wheelchair because they are frequently narrow, potholed, and lack ramps. Cars usually do not respect pedestrians, so cross streets with extreme caution.

The exceptions to the above are airports and high-end hotels. Peruvian hotel chains such as **Libertador** (www.libertador.com.pe) and **Casa Andina** (www.casa-andina.com) stand out for providing accessible rooms in hotels in Trujillo, Lima, Cusco, the Sacred Valley, the Colca Canyon, Arequipa, and Nasca.

PromPeru, the government tourism commission, has launched a major accessibility campaign and now claims that more than a hundred tourist facilities in Aguas Calientes, Cusco, Iquitos, Lima, and Trujillo have been approved for travelers with disabilities. PromPeru lists these wheelchair-accessible places on its web page (www.promperu.gob. pe). Other resources for disabled travelers include **Access-Able Travel Source** (www.access-able.com) and **Society for Accessible Travel and Hospitality** (U.S. tel. 212/447-7284, www.sath.org).

SENIORS

Many organized tours of Peru cater to senior travelers. The major airlines offer discounts for seniors, as do international chain hotels, but other than that, senior discounts in Peru are nonexistent. For visiting the jungle, Amazon cruise boats are an excellent option for people with limited walking abilities.

Good senior agencies include **SAGA Holidays** (www.saga.co.uk), which offers all-inclusive tours and cruises for those 50 and older. **Elderhostel** (U.S. tel. 800/454-5768, www.elderhostel.org) arranges study programs for people 55 and over in countries worldwide, including Peru.

TRAVELING WITH YOUNG CHILDREN

With the right planning, traveling with kids through Peru can be a blast. Kids tend to attract lots of attention from passersby and can cause interesting cultural interactions. By traveling through Peru, children learn a great deal and gain an understanding of how different life can be for people across the world.

Experts suggest that children should be involved in the early stages of a trip in order to get the most out of it. Children's books and movies that deal with the history of the Inca and the Spaniards will help your kids better relate to the ruins they will see later on. Parents should explain to children what they will encounter, prep them for the day's activities, and then hear from them how it went afterwards.

Keeping your children healthy means taking precautions. Make sure your children get the right vaccinations, and watch what they eat while they are in Peru, because the major threat to their health is dehydration caused by diarrhea. Bacterial infection can be prevented by washing children's hands frequently with soap or using hand sanitizer.

For very young children, don't bother bringing your own baby food, as it is cheaper in the country. You will have a hard time, however, finding specialty items like sugar-free foods, which should be brought from home. Outside of Peru's major cities, there is not much selection in supermarkets, so stock up while you can. Always carry a good supply of snacks and bottled water with you, as there can be long stretches where nothing to eat or drink is available.

Pack your **medical kit** with everything you will need for basic first aid: bandages and gauze pads, antibacterial ointment, thermometer, child mosquito repellent (vitamin B acts as a natural mosquito repellent), envelopes of hydrating salts, and strong sunscreen.

Items like Tylenol (*paracetamol infantil*), can easily be found in the local pharmacies, though quality varies. Medical services are very good in Lima and often quite good in the countryside, where city-trained, English-speaking medical students perform residency. Medical care is so cheap in Peru that parents should never hesitate about seeing a doctor. Bring photocopies of your children's medical records.

Your embassy may be of some help, but the best place to contact for advice or help is probably the **South American Explorers Club** (Piura 135, Miraflores, tel. 01/445-3306, www. saexplorers.com, 9:30 A.M.–5 P.M. Mon.–Fri., 9:30 A.M.–1 P.M. Sat.).

Think carefully about your travel arrangements. Kids are likely to enjoy a sensory-rich environment like the Amazon jungle much more than back-to-back tours of archaeological ruins. Buses generally allow children to travel for free until 5 years old and/or if they sit on your lap, but choose flights over long bus rides that could make kids crabby. Choose family-oriented hotels, which offer playgrounds and lots of space for children to run around unsupervised. If you ask for a room with three beds you generally won't have to pay extra. If you have toddlers, avoid hotels with pools, because they are rarely fenced off. Children's rates for anything from movies to museums are common and, even if they are not official, can often be negotiated.

Because parents are often distracted by their children, families can be prime targets for thieves in public spaces like bus stations and markets. Even if you have taught your children to be extra careful about traffic at home, you will have to teach them a whole new level of awareness in Peru. Time moves slower in Peru, and families spend a lot of time waiting for buses, tours, or meals. Be prepared with coloring books and other activities.

Health and Safety

It pays to think ahead about your health before traveling to Peru. With the right vaccinations, a little bit of education, and a lot of common sense, the worst that happens to most visitors is a bit of traveler's diarrhea.

Things get more complicated if you decide to visit the jungle, because Peru, like parts of Africa and Asia, lies in the tropical zone. Travelers who visit the Amazon should be vaccinated against yellow fever, be taking malarial medicine, and take full precautions against mosquitoes.

VACCINATIONS

Vaccination recommendations can be obtained from the **Centers for Disease Control (CDC)** (U.S. tel. 877/394-8747, www.cdc.gov/travel), which recommends the following vaccinations for Peru: **hepatitis A** and **typhoid. Yellow fever** is recommended for people traveling into the jungle below 2,300 meters. Rabies is recommended if you are going to be trekking through areas where the disease is endemic. **Hepatitis B** is recommended if you might be exposed to blood (for instance, health-care workers, plan on staying for more than six months, or may have sex with a local. Travelers should also be vaccinated against **measles** and **chicken pox** (those who have had these diseases are already immune) and have had a **tetanus/diphtheria** shot within the last 10 years.

Unless you are coming from a region in the Americas or Africa where yellow fever is a problem, you are not required by Peruvian law to have any vaccinations before entering the country. The yellow immunizations pamphlet, which doctors tell you to guard ever so carefully, is rarely checked, but you should carry it with your passport. The shots can be quite expensive, in the United States at least, and many of the shots require second or even third visits. Hepatitis A, for instance, requires a booster shot 6–18 months after the initial shot, which most people get after returning

from Peru. Hepatitis B is generally received in three doses, and there are new vaccines now that combine both hep A and hep B in a series of three shots. Rabies is also given in three shots, though both yellow fever and typhoid are single shots.

Most vaccinations do not take effect for at least two weeks, so schedule your shots well in advance. If you are taking multishot vaccinations such as hep B, you will need to receive your first shot five weeks before departing, even under the most accelerated schedule. Getting shots in Peru is easy and a lot cheaper than in the United States, but you will not be protected for the first 2–4 weeks. Places to get shots include **Suiza Lab** (Atahualpa 308, Miraflores, tel. 01/612-6666, www.suizalab.com.pe, 7:30 A.M.–6 P.M. Mon.–Sat., 8 A.M.–2 P.M. daily), **Oficinas de Vacunación** (Independencia 121, Breña, 8 A.M.–12:30 P.M. Mon.–Sat.), and **International Vaccination Center** (Parque de la Medicina s/n, Dos de Mayo National Hospital, 7:30 A.M.–1:30 P.M. Mon.–Sat.).

TRAVELER'S DIARRHEA

Traveler's diarrhea pulls down even the stoutest of Peru travelers eventually and can be very unpleasant. It can be caused by parasites or viruses, but most often it is caused by bacteria carried in food or water. Plenty of other diseases in Peru are spread this way, including cholera, hepatitis A, and typhoid. Nothing is more important for you health-wise than thinking carefully about everything you eat and drink.

Only drink bottled water or water that has been previously boiled. Instead of buying an endless succession of plastic bottles, which will end up in a landfill, travel with a few reusable hard plastic bottles and ask your hotel to fill them with boiling water every morning. Refilling bottles is especially easy at hotels that have water tanks, or *bidones*, of purified water.

PACKING A MEDICAL KIT

Having a small medical kit will come in handy over and over again in Peru, especially in remote areas. Here's a checklist of what should be included:

- antacid tablets (Tums)

- antihistamine (Benadryl)

- diarrhea medication (Imodium)

- motion-sickness medication (Dramamine)

- lots of ibuprofen (Advil)

- lots of acetaminophen (Tylenol)

- Pepto-Bismol (liquid is better)

- insect repellent (12–35 percent DEET or above)

- insect clothing spray (permethrin)

- water purification tablets

- bandages, gauze pads, and cloth tape

- butterfly bandages or Superglue (for sealing gashes)

- Ace bandage

- decongestant spray (Afrin)

- packages of rehydration salts

- antibacterial ointment (Neosporin)

- fungus cream (Tinactin)

- hydrocortisone cream for bug bites

- Moleskin, both thin and foam

- tweezers

- scissors or knife

- syringe and needles

- thermometer

- CPR shield (if you are CPR-certified)

- latex gloves

Your doctor might suggest the following: Advil for pain (no more than 2,000 milligrams per day), Tylenol for fevers over 101.5°F (38.6°C), and Pepto-Bismol for stomach upset and diarrhea (it apparently has a slight antibiotic effect too).

The following antibiotics can be prescribed by your doctor before traveling as well: Keflex (cephalexin) works for systemic infections, like when a cut causes your foot to swell; Zithromax or erythromycin for respiratory infections; and ciprofloxacin for gastrointestinal issues – though it is better to consult a local doctor before taking any of these medicines. Acetazaolamide, commonly known as Diamox, is effective for altitude sickness. If you want to be super-cautious, an Epi-Pen or Ana-Kit that contains epinephrine is the best safeguard against severe allergic reaction to insect stings.

Travelers should also put in their medical kit their brief medical history, including recent allergies and illness. If you take prescription drugs, include written instructions for how you take them and the doctor's prescription as well, just in case you get stopped in customs.

The medical kit only works at the level of the person who is using it. If you can't take a first-aid course, a backcountry wilderness guide like that published by Wilderness Medicine Institute (www.nols.edu/wmi/) will come in handy. Nearly all these medicines, including the antibiotics, can be bought in a pharmacy in Peru without a prescription – either generic or high-quality brands.

Order drinks without ice unless you can be assured it is bagged ice or previously boiled water in order to make ice. Wipe the edges of cans and bottles before drinking or carry straws.

Avoid street vendors and buffets served under the hot sun. Instead, choose restaurants that come well recommended for taking precautions for foreigners. If the kitchen looks clean and the restaurant is full, it is probably all right. Before and after you eat, wash your hands with soap where available. Carry an antibacterial hand sanitizer as a backup.

The safest foods in restaurants are those that are served piping hot. Soups, well-cooked vegetables, rice, and pastas are usually fine. Eat salads and raw vegetables with extreme caution and confirm beforehand that they have been previously soaked in a chlorine solution. Better yet, prepare your own salads with food disinfectants for sale in most Peruvian supermarkets if you have the facilities to cook your own meals.

An exception to the no-raw-foods rule is *cebiche*, which is raw fish marinated in bacteria-killing lime juice. As long as you are in a reputable restaurant, *cebiche* is a safe bet.

Market foods that are safe include all fruits and vegetables that can be peeled, like bananas, oranges, avocados, and apples. Many local fruits are okay as well, including chirimoya, tuna (the prickly cactus fruit), and *granadilla*. Dangerous items include everything that hangs close to the ground and could have become infected with feces in irrigation water. These include strawberries, mushrooms, lettuce, and tomatoes. There are plenty of safe things to buy in the market and, when combined with other safe items like bread and packaged cheese, make for a great lunch.

ALTITUDE SICKNESS

Cusco sits at 3,400 meters, and your main health concern should be altitude sickness. You will know if you're suffering from this illness very soon after your arrival. Symptoms include shortness of breath, quickened heartbeats, fatigue, loss of appetite, headaches, and nausea. There is no way to prevent it, but you can minimize the effect by avoiding heavy exercise until you get acclimatized and drinking plenty of water and liquids in general.

Many travelers carry acetazolamide, commonly known as Diamox, usually prescribed by a doctor in doses of 125–250 milligrams, taken during the morning and evening with meals. In Cusco everybody will say that coca leaf tea or *mate de coca,* taken in plentiful amounts, is the best remedy for *soroche,* the Quechua word for altitude sickness. And it works. A 100-milligram dose of the Chinese herb ginkgo billoba, taken twice a day, seems to work efficiently, too.

If you feel sick, it's good to know that all hospitals and clinics in Cusco have bottled oxygen. If you happen to be in a five-star hotel like Monasterio, Libertador, or Casa Andina Private Collection, they will provide oxygen in the rooms upon request. Have in mind that altitude sickness, if not taken care off appropriately, can develop into **high-altitude pulmonary edema,** with acute chest pain, coughs, and fluid buildup in the lungs, or **high-altitude cerebral edema,** involving severe headaches coupled with bizarre changes of personality. In both cases, these illnesses can lead to death if not treated immediately and adequately.

Hospital Regional (Av. de la Cultura, tel. 084/24-3240) and the **Hospital Lorena** (Plazoleta Belén 1358, Santiago district, tel. 084/22-1581) are the main health centers in Cusco. A bit more expensive, but faster and more reliable, is **Clínica Pardo** (Av. de la Cultura 710, tel. 084/24-0387). In an emergency situation try going to the hospital with a local if you're not fluent in Spanish.

DOGS AND RABIES

There are lots of wild (or at least surly) dogs in Peru, as trekkers in places like the Cordillera Huayhuash soon find out. If you are planning to spend a lot of time trekking in Peru, you should consult with your doctor about getting a rabies vaccine.

There are lots of things you can do to avoid being bitten by a dog. As cute or as hungry as a dog may look, be careful about petting a dog in Peru unless you know the owner. Many street dogs have been mistreated and have highly unpredictable behavior.

If you are walking into an area with dogs, collect a few stones. All Peruvian dogs are acutely aware of how much a well-aimed stone can hurt, and they will usually scatter even if you pretend to pick up a stone, or pretend to throw one. This is by far the best way to stop a dog, or a pack of them, from bothering you.

If you do get bitten, wash the wound with soap and water and rinse it with alcohol or iodine. If possible, test the animal for rabies. Rabies is a fatal disease. If there is any doubt about whether the animal was rabid, you should receive rabies shots immediately.

HYPOTHERMIA

Peru's snow-covered mountains, highlands, and even cloud forests have plenty of cold, rainy days, conditions in which hypothermia is most likely to occur. Watch yourself and those around you for early signs of hypothermia, which include shivering, crankiness, exhaustion, clammy skin, and loss of fine coordination. In more advanced hypothermia the person stumbles, slurs his or her speech, acts irrationally, and eventually becomes unconscious, a state doctors refer to as the "metabolic ice box."

The key to preventing hypothermia is being prepared for the elements, and that starts with clothing. When you go for a hike, pack plenty of different layers in a plastic bag. Remember that cotton is great for evaporating sweat and cooling down on a hot day, but actually works against you in wet, cold weather. Artificial fibers like fleece or polypropylene work when wet because they wick water away from your body. Wool is another good choice because it insulates even when wet. And a waterproof poncho or a Gore-Tex jacket will help keep you dry. Having a lot of food and water is also important, and in demanding conditions you and everyone you are with should be fueling up constantly.

The key to avoiding hypothermia is catching it early. If you or someone in your group is shivering or having a hard time zipping up a jacket, take action immediately. In mild hypothermia, the body is still trying to warm itself, and all you have to do is support that process. Feed the person water and a variety of foods, from fast-burning chocolate to bread and cheese. Have them do vigorous exercises like squatting and standing over and over, or swinging their arms around like a windmill. If the person remains cold, set up a tent and put him or her in a sleeping bag with hot-water bottles. Monitor the person carefully until body temperature returns to normal. A person who was on the edge of hypothermia one day is more susceptible the next, so allow for at least a day or two of rest and recuperation.

SEXUALLY TRANSMITTED DISEASES

HIV/AIDS is a worldwide health problem that is spreading in Peru along with **hepatitis B** and other sexually transmitted diseases. The United Nations officially classifies Peru's AIDS epidemic as low-level and estimated in 2005 that there were between 89,000 and 93,000 people in Peru living with HIV/AIDS. About 74 percent of the adults were men, more than half of whom identified themselves as heterosexual. The number of infected women and children is rising.

Despite state-promoted campaigns that have increased the concept of safe sex in public's mind in Peru, many men still refuse to use condoms. HIV/AIDS and other sexually transmitted diseases may be transmitted just as often in homosexual sex as in heterosexual sex. Travelers should take full precautions before engaging in sex, beginning with the use of condoms.

MEDICAL CARE IN PERU

Peru's health-care system is excellent considering the fact that many Peruvians live in poverty.

Even small villages usually have a medical post, or *posta médica,* which is often staffed with a university-trained medical student completing his or her residency. Midsize cities like Huaraz have a range of health options, including a few government hospitals and a few private clinics. In general, the clinics provide more personalized, high-tech service, but plenty of state hospitals offer in general better health care than what you could ever get in the United States. A country doctor in Peru is probably going to identify your particular stomach ailment faster than a specialist in the United States, simply because the Peruvian doctor has seen your condition many times before.

For serious medical problems or accidents, we recommend that people travel to Lima. The best hospitals are there, and insurance companies abroad are often able to handle payments directly with them (elsewhere the patient is expected to shell out the cash and hopefully be reimbursed later).

Nearly all international medical policies will cover a speedy evacuation to your country if necessary, which is one of the main reasons for getting insurance in the first place. A good resource for advice in medical situations is the **South American Explorers Club** in Lima (Piura 135, Miraflores, tel. 01/445-3306, www.saexplorers.org).

MEDICAL TRAVEL INSURANCE

Most medical insurance will not cover you while traveling abroad, so most Peru travelers buy overseas medical insurance. Go with a reputable insurance company, or you will have trouble collecting claims. Nearly all Peru hospitals will make you pay up front, and then it's up to you to submit your claim.

Some U.S.-based companies that have been recommended by travelers include **Medex Assistance** (tel. 800/732-5309, www.medexassist.com), **Travel Assistance International** (tel. 800/237-2828, www.travelassistance.com), **Health Care Global** by Wallach and Company Inc. (tel. 800/237-6615, www.

wallach.com), and **International Medical Group** (tel. 800/628-4664, www.imglobal.com). Students can get insurance through the **STA** (tel. 800/226-8624, www.statravel.com).

Some companies sell additional riders to cover high-risk sports such as mountain climbing with a rope, paragliding, and bungee jumping. One good company is **Specialty Risk International** (tel. 800/335-0611, www.specialtyrisk.com), which insures for as little as three months. Membership with the **American Alpine Club** (tel. 303/384-0111, www.americanalpineclub.org) is open to anyone who has climbed in the last two years and includes rescue and evacuation for mountain climbers around the world.

PRESCRIPTION DRUGS

Generic medicines are easy to buy in Peru, much cheaper than in the U.S. or Europe, though quality might not always be the same. Travelers used to stock up their medical kit in Peru, but nowadays there are more restrictions with prescribed medicine, especially if you want to purchase it in big pharmacies, hospitals, or clinics. Specific birth control or allergy pills can be hard to find in Peru, unless you go to a private clinic pharmacy.

Though it's tempting, avoid self-medicating. Visiting a Peruvian doctor is inexpensive compared to U.S. and European rates. They are the world's leading experts on bacteria and parasite conditions specific to Peru, anyway, so it's worth it. You can waste a lot of time and money, and negatively affect your health, taking ciprofloxacin, for instance, when another medicine would have been better.

ILLEGAL DRUGS

According to the present Peruvian Criminal Code, the use and possession of drugs for personal consumption is not punished if the quantities are under the amounts stipulated by law (Art. 299: 2 grams of cocaine, 7 grams of marijuana). The problem is that almost no travelers and even very few police know this, and the police will probably still take you to the *comisaría* and charge you until a judge defines the amounts you carry. So to keep it safe, it is highly recommended not to take drugs while in Peru.

The penalties for smuggling out drugs are very strict for **cocaine,** which is common and of very high purity in Peru, and not as cut with all kinds of dangerous chemicals as in the United States and Europe. There is no bail for drug trafficking cases, and the legal process can drag on for up to two years. Your embassy will most likely decline to get involved.

Peru is well known for confidence scams that involve drugs. A typical one generally targets men and can start with a random meeting in the street with an attractive young woman. After conversation and moving to a bar or discotheque the woman will offer up some drugs. Suddenly and unexpectedly, police appear from nowhere and the attractive gal disappears.

What follows is extortion in exchange for not being arrested. The so-called "police" will explain that you could spend the next five years or more in jail unless you give them money. If you don't react, they will take you to the police station. If you decide to offer them money, the police will drive you to a series of ATMs in order to take as much money as possible from your accounts. Several hours later, and after having your bank account cleaned out, you will probably be dropped off in some remote area of Lima. The worst part is that the perpetrators probably are not even real police.

CRIME

Peru is generally a safe country, so travelers should not feel paranoid. But as in any other place in the world, follow common-sense rules and realize that thieves target travelers because they have cash and valuable electronics on them. You will be easy prey for thieves only if you are distracted.

Be alert and organized and watch your valuables at all times. Your money and passport should be carried under your clothes in a pouch or locked in a safety box at your hotel. Keep a constant eye on your luggage in bus stations. When in markets, place your backpack in front of you so that it cannot be slit open. When in restaurants or buses, keep your purse or bag close to you.

Make yourself less of a target. Do not wear jewelry or fancy watches, and keep your camera in a beat-up hip bag that is unlikely to draw attention. Be alert when in crowded places like markets or bus stations, where pickpockets abound. Go only to nightspots that have been recommended. Walk with a sense of purpose, like you belong exactly where you are. When withdrawing money from an ATM, be with a friend or have a taxi waiting.

Experienced travelers can sense a scam or theft right before it happens and, nine times out of ten, it involves momentary distraction or misplaced trust. If someone spits on you, latch onto your camera instead of cleaning yourself. If someone falls in the street in front of you or drops something, move away quickly. If an old man asks for your help in reading a lottery ticket, say no. If a stranger motions you over or offers a piece of candy, keep going. Be distrusting of people you do not know.

At nightspots, do not accept alcohol from strangers, as it might be laced with a sleeping drug. Do not do drugs. If you have been drinking, take a taxi home instead of walking.

Be careful when taking taxis and when changing money. When riding to the Jorge Chávez International Airport in Lima, lock your luggage in the trunk and hold onto your valuables. When traffic becomes heavy on Avenida La Marina, teams of delinquents often break windows and snatch bags before speeding away on a motorcycle.

Information and Services

MONEY

Thanks to ATMs, getting cash all over Peru is about as simple, easy, and cheap as it is in your own country. U.S. banks usually charge a US$3 fee per transaction, but the benefits of using bank cards outweigh the risk of carrying loads of cash. Banks usually charge hefty commissions for cashing travelers checks, but a modest supply is nice to have along in case your bank cards are stolen (check with your bank before you go to find out if it is even possible to replace your bank cards overseas). Credit cards are useful and it's increasingly common to use them to purchase almost everything in big cities. Throughout the country Visa cards are easiest to use in restaurants and hotels, but also ask if establishments accept MasterCard or American Express. If your bank cards get stolen and you spend all your travelers checks, you can always get a cash withdrawal off your credit card. Bottom line: Rely on your ATM card and bring some travelers checks and a credit card or two.

Peruvian Money

The official Peruvian currency is the *nuevo sol* (S/.), which for the last several years has hovered around 2.80 per US$1. Peruvian bills come in denominations of 10, 20, 50, 100, and 200 *soles*. The *sol* is divided into 100 smaller units, called *céntimos,* which come in coins of 1, 5, 10, 20, and 50 *céntimos.* There are also heavier coins for 1, 2, and 5 *soles.* Beware that 2- and 5-*sol* coins look very much alike, the

AVOIDING COUNTERFEIT MONEY

Counterfeit money prevails in Peru. It includes both U.S. bills and Peruvian bills and coins. No counterfeit euros have been detected so far in these last years. Peruvians can recognize counterfeit *nuevos soles* quite easily, either in bills – mostly 100 and 50 notes, but also the 2- and 5-*sol* coins, which are very similar in design but a bit different in diameter. Getting money from an ATM or a bank reduces the risk but not totally. You will know when you have been scammed with a fake note. Depending on the value, it might be easier or harder to pass it on.

Here are a few tips for avoiding counterfeit bills:

- **Feel and scratch the paper.** Counterfeit bills are usually smooth and glossy, while real bills are crisp and coarse and have a low reflective surface. For U.S. dollar bills, many Peruvians scratch the neck area of the person pictured on the bill. The lapel should have a bumpy quality, unless it is an old bill. Hold both ends and snap the bill – it should have a strong feel.

- **Reject old bills.** This includes ones that are faded, tattered, ripped, or taped, especially if they are U.S. notes. You will never get rid of these bills unless you trade them on the street at a lesser rate. Banks will not change them, unless they are Peruvian notes. Counterfeit bills are made of inferior paper and often rip.

- **Hold the bill up to a light.** In both Peruvian and American bills there should be watermarks and thin ribbons that only show up when put against a light source. In the new U.S. $10 and $20 bills, the watermark is a smaller, though fuzzy, replica of the person pictured on the bill. These bills also have thin lines that run across the bill and say "US TEN" or "US TWENTY."

- **With Peruvian bills, look for reflective ink.** When you tilt a Peruvian bill from side to side, the ink on the number denomination should change color, like a heliogram. So far, Peruvian counterfeiters have been unable to reproduce this ink.

only difference being the size (5-*sol* coins are slightly bigger). Currency calculations with today's rate can be made with online currency converters such as **XE.Com** (www.xe.com). Exchange rates are commonly listed on signs in front of banks and exchange houses and are also posted in daily newspapers.

Changing Money

The U.S. dollar, despite being the most common foreign currency to exchange, is far from being the strongest. Nowadays, it is fairly easy to exchange euros in most Peruvian towns and other currencies only in big cities.

Inspect your dollar bills carefully before leaving your country and treat them with care. Even slight rips will cause them to be rejected everywhere you go. In the best case, you might be able to cash a tattered bill on the street for a lower rate, but regardless, US$50 and US$100 bills are difficult to exchange. There are a few banks and money exchange houses in almost all big airports in Peru. Generally speaking, most Peruvians exchange their dollars at exchange houses, called *casas de cambio,* because they give a slightly higher rate than banks. These are usually clustered around the Plaza de Armas or main commercial streets in every city and town. In major cities, representatives of these *casas de cambio* will even come to your hotel to exchange money, depending on the amount.

In major cities, there are also money changers on the street who wear colored vests and an ID card. These people are generally safe and honest, though they will sometimes take advantage of you if you don't know the daily exchange rate. Never change money with unlicensed money changers, who will sometimes have rigged calculators. Whenever you change money on the street, check the amount with your own calculator.

When you change money, check each bill carefully to see that it is not counterfeit. Hand back all bills that have slight rips, have been repaired with tape, or have other imperfections. Insist on cash in 20- and 50-*soles* bills. Unless you are at a supermarket or a restaurant, the 100-*soles* bills are hard to change and you

will end up waiting as someone runs across the street to find change for you.

Money Machines

ATMs, known as *cajeros automáticos,* are now commonplace in tourist towns, even small ones. The most secure ATMs are in glass rooms that you unlock by swiping your card at the door. Most ATMs accept cards with Visa/Plus or MasterCard/Cirrus logos. Banco de Crédito and Global Net are the only machines that accept American Express cards, and Global Net is the only machine that charges a commission to withdraw money. Other ATMs let you off scot-free! Interbank (available in most big cities in Peru) is the only bank with special ATMs that deliver coins. Unlike in Europe or the U.S., ATMs deliver the cash you requested first and then will give your card back. If you forget to pull it out, it will be eaten by the machine and be quite difficult to get back. Thieves sometimes wait for people to take cash out of their ATM and then follow them, sometimes on a motorcycle, to a secluded spot. For this reason, use ATMs during the day.

Banks and Wire Transfers

Banks are generally open 9 A.M.–5 P.M. Monday–Friday, mornings only on Saturday, and are closed on Sunday. Banks are useful for cashing travelers checks, receiving wire transfers, and getting cash advances on credit cards (Visa works best, but MasterCard and American Express are also accepted). Bank commissions for all these transactions vary US$20–30, so it is worth shopping around.

A cheaper option for wire transfers is often **Western Union,** which has offices in many Peruvian cities. Call the person you want to wire money to you and give them an address and phone number where Western Union can contact you. Once your money has arrived, you just go to the Western Union office with your passport to pick it up.

Travelers Checks

American Express is the most widely accepted travelers check and can easily be exchanged in banks. From the United States these checks can be ordered over the phone by calling toll-free 800/721-9768. The best place to change travelers checks in Peru is at **Banco de Crédito,** also known as BCP, which often charges no fee at all. The other banks charge a 2.5 percent commission or a flat fee that can be as much as US$10. *Casas de cambio* charge even higher fees.

Remember to record the numbers of your travelers checks and keep them in a separate place. Some travelers email these numbers to themselves so that they are always available when needed. If you end up not using your travelers checks, they can always be converted into cash back home for their face value.

If your American Express travelers checks get stolen, you can call the company collect either in Peru at 0800/51-531 or in the U.S. at 801/964-6665. You can also go online to www.americanexpress.com to find the nearest office. American Express maintains representatives in Peru in Chiclayo, Trujillo, Lima, and Arequipa. In Lima its representative is Viajes Falabella, which has a half dozen offices in the city, including in Miraflores (Larco 747, tel. 01/444-4239, 9 A.M.–6 P.M. Sun.–Fri.).

Credit Cards

In recent times the use of credit cards has expanded to almost all big cities in Peru for even the smallest purchases. Be sure you ask, though. Not all cards are accepted everywhere. By far, the best card to have in Peru is Visa or MasterCard, though Diners Club and to a lesser extent American Express are increasingly accepted. Apart from their in-country toll-free numbers, most credit cards list a number you can call collect from overseas. Carry this number in a safe place or email it to yourself so that you have it in an emergency.

For Visa cards, you can also look online at www.visa.com or call collect in the United States to 410/902-8022. For MasterCard, see www.mastercard.com or call its collect, 24-hour emergency number in the United States at 636/722-7111. For American Express, see www.americanexpress.com or call the company

in the U.S. at 336/393-1111. To contact Diners Club (www.dinersclub.com) while in Peru call 01/615-1111.

Bargaining

Bargaining is common practice in Peru, especially at markets and shops, and to a minor extent in mid-budget hotels. Bargaining can be fun, but don't go overboard. Have a good sense of what an item should cost beforehand. Ask them how much it costs (*"¿Cuánto cuesta?"*) and then offer 20 percent less, depending on how outlandish the asking price is. Usually vendors and shoppers meet somewhere in the middle. Some people bargain ruthlessly and pretend to walk out the door to get the best deal. On the other hand, a smile, humor, and some friendly conversation works better.

If you have a reasonable price, accept it graciously. There is nothing worse than seeing a gringo bargaining a campesino into the ground over a pair of woven mittens. We might go and have a coffee with the money we save, while the vendor might use it to buy shoes for his daughter!

Discounts

Student discounts are ubiquitous in Peru, so get an **ISIC card** (International Student Identity Card) if you can, and flash it wherever you go. If you are in Peru for a week or two it is usually possible to make up the money you spent on that **South American Explorers Club** membership just in the discounts you are entitled to at hotels, restaurants, and agencies—the hardest part is remembering to ask for it before you pay. The SAE in Lima and Cusco has lists of establishments that accept their discounts.

Tipping

Tipping is a great way for foreign travelers to get money to the people who need it the most—the guides, waiters, hotel staff, drivers, porters, burro drivers, and other front-line workers of the tourism industry. Though not required, even the smallest tip is immensely appreciated. It's also a good way of letting people know they are doing a great job. Tipping is an ethic that varies from person to person.

In restaurants a tip of 10 percent is ideal but not enforced. Try to give the tip to the waiter personally, especially when the table is outdoors or you pay with a credit card. It is not necessary to tip taxi drivers in Peru, but you should give a few *soles* to anyone who helps you carry your bags, including hotel staff or an airport shuttle driver. Assuming you were pleased with their service, you should tip guides, porters, and mule drivers at least one day's wage for every week worked. If they did a great job, tip more. Tipping in U.S. dollars or other foreign currency is not necessarily a good deal for these people, especially if they live away from big cities where they can't exchange the money. Tip in local currency.

MAPS AND TOURIST INFORMATION
Maps
You can buy a range of maps in Arequipa, Cusco, and Huaraz, but the best maps are to be found in Lima. **South American Explorers Club** in Lima and Cusco sells the leading country maps, plus a good selection of military topographic maps. To find topographic maps for remote areas you will have to make a trip down to Lima's **Instituto Geográfico Nacional** (tel. 01/475-3030, www.ign.gob.pe).

Good bookstores generally sell the better national maps, and we especially liked the maps in the back of the *Inca Guide to Peru* and the *Lima 2000* series (scale 1:2,200,00). Many hotels and Iperú offices give out free city maps. If you want to purchase maps before arriving in Peru, the *Lima 2000* map is sold for US$8.95 at www.gonetomorrow.com. Another online map store is www.omnimap.com.

Tourist Offices
The Peruvian government has set up tourist offices—known as **Iperú**—in most major cities, including Tumbes, Chiclayo, Trujillo, Chachapoyas, Iquitos, Huaraz, Lima, Ayacucho, Cusco, Arequipa, Puno, and Tacna. They receive questions and have a website in English, French, German, Portuguese, Italian, and Spanish (tel. 01/574-8000, www.peru.info). They can give you brochures, maps, and basic info.

The Iperú office is also the place to go if you want to file a complaint or need to solve a problem. These can include a bus company not taking responsibility for lost luggage, a tour company that did not deliver what it promised, or an independent guide who is not honest. In an emergency, you should contact the police and also call Iperú's 24-hour hotline (tel. 01/574-8000).

FILM AND PHOTOGRAPHY
Peru is a very photogenic country, and don't be surprised if you shoot twice as much as you were expecting. In Peru, photographing soldiers or military installations is against the law.

Digital Cameras
Memory cards and other accessories are increasingly available in Lima and other large Peruvian cities. Shops that sell cameras and other electronic equipment will usually take a full memory card and burn it onto a compact disc for about US$5—but that requires the toggle cable that comes with your camera. Bring a few large-capacity cards and an extra battery. Unless you have your own laptop, there will be long stretches where you will not be able to download.

Film Processing
When it comes to conventional cameras, nearly every Peruvian city has a photo-processing lab, which is usually affiliated with Kodak. Quality varies, however, and if you are looking for highly professional quality, wait until you return home or get to a big city like Lima, Trujillo, Cusco, Arequipa, or Puno. Developing black-and-white or slide film is limited to big cities too.

Photo Tips
The main issue for photography on the coast and in the highlands is the intense sunlight. The ideal times to photograph are in the warm-

color hours of early morning or late afternoon. Use filters that knock down UV radiation and increase saturation of colors. In the jungle, the main problem is lack of light, so a higher ASA is recommended whether using conventional or digital cameras. If you want to take pictures of wildlife, you will have to bring a hefty zoom and have a lot of time to wait for the shots to materialize. A good source of information on travel photography is **Tribal Eye Images** (www.tribaleye.co.uk). The author offers free tips on choosing equipment and film, general techniques and composition, photographing people, and selling your work. Other sites include www.photo.net/travel and the members-only www.photographytips.com.

Photographing Locals

Before you take a picture of people, take the time to meet them and establish a relationship. Then ask permission to take their photo.

The most compliant subjects are market vendors, especially those from whom you have just bought something. Children in the highlands will ask for money in order to have their picture taken. Adults will even ask if you will be making business selling their portraits.

COMMUNICATIONS AND MEDIA
Mail

Peru's national post office service is **Serpost** (www.serpost.com.pe), and there is an office in nearly every village, or at the very least a *buzón* or mailbox. Postal service in Peru is fairly reliable and surprisingly expensive. Postcards and letters cost US$2–4 to the United States and Europe, and more if you want them certified. Letters sent from Peru take around two weeks to arrive in the United States, but less time if sent from Lima. If you know Spanish, check for a complete list of post offices by region and provinces in Serpost's website (www.serpost.com.pe) under Red de Oficinas. To ship packages out of Peru use **DHL, FedEx** or some other courier service.

If you become a member of South American Explorers, you can receive personal mail at its offices in Lima or Cusco. You can also receive mail at your respective embassy in Lima.

Telephone Calls

International rates continue to drop both from overseas into Peru, and from Peru overseas. Our favorite option for calling Peru is Skype (www.skype.com), as most Peruvians have a Skype account. Even if they don't you can charge your Skype account with money and, via a service called "Skype Out," use Skype to call a Peruvian land line or cell phone. A number of calling cards, which can be purchased online, also make calling Peru incredibly cheap. **Alosmart** (www.alosmart.com) has a search engine for finding the best card depending on the type of calls you are going to make.

If you would like someone from home to be able to reach you, you should consider renting or buying a **cell phone.** In the baggage claim area of the airport, there are cell phone agents who rent phones from Peru's major carriers: Telefónica, Claro, and Nextel. Claro gets the widest service. Buying a cell phone will cost you a minimum of US$30. If you take your cell phone from home with you and it is unlocked, you can buy instead just the sim card for about US$5–10 and have a local number. A new phone comes with a standard number of minutes. Once you expend these minutes, you will need to buy a recharge card, which comes in denominations of US$3.50, US$7, or US$11. You can also charge your phone online. These cards allow callers to call both nationally and internationally—receiving calls is free once you have the phone.

Most towns have public phones on the main square and usually an office of **Telefónica,** Peru's main phone company. The phones are coin-operated, but most people buy telephone cards.

The most popular prepaid card is called 147 and can be bought in denominations of US$3–30 at most pharmacies, supermarkets, and from the Telefónica offices themselves. Also available are HolaPerú cards for international calls. In either case, dialing the United

States is more or less about US$0.80 per minute, and a local call, with 147, is about US$0.15 per minute. Surcharges are applied to all calls made from pay phones, so use your hotel phone or walk into any small store in Peru with the green-and-blue phone symbol above it.

All major **international phone cards** can be used in Peru, as long as you know the access code: AT&T is 0800-5000, MCI is 0800-50010, TRT is 0800-50030, and Sprint is 0800-50020. Worldlink has no direct access in Peru.

The cheapest way to make long-distance calls from Peru, however, is via the **net-to-phone** systems available at many Internet places for as low as US$0.17 per minute calling to the United States or Europe. There can be a lag when calling with most of these services, though Internet cafés that have cable service are usually crystal clear—often even better than a phone!

All long-distance calls in Peru are preceded by a 0 and the area code of that particular region, or department, of Peru. For instance, for calling Cusco all numbers are preceded by 084—these preceding numbers are listed whenever a number is listed in this book. All home phones in Lima have seven-digit numbers, and numbers are six digits in other towns and cities in the rest of the country. All cell phones have nine-digit numbers in all of Peru.

Peru's country code is **51,** and each of the 23 regions in Peru has a different code. Cusco, for instance, is 84. So dialing a Cusco number from the United States would be 011 (used for all international calls) + 51 (country code) + 84 (city code) and then the number. All cities in Peru have two-digit city codes when dialing from overseas, except Lima. When calling Lima from the United States dial 011-51-1 and then the number. When dialing Lima from within Peru, however, you must first dial 01.

To place a direct international phone call from Peru, dial 00 + country code + city code + number. The country code for Argentina is 54, Australia is 61, Canada is 1, Chile is 56, Denmark is 45, France is 33, Germany is 49, Netherlands is 31, Israel is 972, Japan is 81,

PERU'S AREA CODES

Abancay	83
Aguas Calientes	84
Arequipa	54
Ayacucho	66
Cajamarca	76
Chachapoyas	41
Chiclayo	74
Chincha	56
Cusco	84
Huancayo	64
Huánuco	62
Huaraz	43
Ica	56
Iquitos	65
Lima	01
Máncora	73
Nasca	56
Piura	73
Pucallpa	61
Puerto Maldonado	82
Puno	51
Tacna	52
Tarapoto	42
Trujillo	44
Tumbes	72

New Zealand is 64, Norway is 47, Spain is 34, Switzerland is 41, the United Kingdom is 44, and the United States is 1. So for calling the United Kingdom from Peru, callers should dial 0044 before any number, and for the United States 001.

Collect calls are possible from many Telefónica offices, or you can dial the international operator (108) for assistance. The correct way to ask for a collect call is: *"Quisiera hacer una llamada de cobro revertido, por favor."*

The following codes can be called for help: directory assistance 103, emergency assistance in Lima 105, international operator assistance 108, national operator assistance 109, fire 116, and urgent medical assistance 117. The chance of finding an English-speaking operator at these numbers is slim. However, Iperú maintains a 24-hour English-speaking operator at Jorge Chávez International Airport in Lima for emergencies (tel. 01/574-8000).

Fax

Sending a fax from Peru to the United States is expensive, ranging US$2–9 per page to the United States or Europe. Instead of a fax, scan your document and send it as an email attachment. Fax machines are available at most hotels, photocopy stores, and Telefónica offices.

Internet Access

Using a computer is by far the cheapest and most convenient way to communicate in Peru. Internet cafés are everywhere and are popping up in even tiny towns. Using the Internet is cheap (US$0.40–0.70 per hour), and often you can also make cheap net-to-phone overseas calls through **Skype.**

There is a lot that goes into choosing an Internet café, however. First off, make sure it is a high-speed connection, which in Peru is generally referred to as "speedy." Some speedy connections, however, are much faster than others. If your email takes more than a minute or two to open up, we suggest you head elsewhere. Another huge factor is noise, especially with Internet places that cater to schoolkids, who show up each afternoon and shout and scream and wrestle with each other over who gets to use what machine.

Besides speedy, which is a DSL line, Lima and the bigger cities now have faster connections with cable modems and—most important—crystal-clear, dirt-cheap international calls. Sometimes a remote jungle town can have a satellite Internet center, which is also amazingly fast.

Nowadays most upscale and medium-range hotels will have free WiFi access for guests traveling with laptops. In Lima and other touristy cities like Cusco, Arequipa, Trujillo, Puno, or Huaraz, you will find cafés with free WiFi access.

Printed and Online News

Publications in Spanish are headed by *El Comercio* (http://elcomercio.pe/), the largest and oldest standard daily newspaper with major credibility in Peru. It has a variety of supplements and magazines with good information on cultural activities and performing arts, including *Somos,* a weekly magazine published every Saturday. Among a dozen tabloids, two are worth checking out: *Perú21* (http://peru21.pe), with a moderate center political standing, and *La República* (http://larepublica.pe), traditionally left-oriented.

Caretas (www.caretas.com.pe) is a weekly magazine that has been around for more than half a century, founded by the Gibson/Zileri family. It is published every Thursday and contains a good deal of local political content, as well as sections devoted to art, humorous essays, interesting letters to the editor, jokes, crossword puzzles, and great photographs.

DedoMedio (www.dedomedio.com), with its slogan *"la verdad aunque te duela"* (the truth even if it hurts you), is a brilliant monthly publication full of satire, highly acidic content material, great caricatures, and very good written articles about almost any topic you can think of including domestic politics, art, music, etc.

Some useful news websites in English include **Living In Peru** (www.livinginperu.com), which also has classified ads and vast information on cultural activities, tourism, and gastronomy, among other subjects. One of the oldest English-written newspapers in South America, **The Andean Air Mail & Peruvian Times** (www.peruviantimes.com) resurfaced some years ago in the Internet, offering feature articles, op-ed columns, and good overall coverage of what is going on in Peru. The **Expat Peru Network** (www.expatperu.com) also offers local news coverage—actually linked to *The Peruvian Times*— but focuses more on service information such as legal aspects, traveling to Peru, and several discussion forums by topic.

WEIGHTS AND MEASURES

Peru uses the metric system for everything except gallons of gasoline. For conversion information, see the back of this book.

Electricity

The electrical system of Peru is 220 volts and 60 cycles. If you absent-mindedly plug in a 110-volt appliance from the United States into a 220-volt Peruvian outlet, you will start a small fire. All high-end hotels (such as Casa Andina or Libertador, for example) have additional outlets of 110 volts.

You can use 110-volt appliances in Peru with a converter, which can be quite heavy. You can buy one in an electronics shop, though they are cheaper in Peru. Make sure you get the right type, as a hair dryer needs a more robust converter than, say, a digital camera battery charger.

Voltage surges are common in Peru, so it is also a good idea to bring a surge protector from home that can be plugged between your appliance and the converter. Most laptops and digital cameras these days can take either 110 or 220 volts, so check on this before you buy a converter.

TIME ZONES

Peru is in the same time zone as New York, Miami, Bogotá, and Quito. Peru does not use daylight saving time, meaning that its time remains constant throughout the year. The entire country is in the same time zone (GMT -5:00).

RESOURCES

Glossary

abra high pass

aguaymanto an Inca fruit, also known as *capulí*, from which delicious jams, deserts, and other delicacies are made

ají any chili pepper; yellow peppers are *ají amarillo*

ají de gallina creamy chicken stew with yellow chili served over boiled potatoes, garnished with hard-boiled eggs and black olives

aluvión mudslide

anticuchos beef heart grilled brochettes served with an assortment of spicy sauces

arroz con pato duck with rice, originally from the north coast but now found everywhere

café (con leche) coffee (with milk)

camarones freshwater prawns/crawfish

camote sweet potato

cancha roasted corn kernels, a popular snack to nibble with beer, usually served with *cebiche*

canela cinnamon

cañón canyon

causa cold mashed potatoes mixed with yellow chili peppers and a dash of lime juice, layered with chicken, tuna fish, shrimp, or veggies mixed with mayonnaise, avocado, and diced onions

cebiche the trademark of Peruvian cuisine: fish, shrimp, scallops, or squid, or a mixture of all four, marinated in lime juice and chili peppers for five minutes, traditionally served with corn, sweet potatoes, and onions

cebiche mixto *cebiche* with fish and shellfish

cerveza beer; also *chela*

chacana a sacred symbol, also known as the Andean Cross, with varied and complex links to Inca cosmology; a common motif at Inca temples and other sacred sites

chancho/cerdo pig/pork

chela slang word for beer

chicha or chicha de jora drink made from different kinds of fermented corn or peanuts, quinoa, or fruit

chicha morada sweet, refreshing drink made from boiled purple corn and fruit, with clove and cinnamon, served chilled with a dash of lime juice

chicharrón deep-fried pork, chicken, or fish

chifa Peruvian-Chinese food/Chinese restaurant

chilcano a refreshing drink with pisco, ginger ale, lime juice, and a dash of Angostura bitters

chilcano de pescado a fish broth good for hangovers

chirimoya a sweet and pulpy, juicy white fruit with a mushy texture and a bitter dark green skin

choclo fresh Andean corn

choclo con queso steamy hot corn on the cob with slices of cheese and *ají* sauce

chupe Quechua word for a highly concentrated soup with beef, fish, or seafood with potatoes, corn, vegetables, and sometimes milk

cocha lake in Quechua

conchitas negras black scallop delicacy common in northern Peru

cordillera mountain range

crocante de lúcuma a meringue desert made with a fruit called *lúcuma*

culantro cilantro/coriander

cuy guinea pig; stewed, fried, or spit-roasted

granadilla sweet, pulpy passion fruit with a hard shell

guanabana indescribably delicious jungle fruit

guayaba guava

huaca in Quechua, *huaca* is a sacred object that is revered, such as a rock

huacatay black mint

humita fresh corn tamale that can be either sweet or salty

Inca Kola a unique and quite sweet Peruvian pop soda originally made out of lemongrass

juanes tamale stuffed with chicken and rice

jugo juice

kiwicha purple-flowered grain high in protein, which is folded into breads, cookies, and soups

lago lake

laguna lagoon

langostino river or sea shrimp

limón key lime or just lime

lomo saltado popular and inexpensive dish of stir-fried beef loin, with strips of *ají amarillo*, onions, tomatoes, and french fries, served with rice

lúcuma a small brown fruit recognizable by its dark peach color and smoky flavor; a popular ice cream, yogurt, and milk shake flavor

manzanilla chamomile or chamomile tea

maracuyá passion fruit, served as a juice, in a pisco sour, or in cheesecake

masato alcoholic drink made from fermented yuca or manioc

mate de coca coca leaf tea

mazamorra morada pudding-like dessert made from purple corn

mirador lookout point

nevado mountain

ocopa a spicy peanut-based sauce, served over boiled potatoes and garnished with hard-boiled eggs and black olives

pachamanca the utmost Andean meal, made up of beef, pork, alpaca, *cuy*, and chicken cooked together with potatoes, sweet potatoes, and lima beans inside heated stones in a hole in the ground, covered with herbs

paiche Amazon fish; the largest freshwater fish in the world

palmito ribbons of palm heart that look like pasta when served

palta avocado

Panamericana Panamerican Highway

papa potato; Andean tuber originally from Peru and generic name for more than 3,000 different types of potatoes

papa a la huancaina cold appetizer of potatoes in a spicy light cheese sauce with *ají amarillo*

papa rellena fried oblong of mashed potatoes stuffed with meat, onions, olives, boiled eggs, and raisins

pescado fish

pirañas small, vicious, sharp-fanged fish found in oxbow lakes and rivers

pisco grape brandy; distilled spirit

pisco sour cocktail made with three parts of pisco, two parts of lime juice, one part of sugar syrup, mixed with ice, a bit of egg white, and a dash of Angostura bitters

plátano frito fried bananas

playa beach

pollo chicken

pomelo grapefruit; also *toronja*

pongo river gorge that is often dangerous in high water

puna high plains, often grasslands

quebrada narrow valley, ravine

quinoa golden brown, round grain, rich in protein

quipu a system of knotted, multi-colored cords that the Inca used to keep record and transmit data, such as weather forecasts, crop production, and accounting

río river

rocoto a red, bell pepper–shaped chili consumed in Arequipa

rocoto relleno red bell pepper stuffed with meat and spices

sachatomate a red fruit, also known as a *tamarillo*, that has an egg shape, an inside like a tomato, and a sweet, tangy taste

seco de cabrito roasted goat marinated with *chicha*, served with beans and rice

tacu tacu bean and rice patty, fried in a pan and topped with a fried egg, beef or fish stew, or any other kind of garnish

tiradito sashimi-like fish cuts with a chili sauce on top
toronja grapefruit; also *pomelo*
tumbo banana passion fruit

tuna prickly pear from desert cactus
valle valley
volcán volcano
yuca cassava root

Spanish Phrasebook

Even a beginner's grasp of the Spanish language will make your travels more enjoyable. Study the basics before your trip so you will be ready to practice once you arrive in Peru.

Spanish commonly uses 30 letters – the familiar English 26, plus four straightforward additions: ch, ll, ñ, and rr.

PRONUNCIATION
Unlike English, Spanish is a phonetic language. In other words, words are always pronounced exactly as they are spelled. As long as you know how to pronounce the vowels and consonants, you should be able to read Spanish and pronounce it correctly.

Vowels
a like ah, as in "hah": *agua* AH-gooah (water), *pan* PAHN (bread), and *casa* CAH-sah (house)
e like ay, as in "may": *mesa* MAY-sah (table), *tela* TAY-lah (cloth), and *de* DAY (of, from)
i like ee, as in "need": *diez* dee-AYZ (ten), *comida* ko-MEE-dah (meal), and *fin* FEEN (end)
o like oh, as in "go": *peso* PAY-soh (weight), *ocho* OH-choh (eight), and *poco* POH-koh (a bit)
u like oo, as in "cool": *uno* OO-noh (one), *cuarto* KOOAHR-toh (room), and *usted* oos-TAYD (you); when it follows a "q" the **u** is silent; when it follows an "h" or has an umlaut, it's pronounced like "w"

Consonants
b, d, f, k, l, m, n, p, q, s, t, v, w, x, y, z, and ch
pronounced almost as in English; **h** occurs, but is silent, not pronounced at all
c like k as in "keep": *cuarto* KOOAR-toh

(room); when it precedes "e" or "i," pronounce **c** like s, as in "sit": *cerveza* sayr-VAY-sah (beer), *encima* ayn-SEE-mah (atop)
g like g as in "gift" when it precedes "a," "o," "u," or a consonant: *gato* GAH-toh (cat), *hago* AH-goh (I do, make); otherwise, pronounce **g** like h as in "hat": *giro* HEE-roh (money order), *gente* HAYN-tay (people)
j like h, as in "has": *jueves* HOOAY-vays (Thursday), *mejor* may-HOR (better)
ll like y, as in "yes": *toalla* toh-AH-yah (towel), *ellos* AY-yohs (they, them)
ñ like ny, as in "canyon": *año* AH-nyo (year), *señor* SAY-nyor (Mr., sir)
r is lightly trilled, with tongue at the roof of your mouth like a very light English d, as in "ready": *pero* PAY-doh (but), *tres* TDAYS (three), *cuatro* KOOAH-tdoh (four)
rr like a Spanish r, but with much more emphasis and trill. Let your tongue flap. Practice with *burro* (donkey), *carretera* (highway), and Carrillo (proper name), then really let go with *ferrocarril* (railroad).

Accent
The rule for accent, the relative stress given to syllables within a given word, is straightforward: If a word ends in a vowel, an n, or an s, accent the next-to-last syllable; otherwise, accent the last syllable.

Pronounce *gracias* GRAH-seeahs (thank you), *orden* OHR-dayn (order), and *carretera* kah-ray-TAY-rah (highway) with stress on the next-to-last syllable.

Otherwise, accent the last syllable: *venir* vay-NEER (to come), *ferrocarril* fay-roh-cah-REEL (railroad), and *edad* ay-DAHD (age).

Exceptions to the accent rule are always

marked with an accent sign: (á, é, í, ó, or ú), such as *teléfono* tay-LAY-foh-noh (telephone), *jabón* hah-BON (soap), and *rápido* RAH-pee-doh (rapid).

BASIC AND COURTEOUS EXPRESSIONS

Most Spanish-speaking people consider formalities important. Whenever approaching anyone for information or some other reason, do not forget the appropriate salutation – good morning, good evening, etc. Standing alone, the greeting *hola* (hello) can sound brusque.

Hello. *Hola.*
Good morning. *Buenos días.*
Good afternoon. *Buenas tardes.*
Good evening. *Buenas noches.*
How are you? *¿Cómo está usted?*
Very well, thank you. *Muy bien, gracias.*
Okay; good. *Bien.*
Not okay; bad. *Mal* or *no muy bien.*
So-so. *Más o menos.*
And you? *¿Y usted?*
Thank you. *Gracias.*
Thank you very much. *Muchas gracias.*
You're very kind. *Muy amable.*
You're welcome. *De nada.*
Goodbye. *Adios.*
See you later. *Hasta luego.*
please *por favor*
yes *sí*
no *no*
I don't know. *No sé.*
Just a moment, please. *Un momento, por favor.*
Excuse me, please (when you're trying to get attention). *Disculpe* or *Con permiso* (when you're trying to get through).
Excuse me (when you've made a boo-boo). *Lo siento.*
Pleased to meet you. *Mucho gusto.*
What is your name? *¿Cómo se llama usted?*
Do you speak English? *¿Habla usted inglés?*
I don't speak Spanish well. *No hablo bien el español.*
I don't understand. *No entiendo.*
How do you say...in Spanish? *¿Cómo se dice...en español?*
My name is . . . *Me llamo . . .*
Let's go to . . . *Vamos a . . .*

TERMS OF ADDRESS

When speaking with someone of respect, or someone you do not know, use *Usted* for you (formal). Otherwise use *tú* for you (informal).

I *yo*
you (formal) *usted*
you (familiar) *tú*
he/him *él*
she/her *ella*
we/us *nosotros*
you (plural) *ustedes*
they/them *ellos* (all males or mixed gender); *ellas* (all females)
Mr., sir *señor*
Mrs., madam *señora*
Miss, young lady *señorita*
wife *esposa*
husband *esposo*
friend *amigo* (male); *amiga* (female)
boyfriend/girlfriend *enamorado* or *novio* (male); *enamorada* or *novia* (female)
son; daughter *hijo; hija*
brother; sister *hermano; hermana*
father; mother *padre; madre*
grandfather; grandmother *abuelo; abuela*

TRANSPORTATION

Where is . . .? *¿Dónde está . . .?*
How far is it to . . .? *¿A qué distancia está . . .?*
From...to . . . *de...a . . .*
How many blocks? *¿Cuántas cuadras?*
Where (Which) is the way to . . .? *¿Por dónde es el camino a . . .?*
the bus station *el terminal de autobuses*
the bus stop *el paradero de autobuses*
Where is this bus going? *¿Adónde va este autobús?*
taxi *taxi*
public taxi *colectivo*
public van *combi*
three-wheeled motorized bike-taxi *mototaxi*
jungle boat with raised propeller *peke-peke*

mule driver *arriero*
mule, donkey *mula, burro*
the airport *el aeropuerto*
I'd like a ticket to . . . *Quisiera un boleto a . . .*
round-trip *ida y vuelta*
reservation *reserva*
baggage *equipaje*
Stop here, please. *Pare aquí, por favor.*
the entrance *la entrada*
the exit *la salida*
the ticket office *la boletería*
is (very) near; far *está (muy) cerca; lejos*
to; toward *a*
by; through *por*
from *de; desde*
the right *la derecha*
the left *la izquierda*
straight ahead *de frente*
in front *en frente*
beside *al lado; al costado*
behind *atrás; detrá*
the corner *la esquina*
the stoplight *el semáforo*
a turn *una vuelta*
right here *aquí*
somewhere around here *por aquí*
right there *allí; ahí*
somewhere around there *por allá; por ahí*
street *calle; jirón*
avenida *avenida*
highway *carretera*
bridge *puente*
address *dirección*
north; south *norte; sur*
east; west *este; oeste*

ACCOMMODATIONS

Hotel *hotel*
Is there a room? *¿Hay habitación?*
May I (may we) see it? *¿Puedo (podemos) verlo?*
What is the rate? *¿Cuál es la tarifa?*
Is there something cheaper? *¿Hay algo más barato?*
a single room *una habitación simple*
a double room *una habitación doble*
double bed room *una habitación matrimonial*
twin beds *camas dobles*

with private bath *con baño privado*
hot water *agua caliente*
shower *ducha*
bathtub *tina*
towels *toallas*
soap *jabón*
hair dryer *secador de cabello*
toilet paper *papel higiénico*
blanket *frazada; manta*
sheets *sábanas*
air-conditioned or a/c *aire acondicionado*
fan *ventilador*
key *llave*
manager *gerente; administrador*

FOOD

I'm hungry *Tengo hambre.*
I'm thirsty. *Tengo sed.*
menu *carta*
glass *vaso*
cup *tasa*
fork *tenedor*
knife *cuchillo*
spoon *cuchara*
tea spoon *cucharita*
napkin *servilleta*
soft drink *gaseosa*
coffee *café*
tea *té*
boiled water for drinking *agua hervida para tomar*
bottled carbonated water *agua mineral con gas*
bottled uncarbonated water *agua mineral sin gas*
wine *vino*
milk *leche*
cream *crema*
sugar *azúcar*
salt *sal*
black pepper *pimienta*
chili pepper *ají*
cheese *queso*
breakfast *desayuno*
lunch *almuerzo*
fixed lunch menu *menú del día*
dinner *cena*
the check please *la cuenta por favor*

eggs *huevos*
bread *pan*
salad *ensalada*
lettuce *lechuga*
onion *cebolla*
tomato *tomate*
fruit *fruta*
mango *mango*
papaya *papaya*
banana *plátano*
apple *manzana*
orange *naranja*
beans *frijoles*
shellfish *mariscos*
crab *cangrejo*
lobster *langosta*
mussels *choros*
scallops *conchas*
sea bass *corvina*
flounder *lenguado*
squid *calamares*
octopus *pulpo*
trout *trucha*
(without) meat *(sin) carne*
beef; steak *res; bistec*
bacon; ham *tocino; jamón*
fried *frito*
roasted *asada*
grilled *a la parrilla*

SHOPPING
money *dinero*
money-exchange bureau *casa de cambio*
money changer *cambista*
I would like to exchange travelers checks. *Quisiera cambiar cheques de viajero.*
What is the exchange rate? *¿Cuál es el tipo de cambio?*
How much is the commission? *¿Cuánto es la comisión?*
Do you accept credit cards? *¿Aceptan tarjetas de crédito?*
money order *giro*
How much does it cost? *¿Cuánto cuesta?*
What is your final price? *¿Cuál es su último precio?*
expensive *caro*

cheap *barato*
more *más*
less *menos*
a little *un poco*
too much *demasiado*

HEALTH
Help me please. *Ayúdeme por favor.*
I am ill. *Estoy enfermo.*
Call a doctor. *Llame un doctor.*
Take me to . . . *Lléveme a . . .*
hospital; clinic *hospital; clínica*
drugstore *farmacia*
pain *dolor*
fever *fiebre*
headache *dolor de cabeza*
stomachache *dolor de estómago*
burn *quemadura*
cramp *calambre*
altitude sickness *soroche*
nausea *náusea*
vomit; vomiting *vómito; vomitar*
medicine *medicina*
antibiotic *antibiótico*
pill; tablet *pastilla; tableta*
aspirin *aspirina*
ointment; cream *pomada; crema*
bandage *venda*
cotton *algodón*
sanitary napkins *toallas higiénicas*
tampons *tampons*
birth control pills *pastillas anticonceptivas*
condoms *preservativos; condones*
toothbrush *cepillo dental*
dental floss *hilo dental*
toothpaste *crema dental*
dentist *dentista*
toothache *dolor de muelas*

COMMUNICATIONS
long-distance telephone *teléfono de larga distancia*
I would like to call . . . *Quisiera llamar a . . .*
collect *por cobrar*
credit card *tarjeta de crédito*
post office *correo*
general delivery *lista de correo*
letter *carta*

stamp *estampilla*
postcard *postal*
air mail *correo aéreo*
registered *registrado*
package; box *paquete; caja*
string; tape *cuerda; cinta*

AT THE BORDER

border *frontera*
customs *aduana*
immigration *migración*
tourist card *tarjeta de turista*
inspection *inspección; revisión*
passport *pasaporte*
profession *profesión*
marital status *estado civil*
single *soltero*
married; divorced *casado; divorciado*
insurance *seguros*
title *título*
driver's license *brevete; licencia de manejar*

GAS STATION

gas station *grifo, gasolinera*
gasoline *gasolina*
unleaded *sin plomo*
full, please *lleno, por favor*
tire *llanta*
tire repair shop *llantero*
air *aire*
water *agua*
oil change *cambio de aceite*
My...doesn't work. *Mi...no sirve.*
battery *batería*
radiator *radiador*
alternator *alternador*
generator *generador*
tow truck *grúa*
repair shop *taller mecánico*

VERBS

Verbs are the key to getting along in Peru because Spanish is verb-driven. There are three classes of verbs, which end in *ar, er,* and *ir.*
to buy *comprar*
I buy, you (he, she, it) buys *compro, compra*
we buy, you (they) buy *compramos, compran*

to eat *comer*
I eat, you (he, she, it) eats *como, come*
we eat, you (they) eat *comemos, comen*
to climb *subir*
I climb, you (he, she, it) climbs *subo, sube*
we climb, you (they) climb *subimos, suben*

Got the idea? Here are more:
to do or make *hacer*
I do or make, you (he she, it) does or makes *hago, hace*
we do or make, you (they) do or make *hacemos, hacen*
to go *ir*
I go, you (he, she, it) goes *voy, va*
we go, you (they) go *vamos, van*
to go (walk) *andar*
to love *amar*
to work *trabajar*
to want *desear, querer*
to need *necesitar*
to read *leer*
to write *escribir*
to repair *reparar*
to stop *parar*
to get off (the bus) *bajar*
to arrive *llegar*
to stay (remain) *quedar*
to stay (lodge) *hospedar*
to leave *salir* (regular except for **salgo,** I leave)
to look at *mirar*
to look for *buscar*
to give *dar* (regular except for **doy,** I give)
to carry *llevar*
to have *tener* (irregular but important: **tengo, tiene, tenemos, tienen**)
to come *venir* (similarly irregular: **vengo, viene, venimos, vienen**)

Spanish has two forms of "to be." Use *estar* when speaking of location or a temporary state of being: "I am at home." "*Estoy en casa.*" "I'm sick." "*Estoy enfermo.*" Use *ser* for a permanent state of being: "I am a doctor." "*Soy doctora.*"

Estar is regular except for *estoy,* I am. *Ser* is very irregular:
to be *ser*
I am, you (he, she, it) is *soy, es*
we are, you (they) are *somos, son*

NUMBERS
0 *cero*
1 *uno*
2 *dos*
3 *tres*
4 *cuatro*
5 *cinco*
6 *seis*
7 *siete*
8 *ocho*
9 *nueve*
10 *diez*
11 *once*
12 *doce*
13 *trece*
14 *catorce*
15 *quince*
16 *dieciseis*
17 *diecisiete*
18 *dieciocho*
19 *diecinueve*
20 *veinte*
21 *veintiuno*
30 *treinta*
40 *cuarenta*
50 *cincuenta*
60 *sesenta*
70 *setenta*
80 *ochenta*
90 *noventa*
100 *cien*
101 *ciento uno*
200 *doscientos*
500 *quinientos*
1,000 *mil*
10,000 *diez mil*
100,000 *cien mil*
1,000,000 *un millón*

one-half *medio*
one-third *un tercio*
one-fourth *un cuarto*

TIME
What time is it? *¿Qué hora es?*
It's 1 o'clock. *Es la una.*
It's 3 in the afternoon. *Son las tres de la tarde.*
It's 4 A.M. *Son las cuatro de la mañana.*
6:30 *seis y media*
a quarter till 11 *un cuarto para las once*
a quarter past 5 *las cinco y cuarto*
an hour *una hora*

DAYS AND MONTHS
Monday *lunes*
Tuesday *martes*
Wednesday *miércoles*
Thursday *jueves*
Friday *viernes*
Saturday *sábado*
Sunday *domingo*
today *hoy*
tomorrow *mañana*
yesterday *ayer*
January *enero*
February *febrero*
March *marzo*
April *abril*
May *mayo*
June *junio*
July *julio*
August *agosto*
September *septiembre*
October *octubre*
November *noviembre*
December *diciembre*
a week *una semana*
a month *un mes*
after *después*
before *antes*

– Spanish phrasebook adapted from *Moon Pacific Mexico by* Bruce Whipperman.

Quechua Phrasebook

Quechua is spoken throughout Peru's highlands, but especially in the area including Ayacucho, Cusco, and Lake Titicaca. Highlanders in the rural areas of southern Peru tend to speak only Quechua; in areas near major towns and roads, most locals speak both Quechua and some Spanish.

Quechua, or Runasimi as it is referred to by native spakers, is spoken by almost five million people in Peru and eight million throughout Peru, Ecuador, Bolivia, and Argentina. Because the Inca did not have writing, Quechua has only developed a written form in modern times. Quechua is currently receiving a revival in Peru because basic Quechua has become compulsory for all university graduates.

PRONUNCIATION

Quechua has a mixture of occlusive consonants that are separated in simple, glottal, and aspirate. The aspirate consonants are pronounced with a long soft sounds. The simple consonants are much less sharp than the glottal, which are emphasized (as indicated by the apostrophes next to them).

aspirate: ph th chh kh qh
simple: p t ch k q
glottal: p' t' ch' k' q'

NUMBERS

1 *hoq*
2 *iskay*
3 *qinsa*
4 *tawa*
5 *pisqa*
6 *soqta*
7 *qanchis*
8 *pusaq*
9 *isqon*
10 *chunka*
11 *chunka hoq ni yoq*
12 *chunka iskay ni yoq*
13 *chunka qinsa ni yoq*
20 *iskay chunka*
50 *pisqa chunka*

100 *pachaq*

INTERROGATIONS

Who? *Pi?*
What? *Ima?*
Which? *Mayqin?*
Where? *May?*
How much? *Hayk'a?*
When? *Hayk'aq?*
What for? *Imapaq?*

SOME BASIC SENTENCES

How are you? *Imaynallan kashanki?* or *Allianchu?*
I am fine. *Allillanmi kashani?*
What is your name? *Iman sutyki?*
My name is Maria. *Sutiyqa Maria.*
Where are you from? *Maymantan kanki?*
I am from Cusco. *Qosqomantan kani.*
. . . and you? *qanri?*
Where are you going? *Mayman rinki?*

BASIC AND COURTEOUS EXPRESSIONS

hello *napaykullayki*
yes *ari*
no *manan; manan kanchu*
please *allichu*
thank you *añay*
It's freezing! *Alalaw!*
It's really hot! *Akakaw!*
That's really scary! *Atakaw!*
That hurts! *Achakaw!*

QUECHUA-SPANISH CROSSOVER WORDS

As Quechua is spoken thoughout southern Peru, many words have made their way into the Spanish lexicon. Here are some examples:

baby *wawa*
cold *chiri*
no thanks *manan kanchu*
guinea pig *cuy*
brother (slang) *wayqi*
mother earth *Pachamama*

river *mayu*
old, ancient *macchu*
peak *picchu;* also means wad of coca leaves
star *chaska*
woman *warmi*
house *wasi*

The Quechua words for colors are often heard, especially if you have an interest in local naturally dyed textiles.

white *yurak*
black *yana*
red *puka*
blue *anqas*
yellow *q'ello*
green *qomer*

FAMILY
father or sir *tayta*
mother or madame *mama*
sister *panay*
brother *wayqi*
wife *warmi*
husband *qosa*
child *sullk'a wawa*

OTHER USEFUL QUECHUA WORDS
mountain god *apu*
Inca messenger runners *chasquis*
rest place for *chasquis tambo*
lake *cocha*
dried llama meat (jerky) *charqui*
until tomorrow *pakarinkama*
come here *hamuy*
big *hatun*
small *huchuy*
sun *inti*
moon *quilla*
sea *mamacocha*

VERBS
to speak *rimay*
to do *ruway*
to learn *yachay*
to eat *mihuy*
to rest *samay*
to walk *puriy*
to play *pukllay*

Suggested Reading

HISTORY

Burger, Richard. *Chavín and the Origins of Andean Civilization.* London: Thames and Hudson, 1995. A groundbreaking investigation of the Chavín culture, which spread across Peru's highlands 2,000 years before the Inca.

Hemming, John. *Conquest of the Incas.* New York: Harcourt Brace & Company, 1970. This is a masterpiece of both prose and history, in which famed Peru historian John Hemming lays out a gripping, blow-by-blow account of the Spanish conquest of Peru. Hemming, who was only 35 when *Conquest* was published, has written nearly a dozen books about Inca architecture and the native people of the Amazon.

Heyerdahl, Thor, and Daniel Sandweiss. *The Quest for Peru's Forgotten City.* London: Thames and Hudson, 1995. Norwegian explorer Thor Heyerdahl was most famous for piloting the *Kon-Tiki* balsa-wood raft from Callao, Peru, to the Polynesian Islands in 1947. From 1988 until he died in 2002, Heyerdahl's obsession with early ocean travel focused on the inhabitants of Túcume, a complex of 26 pyramids north of present-day Trujillo that was built by the Sicán culture around A.D. 1050. This remains the best work on Túcume.

Kirkpatrick, Sidney. *Lords of Sipán: A True Story of Pre-Inca Tombs, Archaeology, and Crime.* New York: William Morrow, 1992. Shortly after grave robbers unearthed a royal tomb of the Sipán culture near present-day Trujillo, Sydney Kirkpatrick documented the underworld of artifact smugglers and their Hollywood clients. At the center of this real-life drama is Peruvian archaeologist Walter Alva, who struggles against an entire town as he fights to preserve his country's heritage.

MacQuarrie, Kim. *The Last Days of the Incas.* New York: Simon & Schuster, 2007. Peru travelers with time to read just one book should read *The Last Days of the Incas*, written by an Emmy Award–winning author and filmmaker with years of life experience in Peru. MacQuarrie has produced what is, beyond a doubt, the most readable, fast-moving, and factual account of Peru's Spanish conquest. He describes the conquest and its aftermath in detail and integrates both 16th century Spanish chronicles and recent historical research. Unlike the more scholarly *Conquest of the Incas* by John Hemming, *The Last Days* does not end with the collapse of the Inca empire—the final chapters are devoted to 20th-century explorers such as Hiram Bingham, who identified Machu Picchu as the center of the Inca empire, and Gene Savoy, who discovered the real "lost city" of the Inca—Vilcabamba.

Mosley, Michael. *The Incas and Their Ancestors.* London: Thames and Hudson, 1993. This masterly work is still the best general introduction to the history of Peru's early cultures, including the Nasca, Moche, Huari, and Tiahuanaco.

Muscutt, Keith. *Warriors of the Clouds: A Lost Civilization in the Upper Amazon of Peru.* Albuquerque: University of New Mexico, 1998. This book provides a good overview of what archaeologists know of the Chachapoya, a cantankerous cloud-forest empire that was never dominated by the Inca, and is replete with beautiful images of ruins in the remote cloud forest of northeastern Peru.

Protzen, Jean-Pierre. *Inka Architecture and Construction at Ollantaytambo.* Oxford, United Kingdom: Oxford University Press, 1993. Jean-Pierre Protzen spent years at the Inca site of Ollantaytambo in order to understand its historical significance and construction. This hard-to-find book is the best single work on Ollantaytambo, the most important Inca ruin next to Machu Picchu.

Savoy, Gene. *Antisuyo: The Search for the Lost Cities of the Amazon.* New York: Simon & Schuster, 1970. Gene Savoy, who is second only to Hiram Bingham in his knack for sniffing out lost cities, describes in somewhat stilted prose his search for Espíritu Pampa, the last stronghold of the Inca.

Starn, Orin, ed., Carlos Iván Degregori, and Rob Kirk. *The Peru Reader.* Durham, North Carolina: Duke University Press, 1995. This is a great paperback to bring on the airplane or a long train ride, stuffed with an endlessly entertaining and eclectic collection of short stories, anthropological essays, translated chronicles, and a bit of poetry.

Von Hagen, Adriana, and Craig Morris. *The Cities of the Ancient Andes.* London: Thames and Hudson, 1998. Writer Adriana von Hagen, daughter of the renowned German-born Peruvianist Victor von Hagen, and a curator of New York's America Museum of Natural History teamed up for this highly recommended introduction to Peru's major archaeological sites. This is the most concise and accessible history of Peru's ancient cultures, written around the centers and cities they left behind.

CHRONICLES

Cieza de León, Pedro. *The Discovery and Conquest of Peru: The New World Encounter.* Durham, North Carolina: Duke University Press, 1999. Pedro Cieza de León arrived in Peru in 1547, wide-eyed at the age of 27, and proceeded to explore every nook and cranny, describing everything as he went. He is the first Spaniard to describe Spanish mistreatment of Peru's natives. His reliable voice paints the Spanish-Inca encounter in simple and clear language.

Garcilaso de la Vega, Inca, and Harold Livermore, translator. *Royal Commentaries of the Inca and General History of Peru.* Austin, Texas: University of Texas Press, 1966. Inca Garcilaso was the son of a conquistador and an Inca princess who moved to Spain in his youth and spent the rest of his life documenting the myths, culture, and history of the Inca. Though criticized for historical inaccuracies and exaggeration, Inca Garcilaso's 1,000-page *Royal Commentaries* contains subtitles that make this work easy to thumb through.

Poma de Ayala, Felipe Guamán. *Nueva Crónica y Buen Gobierno.* Madrid: Siglo XXI, 1992. This magnificent 16th-century manuscript has become the New World's best known indigenous chronicle since it was discovered in the Royal Library of Copenhagen in 1908. It is a 1,200-page history of the Spanish conquest, told from the Andean point of view in an eclectic mixture of Quechua and Spanish. Its harangues against Spanish injustice are complemented by 400 drawings made by Poma de Ayala, which accompany the text. Parts of this text, which was intended as a letter to Spanish King Phillip III, have been translated into English and are published on the Internet at http://www.kb.dk/permalink/2006/poma/info/es/frontpage.htm.

LITERATURE

Alarcón, Daniel. *War by Candlelight. Story Collection* New York: Harper Perennial, 2006. Born in Peru and raised in Birmingham, Alabama, Alarcón returned to Peru on a Fulbright. As a result he wrote a series of short stories that evoke the sorrows and beauty of a ravaged land with a precision and steadiness that stand in inverse proportion to the magnitude of the losses he so powerfully dramatizes.

Floods and earthquakes destroy what little equilibrium remains in a relentlessly violent world in which the authorities and the rebels are equally vicious and corrupt.

Alegria, Ciro. *Broad and Alien Is the World.* Chester Spring, Pennsylvania: Dufour Editions. This award-winning, lyric novel (*El Mundo Es Ancho y Ajeno,* 1941) was written by a celebrated Peruvian novelist who spent his career documenting the oppression of Peru's indigenous peoples. Look also for Alegria's other classic, *The Golden Serpent (La Serpiente de Oro).* The Spanish versions of these works are available in most bookstores in Peru.

Bryce Echenique, Alfredo. *A World for Julius.* University of Wisconsin Press, 2004. Bryce Echenique explores Peruvian society while describing a world of illusion created for little Julius, who eventually will have to fit perfectly in this society. A true masterpiece from one of Peru's top novelists.

Vargas Llosa, Mario. *Aunt Julia and the Scriptwriter.* New York: Penguin, 1995. This autobiographical tale of taboo mixes radio scripts with the steamy romance that a young radio writer carries on with his aunt—this is Vargas Llosa with Julia Urquidi, who became his first wife. This was one of Vargas Llosa's first novels revealing a glimpse into highbrow Lima society.

Vargas Llosa, Mario. *Captain Pantoja and the Secret Service.* New York: Harper Collins, 1978. This is the funny and ludicrous story of a faithful soldier, Pantaleón Pantoja, and his mission to begin a top-secret prostitution service for Peru's military in Iquitos, Peru. His problem is that he is too successful.

Vargas Llosa, Mario. *Conversation in the Cathedral.* New York: Harper Perennial, 2005. This is one of Vargas Llosa's masterworks. *Conversation in the Cathedral* takes place in 1950s Peru during the dictatorship of Manuel A. Odría. Over beers and a sea of freely spoken words, the conversation flows between Santiago and Ambrosio, who talk of their tormented lives and of the overall degradation and frustration that has slowly taken over their city. Through a complicated web of secrets and historical references, Vargas Llosa analyzes the mental and moral mechanisms that govern power and the people behind it. It is a groundbreaking novel that tackles identity as well as the role of a citizen and how a lack of personal freedom can forever scar people and a nation.

Vargas Llosa, Mario. *The Green House.* New York: Harper Perennial, 2005. Vargas Llosa's classic early novel takes place in a Peruvian town, between desert and jungle, where Don Anselmo, a stranger in a black coat, builds a brothel, bringing together the innocent and the corrupt: Bonifacia, a young Indian girl saved by the nuns, who becomes a prostitute; Father García, struggling for the church; and four best friends drawn to both excitement and escape.

TRAVEL AND EXPLORATION

Bingham, Hiram. *Phoenix: Lost City of the Incas.* Edited by Hugh Thomson. London: Phoenix Press, 2003. Bingham's classic description of how he discovered Machu Picchu lends historical detail to Peru's stand-out attraction and also explains why Bingham went on to become the leading inspiration for movie character Indiana Jones.

Kane, Joe. *Running the Amazon.* New York: Vintage, 1990. Starting from a glacier at 17,000 feet, Joe Kane and a team of adventurers attempted the never-before-done feat of navigating the entire length of the Amazon River from source to mouth. The story begins as an accurate description of life in Peru's highlands and ends with the difficulties of managing personalities in a modern-day expedition.

Lee, Vincent. *Sixpac Manco: Travels Among the Incas* (1985). This self-published book is a must-read for Vilcabamba explorers and is available at the South American Explorers Club in Lima. It is out of print, but used copies can be found at Amazon.com or other Internet sites that sell used books. The book comes with highly accurate maps of the area around Espíritu Pampa and Lee's amusing, shoot-from-the-hip adventurer's attitude.

Mathiessen, Peter. *At Play in the Fields of the Lord.* New York: Vintage, 1991. Set in a malarial jungle outpost, this Mathiessen classic depicts the clash of development and indigenous peoples in the Amazon jungle. It was made into a motion picture as well.

Muller, Karin. *Along the Inca Road, A Woman's Journey into an Ancient Empire.* Washington, D.C.: National Geographic, 2000. The author traces her 6,000-mile journey along Inca roads in Ecuador, Peru, Bolivia, and Chile. Along the way she shares her insights about modern exploration and Inca history.

Schneebaum, Tobias. *Keep the River on Your Right.* New York: Grove Press, 1998. In 1955, New York intellectual Tobias Schneebaum spent eight years living with the Akarama tribe in the remote Madre de Dios jungle. His book describes his participation in homosexual and cannibalistic rituals and became an immediate jungle classic when it was published in 1969.

Shah, Tahir. *Trail of Feathers: In Search of the Birdmen of Peru.* London: Orion Publishing, 2002. A 16th-century mention of Inca who "flew like birds" over the jungle leads one journalist on a quest to unlock the secret of Peru's so-called birdmen. His journey takes him to Machu Picchu, the Nasca Lines, and finally into the Amazon itself.

Thomson, Hugh. *The White Rock, An Exploration of the Inca Heartland.* New York: Overlook Press, 2001. British documentary filmmaker Hugh Thomson returns to Vilcabamba, where he explored in his early 20s, to weave a recollection of his travels together with an alluring blend of Spanish chronicles and Inca history. It contains vivid, sometimes scathing, depictions of local personalities and makes for a fast, exciting way to read up for a Peru trip.

TRAVEL GUIDES

Frost, Peter. *Exploring Cusco,* 5th ed. Lima: Nuevas Imágenes, 1999. This book continues to be the best-written, most readable historical and archaeological approach to the Cusco area, written by longtime Cusco resident Peter Frost.

Wust, Walter, et al. *Inca Guide to Peru.* Lima: Peisa, 2003. This excellent highway guide, sponsored by Mitsubishi, contains the country's best road maps and detailed descriptions of all the driving routes. There is also some historical and cultural information on each of Peru's main destinations, though little information on hotels and restaurants. This company has also published *Guia Inca de Playas,* which runs down all the remote camping and surfing spots along Peru's coast from Tumbes to Tacna. These books are for sale in Ripley department stores and most Lima bookstores.

Zarzar, Omar. *Por los Caminos de Peru en Bicicleta.* Lima: Editor SA, 2001. This is a guide to Peru's best mountain-biking routes. Though written in Spanish, the maps and itineraries are useful even for non-Spanish speakers.

BIRDING

Clements, James, and Noam Shany. *A Field Guide to the Birds of Peru.* Temecula, California: Ibis Publishing Company, 2001. Though much criticized by bird-watchers for its faulty pictures of certain birds, this US$60 tome catalogs nearly 1,800 birds known to reside in, or migrate to, Peru. This is the best alternative for birders unable to afford *Birds of Peru.*

Krabbe, Nils, and John Fjeldsa. *Birds of the High Andes.* Copenhagen: Denmark Zoological Museum of the University of Copenhagen, 1990. Real birders consider this such a must-have masterpiece that they are willing to shell out US$150 for it. It includes all the birds you are likely to encounter in the temperate and alpine zones of Peru.

Schulenberg, Thomas, and Douglas Stotz, Daniel Lane, and John O'Neill. *Birds of Peru (Princeton Field Guides).* Sanibel Island, Florida: Ralph Curtis Books, 2007. This long-awaited bible of Peru birding is coveted by every professional bird guide in Peru. It represents a huge step forward and was a colossal undertaking, as reflected by its beautiful color renderings of birds and its US$300-plus price tag.

Valqui, Thomas. *Where to Watch Birds in Peru,* 1st ed. Peru, 2004. This comprehensive self-published guide to birding in Peru explains not only what birds you'll see where, but how to get there and where you might stay along the way. This is an excellent resource, and there's nothing else like it on the market. More information about this book may be found at www.granperu.com/birdwatchingbook.

Walker, Barry, and Jon Fjeldsa, illustrations. *Field Guide to the Birds of Machu Picchu.* Lima: Peruvian National Trust for Parks and Protected Areas. This portable guide, written by Cusco's foremost bird expert and owner of Manu Expeditions, is widely available in Cusco. At US$30 it is an excellent value, with 31 superb color plates and descriptions of 420 species.

PHOTOGRAPHY

Milligan, Max. *Realm of the Incas.* New York: Universe Publishing, 2001. English photographer Max Milligan spent years trekking to the remote corners of Peru to capture images that range from the sacred snows of Nevado

Ausangate to the torpid meanderings of the Río Manu.

Weintraub, Adam L. *Vista Andina. A Photographic Perspective on Contemporary Life in the Andes.* PhotoExperience.net, 2010. Seattle–based photographer Adam Weintraub explores Cusco and surroundings through his lens, attempting a journalistic and zealous look into the intimate world of the city's inhabitants.

FOOD

Acurio, Gastón. *Peru: Una Aventura Culinaria.* Lima: Quebecor World Peru, 2002. This large-format photo book written in Spanish profiles Peru's array of foods in chapters titled Water, Land, and Air. It includes a range of recipes and profiles of Peru's leading chefs and is available in Lima bookshops.

Custer, Tony. *The Art of Peruvian Cuisine.* Lima: Cimino Publishing Group, 2003. This book has high-quality photos and an excellent selection of Peruvian recipes in both Spanish and English.

Morales, Edmund. *The Guinea Pig: Healing, Food, and Ritual in the Andes.* Tucson, Arizona: University of Arizona Press, 1995. This is the first major study, with good pictures, of how Andean highlanders not only eat guinea pig but also use it for medicinal and religious purposes.

PromPeru. *Peru Mucho Gusto.* Lima: Comisión de Promoción del Peru, 2006. This Spanish-English book is the latest of Peru's glamorous large-format cookbooks. Starting with the history of the country's cooking, the book gives a general overview of Peru's traditional cooking. The last chapter is dedicated to the creative chefs who will lead Peru's cooking into the future. Available in Lima bookstores.

SPIRITUAL AND ESOTERIC

Milla, Carlos. *Genesis de la Cultura Andina,* 4th ed. Cusco: Amana Wayra, 2006. If you can read Spanish, this book presents esoteric theories based on many of Peru's ancient ceremonial centers. Milla's latest book, 2003's *Ayni: Semiotica Andina de los Espacios Sagrados,* from the same publisher, focuses on astrology. Carlos Milla can be reached in Cusco at cmilla@viabcp.com.

Villoldo, Alberto, and Erik Jendresen. *The Four Winds: A Shaman's Odyssey into the Amazon.* New York: Harper Collins, 1991. Even Peru's shamans respect this work, which documents the author's spiritual initiation into Amazon rituals.

WEAVING

Heckman, Andrea. *Woven Stories: Andean Textiles and Rituals.* Albuquerque: University of New Mexico Press, 2003. A series of ethnographic essays on Andean life and weaving by a researcher with two decades in the field.

Pollard Rowe, Anne, and John Cohen. *Hidden Threads of Peru: Q'ero Textiles.* London: Merrell Publishers, 2002. In vibrant pictures and concise prose, this book documents the extraordinary weavings of Q'ero, a remote town in south Peru where the authors have been researching for nearly four decades.

CHILDREN

Hergé, *The Adventures of Tintin: Prisoners of the Sun,* 1949. Copenhagen: Egmont Books Ltd., 2002. In this Hergé classic, a sequel to *The Seven Crystal Balls,* Tintin, Captain Haddock, and Milou catch a steamer to Peru to rescue a kidnapped professor. The adventure leads them through the Andes and the Amazon, which are depicted in fascinating detail and through the romanticized lens of the mid-20th century.

Internet Resources

TRAVEL INFORMATION
Andean Travel Web
www.andeantravelweb.com
This is the best of several websites in Peru that evaluate hotels, restaurants, and agencies.

The Latin American Network Information Center
http://lanic.utexas.edu/la/peru
The largest single list of links on Peru has been compiled by the University of Texas.

Living in Peru
www.livinginperu.com
This, along with www.expatperu.com, is a directory of resources for foreigners living and traveling in Peru.

Peru Links
www.perulinks.com
This huge website of links lists tons of hard-to-find Peru websites, including gay and lesbian clubs, alternative medicine, chat rooms, etc.

The Peruvian Times
www.peruviantimes.com
Lima's oldest English-language publishing house, which until recently published the *Lima Times,* has an interesting website with tips on arriving in Lima, photos, links, and a directory of expatriate associations.

South American Explorers
www.saexplorers.org
This web page for the South American Explorers Club has books for sale, information on insurance providers, an online bulletin board with cars for sale and apartments for rent, and interesting links.

FLIGHT INFORMATION
Lima Airport
www.lap.com.pe
This is the home page of the Jorge Chávez International airport in Lima.

Tráfico
www.traficoperu.com
This agency newsletter is an updated list of all international and domestic flights in Peru.

ECOTOURISM
GORP
www.gorp.com
This joint production of Away.com, Gorp, and Outside Online has hundreds of travel stories on Peru, a list of top 20 travel destinations, and links to tour operators.

Planeta
www.planeta.com/peru.html
This ecotourism site includes articles, essays, and links to responsible tour operators.

SURFING
Peru Azul
www.peruazul.com
Peru's most popular website for surfing and ocean conditions along the coast is for Spanish speakers only.

ANDEAN CULTURE
Culture of the Andes
www.andes.org
A labor of love from Peru fanatics Russ and Ada Gibbons, this site focusing on Andean culture includes short stories, jokes, music, songs in Quechua, poetry, and riddles.

Index

List of Maps

Acknowledgments

In preparing the first edition of *Moon Cusco & Machu Picchu,* we relied on three very hard-working researchers, Gabriela Holland, Fiona Cameron, and Celine Wald. This book was possible because of these hard-working updaters and the extraordinary people they met along the way. Gabriela, who grew up in Ollantaytambo has recently returned to Peru after a long time abroad. She infused this book with new elements of Peruvian culture, such as Cusco's rich tradition of street food. Fiona did the Salcantay trek in order to capture it for the book, and Celine proved to be a very capable restaurant critic.

In the Cusco area, we want to thank Raúl Montes, Richard Webb, Wendy Weeks, Joaquín Randall, Kennedy Leavens, Adela Arenas, Marcela Zúñiga Sáenz, Carlos Zevallos, Rafael Casabonne, and Ulrike in Pisac, along with her next-door neighbors Fielding and Roman Vizcarra. Nicholas Asheshov is one of the great experts on Peru and, along with his wife María del Carmen, he contributed immeasurably as always.

We also want to thank the kind and professional staff at Avalon Travel. Publisher Bill Newlin and Associate Publisher Donna Galassi placed their complete trust in us. Our Editor, Erin Raber, guided us expertly and was exceedingly patient and professional. Thanks also to Cartography Director Mike Morgenfeld, Map Editor Albert Angulo, Graphics Coordinators Lucie Ericksen and Darren Alessi, Editorial Director Kevin McLain, Acquisitions Director Grace Fujimoto, and Production Director Jane Musser.

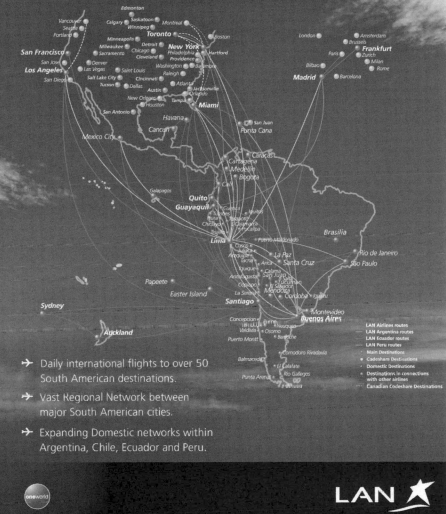

www.moon.com

DESTINATIONS | ACTIVITIES | BLOGS | MAPS | BOOKS

MOON.COM is ready to help plan your next trip! Filled with fresh trip ideas and strategies, author interviews, informative travel blogs, a detailed map library, and descriptions of all the Moon guidebooks, Moon.com is all you need to get out and explore the world—or even places in your own backyard. While at Moon.com, sign up for our monthly e-newsletter for updates on new releases, travel tips, and expert advice from our on-the-go Moon authors. As always, when you travel with Moon, expect an experience that is uncommon and truly unique.

MOON IS ON FACEBOOK—BECOME A FAN!
JOIN THE MOON PHOTO GROUP ON FLICKR